INSIDE THE MIDDLE EAST

INSIDE THE MIDDLE EAST

MAKING SENSE OF THE MOST DANGEROUS AND COMPLICATED REGION ON EARTH

AVI MELAMED

FOREWORD BY LUCY AHARISH

Skyhorse Publishing

Skyhorse Publishing books may be purchased in bulk at special discounts for sales promotion, corporate gifts, fund-raising, or educational purposes. Special editions can also be created to specifications. For details, contact the Special Sales Department, Skyhorse Publishing, 307 West 36th Street, 11th Floor, New York, NY 10018 or info@skyhorsepublishing.com.

Skyhorse® and Skyhorse Publishing® are registered trademarks of Skyhorse Publishing, Inc.®, a Delaware corporation.

Visit our website at www.skyhorsepublishing.com.

10 9 8 7 6 5 4 3 2 1

Library of Congress Cataloging-in-Publication Data is available on file.

Cover design by Rain Saukas

Print ISBN: 978-1-63450-572-7
Ebook ISBN: 978-1-63450-976-3

Printed in the United States of America

I dedicate this book to my children: my daughter, Sapir, and my son, Nimrod, who are two Israeli, Jewish young people in the Middle East of the twenty-first century. I do not know where their paths will lead them, but I hope that they will have the privilege of seeing a new, better Middle East in which everyone can look forward to a future of hope.

TABLE OF CONTENTS

FOREWORD

THIRTY-FOUR YEARS AGO I WAS BORN in Dimona, a small, predominately Jewish town in southern Israel. Ten years earlier my parents had made a very courageous decision. They'd decided to leave their home, their family, and their familiar environment in Nazareth, a predominantly Arab town in northern Israel with a large Muslim and Christian population, to move to Dimona to build a new and better life for their family.

Growing up as the only Muslim girl in school was not a walk in the park. One of my earliest memories is sitting with my mother in our small living room the night before I went into first grade. She told me something I'll never forget: "You are an Arab, a Muslim Arab, you are not Jewish. But that doesn't mean that you are less than anybody else. You have different beliefs and different customs—but you are a human being. Always be proud of who you are and what you represent, and don't let anyone tell you otherwise." It was an important conversation for me and especially for my mother, because that year I had a school vacation that will leave a scar for the rest of my life.

It was in 1987, a very hot sunny Saturday morning. My uncle came with his wife and their two sons to visit us, and they really wanted to travel to the Gaza Strip. My father hesitated, knowing that the security situation was not very good there. After some persuading, my father relented and my mother, my father, my aunt and uncle, my cousin, and I set out for a Saturday drive.

I used to love those trips to Gaza. It was so different than Dimona. But so familiar at the same time. The beautiful coastline was pure and blue and I can still taste the kebab sandwich . . .

But that day was different. All the shops that we used to buy from were closed and the old man that used to sell us fish was sick. Before we started heading back, we made one last stop in Bambino, a children's clothing store. The owner of the shop was on his way out and wanted to close but decided to stay open when he saw us pull up. He told my father that the business was slow because of the "situation." "They are calling it an '*intifada*,'" he said, "it doesn't look good." Before we left he leaned toward my father and said: "Do me a favor. Until you leave Gaza keep your windows closed or just give a sign so they know you're an Arab—hold a newspaper or something . . ." My father waved at him and said in Arabic, "Leave it to God." My father owned a yellow three-door BMW with no air conditioning, and because it was so hot the windows were open. The road was packed with cars. I looked outside and I saw a man holding something in his hand coming toward us. There was something about him that really scared me, so I started squirming my way down the back seat. My mom noticed and yelled, "Lucy, sit up straight!" I kept watching the man getting closer and closer and looking at me; our eyes met and in the background I heard my mom again saying, "Lucy, sit up straight!" The third time I heard her voice, I heard a big explosion. It started getting hotter in the car and then suddenly my face hit the ground. I looked to the side and I saw my mother laying on the ground, holding my aunt and crying. I saw my father pointing a fire extinguisher at my uncle who was holding my cousin who was on fire. My father yelled, "HELP US!" at the people who had gathered to watch the horror. "WE ARE ARABS JUST LIKE YOU!" But they just stood there. And in a few minutes two Israeli Army jeeps arrived and rescued us.

After a series of surgeries, my cousin healed. But the scars in my head are still there. I hated the Palestinians. I didn't want to understand them. I wanted them to vanish. When my father heard me saying things like that he used to say to my mother, "She'll grow up and she'll understand that the world is not black and white." Today I understand that that was one of the reasons my mother had that conversation with me the night before I went to first grade.

The kids in school knew that I was Arab. Because I had nothing to be ashamed of, I proudly shared my identity with all my friends. But then I started getting picked on and beaten up almost every day. And I understood that it was because I was "different." I was not the "fat" girl. I was not the girl with the braces. I was not the girl with the glasses. I was the Arab girl. And the Arab girl understood very quickly that she needed to excel in everything she did in order to survive. And so I did. I had no choice. My parents made it very clear that a failure was unacceptable. I participated in every school activity. I sang in the school choir. I played the flute in the city's orchestra. I participated in every single ceremony. I finished first in my class every single semester. In high school it was even harder. . . . It was the 1990s and Israel was shaken almost every week with another suicide bomber that blew himself up on a bus and murdered tens of people. After every terror attack, all I wanted to do was stay home. I didn't want to face my schoolmates who blamed me because I was one of "them." My friends never looked at me differently, but others did. I remember them standing right in front of me yelling, "terrorist," "filthy Arab get out of here," and "we don't want you here."

Despite their words, or perhaps because of them, I finished first in my class, graduating with honors and majoring in theater and Middle Eastern studies. I wanted to be an actress. I wanted to make people laugh, to make them feel, think, and express themselves. So I went to the university to study Theater Studies and Political Science. Why? Because I was once told that in order to be a good politician you need to have good acting skills. But I really only wanted to be an actress.

I moved to Jerusalem in 2000, the beginning of the second intifada. It was my first encounter with Palestinians since that day in Gaza. It was in this chapter of my life that I discovered how and why it's not black and white. . . . My mother's wise words proved true.

I have always asked myself what would have happened if I had not been born a woman. If I had not been born an Arab woman. If I had not been born an Arab Muslim woman. If I had not been born an Arab Muslim woman in a small Jewish town in the south of Israel. If I had not been born in the Middle East. These questions have become even more relevant with the tremendous chaos surrounding us here inside the Middle East.

My multifaceted identity is, to a large degree, a reflection of the multifaceted identity of the region I was born in.

I'm a journalist now. And as a journalist, in this chapter of my life, I had the honor of meeting Avi Melamed. I met him almost three years ago, just when I started anchoring the Prime Time Evening Edition on the internationally broadcasted i24news. My many encounters with Avi, an Israeli Jew with a unique and rare understanding of the Arab world—as well as the Arabic language—contributed yet another dimension to my understanding that it is not black and white. With his calm voice, vast knowledge, profound perspective, and accurate analyses, Avi was able to take my hand and the hands of the viewers and navigate us through the wreckage of what was left of the Middle East. Time after time, Avi methodically revealed layer after layer of a multifaceted, multidimensional, multi-identity Middle East *that is never black and white.* The Middle East is a place, as Avi taught me, where "One plus one never equals two."

The question mark that Avi would leave with me and viewers after he'd step out of the studio was not a normal one. The question mark was not one that kept me wondering what he meant, rather it generated more questions that I wanted answers to. It's a question mark that keeps me excited, intrigued, interested, and thinking. Each time I got to host Avi on my show, I got the front row seat to the best lecture in town, what he masterfully presents here, in *Inside the Middle East.*

—Lucy Aharish

PREFACE

In December 2010, a Tunisian peddler set himself on fire. The unprecedented events that followed—a revolutionary shift in the cultural, economic, political, and social tectonic plates of the Arab world—engulfed the region at the end of the first and the beginning of the second decade of the twenty-first century. Some people call this the "Arab Spring." Others use a term less commendable-sounding; they call it the "Arab Winter." I join those who call it the "Arab Awakening." It was akin to a smoldering volcano whose eruption was the result of the chaotic situation that had prevailed in the Arab world—a condition previously held in check by a layer of oppression and repression. The Arab Awakening was when that layer ripped open, and chaos exploded onto the surface with all its might.

In the time that has elapsed since December 2010, the face of the Middle East has changed beyond recognition. Many of the "borders" are no longer relevant. Iraq, Syria, Libya, and Yemen have fallen apart in a violent process. Lebanon is on a perilous slope toward disintegration. In Algeria, Egypt, and Tunisia, a dramatic political shake-up is underway. In Bahrain, Jordan, and Morocco, the Arab Awakening has accentuated and deepened the internal unrest. And militant Islamist factors, inspired by what they view as the right translation of the Islamic faith, and guided by a vision of restoring the early medieval Islamic caliphate, are building emirates across the Middle East—stretching from Iraq through Syria, the Sinai Peninsula, and Yemen, and across the northern belt of the Sahara desert all the way to Africa's western shores. Arab societies have been thrust into a powerful whirlpool as they struggle to define their identity, path, and direction. Arab regimes that had been part of the landscape for decades—like those of Zine al-Abidine Ben Ali, in power in Tunisia from 1987–2011; of Ḥosinī Mubārak, in power in

Egypt from 1981–2011; and of 'Alī 'Abd Allāh Ṣāliḥ, in power in Yemen from 1978–2012—have fallen.

There are people who claim that the Arab Awakening was responsible for the chaos in the Middle East. Many people in the West even seemed surprised by it, caught off-guard. This intrigued and concerned me, and my career has been heavily shaped by my need to help Westerners understand the unfolding events. The uprising should have been internationally predictable. The fact that it shocked so many people was one of the reasons I wrote this book.

It's important for me to stress that this book does not purport to present a deep and all-encompassing academic analysis of the Arab world or the Middle East. In this book, I attempt to condense the wide array of processes, trends, and events that have taken place and are currently taking place in the Arab world into a general picture that is clear, yet also expresses the complexity of what is unfolding. My intention is, in the most modest way, to explain the background of the central events taking place in Arab societies; to examine the streams of thought shaping Arab societies; to outline the limitations and constraints of its major players (states as well as movements); and to assess the possible and likely results and repercussions of what is currently taking place within the Arab world.

The overwhelming majority of the information I present in this book is based on the knowledge I gained about the Arab world during the course of my career, from my own professional experiences, a variety of contacts—both personal and professional—throughout the Arab world, and a wide range of media and professional resources, primarily in Arabic, from within the Arab world. My view of the Arab world is a critical one, but it is not condescending and it is not hostile. The insights I offer are based on an analytic examination that has been constructed on the basis of a great deal of continually updated cumulative knowledge, a constant acquisition of further information, and a relentless pursuit of further understanding. My analysis is subject to the rigorous standards of professionalism that I have adhered to throughout my intelligence, advisory, policy, and educational careers, and it is firmly grounded in an obligatory humility due to my awareness that, despite my best efforts to continually learn and understand more about the Arab world, I am not immune to mistakes or faulty readings.

There is one chapter in the book, Chapter Eleven, which reflects my personal perspectives—as opposed to the professional analysis on which the book is based. In this chapter, I offer my thoughts about the cultural, emotional, and psychological environment that gave birth to the involvement of Westerners in the campaign to delegitimize the State of Israel. It is important to me to point out that the thoughts and insights that I present in this chapter are my own. I am not—nor have I ever been—a member of an Israeli political body, and I am not—nor have I ever served as—an official spokesperson for the State of Israel. Since this book is an honest attempt to present a professional analysis in the most objective way possible, I debated whether this chapter was appropriate to include. I decided to include it because I believe the insights I suggest are important for a better understanding of the manner in which knowledge about the Middle East is shaped in the West and the repercussions of that process on relations between the West and the Arab world, which is the central focus of Chapter Eight.

Over the span of my career, I have had the honor of briefing thousands of people around the world, from high school students to senior diplomats, military leaders to media professionals and politicians. Based on my experience I have developed the following thesis:

The domestic and foreign policy of Western governments is largely shaped by academics, large corporations, media, non-governmental and nonprofit organizations, and politicians. The conversations and thinking within these circles play a significant role in shaping policy. With regard to the Middle East, a disturbing process has taken place over the last generation. People in these circles, and other mediators of knowledge perceived as expert interpreters of the region, have developed concepts, narratives, and theories regarding the Middle East, but because these "guides" almost never speak or read Arabic, they are dependent on mediated, translated, and sometimes deliberately manipulated information. This compromises their ability to critically evaluate the information they are provided and prevents them from having their finger on the pulse of significant events and developments. The "reality" they present, at best, reflects a small part of the picture—yet it creates a "looping echo chamber" that percolates into public discourse.

The concepts they communicate become "the facts," the narratives they convey become "the reality," and the theories they create become "the truth."

Unfortunately and dangerously, these Western narratives are often based on a reading that does not accurately reflect or appropriately dialogue with unfolding events. The reality on the ground is often quite different, and this false reading presents two clear challenges: one connected to the United States and one connected to Israel. For the United States, this phenomenon has resulted in accumulating failures of American policy in the Middle East. For Israel, it has resulted in critical rhetoric and forceful attacks—the Boycott, Divestment, and Sanctions (BDS) campaign, for example, which is not only an international attack on Israel's economy but also a challenge to Israel's right to exist.

This book has been developed for a variety of audiences in the West and I hope it serves as a sort of road map or GPS to help all levels of analysts—mediators of knowledge and laymen, novice students and experts—navigate the region and understand where the Middle East is going as we get deeper into the twenty-first century. My intention is to present views that are rare in Western conversations about what is unfolding in the Middle East; to elucidate extremely complicated subjects in an intellectual yet digestible way; and to deal with the most political issues and yet present them in an apolitical manner. I hope that all readers, regardless of their background, education, views, or faith, will see this book as a tool that offers them an additional layer of knowledge and understanding of this very complicated yet critically important region.

I made a great effort to be certain that the information I present, as well as the quotations and translations, are precise and reliable. I have tried to be as accurate as possible and use the sources and figures I believe to be the most reliable at the time of writing, as well as to maintain the intended meaning of the quotes throughout that I have translated from Arabic to English. If any supplied content is imprecise or mistaken, I take responsibility for it. This principle also applies to the conclusions, predictions, and insights I suggest.

I began writing this book in the second half of 2014 and the final editing was done in January 2016. My biggest challenge in writing this book has been to update—in real time—the information and some of the predictions I have made. I am happy to say that in all of the cases throughout my writing and editing in which I had to update my predictions, it was because they had come true. I share all this with you to provide a framework for the arguments, analyses, and insights that follow.

It may be helpful to describe my own position in this "arena." I am an Israeli, a Jew, and a Zionist. I am the fourth generation of my family to be born in Israel—Jerusalem to be exact. My ancestors lived in the old city of Jerusalem in the nineteenth century. My family's roots are deep in this region, from Jerusalem to Iraq to Turkey, but also as far as Italy and Spain. My grandparents spoke Arabic in addition to Hebrew. Growing up in Jerusalem, many of the games we played as children had Arabic names. Arabic was a natural part of my landscape as a child, and my childhood in Jerusalem was a magical and sweet time filled with powerful and meaningful memories that I carry with me every day. Later, I served in a field intelligence unit in the Israeli Defense Forces. I have held positions connected to the Arab sector both in Israel and beyond its borders in my service to the State of Israel, including my work in Israeli intelligence. And I have had formal academic education in the field of the Middle East.

I have acquired the bulk of my knowledge, understanding, and point of view during my thirty-year career as a Middle East and Arab affairs expert. For many years of my life I operated daily in Arab communities, working in the fields of counterterrorism, intelligence, civil policy, and policy development and implementation. I spent another twelve years as an intelligence analyst and advisor, working both within Israeli intelligence and independently, and a further seven years teaching contemporary Middle Eastern affairs and Arabic. In the course of my pursuits, I have become fluent in the Arabic language and intimately familiar with the social and cultural norms and codes of Arab society. My years of work and my decision to continue in the field after retiring from my formal positions have compelled me to engage in an ongoing, dedicated, daily study of what is happening in Arab societies—from cultural, economic, political, and social angles—and I feel confident in saying that I have developed a deep, intimate, and unique understanding of Arab societies. My decades of experience have enabled me, in all of my positions and most recently as an independent Middle East strategic intelligence analyst and the Eisenhower Institute's Fellow of Intelligence and Middle East Affairs, to take pride in a long and proven record of precise analyses and interpretations concerning developments in the Arab world, the ramifications of those developments, and their impact on the region.

We are about to embark on a journey into the dramatically changed Middle East of the second decade of the twenty-first century. I am honored to be your guide and private analyst. I hope my insights help you understand this complicated, fascinating, and critical region. It is closely tied with my personal history, very close to my heart, and critically relevant for all of us.

CHAPTER ONE

THE DISTORTED COMPASS

In 2014, Salman Masalha, an Israeli Druze scholar, wrote that Mohamed Bouazizi, the peddler who lit the fire of the Arab Awakening, was "an agent of the CIA and perhaps even of the Israeli Mossad [one of Israel's intelligence agencies]." He wrote that "the millions of people who went out to demonstrate and to spread the Arab Awakening throughout the Arab world were actually agents of the CIA and of the West." These claims were part of an article he wrote titled "The Crazy Person Speaks and the Wise Person Listens."[1]

Masalha was not reflecting his own beliefs. He was referring—with despair, frustration, and sorrow—to the fact that many people in the Arab world actually think these things are true. He expressed sadness at the fact that there are many people in the Arab world who believe that the millions of people who took to the streets to demand change and a better future, many of whom did so at the cost of their lives, are believed to have been "acting as emissaries of the CIA or the countries of the West in a plot intended to undermine the resistance axis."[2]

Masalha shares these claims to examine the question, "Why are Arabs—more than all other nations—absolutely convinced that all of the problems of the Arab world have their source in local or foreign plots?"[3] In his opinion, the answer is that none of the regimes that have risen in the Arab world, nor their consequences, are a result of the free choice of the individual in Arab societies. Masalha wrote that the ongoing war in Syria has "revealed the face of those [in the Arab world] who in the name of the fake slogan of nationalism actually enhanced an Arab fascist and racist ideology, which was disguised with slogans [promoting things] such as 'the resistance.'"[4]

To substantiate his point, Masalha highlighted how the regime of Bashar al-Assad, the president of Syria, strives—through the use of demagoguery, rhetoric, and meaningless slogans—to not only avoid taking responsibility for the tragedy that it is creating but to go so far as to hold the Syrian people, who are only seeking freedom and a better future, responsible for the devastating results. What is even worse, he adds, is that there are so many people in the Arab world who continue to accept the claims, slogans, and propaganda of the Assad regime without doubt, while their hearts "remain impervious to the tragic murder of thousands of men, women, and children, the hundreds of thousands of wounded, the millions of refugees, and the enormous destruction."

Masalha concluded his article with a searing statement: "Every Arab should hang his head and be ashamed . . . every Arab should look in the mirror and ask, 'How did we reach this miserable state? Everything that happened to us has been the work of our own hands.'"[5]

Masalha is touching on a raw nerve. Arab academics, intellectuals, journalists, and politicians are pondering a similar question—and it's not rare for them to use descriptions such as "sick" when describing the unfortunate state of the Arab world.[6, 7] To understand this, it helps to establish what these "diseases" are and to be clear on their symptoms.

One disease is the deeply-rooted belief in *al-muamira* (the conspiracy). This refers to the perception in the Arab world that Muslims, particularly Arab Muslims, are victims of local and foreign plots against them, and that the responsibility for the dismal state of the Arab world does not lie with the Arabs, but with places such as the United States, Europe, and Israel. Arabs who believe in al-muamira believe they are victims of things like imperialism, colonialism, and racism. In an article titled "The Theory of the Plot—The Theory that Will Never Die," Abdulrahman al-Rashed wrote about this disconcerting belief: "I am not saying that there are no plots at all, but in the overwhelming majority of cases this is an excuse used as a card that is brandished by various factors in the Arab world to justify failures or emergency measures, and we [Arabs] have only ourselves to blame."[8]

Other examples of the concept of "conspiracy" embedded in Arab thinking are:

In 2011, when Muammar al-Qaddafi was facing increasing calls to step down from his role as leader of Libya, he tried to coalesce the Libyan people against an enemy he said was outside, saying, "There is a conspiracy to control the Libyan oil and to control the Libyan land, to colonize Libya once again . . . This is impossible, impossible. We will fight until the last man and last woman . . . to defend Libya from east to west, north to south."[9]

In the spring of 2012, during the first months of the riots in Syria, the Assad regime claimed that Christians from Lebanon were behind the events in Syria; after, the regime blamed the Israeli Mossad; and later, it blamed intelligence agencies of the West.[10, 11]

In August 2012, a Salafi-Jihadi group attacked an Egyptian border patrol outpost in Sinai. The attack occurred in the evening, when the Egyptian soldiers were eating at the end of a fast day during the month of Ramadan. Sixteen Egyptian soldiers were killed in the attack. The attackers then infiltrated Israeli territory and were killed by the Israeli army. Arab commentators and news reporters, the Muslim Brotherhood in Egypt, and some retired senior officers of the Egyptian army claimed that the attack was an Israeli plot.[12, 13, 14, 15]

In December 2013, then Grand Mufti of Lebanon Mohammed Rashid Qabbani visited a Sunni mosque in Lebanon. While there, he was attacked by worshipers because of his support for Hezbollah[16] and had to be rescued by the Lebanese army. Ironically, the next month he proclaimed that the Arabs must "save their countries from the American plots that are meant to sow schisms and hatred between brothers."[17]

In an article by Lebanese journalist Basim al-Jisr' titled "The Conspiracy of the Arabs Against Themselves," Jisr wrote: "The real plot is that of the Muslim and Arab world against itself because it has not been able put an end to the religious, ethnic, social, and political divisions within it."[18]

Another disease of the Arab world is the ocean of demagoguery, fiery speeches, rhetoric, and slogans in which it has drowned itself, spewing phrases such as Arab brotherhood, Arab socialism, Arab solidarity, Arab unity, resistance, the liberation of Palestine, a unification of the lines, and Islam is the solution. These phrases have been propagated by generations of academics, artists, intellectuals, media figures, politicians, and religious leaders.

The narratives and rabble-rousing serve economic and political interests and have granted a perceived legitimization and immunity to dictatorial regimes and brutal rulers in the Arab world. Demagoguery and slogans have been an effective tool for governments and rulers to avoid responsibility and accountability and to distract the public's attention from the dismal reality of Arab societies—a reality the Arab leaders, dictators, and government officials are responsible for creating and perpetuating.

On August 2, 1990, an Iraqi regime led by Iraq's then president, Saddam Hussein, invaded Kuwait, triggering the first Gulf War (August 1990–February 1991), in which a coalition of Western powers and Arab states assembled to force Hussein to withdraw from Kuwait. During the war, the Iraqi dictator oversaw an attack against Israel with scud missiles. Hussein hoped to create an Israeli retaliation that would lead to the disintegration of the Arab-Western coalition. He declared that by shooting missiles at Israel he was fighting against American and Israeli aggression. He's quoted as saying, "By God, we will make the fire eat up half of Israel if it tries to do anything against Iraq."[19] Other lines of his include:

> "Fight them with your faith in God, fight them in defense of every free honorable woman and every innocent child, and in defense of the values of manhood and the military honor . . . Fight them because with their defeat you will be at the last entrance of the conquest of all conquests. The war will end with . . . dignity, glory, and triumph for your people, army, and nation."[20]

> "What remains for [George W.] Bush and his accomplices in crime is to understand that they are personally responsible for their crime. The Iraqi people will pursue them for this crime, even if they leave office and disappear into oblivion. There is no doubt they will understand what we mean if they know what revenge means to the Arabs."[21]

> "We will chase [Americans] to every corner at all times. No high tower of steel will protect them against the fire of truth."[22]

Through firing fiery rhetoric at Israel and the West, Hussein was trying to divert attention from the fact that his troops had brutally occupied Kuwait. In August 1990, Saddam declared that the army would leave Kuwait only if Israel withdrew from all Arab lands it occupied in Palestine, Syria, and Lebanon.[23] Many Arabs and Palestinians were receptive to Hussein's spin. Crowds of Palestinians cheered him by chanting the slogan (which rhymes in Arabic), "Hey Saddam / Hey dear friend / Give a beating / to Tel Aviv."[24] Ironically, some of the missiles launched by Hussein landed in areas populated by Palestinians. This, however, did not prevent Palestinian leader Yasser Arafat from expressing open support for Hussein, and later the Palestinians paid dearly for this. Following the war, some four hundred thousand Palestinians who worked in Kuwait were expelled by the Kuwaiti government.[25] In 2004, Palestinian leader Mahmoud Abbas formally apologized to Kuwait for the Palestinians' support of Saddam Hussein.[26]

More recently, when the riots in Libya that led to the ousting of the Libyan dictator Muammar al-Qaddafi began in 2011, Qaddafi tried to incite the masses, hoping to divert their attention and save his government by calling upon his nation to "go forth and liberate Palestine."[27] Like other Arab rulers, Qaddafi hoped that anti-Israel rhetoric would help him divert the growing discontent of his people and save his own skin. It didn't work.

Saudi writer 'Abd al-Salam Wa'il referred to the "Israel phenomenon" in a 2013 article titled "Israel, the Everlasting Arab Treasure." In it he wrote:

> Israel is a bounty for Arab dictators who use the Palestinian-Israeli conflict to rule their countries and make a lot of money by issuing hollow threats to Israel. Israel is a card used and manipulated by Arab rulers for their purpose on issues that Israel had nothing to do with. The Israeli-Palestinian conflict is a card used by Arab rulers to gain legitimacy while delegitimizing their political opponents.[28]

Lebanese author, journalist, and political analyst Samir Atallah wrote in 2014 that the "Arab regimes that led the Arab nation with slogans and speeches and proclamations and revolutions left the Arab nation poor and despondent, and now those regimes that oppress and exploit their people are sending their subjects to drown in the sea or to drown in the mud or to turn to prostitution in the bitterness of their despair."[29]

Another disease of the Arab world is the culture of whitewashing and sweeping controversies and tensions under the rug. Deep conflicts among groups within Arab societies throughout the regions have often been ignored. One of the most common means of covering up the divisions—side by side with hollow slogans and rhetoric—has been to create fancy constitutions lauding the religion and culture of Islam and laden with all the buzzwords like freedom, liberation, and unity. A constitution should express consensus, an agreement on basic principles and values that a majority of the sectors of society share. When four Arab states that are violently disintegrating—Syria, Iraq, Libya, and Yemen—have constitutions, and other Arab states, like Egypt and Lebanon, which also have constitutions, are struggling with serious political violence and instability, it becomes clear that the constitutions in the Arab world do not reflect consensus and are not strong enough to secure their states' integrity and social fabrics. Constitutions in the Arab world are at best plastering a challenging, fragile reality.

These diseases have prevented the creation of the mechanisms necessary for the development of a healthy, strong, and dynamic civil society. One of the other symptoms of the absence of mechanisms that encourage productive and respectful debate is the verbal and physical violence that has become prevalent in political and public discourse in Arab society. Houses of parliament and television stations in the Arab world sometimes appear to be more like boxing rings in which publicly elected officials, media personalities, intellectuals, and others curse, hit, and even throw shoes at one another, which is considered a serious insult in Arab culture. In 2008, Iraqi journalist Muntazer al-Zaidi bade an angry farewell to President George W. Bush by throwing a shoe at him on his last visit to Iraq.[30] In another case, a Jordanian representative of Parliament drew his gun in a television studio.

Abdulateef al-Mulhim, a Saudi journalist and retired commodore in the Royal Saudi Navy, described in an article titled "Arab Spring: Mirror, Mirror on the Wall" how the Arab world does not want to recognize the problems it has. He wrote:

> The Arab world never looks at mirrors. We don't like to say mirror, mirror on the wall because mirrors don't lie and we don't want to know the truth. We can't handle it. We never blamed our systems for the many failures to develop the Arab mind. We talk about Sykes-Picot [the secret 1916 agreement dividing the Ottoman Empire for the United Kingdom and France], imperialism, and Zionism, but we never look at the mirrors on the wall.[31]

The diseases of the Arab world have perpetuated and deepened a culture of double standards, self-denial, evasion, and transfers of responsibility. Al-Mulhim described this as "decades of hiding from reality, chasing a mirage of enemies, conspiracies, and blaming the outside world."[32]

Instead of looking inward and encouraging critical thinking, reflection, and open and analytical discussions to address its enormous challenges, the Arab world has chosen an approach that has dictated uniformity of thought and strangled expressions of constructive criticism and change.

Here is an example: In March 2014, an eight-minute-long film named *Yarmouk* created by an Israeli director of Palestinian descent, Mohammad Bakri, was posted on YouTube. The film tells the tragic story of the largest Palestinian refugee camp in Syria, al-Yarmouk, which functions as a very densely populated residential suburb of Damascus. In the only scene in the film in which there is dialogue, the father (implied to be a Palestinian) and his daughter are sitting in an old car that is facing a luxury Mercedes. There is a man (implied to be a sheikh from the Gulf) dressed in traditional Arab clothing in the back seat of the Mercedes. The driver of the Mercedes gets out of the car and goes over to the father's car. He gestures to the daughter to open her mouth and he examines her teeth. He then pays the father money, but the father protests and says that the agreed fee was higher. In response, the man says, "The fee didn't include treatment for rotten teeth."

The scene depicts a transaction in which the father is selling his daughter to another Arab to be able to buy food for his family who is suffering from hunger. The sale of the daughter addresses one of the tragic aspects of the war in Syria: the huge wave of poor refugees it has created. Most of them are living in improvised refugee camps, in wretched conditions, and are engaged in a daily struggle to survive. This extreme distress has led to many Syrian families "marrying" their daughters to men from all over the Arab world (and mainly from the Gulf) in exchange for money.

To comprehend this phenomenon, it helps to understand the cultural context. One of the core values in Islamic and Arab culture is known by the term *al-'ard;* its literal translation is "display" or "exhibit," and it is a reference to female valor—the importance of a woman's good name and purity. Islam considers women to be the face or facade of the family. A family's honor is dependent on the perception of the women in it. Any kind of "moral misbehavior" or "immoral actions" attributed to a woman in the family—such as adultery, drug addiction, prostitution, or sexual relations before marriage—tarnishes the family's good name and disgraces its honor. The blight can only be removed by severely punishing the woman, even killing her. To avoid this and keep a family's good name intact, and also for much-needed money, it's common for Syrian families to arrange marriages for their daughters.

In Muslim culture there are contracts for "limited duration marriages" or "temporary marriages," which are legal according to the sharīʿah, the Islamic religious code. In Shiite Islam, these marriages are known as *zawaj al-mutʿah* (a marriage of pleasure). Sunni Islam forbids this kind of marriage, yet a similar phenomenon they call *zawaj al-misyar*, a "travel (tourist) marriage," is legal. Both Shiite and Sunni values allow for the marriage of girls at a young age and the marriage contracts often have expiration dates. In 2010 it was reported that forty-two thousand marriages of girls between the ages of ten and fourteen were formally registered in Iran.[33] In 2013, a Jordanian Salafi cleric issued a *fatwā*, an Islamic religious ordinance, ruling that due to the large number of men killed and the growing vulnerability of women as an outcome of the war in Syria, a man can marry fifty women through a contract known as a *milk al-yamin*, a property by oath. This agreement defines the obligations of the man to the woman, her children, and her relatives—and the woman, in return, agrees to become his slave in a ceremony conducted by an ordained Muslim cleric. In the ceremony the woman recites the phrase, "I do hereby proclaim that my soul is your property."[34]

The film *Yarmouk* highlights another unfortunate result of the war in Syria: the poor living conditions of Palestinians living in the Yarmouk refugee camp. In October 2015, the Action Group for Palestinians of Syria[35] reported that the camp had been under siege by Assad's forces for more than eight hundred days and nearly two hundred people had died as a result of starvation or a lack of medications. It's been reported that inhabitants of the camp have had to eat stray cats and dogs to survive.[36, 37] In April 2015, the International Union of Muslim Scholars launched an emergency campaign called "Save al-Yarmouk Camp."[38, 39]

The film was met with widespread criticism from Palestinians and non-Palestinian Arabs alike. Palestinians blamed Bakri for what they perceived as him humiliating them. One Facebook user wrote that he was "undermining the suffering of the Palestinian refugees by emphasizing the tragedy of Syrian female trafficking."[40] Non-Palestinian Arabs viewed the film as having been intended to be an allegory of the gloomy situation of the entire Arab world. They believed this for a variety of reasons, including that the film ends with a line from Bakri—"to the Arab nation"—and, accordingly, expressed that they too felt humiliated. One commentator wrote that the film "diminished the tragedy of the Syrian refugees while emphasizing the suffering of Palestinian refugees."[41]

In response, Bakri issued a statement expressing his apologies and quickly pulled the film from YouTube.[42] He stated: "Had I been able to, I would have gone myself to the al-Yarmouk refugee camp . . . All I wanted was to draw the world's attention to the tragedy of the al-Yarmouk camp."[43, 44] His apology and the pulling of the film were surprising given that the film is on-point and reflects reality. The harsh conditions in the camp have led to a severe humanitarian crisis, and Arab and non-Arab organizations are documenting the tragedy of Syrian female trafficking in the Arab world—as well as the exploitation and sexual abuse of Syrian women in the Gulf states, Lebanon, Syria, Turkey, and other places.[45, 46, 47, 48]

The pressure on Bakri, which may likely have included threats and not just verbal criticism, is reflective of the refusal of many people in the Arab world to look in the mirror. Not for the first time, Arabs prefer to kill the messenger rather than admit and resolve the situation.

Another dynamic of the *Yarmouk* episode relates to the fact that Mohammad Bakri became famous for a documentary titled *Jenin, Jenin* that he produced and directed. *Jenin, Jenin* documented the alleged war crimes committed by Israeli soldiers during a military operation in a Palestinian refugee camp in Jenin in April 2002. The true story of Jenin is that following a massive wave of Palestinian suicide bomber attacks on Israeli civilian targets, Israel launched a military campaign to restore security and control in the West Bank, where the overwhelming majority of Palestinian suicide bombers were dispatched from to carry out their missions. The Jenin refugee camp is in the northern part of the West Bank, and for twelve days, April 2–14, 2002, fierce military clashes took place between the Israel Defense Forces and Palestinian militants inside it.

Following the clashes, the Palestinians accused Israel of genocide, claiming that the Israeli attacks killed hundreds of Palestinian civilians, including babies. An official report published in July 2002 by Kofi Annan, then the United Nations Secretary General, dismissed this claim as unsubstantiated and supported previously published accounts that said fifty-two Palestinians had been killed in the Jenin refugee camp, along with twenty-three Israeli soldiers.[49]

Israeli soldiers who'd been involved in the fighting in Jenin accused Bakri of deliberately misrepresenting the events, and the Israeli film censorship board ruled that the movie should not be publically screened. Bakri and Israeli human rights organizations appealed to Israel's supreme court, which in 2003 dismissed the ruling—not because it supported the film, but because of Israel's commitment to individuals' freedom of self-expression.

The legal battle, however, did not end there. Israeli soldiers who had fought in Jenin and families of Israeli soldiers who had been killed in Jenin filed a lawsuit accusing Bakri of defamation. The appeals were discussed in two Israeli courts until finally, in 2011, the Israeli supreme court rejected the lawsuit. The court again protected Bakri; however, its judges decisively ruled that the film was deliberately distorted and replete with lies. Judge Dalia Dorner said, "The fact that the movie includes lies does not justify preventing its screening."[50]

In a way, the story of Bakri's films, *Jenin, Jenin* and *Yarmouk*, is also the story of the differences between Israel and the Arab societies. Israel, as a democratic society, enables freedom of speech and pluralism, even if it is hard to swallow and offensive to many people. Arab societies refuse to face criticism and prefer to shoot the messenger until the message goes away—or in this case, is pulled from YouTube. If Arab societies enabled criticism, dialogue, and the sharing of different opinions, they might be in a better place today. Disturbingly, they all too often promote ignorance at all costs and in so doing fail to make rational assessments and logical connections. In essence, they fail, by choice, to accept reality and purposefully distort it.

The Arab mindset's perception of reality is all too often not subject to an analytical process based on the rational analysis of facts, logical connections, the chronological order of events, actions and reactions, and causes and outcomes. It allows, evens encourages, cause to be turned into effect; defeat to be turned into victory.

Noted Egyptian political science analyst and news executive Abdel Monem Said reflected in an article titled "Concerning Defeat and Victory" that in 1968, when he began his work as a journalist, he was amazed to discover that the 1967 War, the Six-Day War, in which Egypt suffered a bitter defeat, was perceived within Egyptian intellectual circles as a victory.[51] The logic behind this outlook was the perception that the war was an American-Israeli plot that was meant to lead to the ousting of Egyptian President Gamal Abdel Nasser—and the fact that Nasser stayed in office "proved" the Egyptian victory. That mindset, he lamented, has persisted since 1967; and the same distorted way of thinking in the Arab world, which ignores outcomes and facts, was also manifested after the war between Hezbollah and Israel in 2006 and again after the military confrontation between Israel and Ḥamās during July and August of 2014.

In an article titled "The Arab Spring and the Israeli Enemy," Saudi journalist Abdulateef al-Mulhim wrote:

> Why didn't the Arab states spend their assets on education, healthcare, and infrastructures instead of wars? . . . The Arab world wasted hundreds of billions of dollars and lost tens of thousands of innocent lives fighting Israel, which it considered its sworn enemy, an enemy whose existence it never recognized. The Arab world has many enemies and Israel should have been at the bottom of the list. The real enemies of the Arab world are corruption, lack of good education, lack of good healthcare, lack of freedom, lack of respect for the

> human lives, and finally, the Arab world had many dictators who used the Arab-Israeli conflict to suppress its own people.[52]

Abdel Monem Said, Abdulateef al-Mulhim, and other Arab journalists are willing to accurately and publicly assess the flaws of the Arab world, but so many of its other journalists and politicians continue to brainwash the Arab people with their distorted perceptions of reality. One of these journalists is Abdel Bari Atwan, of Palestinian origin, who was, until July 2013, the editor-in-chief of the widely-distributed Arab newspaper *Al-Quds Al-Arabi*, and whose distorted perception of reality can be found in many of his articles. In his article "Sinai Is the Nightmare of Israel," Atwan wrote that "Israel is the source of all of the problems, the troubles, and the instability of the Middle East."[53] The article was published in September 2012, at a time when tens of thousands of Syrians were being openly murdered by the Assad regime. An equal amount were being killed in nonstop violence in Iraq, Libya, the Sudan, and Yemen; demonstrations were flooding city streets across the Arab world; educational, physical, and social infrastructures were collapsing throughout the Arab world; and public and personal security did not exist in many cities, towns, villages, farms, mosques, schools, markets, streets, and even private homes throughout the region. Placing the blame on Israel for what was happening in the Middle East, as Atwan did, is a quintessential expression of a distorted reading of reality.

Atwan lives in London. He is one of the most veteran journalists in the Arab world—and among the most controversial. Since leaving *Al-Quds Al-Arabi*, he has become the editor-in-chief of a new Arabic news site, *Rai al-Youm* (*Today's Opinion*), and he continues to be a welcome guest-of-honor and contributor to many media outlets in the West, like BBC and the *Guardian*.[54, 55] He is certainly aware of what is truly going on in the Middle East, so why does he propagate a distorted explanation of reality? A partial explanation lies in the fact that Atwan is deeply hateful of the State of Israel, a sentiment he unabashedly expresses in his articles and public appearances. In a 2007 interview he gave on the Lebanese television station ANB, he expressed his hope that, "God willing, Iranians will attack Israel." He said, "[I]f Iranian missiles hit Israel, I will dance in [London's] Trafalgar Square."[56]

More recently, in a January 2015 appearance on Lebanon's Al Mayadeen television station, he said:

> In my view, jihad must be directed first and foremost against the Israeli enemy. This is the enemy about which there is consensus. Arabs who do not think that Israel is an enemy are neither Arabs nor Muslims. Our compass must point toward that enemy. All our guns must be pointed toward that enemy regardless of our differences because this is the only thing that unites us.[57]

Atwan knows that Israel is not the source of all of the Arab world's problems, but he also knows that he can get away with his outrageous claims because many people in the Arab world really think this way and will condone, embrace, and even spread this mindset.

The Resistance

One of the most powerful slogans used in the political and cultural discourse in Arabs societies is the slogan of *al-muqāwamah*, "the resistance."

Inspired by the armed groups who helped the Allies fight the Nazi regime in Europe, particularly in France, the concept of "the resistance" in its Middle Eastern version first appeared in Algeria when it was under French rule. It fueled nationalist sentiments and sparked an uprising in 1954, which resulted in the independence of Algeria in 1962, ending 125 years of French rule.

The core of "the resistance" is the promotion of a proactive struggle against the existing political order, borders, and arrangements that were determined following World War II as well as a struggle against the West and Israel. It's also meant to lead to the transformation of Arab and Muslim society through reinforcing the foundation of its defining element, Islam. Al muqāwamah provides feelings of dignity, hope, self-worth, and pride on both a personal and a nationalist level.

In the 1950s, the resistance in Algeria inspired Arab societies who were contemplating their own political identities and the meaning of concepts like Arab nationalism, pan-Arab nationalism, Arab socialism, and political Islam. Later, the discussion of these concepts was warmly embraced in a wide range of Arab circles. Part of the discussion involved the Arab-Israeli conflict.

Arab armies had suffered a humiliating defeat in the 1967 Six-Day War against Israel, which had been launched by Egyptian President Gamal Abdel Nasser, Syrian President Ḥafiz al-Assad, and Jordanian King Ḥussein ibn Ṭalāl, whose shared goal was to destroy Israel. In just six days, the Arab armies were badly defeated, and Egypt, Syria, and Jordan lost territory. Following the war, Israel occupied the Gaza Strip and the Sinai Peninsula, which were ruled by Egypt; the West Bank and East Jerusalem, which were ruled by Jordan; and the Golan Heights, which was ruled by Syria.

The defeat shocked the Arab masses and generated a process of self-criticism among Arab intellectuals. Egyptian author and 1988 Nobel Prize winner Naguib Mahfouz wrote of how profoundly impacted he was by the defeat; Syrian poet Nizar Qabbani wrote a poem named "Notes on the Book of Defeat" (1968) describing it; and Syrian scholar Sadiq Jalal al-Azm explored the roots of the defeat in his book *Critique of Religious Thought* (1969).

After the Six-Day War, a gloomy atmosphere pervaded the Arab world, and allegiance to "the resistance" was perceived to be even more important. It was considered a way to end the poverty and unemployment rocking Arab societies, to restore pride, and to offer a path to rehabilitation and recovery; in essence, a way to cure all problems. Other major tenets of the resistance were the centrality of Islam, a reference to the core of the individual as well as the collective identity, the proactive struggle to spread Islam, the rejection of the West and its values, and the restructuring of the current political structure and borders. Militant Islam completely rejects the origin of the resistance: the desire for an independent national state.

The resistance was widely, publicly adopted and warmly welcomed by the Palestinian National Movement, which began in the twentieth century as a struggle against Zionism and the British mandate (1920–1948). The mandate had been set up by the League of Nations to govern the territory of Palestine/the land of Israel, which had been ruled by the Ottoman Empire until the end of World War I.

When the Palestinians embraced the concept of the resistance, they recast it as an adherence to the use of violence as a way of life, one marked by determination, patience, and total sacrifice. The concept of resistance became the central tenet in an uncompromising fight against Israel until its extinction.

It was until just a few years ago that images of Syria's president, Bashar al-Assad, and Lebanese political leader and former secretary-general of Hezbollah Hassan Nasrallah, adorned streets and stores in the Arab world. For many Arabs, Assad and Nasrallah symbolized the "victory" of the "path of resistance" over Israel and the West. They were considered the spearheads of the resistance. In the eyes of many Arabs, Israel's withdrawal from Lebanon in 2000, which ended eighteen years of Israel's military presence in Lebanon, was due to the fact that Israel was defeated militarily by Hezbollah.

This adoration wasn't a universal sentiment—there were people who criticized Assad and Nasrallah's methods and leadership and voiced extreme suspicion over their motives. The critics had not forgotten that Hezbollah had conquered West Beirut, the capital of Lebanon, by force in 2008. They had not forgotten the involvement of Hezbollah and Assad in the assassination of their political opponents in Lebanon and Syria. And they had not forgotten the mass demonstrations in Lebanon from February–April 2005, called *thawrat al-Arz* (the cedar revolution), that had accused Syria of being behind the February 2005 murder of Lebanese Prime Minister Rafiq al-Hariri and had resulted in the withdrawal of Syrian forces from Lebanon in April 2015.

When the war in Syria broke out, it put the blind admiration that existed for Assad and Nasrallah into question. Before the shocked eyes of the Arab world, "the resistance" became a slogan that was used to justify the indiscriminate killing of Syrian citizens, including the elderly, women, and children, by the Assad regime and its allies—Hezbollah and Iran—and to authorize the rape of Syrian women by militias of the Assad regime.[58, 59, 60] It bestowed the stamp of approval on the destruction of Syrian cities and villages and the transformation of millions of Syrian citizens into refugees.

The yellow flag of Hezbollah bears the slogan, "The Islamic Resistance in Lebanon." Hezbollah flags found in the possession of Hezbollah militants slain in Syria have been imprinted with the phrase, "The Islamic Resistance in Syria." The resistance is no longer about fighting Israel and has instead become about fighting Syrians—and this has shaken the Arab world to its core. "The resistance"—the slogan that only yesterday was, as far as many members of the Arab world were concerned, the light that would show the right path—has revealed itself as a fabrication, a cynical and manipulative lie. It's shown itself as a compass that has purposefully distorted and misled.

A long line of writers, intellectuals, and politicians in the Arab world talk openly about this deception and fraud.[61, 62, 63, 64, 65, 66] Jordanian businessman and journalist Dr. Fateen al-Baddad wrote in a 2014 article that "Nasrallah keeps on selling us stories about resistance while his militants in the service of the Iranian butcher are starving Palestinians who eat cats in the Yarmouk camp . . . How long," he asked, "will this person [Nasrallah] continue to deceive and tell us stories and slogans about resistance and conspiracies while he and his master, the Iranians, are destroying the region?"[67]

Al-Quds Day, an annual event held on the last Friday of Ramadan, was initiated by the Islamic Republic of Iran in 1979 to express solidarity with the Palestinian people and oppose Zionism and Israel's existence. In Iran, several other Arab countries, and Muslim communities elsewhere in the world, it is marked by demonstrations against Israel and showcases of solidarity with the Palestinian people. On al-Quds Day in July 2015, as Hezbollah was facing mounting losses in fierce battles in the southwestern Syrian town of al-Zabadani, Nasrallah delivered a televised speech in which he said:

> The road to al-Quds [Jerusalem] passes through Qalamoun, Daraa, al-Zabadani, Homs, Aleppo, al-Ḥasakeh, Swaida, and other [Syrian cities] because if Syria was lost, Palestine would be lost too. . . . Every martyr falling for us in Syria and laid to rest here in Lebanon is a martyr for the sake of Syria, Lebanon, and Palestine. . . . After God, Iran is the only remaining hope to free Palestine. . . . If you are an enemy of the Islamic Republic of Iran, then you are an enemy of Palestine.[68]

In response to Nasrallah's comments, a Twitter hashtag was created whose meaning translates to, "the road to Jerusalem does not pass through al-Zabadani, Hassan Nasrallah."[69, 70] In response to his speech, one Twitter user wrote that "the way to Jerusalem does not pass through the scalps of Syrians." Another wrote, "Perhaps we should begin on the road to Jerusalem by going through Iran and we'll do it the exact same way the Iranians are doing it in Syria."

The name Nasrallah means "Allah's triumph," and as an expression of the growing anger toward Hassan Nasrallah, people in the Arab world have used insulting nicknames for him on Twitter. Some of the names translate to "Satan's Servant" or "The Piper"; others use Hassan but have changed his last name to *Nasrallahat*, which means "triumph of goddesses" and insinuates that he is pagan and not Muslim.

Today, much of the admiration in the Arab world for Assad and Nasrallah has been replaced by a burning hatred. Hezbollah flags are publically burned; posters and billboards that only yesterday hailed Assad and Nasrallah as heroes now portray them as monsters, wolves, and bloody predators.

Muna Fayad, a human rights activist and former assistant professor of psychology at the Lebanese University in Beirut, implored Nasrallah in an article titled "What Nasrallah Has to Hear" to remove his fighters from Syria and "return to the path of resistance against the real enemy—Israel."[71] The reactions of Arab readers to the article have largely been expressions of sarcasm. One reader asked, "How can Hezbollah continue to operate undisturbed in Lebanon as an Iranian agent?" and answered sarcastically, "There is nothing preventing it because Lebanon has stopped existing as a state since Hezbollah took it over in the name of the resistance."[72]

The reality is that Lebanon has been taken hostage by Hezbollah under the pretext of "the resistance" and that Hezbollah does not truly care about the Lebanese government or its people. A number of facts demonstrate this:

1. Hezbollah refuses to turn over senior personnel who are wanted by the Special Tribunal for Lebanon as persons of interest in the 2005 murder of Lebanese Prime Minister Rafiq al-Hariri.

2. The 2006 war with Israel that Nasrallah initiated resulted in enormous damage to Lebanon.

3. The weapons that Hezbollah describes as "the weapons of the resistance" were used by it to conquer West Beirut in 2008.

4. The weapons of the resistance are actually being used by Hezbollah's militants to kill Syrians.

> 5. Hezbollah refuses to comply with the repeated requests of Lebanese politicians and leaders to disarm on the pretext that the weapons of the resistance are meant to protect Lebanon from alleged Israeli plots. This is in spite of the fact that Israel completely withdrew from Lebanon in 2000, in full compliance with United Nations rulings, and has no presence on Lebanese soil.

Yet, despite the facts, there are still people in the Arab world who adamantly stand by Hezbollah and are committed to "the resistance" it promotes. Many of them truly believe that Israel wants to conquer Lebanon. A possible explanation was provided by Iraqi journalist Hadir Taher, who wrote in his article "It Is Because of My Admiration for Israel that I Had to Cut Relationships with My Friends" that "time and time again, Arab media brainwashed us that Israel desires to occupy the Middle East regardless of the fact that Israel withdrew from Egyptian, Jordanian, and Lebanese lands and is willing to negotiate withdrawals from other lands as well."[73]

Experiencing the world through the lens of conspiracies, seeing the world through a shift of responsibilities to the other, and being immersed in deeply embedded hollow slogans and inciting demagoguery continues to be a broken compass by which the Arab world navigates. And this is why the Arab world has lost its way. To confront and overcome their immense problems, Arab and Muslim societies must change their political and cultural discourse. A change like this is possible, but it is complicated and will take time. If people like Abdel Bari Atwan continue to shape the conversation, the Arab world will go more and more off-course. And the price of this—both for Arab societies and their neighbors—will continue to rise.

Thankfully, the Arab Awakening offers hope. It symbolizes the beginning of the disengagement of the Arab world from demagoguery, rhetoric, and slogans.

In April 2014, a reconciliation agreement was signed, for the fourth time, between the two central powers in Palestinian society: the Fatah Palestinian Organization and Ḥamās. According to the agreement, which is based on previous agreements signed between the sides, a Palestinian unity government will be formed and elections to a newly created Palestinian parliament will be held in the West Bank and the Gaza Strip. Initial discussions of this Palestinian schism followed a violent coup that Ḥamās perpetrated in the Gaza Strip in 2007, in which it violently overthrew the Palestinian Authority. The inner Palestinian split has been one of the the central subjects on the agenda of the Palestinian public, which is eager to put an end to the rift. Each of the previous times that a reconciliation agreement was announced, the speeches and slogans of leaders on both sides were laden with hackneyed clichés, such as "Palestinian brotherhood" or "shared destiny," and were accompanied by expressions of excitement and joy in the Palestinian cities. Processions and rallies were held, and sweets were given out to mark the events. But after the signing of the latest agreement, the picture was completely different: the slogans and festive processions were replaced by a sober, skeptical view among many Palestinians. They weren't convinced that the conciliation agreement would succeed.

Young Palestinians from both camps—who were accustomed to disappointment from previous failed attempts at conciliation—established a Facebook page named "The Reconciliation Meter" to track the status of the implementation of the agreement requirements.[74]

The reaction on the Palestinian street to the agreement reflected a process of maturation, and similar processes are happening throughout the Arab world as it begins a new chapter on a long, difficult, even dangerous path. Masalha may have been right when, in referring to the fake slogans of the Arab world, he said "that merchandise no longer has buyers in the young Arab market."[75]

CHAPTER TWO

THE ARAB AWAKENING: SCREAMS OF ANGER

DECEMBER 17, 2010. A NEW DAY dawned over the Tunisian village of Sidi Bouzid. In a small stucco house, a young man, Tarek al-Tayeb Mohamed Bouazizi, a street vendor, was getting ready for work. Bouazizi had never finished high school because, from an early age, he had to work to support his family. In that respect, Bouazizi was no different than millions of other young men of his generation in the Arab world.

By the time the sun set that day, Bouazizi would be hospitalized in critical condition after having deliberately set himself on fire, protesting the fine he was given by municipal authorities for the illegal peddling of fruits and vegetables. There are uncorroborated reports that he was beaten by the female inspector who fined him. Whatever the story, the frustration, the anger, and the absence of hope that he would be able to eke out a living and have a future with honor broke Mohamed Bouazizi's spirit.

Bouazizi died from his injuries, but his death granted him eternal fame. The flame he ignited on his body became a mighty and destructive fire that spread across the Middle East, generating a process of change of historic proportions that would influence the lives of hundreds of millions of people. It was an outcry, an outpouring of anger and frustration, and, most of all, it was a demand for change. The Arab Awakening is the scream of people throughout the Arab world who are demanding that their leaders and governments offer real solutions to their real problems. Like Bouazizi, they demand a future with honor and hope.

And indeed, the Arab world is facing enormous challenges. By every criterion—civil rights, development, education, employment, housing, literacy, personal safety, poverty, public services, scientific research, etc.—the majority of the Arab world, the twenty-two countries representing more than $369.8 million with a GDP of $2.853 trillion,[1] is in a dismal state.

The Freedom House, a US advocacy group that studies political freedom and human rights, publishes an annual *Freedom in the World* report, a large-scale assessment of civil liberties and political rights in countries around the world. According to its 2015 report, "Ratings for the Middle East and North African region were the worst in the world."[2]

The report's key findings stated that "a troubling number of large, economically powerful, or regionally influential countries moved backward." Egypt, the most populous country in the Middle East, and Turkey were on this list. The "Worst of the Worst" countries included Saudi Arabia, Somalia, Sudan, Syria, and the nearby countries of Turkmenistan and Uzbekistan.[3] Syria, a dictatorship it called "mired in civil war and ethnic division and facing uncontrolled terrorism," received the lowest Freedom in the World score of any country in over a decade.

One of the underlying problems in Arab territories is the poor educational system. In January 2014, the Arab League Educational, Cultural and Scientific Organization reported that the "illiteracy rate in Arab countries exceeded 19 percent or nearly 97 million."[4] A 2014 report by the International Monetary Fund stated that 39 percent of the workforce in the Middle East and North Africa region is "inadequately educated." This is the highest percentage among the world's regions.[5]

Unemployment is also widespread. At the February 2014 Arab Forum for Development, sponsored by the World Bank in partnership with the Kingdom of Saudi Arabia and the Arab Labor Organization, Inger Andersen, vice president of the Middle East and North Africa region at the World Bank, stated:

> The unemployment numbers are staggering. The Arab region persistently ranks higher than any other region and overwhelmingly reflects the numbers of youth and women. Joblessness is as high as 54 percent, which includes inactive and unemployed individuals

> between the ages of fifteen and sixty-four. Three of four working-age women do not participate in the labor force and constitute over 80 percent of the inactive population in the region.[6]

In an October 2014 interview, Andersen described the poverty prevalent throughout the region. She said:

> If we just look at the poverty delineator of [the number of people living on less than] 1.25 [US dollars per day]—then MENA [the Middle East and North Africa] has achieved the [goal of] eradicating extreme poverty. But that doesn't really quite work; if we take it up to two dollars a day, then all of a sudden we are at 13 percent [of the population living in poverty]. It is only 3 percent at 1.25 dollars. But if we take it up to four dollars—in the MENA region living on four dollars a day is impossible—then we are talking 53 percent. Then all of a sudden we begin to see that any little crisis, any little thing, can cause more people to fall into poverty, and cause more people to fall into extreme poverty. And that of course is the tragedy of the conflict we see in the Mashriq [the vast region extending from the western border of Egypt to the eastern border of Iraq], the turmoil we are seeing in Libya, as well as what we have witnessed in Yemen: that any little thing can then have a massive impact on nearly half the population when we are talking about [living] on four dollars a day, when 53 percent [of people] are living below that.[7]

To get perspective on the scope of the problems in the Arab world, let's first look at Saudi Arabia, the richest Arab state and one of the wealthiest countries in the world, and Egypt, the most populous Arab state.

Saudi Arabia

On the 2015 *Forbes* list of the world's billionaires, ten were Saudi nationals, with a combined fortune of $51.9 billion. Saudi Arabia has approximately 266 billion barrels of oil reserves, plus an additional 2.5 billion barrels in the

Saudi-Kuwaiti shared neutral zone. With 16 percent of the world's proven oil reserves, Saudi Arabia is the largest exporter of total petroleum liquids, maintains the world's largest crude oil production capacity, and is the second largest petroleum exporter of oil to the United States, after Canada.[8] According to the Organization of the Petroleum Exporting Countries, in 2014, Saudi Arabia's exports totaled $377,013,000. Of that, petroleum exports equaled $321,723,000.[9] On the surface, Saudi Arabia seems a prime example of a wealthy, thriving country. Within, things are much different.

In April 2013, the office of Saudi Prince al-Walīd ibn Ṭalāl ibn ʿAbd al-ʿAzīz Āl Saʿūd', better known as bin Ṭalāl, warned officials via his office's Twitter account that "there are five ticking time bombs in Saudi Arabia: a lack of diversity in sources of income, a diminishing need for oil, high population growth, the housing crisis, high unemployment, and poverty."[10]

Saudi Arabia is a country of more than twenty-seven million people.[11] Most of them are young people, at or approaching working age—80 percent of Saudi citizens are younger than forty, about 67 percent are under thirty, and 35 percent are under fifteen[12]—and the majority are educated. Unlike most of the Arab world, Saudi Arabians increasingly have access to education. In 2014, the average literacy rate for Saudis older than fifteen was 87 percent. And literacy is not gender limited. Eighty-two percent of Saudi women are literate. They're even increasingly able to access higher education. In February 2015, Al Arabiya, the Saudi-owned pan-Arab television network, reported that "64 percent of bachelor's degree graduates from public and private universities in the Kingdom in 2010, 2011, and 2012 were women."

But even with education, employment is not guaranteed. According to the Saudi Statistics Authority and the Saudi Ministry of Labor, the rate of unemployment in Saudi Arabia in 2014 was 11.7 percent.[13] Other estimates quote unemployment as high as 25 percent.[14] It's said that at least 11.2 percent of Saudi males are unemployed and that despite accounting for 51 percent of Saudi graduates, Saudi women occupy only 13 percent of private and public positions occupied by nationals.[15] The statistics include women with undergraduate, graduate, and postgraduate degrees and those who studied in Saudi Arabia as well as those who studied abroad. It's also particularly hard for immigrants to get employment, and a heavy 30 percent of Saudi Arabia's population is immigrants,[16] people highly unlikely, given the country's strict laws, to ever become citizens.[17]

The housing crisis is also an ever-increasing problem. There is a staggering lack of housing for young couples in Saudi Arabia. In January 2015, a reported 70 percent of Saudis were affected by the country's housing crisis. According to an article on the Middle East news website *al-Araby al-Jadeed* (*The New Arab*), "The Saudis are suffering from the biggest housing crisis in decades. Unofficial statistics claim that 60 percent of Saudis don't have homes and that about 30 percent of homeowners live in inadequate housing." A member of the Real Estate Committee of the Council of Saudi Chambers of Commerce stated that the Saudi Building Ministry completely failed to meet the program designed by the late king of Saudi Arabia Abdullah bin Abdulaziz al-Saud to build five hundred thousand housing units.[18]

Let's look now at Egypt, the most populous Arab state.

Egypt

On February 9, 2015, Egypt's Central Agency for Public Mobilization (CAPMAS) reported that the population of Egypt had reached eighty-eight million. It reported that 5,695 babies are born in Egypt every day, which equals a baby being born every fifteen seconds. The report stated that in less than six months, between August 2014 and February 2015, Egypt's population grew by more than one million people.[19] The skyrocketing population goes hand-in-hand with a young population. According to CAPMAS, 75 percent of Egyptians are under age forty, 61 percent are under thirty, and 31 percent are under fifteen.[20]

Like Saudi Arabia, Egypt also has great wealth within its borders. It, too, had ten nationals featured on *Forbes*'s 2015 list of the world's billionaires. Its listed billionaires had a combined fortune of $23.45 billion.[21] And like the Saudi ones, most of their fortune is from oil profits.

In the US Energy Information Administration's 2014 country brief, it states, "Egypt is the largest non-OPEC [Organization of the Petroleum Exporting Countries] oil producer in Africa and the second largest dry natural gas producer on the continent." However, the profits from oil are unsustainable. It noted that "one of Egypt's main challenges is to satisfy increasing domestic oil demand amid falling production. Total oil consumption grew by an annual average of 3 percent over the past ten years, averaging almost 770,000 bbl/d [barrels per day] in 2013. Egypt's oil consumption has outpaced production since 2010."[22]

Egypt has a much higher illiteracy rate than Saudi Arabia. In 2014, CAPMAS reported that 25.9 percent of Egyptians were illiterate. The rate of illiteracy among women in Egypt is almost double that of men—18.5 percent of men and 33.6 percent of women cannot read or write—and nearly 30 percent of youth over fifteen are illiterate.[23] One study found that "34 percent of [Egyptian] jobs require a technical education, but only 11 percent of the graduates have this level of qualification."[24]

Alarming rates of unemployment and poverty also shake the Egyptian way of life. The World Bank's January 2014 *MENA Quarterly Economic Brief* described the unemployment situation in Egypt, focusing both on the reasons for the continued strain—"political instability" and "escalated violence"—and what would be necessary to prevent its continued increase. It read:

> Unemployment rates have been increasing, reaching 13.4 percent in the third quarter of 2013. . . . This figure includes only registered workers and does not take into account the informal economy where unemployment is believed to be higher than the official rate. The period July to September 2013 alone saw an additional 30,000 unemployed Egyptians due to ongoing political instability and escalated violence. Official data show between 700,000 to 800,000 new job seekers entering the job market every year, some of whom will add to the already large stock of unemployed standing at 3.6 million. Estimates by the World Bank show that the economy needs to grow by at least 6 percent to make a dent in the unemployment rate by 2020.
>
> The gap between female and male unemployment rates, which pre-dates the 2011 revolution, has widened sharply. The male unemployment rate stood at 9.8 percent, while that of females reached 25.1 percent as of [the] end [of] September 2013. Data from the recent labor survey in Egypt show that approximately 74 percent of the unemployed are between 15 and 29 years old, of which 42 percent are in the age

> group of 20–24 year-olds. More than 76 percent of the unemployed are educated, with 30 percent having university degrees and above.[25]

Regarding poverty, the report notes that official data shows rates are high, and increasing:

> The poverty headcount (number of people living under the national poverty line of EGP 3920 [$569] per person annually) has increased to 26.3 percent in 2012/13 compared to 25.2 percent in 2010/11. The extreme poverty headcount (defined as EGP 3570 [$518] per person) increased tenfold after the 2011 revolution reaching 4.4 percent in 2012/13.[26]

In January 2015, CAPMAS and the United Nations Children's Fund (UNICEF), published a document stating, "Child poverty has grown continuously in Egypt over the past fifteen years, with a marked acceleration since 2010/11." In 2012 and 2013, 9.2 million children (age 0–17) lived in monetary poverty in Egypt. An additional 7.5 million children were vulnerable to extreme poverty, living somewhere between the national lower and upper poverty lines.[27]

Housing in Egypt is also a problem. In February 2015, Egypt's National Council for Human Rights accused the Egyptian government of not doing enough to solve the country's housing crisis, stating that more than 15.5 million Egyptians are living in shacks in slums and 1.5 million are living in cemeteries. The council argued that there is a need to build 450,000 housing units every year in Egypt.[28]

Israel

By all modern criteria, the Arab world is in a deep and serious crisis. Academics, intellectuals, journalists, politicians, and social activists in the Arab world speak openly and with great pain about its dismal state. In this context, Israel serves as a model for comparison of the dire situation in the Arab world.

In the spring of 2013, Khalil Ali Haidar, a Kuwaiti journalist, wrote that "an Israeli earns, on average, ten to twenty times what an Arab earns and enjoys a thousand times the freedom that the Arab has."[29] A month later, Dr. Hussein Amar Toka, a former Jordanian ambassador to Libya and a senior strategic analyst, wrote that "Israel manufactured so many satellites at a time when the Arab world manufactured nothing, nothing, nothing."[30]

Dr. Amal al-Hazzani, an assistant professor at King Saud University in Riyadh, Saudi Arabia, made a speech in 2011 that focused on Israel's place within the academic ranking of world universities. She noted the technological and scientific accomplishments of Israel as compared to the total failure of the Arabs in this arena. In explaining why she chose Israel as a source for comparison, she said:

> It is the only scientifically superior [country] in the Middle East, with scientists who just two days before won a Nobel Prize in Chemistry, and although it is not rich in oil and its security is unstable. . . . [I]t ranks highly in the fields of mathematics and computer science. Five Israeli universities are at the forefront of the top one hundred universities in the world. . . . [A] stunning achievement in record time . . . [W]hile Israel is succeeding, Arab states top the list of the least developed countries.[31]

The Scream of Anger

The smoking volcano of corruption, illiteracy, lack of services, poverty, unemployment, violence, etc. has erupted into an inevitable outcry of anger and frustration. In 2012, Syrian artist Rudy Khalil created an exhibition of nine posters to represent the Arab people's cry. He named the series "The Scream of Anger", and in an interview he gave to Al Jazeera, a Qatari-based news network, he explained that each poster stood for one Arab state that is in a "revolutionary phase as an outcome of the Arab Awakening." Khalil said the series expresses his belief that "the Arab Awakening is a scream of liberation that will inevitably result in a better, enlightened reality for the Arab world."[32] To understand the viability of Khalil's vision, it's necessary to journey deep into Arab society.

CHAPTER THREE

POLITICAL ISLAM: BELLY DANCING IN THE DRIVER'S SEAT

THE TERM "POLITICAL ISLAM" REFERS TO movements and parties in the Muslim world that have the following things in common:

- Their ultimate goal is to create a global Islamic cultural, political, and religious entity known as a *khalifa*, caliphate, in which no independent or sovereign state exists.
- They believe the caliphate should be governed and ruled by their definition of Islam's moral and religious laws, called *sharīʿah* (the path).
- The ruler of the caliphate will be the *khalif*, the highest executive position in the caliphate.
- The khalif will be monitored by the Supreme Council, Majlis al-Shura, which will make sure that the khalif governs according to the sharīʿah.
- They believe sharīʿah is the "master plan" given by Allah to mankind and the manifestation of Allah's ultimate will, and that it should therefore govern all areas of life, public and private, and be the only source of all legislation.
- They believe that any differing political philosophy (communism, democracy, socialism, etc.) is unacceptable because it is man-made, in defiance of Allah's will, and therefore imperfect, unjust, and doomed to fail.
- They reject democracy but consider it legitimate to use democratic elections and democratic government systems, such as parliamentary and multi-party political systems, as tactical tools to achieve their ultimate goal of creating a global caliphate.

- They oppose, and their values are in direct conflict with, Western values such as gender equity, homosexuality, liberalism, pluralism, and secularism, and they have little tolerance for freedom of expression, freedom of religion, freedom of thought, human rights, individualism, and liberty.
- They view Western values as an imminent and existential threat to Islam.
- They garner support and strengthen their power base by creating economic, educational, social, and welfare programs that benefit the broad public, especially people on the lower end of the socio-economic scale.
- They create educational and religious programs and institutions to embed the values of political Islam into as many people as possible, and they use these platforms to percolate and spread their ideology as much as possible.
- They have and require an absolute and uncompromising opposition to the existence of the State of Israel, and they refuse to recognize a Jewish nation. They justify their animosity with Islamist theology, believing that Judaism was once a "valid religion," but that the Jews betrayed Allah's master plan for mankind and therefore Allah punished the Jews, dispersed them in the world, and provided Islam to guide mankind.
- They believe that a Jewish state is a direct defiance of Allah's will.

The most prominent representative of political Islam is al-Ikhwān al-Muslimūn, the Muslim Brotherhood, the biggest mass movement in the Muslim Sunni world. The Muslim Brotherhood was founded in Egypt at the end of the 1920s by Ḥasan al-Bannā', an Egyptian teacher and *iman* (preacher) who was alarmed by what he perceived to be a Western threat to Islam and an attack on Islam's codes, morality, and values—things ranging from male-female social interactions and women's liberation to movie theaters, music, and Western dress. He created the Muslim Brotherhood as a revolutionary group to restore the caliphate through education, preaching, indoctrination, and proselytization. The process is known as *da'wa* (a "call" or "invitation").

Another major group within political Islam is the Salafi movement. *Salaf* means the past of something—its origin, roots, and primal source. Salafi thinkers and theologians believe that Islam will flourish again once its followers adopt the Islamic codes as they were in the time of the Prophet

Muhammad—Abū al-Qāsim Muḥammad ibn'Abd Allāh ibn'Abd al-Muṭṭalib ibn Hāshim—and his first four successors, *al-khulafā'u ar-rāshidūn* (the righteous caliphs who lead the path).

The ideologies of the Salafi movement and the Muslim Brotherhood have a lot in common. However, the Muslim Brotherhood leaves room for a more flexible translation and implementation of Islamic religious law and thus sometimes adopts a more pragmatic approach toward different aspects of everyday life. Salafis tend to be less flexible, ultraconservative. They believe in a tough, dogmatic implementation of Islamic religious law.

Political Islam's Political Parties

Political Islam did not incite the Arab Awakening; however, as it unfolded, it became clear to its adherents and leaders that it was a source of great opportunities—one of which was the opportunity to create political parties. With their own political parties, the Muslim Brotherhood and the Salafi movement would be eligible to compete in elections. In Tunisia, the Muslim Brotherhood created the Nahḍah ("Awakening" or "Renaissance") Party in March 2011. In Egypt, it created the Ḥizb al-Ḥurriya Wal-'Adala (the Freedom and Justice Party) in April 2011. In Kuwait, its al-Haraka al-Dosturiya al-Islāmiyyah (Islamic Constitutional Movement), known by its Arabic acronym, *Hadas*, developed in 1991. In Jordan, its Jabhat al-'Amal al-Islami (the Islamic Action Front) developed in 1992. And other countries stretching from the Arab Gulf to North Africa were developing their own offshoots. The Salafi movement in Egypt also had its own party, the an-Nour ("the Light") Party.

For political Islam, the creation of these parties was an important move. As the first waves of the Arab Awakening were rolling across the Arab world in 2011, the parties began to gain popularity, even taking power in some countries.

Tunisia, October 2011: In Tunisia's first free election, the Muslim Brotherhood's Nahḍah Party wins the most seats in Tunisia's newly created Tunisian Constituent Assembly and becomes the largest party in the Tunisian government.

Egypt, November 2011–January 2012: The Muslim Brotherhood's Freedom and Justice Party and the Salafi an-Nour Party win an overwhelming majority of seats in the Egyptian Parliament.

Kuwait, February 2012: The Muslim Brotherhood's Islamic Constitutional Movement, *Hadas*, and the Salafi movement increase their seats in the Kuwaiti parliament from nine to twenty-three.[1]

Egypt, June 2012: The Muslim Brotherhood candidate, Mohammed Morsi, the chair of the Freedom and Justice Party, wins the presidential elections and becomes the president of Egypt.

Syria, April 2013: About two years after the Syrian Civil War began, the Muslim Brotherhood formally announces the renewal of its activity. This comes after more than forty years of suppression by the late Syrian President Ḥafiz al-Assad, the father of the current president, Bashar al-Assad.[2]

From 2011–2013, across the Arab world—Tunisia, Egypt, Kuwait, Syria, Jordan, the West Bank and the Gaza Strip, Algeria, Libya, Morocco, and Qatar—the Muslim Brotherhood and Salafi movements gained momentum. In February 2013, Algeria's minister of religious affairs said that 80 percent of the mosques in Algeria were influenced by Salafi preachers.[3]

The more powerful political Islam became, the more its intolerant face was exposed. In November 2012, a senior Salafi leader in Egypt demanded the demolishing of Egypt's pyramids and sphinx, arguing that they were pagan, non-Islamic symbols.[4] In April 2013, a senior clergy member of the Muslim Brotherhood ruled that it was prohibited to wish Christians in Egypt a "Happy Easter."[5] In March 2012, Salafi activists in Tunisia replaced the Tunisian flag atop the entrance to Manouba University with the Salafi flag, resulting in violent clashes between students.[6] In 2013 Salafi activists began patrolling the streets in Tunisia, acting as a moral police force to impose strict code of Islamic dress.[7] In Jordan, they stormed Halloween parties, declaring the holiday an infidel ceremony offensive to Islamic values.[8]

In March 2013, the Muslim Brotherhood rejected a United Nations declaration calling for an end to violence against women and the safeguarding of women's rights—including those of lesbian and transgender women. The Muslim Brotherhood described the charter as a threat to the societal structure and moral values of the Muslim world, arguing that it would lead to the "complete disintegration of society."[9] In an announcement published on its website, the Muslim Brotherhood listed ten reasons for its objection, explaining that the suggested charter stood for ideas such as female equality, LGBT rights, legalization of prostitution, and others that are in full contrast with Islamic values, so are completely unacceptable.[10]

The major contributing factors to the success of political Islam at the beginning of the Arab Awaking were:

- *Community support*: From its early days, the Muslim Brotherhood and, to a lesser extent, the Salafi movement had been building far-reaching economic, educational, social, and welfare programs. They built, funded, and managed schools, religious study programs, and youth centers. They ran medical clinics and provided material and financial aid to the needy: orphans, widows, and others. These activities provided a wide base of emotional and political support, particularly for the Muslim Brotherhood.
- *Organization, presence, and infrastructure*: An efficient organizational structure and a large and broad infrastructure with a clear set-up and hierarchy, defined roles and responsibilities, and a clear succession plan provided steady footing. Mosques were used for religious purposes and as community centers and held administrative offices and the parties' headquarters. Today the Muslim Brotherhood in Egypt has thousands, some claim tens of thousands,[11] of mosques that are used for religious events, praying, preaching, and classes, as well as for community gatherings, meetings, and social get-togethers. They also house the offices of the Egyptian branch of the Muslim Brotherhood.
- *A vision that resonates*: Political Islam offers a way of life and a vision for dealing with the challenges that the people of the Arab world are facing. The Muslim Brotherhood's slogan, "Islam is the solution," is well-known in the Arab world, commonly spoken and frequently appearing on signs and billboards.

The Muslim Brotherhood and the Salafi movement saw tremendous growth; however, they were quick to lose office in Egypt and Tunisia, and the momentum they gained in other countries did not last long.

Political Islam's Dilemma

The Muslim Brotherhood's success paradoxically guaranteed its failure. As the Muslim Brotherhood took political power in Egypt and Tunisia, it became clear that solutions, not slogans, were necessary to maintain public support. The Muslim Brotherhood's slogan, "Islam is the solution," helped get its parties elected, but when no concrete solutions were provided, the public became disillusioned. Talking about change was insufficient—actual change was needed. The Arab Awakening had put political Islam, primarily the Muslim Brotherhood, in a place it had never been before, the driver's seat, but it wasn't sure how to steer. It had promised, and, once in office, was expected to deliver, solutions to problems such as mounting economic and social turmoil—but it had no concrete plans for doing so.

There is irony in history. About a year before the flames of the Arab Awakening ignited in Egypt, representatives of the younger generation of the Muslim Brotherhood recommended to its senior leadership that they change their slogan from "Islam is the solution," which had been with the movement since its beginnings. The younger generation, which is very active in universities throughout the Arab world, and in Egypt, in particular, understood that big changes were brewing and that the slogan needed to be revised because it did not resonate with large sectors of the public. The senior leadership, however, disregarded the concern.

Following the downfall of President Ḥosnī Mubārak in 2011, divisions within the Muslim Brotherhood's branch in Egypt became more pronounced. Many young members of the Muslim Brotherhood movement established a new political party, Ḥizb al-Wasat al-Jadid (the Party of the New Center), which was more moderate.[12] In addition, reports indicated that during 2012, tensions within Egypt's Muslim Brotherhood movement grew more virulent, resulting in the resignation of senior members.[13, 14, 15]

Finally, in the months between the Muslim Brotherhood's election to the Egyptian parliament in early 2012 and the country's presidential elections in June 2012, the leaders began to understand that the movement's slogan did not serve them any longer. They recognized what the younger generation had told them years ago—that the overwhelming majority of people in the Arab world were no longer interested in hearing slogans about a solution and instead wanted actual, clear, and immediate solutions to their real and growing problems. And so, in Egypt's 2012 elections, following President Ḥosnī Mubārak's ousting after three decades of rule and two-and-a-half weeks of civil disobedience—demonstrations, marches, riots, and strikes—the Muslim Brotherhood campaign slogan became "We are working for the welfare of Egypt." Its new lingo used terms such as "development," "justice," and "welfare," and the words became part of the names of Muslim Brotherhood parties throughout the Arab world. The slogan "Islam is the solution" was stored.

But even the new slogan and buzzwords were insufficient. The Arab world didn't want rhetoric; it wanted an action plan, and it wanted results.

Mohammad Morsi's Short Presidency

A short time after Mohammad Morsi's election as president of Egypt, on June 30, 2012, an organization of Egyptian young people arose by the name of Zabatak (literally, "I'm watching you"), and set up a website called the Morsi Meter.[16] The site followed the pace of the implementation of the sixty-four promises that Morsi had made to the Egyptian people during his election campaign. The subjects ranged in scope from things such as his promised supply of pita bread to transportation and traffic solutions, the improvement of personal safety, security, public order, energy solutions—especially regarding the supply of gas to the home and increasing the availability of fuel—and activities that would promote the awareness of issues like the quality of the environment.

The young people granted Morsi one hundred days to make good on his promises. One year later, on July 3, 2013, Morsi was ousted—partially because, as far as Egyptians were concerned, he failed to deliver the goods he promised. No leader could have provided immediate answers to Egypt's enormous problems—but, still, the public's patience had run out. In the same month Morsi was ousted, Tariq Alhomayed, one of the most senior journalists in the Arab world and the former editor-in-chief of *Asharq al-Awsat*, emphasized the impatience of the Egyptian people in an article he wrote titled "Egypt Is Uniting." In it he stated, "The masses need solutions, not hollow and empty slogans." A year later, Lebanese journalist Khairallah Khairallah wrote, "The Muslim Brotherhood [in Egypt] has no path or solutions to hardships."[17, 18]

When the Egyptian Army ousted Morsi, it was because of growing dissatisfaction with his rule and a resulting chaos on the streets, which the army determined he could not control. In a military coup, the army created a temporary government, arresting Morsi and Muslim Brotherhood activists in the process. In December 2013, the Muslim Brotherhood movement in Egypt was declared a terrorist organization by the Egyptian government. However, the political party of the Muslim Brotherhood was not classified as one.[19]

A year and a half later, in May 2015, Morsi, the executive leader of the Egyptian branch of the Muslim Brotherhood, Mohammed Badie, the supreme guide of the Muslim Brotherhood, and many other party members were sentenced to death. At this point they are still in prison, but none have thus far been executed. Some of the death sentences have been reduced to lifetime imprisonment.

In addition to Morsi's failure to deliver solutions, he made a wealth of devastating mistakes. One mistake was the strategy he used to gain support among Egyptians whose values and worldviews were different from, or in opposition to, political Islam. This strategy was his distancing himself from the Salafi movement, which he did in spite of the fact that cooperation between the Muslim Brotherhood and the Salafi movement would have been natural, given their shared ideology. In doing so, the Muslim Brotherhood not only lost a potential political partner, it created a political enemy. The Salafi movement bore a grudge against the Muslim Brotherhood and revenge was not long in coming. When Morsi was removed from office, the Salafi movement hurried to express its support for his ousting.[20]

Another of Morsi's mistakes was that he created a hostile relationship with the Egyptian Army. There was a growing suspicion in the army that Morsi was looking to repeat actions of his Muslim Brotherhood counterpart, President Recgep Tayyip Erdoğan of Turkey, who, after taking his former title of prime minister in 2003, had done a complete overhaul of the Turkish Army. The overhaul included arresting and ousting many officers to avoid opposition that might threaten his rule. Erdoğan was Morsi's role model and the first world leader to congratulate Morsi on his victory. This created early hostility and suspicion from the Egyptian Army, and Morsi never worked to assuage their fears.

A third mistake was that Morsi knew that many Egyptians did not identify with political Islam—it's why he distanced himself from the Salafi movement—but he, nevertheless, tried to lead Egypt toward a more "Islamic" course in accordance with political Islam's values. This raised concern and resentment among large sectors of the Egyptian population, particularly Christian Copts, women, and young people.[21, 22] His biggest move toward what was perceived to be a "Muslim Brotherhood–style Islamization" of Egypt was his attempt to write a new constitution for Egypt—one that left many segments of the population feeling alienated and disgruntled. The constitution was interpreted by many Egyptians to be an aggressive attempt by the Muslim Brotherhood to force its hard-line ideology on Egypt. The rejection of Morsi's constitution became widespread and virulent,[23] and some of its detractors even came from the other side of Egypt's political map. Muhammad al-Zawahiri, the leader of the Salafi-Jihadi movement in Egypt and the brother of Ayman al-Zawahiri, the leader of al-Qaeda, announced that the constitution was invalid because it viewed the people, not sharīʿah—the will of Allah—as the source of sovereignty.[24]

The outcome of Morsi's mistakes—his lack of sufficient action, his alienating the Muslim Brotherhood's most natural partner, the Salafis, his angering of the army, and his estranging of significant segments of the Egyptian population—was disastrous for him. He was left with waning public support and no political allies, a situation exacerbated by the fact that the rule of the Muslim Brotherhood was perceived by many Egyptians to be a dictatorial rule and therefore illegitimate, despite the fact that the party had won a democratic election.

At the end of the one hundred "Days of Grace" period allowed by Zabatak, it, together with other Egyptian political bodies and nonprofit organizations, launched a campaign called *Tamarod* (Uprising), which organized the social unrest that the Egyptian Army used as justification for removing Morsi from power.

Beyond Egypt, the Muslim Brotherhood's political parties in Tunisia, Jordan, Kuwait, and the United Arab Emirates also faltered.

In Tunisia's October 2014 parliamentary elections and its November–December 2014 presidential elections, its Muslim Brotherhood party, Nahḍ ah, was defeated by its major opponent, the Nidā' Tūnis (Call of Tunisia). Nidā' Tūnis is Tunisia's national/civil society–affiliated camp, which seeks a modern nation state, in which political and personal rights are anchored in legislation whose substantial—if not main—source of inspiration is civil, not hard-line Islamic law. The defeat was a clear message that the majority of Tunisians reject the path and vision of the Muslim Brotherhood. Following the elections, the Nahḍah Party was part of the new government but played a minor role.[25] But in November 2015, thirty-two members of the Nidā' Tūnis coalition resigned from the government, making the Muslim Brotherhood party, Nahḍah, the largest party in the Parliament. Yet, when the leader of the Muslim Brotherhood in Tunisia, Rashid al-Ghannushi, was asked if the movement planned to take advantage of the political crisis and take control of the government, he cautiously replied that it was not a crisis but merely a slight turbulence that would be over soon, and that the Muslim Brotherhood movement was interested in maintaining the stability of the state above all else.[26]

In Jordan, the political branch of the Muslim Brotherhood, Jabhat al-'Amal al-Islami, was publicly embarrassed in January 2013 when it protested the country's parliamentary elections. It called for a boycott of the elections, demanding that King Abdullah II transfer more power to the people, and held demonstrations and launched campaigns to rally the public to join the boycott.[27, 28] The organization believed it was influential enough that it could cause the cancellation of the elections. This proved a fatal mistake. The elections went on as scheduled and the failure boosted tension inside the movement and party. It generated a process that resulted in a formal split in March 2015 within the Muslim Brotherhood movement in Jordan and the establishment of a new movement, the reformist wing al-Janah al-Islahi, under the leadership of Abd al-Majid al-Zneibat, the previous leader of the Muslim Brotherhood movement in Jordan (1994–2006). The reformist wing has committed to limit its activities to preaching, and accordingly and not surprisingly, received the formal blessing of the Jordanian government. It is even registered as a Jordanian NGO and as such is subject to governmental inspection and monitoring. In November 2015, a number of senior members of Jordan's Muslim Brotherhood resigned from the movement.

The Muslim Brotherhood's Balancing Act: Belly Dancing in the Driver's Seat

While in power in Egypt, the Muslim Brotherhood found itself facing an enormous dilemma, one that it still wrestles with today. It realized that if it continued to cling to its extreme hard-line ideology, which openly discriminates against homosexuals, other religions, and women, and professes anti-Israeli and anti-Semitic sentiments, it would be perceived by the international community, particularly the West, as a non-pragmatic, extreme element. Being characterized this way would make it difficult to attract foreign aid and monetary investments—an overwhelming majority of which come from the West. Without foreign aid and investments, it would be impossible for the Muslim Brotherhood to fulfill its promise to solve economic challenges and social hardships.

But if it were to compromise on its ideology, it risked being weakened politically as a result of a loss of support by voters disappointed by its ideological compromises. The disappointed supporters of the Muslim Brotherhood might even have punished the organization by supporting the Salafi movement instead. The Salafi movement was not attempting to secure political power, and thus was not restricted by the need to exercise political flexibility and compromise ideologically in order to form a government.

In an attempt to deal with this dilemma, the Muslim Brotherhood created a "belly dancing policy." The model, used in Egypt and beyond, was to work on two parallel channels: the movement itself would be active on one channel and the movement's political party would work on the other channel. The ultimate authority stayed in the hands of the Supreme Council—the highest executive body of the Muslim Brotherhood. The logic was that by separating into two units, the Muslim Brotherhood movement could stick to its ideology in rhetoric and activity in order to placate its base and ensure the continued support of its natural supporters, while its political parties would, by functioning as distinct units, have much more room for pragmatic maneuvering. This was essential for internal needs, such as maintaining its followers' loyalty, and for external needs, like placing the Muslim Brotherhood on the international stage as a pragmatic body that the international community could negotiate and do business with.

While in power, both the Egyptian and Tunisian Muslim Brotherhood governments had to constantly maneuver between the "pragmatic arena" and the "ideological arena." There are many examples of this "belly dance," and it characterized the short-lived governing era of the Muslim Brotherhood in both countries. One especially illustrative example was Egypt's peace agreement with Israel. The Muslim Brotherhood—as part of its core ideology—is on the front line of the Arab world that opposes all relations with Israel and calls, at every opportunity, for the cancellation of the peace agreements signed between Israel and its neighbors Egypt and Jordan; but once elected president of Egypt, Morsi made it clear that even though he was part of the Muslim Brotherhood, he would honor the peace treaty with Israel established in 1979.[29] His commitment to this happened at the same time as the leader of the Muslim Brotherhood movement in Egypt was calling for a "jihad to free Jerusalem."[30]

In most cases the activity on the two channels was coordinated. However, there were episodes when the inner tension between ideology and political needs clashed—for example, the wave of protests in the Arab world following the broadcasting on YouTube of the movie *The Innocence of Muslims*[31] in September 2012. The Muslim Brotherhood's response to the broadcasting of the movie was its call for mass demonstrations in front of every major mosque in Egypt; but the very next day, it announced the abolishment of the planned protests. It is likely that Morsi urged the movement to back down. On September 13, 2012, there was an attack on the US embassy in Cairo that nearly caused a diplomatic crisis between Egypt and the United States, and Morsi was eager to restore calm. Both he and the Muslim Brotherhood movement knew that Egypt needed the support of the United States and that an internal chaos would not help attain this.

These examples offer insight into the Muslim Brotherhood's mentality: *it is willing to make its ideology subordinate to pragmatic considerations for its political benefit.* In the case of the peace treaty with Israel, Morsi knew that if he dissolved it, he was not only damaging the Muslim Brotherhood's attempt to gain international approval as a reliable counterpart, he would also have faced tough retaliation from the United States and the rest of the international community that would have threatened the endurance of the party's rule.

The Future of the Muslim Brotherhood

The Arab Awakening offered political Islam a historic opportunity to take a meaningful step in the direction of actualizing its vision, but the leaders of political Islam, especially within the Muslim Brotherhood, mismanaged the opportunity and no amount of "belly dancing" was enough to keep them in power. Had the Muslim Brotherhood created alliances with natural partners, like the Salafis, and courted alliances with other potential partners, it might have been able to show that it could deliver results. Instead, it estranged major segments of the public and alienated political opponents and potential partners.

Today, the Muslim Brotherhood, and, to a lesser extent, the Salafi movement, is experiencing a deep crisis. Saudi Arabia, the United Arab Emirates, and Egypt have decreed the Muslim Brotherhood to be a terrorist organization and the Muslim Brotherhood's activities in Jordan and in the Gulf states, even Qatar—which is a major sponsor of the Muslim Brotherhood—are limited and controlled. Defeated politically, facing growing constraints, and experiencing fragmentation resulting from the need to bridge the growing tension between ideology and practicality, today's political Islam is at a crucial crossroads.

But despite its setbacks, political Islam is by no means down for the count; it is too deeply planted in the broad avenues of the Arab world. In August 2015, the movement was estimated to have some five hundred thousand members in Egypt.[32] The widespread educational, economic, and social programs that the Muslim Brotherhood created, and still runs, provide this enduring support.

The Muslim Brotherhood and the Salafis are also marathon runners—the Arabic terms *sabr* (patience) and *tamkin* (to make possible) are among their core values and symbolize their goal of actualizing a global caliphate. For them, the realization of this goal justifies temporary political and ideological compromise; the end justifies the means.

At this stage and in the foreseeable future, the Muslim Brotherhood will continue to focus on reorganization and a political strategy that will preserve its core values, yet also enable it to be attractive to voters who demand real solutions to the challenges of Arab societies. As a result of the need to reconcile ideology with practicalities, struggles between the pragmatic camp and the ideological camp within political Islam will continue. This power struggle is likely to result in the strengthening of the pragmatic camp within political Islam.

For those members of the Muslim Brotherhood who are unwilling to compromise their values or work with those open to compromise, the Salafi movement or other entities that to large extent are offspring of political Islam may become increasingly desirable.

CHAPTER FOUR

MILITANT ISLAM: BIN LADEN IS BOTH DEAD AND ALIVE

In a 2012 article titled "The bin Laden Movie,"[1] Lebanese journalist Diana Moukalled wrote, "Osama bin Laden died when Bouazizi set himself on fire."[2] Saudi writer Hussein al-Shabakshy shared these sentiments in May 2011, shortly after bin Laden was killed, when he proclaimed:

> Today, what matters is Mohamed Bouazizi and the movement for freedom. Osama is gone—Bouazizi lives on. Who will win? Bouazizi, of course! Turn the page and cast aside the book of al-Qaeda and its stalwarts.[3]

In many ways, the Arab Awakening symbolized the ideological defeat of the murderous way of Osama bin Laden and his successors. Contemporary Sunni militant Islam is rooted in the two main representatives of political Islam: the Muslim Brotherhood and the Salafi movement.

Since the early days of the Muslim Brotherhood, it has had—in addition to its educational, social, and welfare initiatives—a violent yet largely confidential terror arm operating under the code name al-Nizam al-Khass (the Special Apparatus). Throughout its history, the conflict between the Muslim Brotherhood's vision of a global caliphate ruled according to sharīʿah law and the model of modern national statehood has led to collisions—sometimes violent ones—between the Muslim Brotherhood and state governments; al-Nizam al-Khass is utilized when necessary to promote its agenda.

The Muslim Brotherhood has a history of using violence against the Egyptian government, and the Egyptian government has a history of using violence against the Muslim Brotherhood. In Egypt, in 1948, members of al-Nizam al-Khass assassinated the Egyptian prime minister Maḥmūd Fahmī al-Nuqrāshī. In the 1950s, they attempted to assassinate Egypt's President Gamal Abdel Nasser, but failed. Ḥasan al-Bannā', the founder of the Muslim Brotherhood movement, was assassinated in 1949, allegedly by Egyptian government agents; and over the years, the organization's leaders and activists have been arrested and tortured, sometimes executed, by the Egyptian government.

One of the Egyptian government's targets was Sayyid Quṭb, an author and educator who was one of the leaders of the movement in the 1950s and 1960s. Quṭb's radical hard-line ideology, which not only included the use of violence but made it mandatory, laid the foundations for contemporary militant Islam and was seen as a threat to the government. He was hanged in 1966, convicted of plotting to assassinate President Nasser.

Sayyid Quṭb's ideology called for:

- Making sharī'ah the one and only law.
- Toppling any regime that does not implement sharī'ah law.
- Proactively and violently creating a global caliphate.
- Unwaveringly opposing Western values.
- Eliminating the State of Israel and Jews.

Quṭb and other radical Islamist thinkers, like Mawlana Abū'l-A'lā Mawdūdī, laid the foundations for the emergence of "Islamic fundamentalism." The Arabic word for the phenomenon is *usuliya* (the root, the origin) and Islamic fundamentalists are called *usuliyun.*

Modern Islamic fundamentalism has two branches. One branch is the camp of non-militant Islamist fundamentalists whose members adopt the strict implementation of sharī'ah law but do not strive to impose it on others by the use of force; instead, they use preaching, educating, and political action. Some fundamentalist groups, like the Egyptian group al-Quṭbiyun, which was created in the 1960s and named after Sayyid Quṭb, or Ahl al-Khaf (People of the Caves), choose to physically segregate themselves.

This separation aims to defend their way of life, norms, and values from the surrounding society that is—in the eyes of fundamentalists—morally decadent and corrupt.

The other branch of Islamist fundamentalism is militant Islam. Militant Islamists are often called *usuliyun mutashaddidun* or *al-mutashaddidun al-Islamiyyun* (extreme fundamentalists or extreme Islamic fundamentalists).

Militant Islamists and fundamental Islamists reject Western values and strive for the creation of a global caliphate. They call for a return to the ideals and laws of pure early Islamic sharīʿah, and they adhere to and apply a strict and dogmatic Islamic orthodoxy. For militant Islamist groups, such as al-Jama'ah al-Islamiya, Islamic Jihad, ISIS, and al-Qaeda, violence is a necessary tool to use to proactively impose the ideological objectives of fundamentalist Islam.

Takfir Ideology

In the late 1960s, an additional radicalization took place within the militant ideology with the development of the concept of *takfir*. It was at this time that a group in Egypt appeared called al-Takfīr wa al-Hijrah (Excommunication and the Holy Flight or Excommunication and the Migration),[4] which was founded by Shukrī Muṣṭafā. Muṣṭafā saw violence and terrorism as a necessary means for "purifying infected Islam" and as a step toward the realization of the caliphate.[5]

Takfir is an extreme school of thought within militant Islam—likely one unforeseen by Quṭb or the early Salafi thinkers. It has taken violence to even more extreme levels and relates to a basic concept in Islam known as *kāfir billah* (heresy).

Islam means the total emotional, intellectual, physical, and spiritual willingness of a person to subdue himself or herself to the concepts of monotheism and Allah. A Muslim, then, is a person who fully submits to Allah's rule. Islam argues that the world is divided into two major groups: Muslims who adopt Allah's rule and people of all faiths who do not. Those who do not are *kuffār* or *kāfirun,* heretics.

Takfir ideology argues that in addition to non-Muslim infidels, there are people who claim to be Muslims, but do not fulfill the commandments of Islam in the "true and correct" manner and, therefore, should not be seen as

Muslims but instead as *kāfirun*. These people are considered the worst enemies of Islam, whose danger is even greater than that of non-Muslims. It's considered necessary to fight against both. The *takfir* ideology believes that Muslim infidels are corrupting Islam and its values from within, and as long as Islam is not pure, the ultimate goal, establishing Allah's dominion on earth, cannot be realized. *Takfir* ideology believes that Islam must be purified of "Muslim impersonators," and the result has been the emergence of militant Islamist groups who murder Muslims indiscriminately in the name of *takfir*.

The overwhelming majority of the victims of militant Islamist terrorism are Muslims. The West states this cautiously,[6] even though Arab thinkers have been saying it loudly and openly for many years. In an article by Kuwaiti journalist Dalaa al-Mufti, he gave sample statistics of the daily death toll caused by adherents of militant Islam and declared that "Militant Islam and jihad brought catastrophe on the Arab world."[7] Arab journalist Huda al-Husseini reported in October 2013 that al-Qaeda was responsible for the killing of more than eight thousand people between 1998 and 2011, and that almost all of its attacks took place in Muslim and Arab states.[8]

Salafi-Jihadi Militant Islam

The ideology of militant Islamist groups is rooted in the Muslim Brotherhood's ideology or the Salafi ideology. The Muslim Brotherhood's ideology led to the development of terror organizations such as the Egyptian Jihad, al-Jama'ah al-Islāmiyyah (the Islamic Group), and Ezzedeen al-Qassam Brigades, the armed-militant wing of Ḥamās (the acronym for Ḥarakat al-Muqāwamah al-'Islāmiyyah, the Islamic Resistance Movement). Ḥamās is a Palestinian Islamist organization that defines itself as the branch of the Muslim Brotherhood in Palestine.

Quṭb's radical hard-line philosophy and teachings combined with the Salafi's ultra-conservative ideology gave birth to the militant Islam Salafi-Jihadi ideology of al-Qaeda, Global Jihad, ISIS, Islamic Jihad, Jabhat al-Nusra, and dozens of other militant Islam organizations. Quṭb's voice echoed clearly in the messages of Osama bin Laden, the Saudi-born founder of al-Qaeda; Ayman al-Zawahiri, the Egyptian-born current leader of al-Qaeda; Anwar al-Awlaki, the US-born former leader of al-Qaeda; Abū Bakr al-Baghdadi, the Iraq-born current leader of ISIS; and other militant Islam leaders.

Analyses, reports, research, and information on militant Islam could fill volumes. Instead of attempting to undertake a comprehensive review, let's focus on its evolution, some of its basic concepts, and one of its major streams, the Salafi-Jihadi ideology—the school of thought that guides, inspires, and motivates many of the major militant Islamist groups, including al-Qaeda, Boko Haram, Islamic Jihad, ISIS, Jabhat al-Nusra, and dozens of others operating today.

The core belief of Salafi-Jihadi ideology is that Islam will thrive again once it adopts the codes, laws, and values as they were in the time of the Prophet Muhammad and his first four successors, the rightly-guided caliphs. To implement the codes, law, and values, Salafi-Jihadi calls for proactively and violently spreading and implementing its ideology.

The core difference between political Islam and militant Islam when it comes to the creation of the caliphate is that while political Islam's core concept is *tamkin*, the need to focus today on creating the conditions and *laying the foundations for a future* global caliphate; militant Islam's core concept is *takwin*, the need for the *immediate establishment* of a global caliphate. Takwin represents the belief that it is necessary *now* to establish a global caliphate—and that the realization of this goal requires uncompromising ideological rigidity.

The values and goals of Salafi-Jihadi militant Islam are:

- To urgently establish a global caliphate in which every aspect of life is governed by a strict orthodox interpretation of sharī'ah.
- To overthrow all current political structures in the Muslim and Arab world because the current governments and rulers do not rigidly enforce sharī'ah and are therefore illegitimate.
- That the use of violence is justified, even critical, to establish the caliphate; that all means necessary to achieve the caliphate are acceptable.
- That it's necessary to wage war on the West and its values because they threaten the Islamic religion and Islamic civilization.
- That it's necessary to wage war on the Jews and the State of Israel.
- That it's necessary to wage war on Shiites.

- That the total devotion and commitment of the individual is needed to achieve the objectives of the ideology.
- The concept of *talb a-shahada* (the quest for martyrdom) and its importance.

In militant Islam there is a much higher and nobler objective than living a fulfilling life, the establishment of Allah's rule over the human race. Muslims are expected to not only be *willing* to sacrifice their lives, but also to *want* to sacrifice their lives.

In southern Israel there is a respectful memorial site commemorating Egyptian soldiers who were killed in wars with Israel. At the site is a stone monument decorated with the Egyptian flag. A famous verse taken from the Koran—the Muslim's sacred book—is carved in the stone: "*wala Tahsabana lazina kutilu fi sabil Allah amwatah bal ahya inda rabihim yurzakun.*" The translation is: "Think not of those who are killed in the Way of Allah as being dead. Nay, they are alive, with their Lord, and they have provision." The original reading of the verse was that it was meant to offer comfort and solace to people who lost loved ones in battle. Militant Islam uses the verse in its marketing, propaganda, and recruitment and to encourage people to pursue martyrdom—to kill and get killed.

Jihad

The other core value of militant Islam is *jihad* (an effort). Jihad comes from the broad Arabic concept of *jihad fi sabil Allah* (an effort to implement Allah's way).

In the very early phases of Islam, jihad referred to an intensive spiritual journey of Muslims to reach a higher degree of inner purity in their beliefs and a more pure worship of Allah; today, it's much more violent.

Prophet Muhammad and his first disciples were persecuted by powerful Arab tribes and forbidden to preach and practice Islam. In fear of their lives and yearning to practice their religion free of punishment and retribution, they fled Muhammad's hometown, the city of Mecca, and found refuge in the ancient Saudi city of Yathrib, located some two hundred miles north of Mecca. Shortly after their arrival, the city's name was changed to Madīnah al-Nabi (the City of the Prophet), and later, simply, al-Madīnah (the City)—in English, Medina. Today it is one of Islam's three sacred cities.

Muhammad fled Mecca in 622 CE, which is year 0 in the Muslim calendar, the *hijri* or *hijra* (the "migration" calendar). Due to the persecution and harsh conditions that the first Muslims endured, jihad evolved to not only be the spiritual journey of the believer but also the willingness of Muslims to sacrifice materially and physically, and to suffer stressful and uncomfortable conditions in order to practice their faith and fulfill their religious duties.

During the seventh century, Muhammad and his followers, through the use of military campaigns, expanded Islam's influence and control throughout the Arab Peninsula and northward toward Iraq and Syria. This is when a new dimension was added to the concept of jihad—it became not only about the willingness to die while *defending* Islamic values, but it also began to represent a willingness to die as an *offensive* act used in proactively spreading Islam, expanding its territory, and imposing Islamic rule.

A Global Movement

There are many militant Islamist groups operating around the world, most powerfully and visibly in the Middle East, Africa, and Central and Southeast Asia. In Australia, Europe, and North America, their activity is mostly underground. The activists' shared goals are to spread militant Islam's ideology, recruit supporters, and build terror cells. The terror cells can either act independently or together to plan and execute terror attacks. The September 11, 2001, attack on the United States by al-Qaeda—the largest terrorist attack in history, in which 2,997 victims were killed—as well as the terror attacks in Madrid, London, Paris, and San Bernardino, California, were painful manifestations of the severe global threat that Salafi-Jihadi militant Islam presents.

Of the militant Islamist groups, the average Westerner is likely most familiar with the names al-Qaeda and ISIS. Al-Qaeda, which in Arabic means "the base," "the foundation," or "fundamental," was established by Osama bin Laden in the late 1980s. It is a global Islamist Salafi-Jihadi militant organization and an old player in militant Islam compared to more newly developing militant Islamist groups like ISIS.

ISIS—whose acronym is for the Islamic State of Iraq and Syria or the Islamic State of Iraq and ash-Sham (ash-Sham is the Arabic name that for centuries referred to a geographic area consisting of what is today Israel, Jordan, Lebanon, and Syria)—is also commonly referred to as ISIL—the Islamic State of Iraq and the Levant or just IS-Islamic State. In Arabic it is *al-Dawlah al-Islāmīyah*—the Islamic State (IS)—or *al-Dawlah al-Islamīyah fī al-'Irāq wa-al-Shām*—the Islamic State of Iraq and ash-Sham—but is primarily referred to in the Arab world and in Israel by the acronyms *Da'ish*, *Da'eesh*, or *Daesh*.

Al-Qaeda, ISIS, Global Jihad, and all other Salafi-Jihadi groups share the same message: *Kill and get killed for the glory of Islam and Allah's rule*. Anwar al-Awlaki, al-Qaeda's leader, was quoted in the al-Qaeda magazine *Inspire* as saying, "The killing of women and children, as well as the use of weapons of mass destruction, is legitimate and justified."[9] This is the message that Osama bin Laden; Sheikh Abdullah Yusuf Azzam, the founder of Global Jihad and the man credited with creating what bin Laden formed into al-Qaeda; Ayman al-Zawahiri, the former leader of Egyptian Jihad and the current leader of al-Qaeda; Abū Bakr al-Baghdadi, the leader of ISIS; and others like them offer the Muslim world.

Militant Islam and the Arab Awakening

The Arab Awakening symbolized the ideological defeat of Osama bin Laden and what he, his successors, and other adherents of militant Islam stand for because the vision at the heart of the Arab Awakening is opposite theirs—it is one of a better life, a future, and hope. The overwhelming majority of Muslims do not want to die for the sake of religion or Allah's rule—they want a future of dignity and prosperity for themselves and their children. In the minds of militant Islam's practitioners, the objectives motivating the Arab Awakening were both in full contrast to their own and also manmade—and thus in complete defiance of Allah's will.

However, while on an *ideological level*, the Arab Awakening symbolizes the defeat of bin Laden and his path, on an *operational level*, the Arab Awakening has caused the terrorist path of bin Laden and his successors to gain momentum.

In May 2015, Arab journalist Tariq al-Humaid wrote that "bin Laden viewed the Arab Spring as the most important event in the Muslim world over the last centuries . . . [and] accurately recognized that the Arab Spring offers militant Islam an opportunity and a stage."[10]

Chaos in the Arab world is what caused the Arab Awakening—and the Arab Awakening in turn generates chaos. And chaos is the strategic ally of bin Laden and those who succeed him because the more that chaos grows, the more powerful militant Islam becomes.

The disintegration of states like Iraq, Libya, Syria, and Yemen, the growing instability of states such as Algeria, Egypt, Jordan, Lebanon, and Tunisia, and the lack of proper borders throughout the region are good news to bin Laden's successors. They present a large playing field in which militant Islam can expand, physically taking over and expanding its influence into a wide range of geographical areas, including parts of Iraq, Syria, Libya, Nigeria, North Africa, Somalia, the Sinai Peninsula, the Gaza Strip, and Yemen.

Militant Islam exploits chaos to grow, build momentum, and deepen its hold on its followers. It does this through violence and terror that brings anarchy, which in turn creates more violence and terror. It is a vicious cycle that serves militant Islam well because it allows militant Islamist groups to establish themselves and accumulate power in parts of the Arab world that have been neglected, communities with illiteracy, poverty, and violence. With neglect, a communal hopelessness develops and the result is vulnerability—a situation in which people can be easily overtaken.

Political Instability, Case Example: Iraq

Most Iraqis are Shiite Muslims, about 60–65 percent.[11] The second largest religious group in Iraq is Sunni Muslims. Sunni Muslims, who are mostly based in central and western Iraq, account for roughly 35 percent of the Iraqi population.[12]

During the rule of Saddam Hussein—who was Sunni—Iraqi Shiites (as well as Kurds) were discriminated against and oppressed. Following the 2003 overthrow of Saddam Hussein, a new, predominately Shia government came into power in Iraq and the balance of power was reversed. The prime minister who followed Saddam Hussein, Nūrī al-Mālikī, was Shiite, and his successor, the present prime minister, Haider al-Abadi, is also Shiite. Since 2003, the Iraqi Sunnis have found themselves being discriminated against and oppressed.

In 2013, the growing anger, bitterness, discontent, and frustration of Iraq's Sunni minority led to outbursts of violence in the predominately Sunni province of al-Anbar, in western Iraq. With a population of about two million people, al-Anbar is the largest province in Iraq, with borders that begin in Bagdad and extend to Syria, Jordan, and Saudi Arabia. In 2013, violence led to a large-scale uprising of the Sunni tribes' militias.[13, 14, 15] By the end of 2013, the combat was primarily in the district's two major cities: al-Ramādī, seventy miles west of Bagdad, and al-Fallūjah, forty miles west of Bagdad—and the Iraqi government was quickly losing its ability to enforce its authority anywhere in the country. Shiite militias took control in southern Iraq; the Kurds for all intents and purposes established Kurdish autonomy in northern Iraq; and the Sunni tribes in central and western Iraq were battling the Shiite government. The state of Iraq, embroiled in chaos and violence, was disintegrating.

This was the situation in Iraq when, in April 2013, ISIS was forming.[16] Within a year, it ruled over sections of three central Iraqi districts, al-Anbar, Diyala, and Saladin, all predominately populated by Sunnis.

In June 2014, ISIS conquered the city of Mosul, 250 miles north of Baghdad, and expanded its control westward, crossing the Iraqi-Syrian border and occupying parts of the districts of Dayr al-Zawr and al-Raqqah, in northeastern Syria. Abū Muḥammad al-'Adnānī, a senior ISIS leader and its official spokesman, announced the establishment of the "Islamic State" in these areas.[17] In May 2015, ISIS also occupied the city of Palmyra, in central Syria.

A large part of ISIS's power is rooted in two Iraqi Sunni sectors: the tribes in the central part of Iraq and Iraqi soldiers and officers who served in the Iraqi military during Saddam Hussein's rule and lost their jobs and status following the dismantling of Hussein's military after the United States occupied Iraq. These groups are frustrated and seeking revenge.

The appearance and achievements of ISIS in such a short amount of time are a result of the chaos, poverty, violence, and despair coupled with a lack of governance and clear borders.

Political Instability, Case Example: Libya

Libya is a country of about six and a half million people,[18] is overwhelmingly Sunni, and is based on tribes—dozens of tribes—who are mostly Bedouins of Arab origin, called Berbers, or members of the Tuareg tribes. Both the Berbers and the Tuareg are from North Africa; the two largest tribes, Warfalla and Magarha, and another significant tribe, Zuwayya, reside mostly in the eastern part of Libya, where most of the country's oil and gas fields are located.

Libya gained independence from Italy in 1951 and was ruled from 1951–1969 by King Idrīs, its first and only king, who claimed he was a direct descendant of the Prophet Muhammad. In 1969, Muammar Qaddafi, then a Libyan army officer who was a member of the tribe Qadhafah, a relatively small tribe from the area of Sirte, in north Libya, led a military coup against Idrīs. When Qaddafi took power, he led a brutal dictatorship for more than forty years.

The events of the Arab Awakening did not skip Libya. The riots and demonstrations that broke out in the country in 2011 were met with brutal oppression from Qaddafi's forces and led to a civil war and a power struggle between its major tribes. In October 2011, Qaddafi was killed by the rebels—members of the Warfalla, Magarha, and Zuwayya tribes.

At present, bloody battles continue to rage between the tribes and Libya is divided into areas controlled by different tribes. Militant Islamist groups operating in North Africa take advantage of the chaos to increase their presence and influence in Libya. Some Libyan militant Islamist groups have sworn allegiance to ISIS and established strongholds in the coastal city of Sirte, in north Libya. To add to the chaos, descendants of King Idrīs call for the restoration of a monarchy in Libya.

Ongoing Violence, Case Example: Iraq

According to Iraqi statistics, in March 2015, Iraq's population was close to thirty-six million people,[19] making it the fourth most populated country in the Arab world. More than 25 percent of Iraqis are unemployed and 25 percent are living below the poverty line.[20] Almost 20 percent of Iraqis over the age of fifteen are illiterate.[21]

According to the United States Agency for International Development (USAID) and the United Nations Office for the Coordination of Humanitarian Affairs (OCHA), in November 2015 there were 3.2 million Iraqis internally displaced—refugees in their own land—as a result of the conflict with ISIS.[22, 23] OCHA also reports that more than 8.6 million Iraqis are in need of humanitarian assistance.[24]

In addition to unemployment, poverty, illiteracy, and displacement, incessant violence and terror also plague the country, having been perpetrated by groups like Sunni and Shia militias and various criminal organizations. Between 2003 (the Unites States' entrance into Iraq) and 2010, approximately 110,000 people—most of them civilians—were killed in terrorist attacks in Iraq—twelve thousand of them were killed by more than one thousand suicide bombings.[25, 26] According to a 2013 United Nations report, in April 2013 alone there were 712 Iraqis killed in terror attacks, most of them in Baghdad.[27] Another report cited the death toll in Iraq during July 2013 to be more than eight hundred people.[28] In October 2013, more than three hundred cars exploded in Iraq, killing more than nine hundred people.[29] In November 2013, about 950 Iraqis—most of them civilians—were killed.[30] In total in 2013 in Iraq, there were 2,501 terror attacks, killing 6,387 people and injuring 14,976.

In an article titled "Death in Iraq Has Become Just a Statistic," the Iraqi journalist Mustafa al-Kadhimi wrote:

> The Iraqis have simply surrendered and accept, with a resignation born of despair, nonstop killing in their cities. What is amazing is the fact that those who have been appointed to protect the citizens profess a kind of perverted pride in the fact that most Iraqis killed are civilians, since, in their view, this is proof that the terrorists cannot hurt military and security targets because they are well protected.[31]

The fighting, terror, and barbaric bloodshed in central and western Iraq, which follows the emergence of ISIS in Iraq, in April 2013, has resulted in thousands more people being killed and millions displaced.

In 2014 in Iraq, there were 3,370 terror attacks—bombings, explosions, suicide attacks, armed assaults, kidnappings, and assassinations; 9,929 people were killed and 15,137 were injured. Almost half of the attacks were against private citizens and property. The number of hostages taken in terror attacks in Iraq increased from 207 in 2013 to 2,658 in 2014.[32]

For perspective, in 2014, there were 1,591 terror attacks in Afghanistan, 662 in Nigeria, and 232 in Syria. There were 13,463 attacks worldwide, up from 9,964 in 2013, and the number of hostages taken in terror attacks increased from 3,137 in 2013 to 9,428 in 2014.[33]

On May 14, 2015, the special representative for Iraq and the head of the United Nations Assistance Mission for Iraq (UNAMI), Ján Kubiš, described the "unpredictable, unstable security situation" within Iraq to the United Nations Security Council. Kubiš said, "Violence continues to take a terrible toll on the men, women, and children from all of Iraq's communities. Since June last year until the end of April 2015, more than forty-four thousand civilian casualties have been reported, including at least 15,219 killed and 29,493 wounded."[34] Between April and June 2015, more than twelve hundred Iraqi civilians were killed and more than one thousand were injured.[35]

In September 2015, USAID released a document revealing that in August 2015 approximately 1,325 Iraqis, including 585 civilians, were killed in armed conflict, terrorism, and other violence, and more than eighteen hundred people were injured, including approximately eleven hundred civilians.[36] In the same month in Baghdad, the worst-effected governorate, 320 civilians were killed and approximately 750 were injured.[37]

In a joint statement delivered on December 3, 2015 by Ján Kubiš and UNICEF's representative in Iraq, Peter Hawkins, they announced that 189 Iraqi children had been killed and 301 injured since the beginning of 2015, and that hundreds of people have been deprived of access to basic healthcare and educational services because of attacks on medical facilities and schools.[38] In the same statement they added that in the month of November 2015 alone, 888 Iraqis, almost half of them civilians, were killed, and another 1,237 were wounded in acts of terrorism, violence, and armed conflict.[39]

The Birth of the Murderous Mentality

Children and young adults in the Arab world have grown up in a physically and mentally chaotic environment. They live in neglected, underachieving Arab societies stricken with fear and violence, and they are looking for a way out of the confusion, frustration, and misery.

This despair has made them an easy target for radical, charismatic leaders who channel their own anger and despair into a path of violence in the name of a distorted ideology.[40] Given the desperation, terrorist groups haven't had to work hard to recruit new followers. Young people growing up in Arab societies crippled by poverty, fraught with illiteracy, and engulfed in chronic violence are not equipped with the tools and skills needed to help them navigate their lives. They view themselves as powerless—and the preachers and radical leaders prey on this, offering them a path and a direction, one colored with visions of heaven and promises of virgins who will take care of their needs. They promise an afterlife of indulgences for those who ask to die as martyrs for the glory of Islam and Allah's rule. The charismatic Muslim preachers and leaders also provide weapons. With them, the young people begin, for the first time, to feel powerful.

It takes years and resources to develop artists, doctors, scientists, and teachers—it takes minutes to teach a person to shoot and kill.

Saudi Shiite poet Kawthar al-Arbash wrote in her article "How Do You Produce an ISIS Member Before the Age of 20?":

> Teach him to condescend, encourage him to despise other people, oppress his self-esteem, teach him blind obedience by terrorizing him, fill his mind and heart with horror stories of hell and death, and eliminate his ability to see all aspects of beauty, mercy, compassion, and empathy. That way you produce a terrified seventeen-year-old person with low self-esteem and a lack of compassion and mercy who becomes easy prey for ISIS and within three months turns into a brutal murderer.[41]

In October 2014 when ISIS announced that one of its fighters, a ten-year-old boy, fell in battle, they described him as a *shahid*, a martyr. The boy was from the United Arab Emirates and was known by the nickname "the Lion Cub of

Baghdadi"—likely a tribute to ISIS's leader, Abū Bakr al-Baghdadi. It's been said that the boy was killed with his father, who was also a fighter for ISIS, during a United States air raid on ISIS targets in Syria.[42] Photographs circulated after the child's death show him holding a weapon and being embraced by his proud father. The ISIS subtext here is clear: *You may think you're powerless, but with ISIS you'll be powerful. You'll have an identity, a path (jihad), a vision, and destiny. You'll also have the tools (a weapon in your hand), and your sacrifice won't be in vain. You'll be a martyr, a shahid, with all the benefits that come with it.* Reports indicate that ISIS is recruiting and paying a salary to thousands of children—mostly ones from Iraq and Syria, many of whom are orphans—and developing them into cruel, devoted militants.[43, 44] In April 2015, a UNICEF representative for Yemen reported that one third of the fighters in Yemen are children.[45]

This dangerous circuit supplies groups like al-Qaeda and ISIS with a steady stream of militants. There is a continuous increase in the number of young people enlisting in the ranks of militant Islamist groups and reinforcing their strength. In early 2014, the number of ISIS militants was reported to be eight thousand.[46] In September 2014, a CIA spokesperson estimated the number of ISIS militants to be between twenty thousand and 31,500.[47] Because of their ability to recruit young people, militant Islamist groups easily expand their ranks and increase their abilities—and with this, increase the threat they present.

The murderous ideology, political vision, and weapons also appeal to young people from non-Muslim states—primarily in Europe, and to a lesser extent in the United States, Canada, Australia, and China—who were born Muslim or converted to Islam. In 2013, reports suggested that the number of foreigners joining militant Islamist groups varied between dozens and hundreds.[48] In December 2013, the French minister of interior affairs declared that there were two thousand Europeans fighting within the ranks of al-Qaeda in Syria.[49] In June 2014, it was estimated that twelve hundred foreign fighters from eighty-one countries had made their way to Syria.[50] In September 2014, the United Nations Security Council adopted Resolution 2178, condemning violent extremism. As part of this, it declared that its member states will, consistent with international law, prevent the "recruiting, organizing, transporting, or equipping of individuals who travel to a state other than their state of residence or nationality for the purpose of the perpetration, planning of, or participation in terrorist acts."[51] In February 2015, the head of the International Criminal Police Organization (INTERPOL) announced that some twenty thousand foreigners had joined militant Islamist groups in Syria and Iraq.[52] It's now estimated that the number of foreign fighters in Syria may have surpassed thirty thousand, and that they're from eighty-six countries.[53, 54]

Lack of Governance, Case Example: Sinai Peninsula

The Sinai Peninsula is located between the Suez Canal and the Arabian Peninsula. Though geographically isolated, it links Africa with Asia and connects politically important states, such as Egypt, Israel, Jordan, and Saudi Arabia.

The Sinai Peninsula is a major asset for Egypt. Luxury hotels and tourist resorts, which are located mostly in the eastern and southern part of Sinai, are a major component of one of Egypt's major income sources: tourism. In Egypt, tourism revenues once accounted for $12.5 billion a year. At its peak, according to Egypt's ambassador to Germany, some 1.2 million tourists from Germany alone visited Sinai annually.[55] In 2013, income in Egypt generated from tourism was $5.9 billion. In the first half of 2014, about 4.5 million tourists visited Egypt and the income generated was around $3 billion.[56] The tourism industry in Egypt directly employs two million people and provides an income for twenty million Egyptians.[57] In 2012, Egypt opened a port in Taba, a small Egyptian town on the eastern shore of the Sinai Peninsula. It was designed to accommodate the entrance of 350,000 tourists a year, and it was estimated that it would draw an added annual revenue of $250 million.[58]

The natural gas pipeline that passes from Egypt to Jordan and Israel runs through the Sinai. Egypt provides Jordan with one hundred million cubic feet of natural gas a day, and the revenue of this is $450 million annually.[59] The Suez Canal that connects the Mediterranean Sea and the Red Sea is located in the western part of the Sinai Peninsula. Egypt has recently undertaken a massive engineering project aimed at widening the canal to increase the volume of ships using it. Reportedly, the Suez Canal generates an annual revenue of $5 billion, and this is expected to grow to $13.5 billion by 2023.[60]

Given the wealth the Sinai Peninsula brings, it would be logical for Egypt to proactively protect and care for it—but it's failed to do so. The central and northern Sinai Peninsula under Egyptian rule are remote, neglected, and sinking in poverty. The land has become a kingdom of terrorism and crime, in which Bedouin tribes work with militant Islamist groups. Its wild, wide deserts, mountain ranges, valleys, and caves provide ideal conditions for terrorists and outlaws and a fertile ground for crime and terror.

The northern Sinai, one of Egypt's poorest districts, is populated by ten major Bedouin tribes who live in the heavily populated urban cities located very close to the Egypt-Gaza Strip border: the towns of al-'Arīsh, Rafah, and Sheikh Zuweid.[61] Taking advantage of the lack of Egyptian governance—manifested by inferior governmental services, poor infrastructure, and only a partial enforcement of law and public order since the Israeli withdrawal from the Sinai in the early 1980s, a result of the 1978 Camp David Accords—the Bedouin tribes took de facto control of the region. Under this, a large industry of smuggling—of items such as ammunition, cars, drugs, merchandise, weapons, women, and terrorists—is flourishing and has become a highly lucrative business—one which the Bedouins have no intention of giving up. Today's Sinai Peninsula is a crossing point for a massive smuggling route that connects North Africa and Europe with West Africa, going northeast through the Sahara, to the eastern basin of the Mediterranean Sea, to the Gaza Strip, Israel, Jordan, and Syria, and eastward toward Iraq.

The Egyptian government is well aware that militant Islamist groups in the Sinai Peninsula have become a serious threat to Egypt's national security. Egypt's intelligence estimates that there are thirteen militant Islamist groups in Sinai.[62] According to different assessments, the number of militants varies from five hundred to seven thousand,[63, 64] comprising both Egyptians and foreigners coming from countries like Algeria, Iraq, Libya, Saudi Arabia, and Yemen.[65, 66, 67] And Egypt pays dearly for this.

In an October 2004 attack by militant Islamist groups on hotels in the eastern Sinai Peninsula, thirty-four people were killed and 171 were injured. In September 2013, a Salafi-Jihadi group in Sinai claimed responsibility for shooting a rocket-propelled grenade onto a ship in the Suez Canal.[68] In May 2015, the gas pipeline in the Sinai was blown up for the thirtieth time.[69] In September 2015, a group of Mexican tourists eating lunch on a sand dune in the western desert were killed when the air force bombed them, believing they were militants.[70] In November 2015, a Russian commercial aircraft that took off from the famous tourist resort of Sharm el-Shiekh, in southern Sinai, crashed after breaking apart in midair. All 224 people on board were killed. The destruction of the plane was likely caused by a bomb in a soda can planted by ISIS; it claimed responsibility.

Terror in the Sinai has long been a challenge for Egyptian authorities. Egypt's army is conducting a complicated ongoing war in the Sinai Peninsula in an attempt to uproot the kingdom of terrorism and crime that has been established there, but it is not an easy task. Hundreds of Egyptian soldiers and police officers have been killed by militant Islamist groups, operating mostly in the northern part of the Sinai Peninsula. The militants attack places like Egyptian army bases, government facilities, courts, and police stations, even the gas pipeline to Jordan. A spokesperson for the Egyptian military said the ongoing Egyptian campaign in the Sinai, titled *Haq al-Shaid* (the Martyr's Justice), had by September 2015 resulted in the killing of more than five hundred Islamic militants and the arrest of hundreds.[71] Yet analysts have raised serious doubts regarding the Egyptian government's capability to put an end to the terror in Sinai.[72]

Lack of Borders

Also helping militant Islam spread is the lack of physical borders between countries. Thousands of miles of deserts, forests, and mountains are wide open, free of monitors or barely monitored. At any given moment, caravans of ammunition, drugs, employment seekers, smuggled merchandise, terrorists, weapons, and women are crossing the Middle East from Libya to Egypt, from Sudan to Sinai, from Iraq to Syria, from Syria to Lebanon, from Yemen to Saudi Arabia, from Turkey to Syria, and elsewhere.

Salafi-Jihadi-run corridors crisscross the region. A horizontal (east-west) corridor stretches from Iraq through Jordan, the Gaza Strip, Egypt (specifically the Sinai Peninsula), Libya, Tunisia, and Algeria, and ends in Morocco in western Africa. Starting in North Africa, a vertical (north-south) corridor stretches south toward

Mali, Niger, and Nigeria; northern Nigeria is the home of Jamā'at Ahl al-Sunna lil-Da'awah wa al-Jihād (the Sunni Group of Indoctrination and Jihad), better known as Boko Haram ("Western Values Are Forbidden"). The corridor ends in Somalia and Yemen off the shores of the Indian Ocean. Somalia and Kenya also have a strong Salafi-Jihadi axis. This is where a branch of al-Qaeda named Ḥarakat al-Shabāb al-Mujāhidīn (the Movement of the Young Jihadists), better known as al-Shabaab, operates. When ISIS stormed its way from Iraq into Syria in 2013, it didn't have any tangible obstacles in its way. ISIS literally just walked in.

On Egypt's western side, it has a nearly seven-hundred-mile-long border with Libya that is barely monitored.[73, 74] On its northeast side, it has a short eight-mile border with the Gaza Strip. This tiny area has a massive network of tunnels that connect the northern Sinai to the Gaza Strip. The tunnels were dug by Ḥamās from the Gaza side and by Bedouin smugglers from the Egyptian side. For many years Egyptian authorities allowed them to operate, but in recent years, especially after the ousting of President Morsi, Egypt has undertaken a serious effort to locate and destroy the network. In February 2014, an Egyptian military spokesman announced that Egypt had demolished 1,275 tunnels.[75] Egypt also created a buffer zone that is the full length of the Gaza border and about half a mile wide.[76] In December 2014, the Egyptian governor of North Sinai announced that 680 houses of Egyptian citizens were demolished for the purpose of creating this buffer zone, adding that troops found connections to the tunnels in 122 of the 680 houses they demolished. He declared that in order to create the buffer zone, 290 houses were evacuated and their owners received a sum of more than $13 million as compensation.[77] In May 2015, Egypt's president, Abdel Fattah al-Sisi, announced that 80 percent of the tunnels discovered in the buffer zone had been demolished and a huge amount of explosives and weapons had been discovered inside the tunnels.[78] In September 2015, as part of its effort to thwart tunnel traffic, Egypt began pumping water into the tunnels. Sisi said the "measures aim to protect the Egyptian border and preserve Palestinian and Egyptian national security"[79] and were being carried out in cooperation with the Palestinian Authority, led by President Mahmoud Abbas, which is the governing authority in the West Bank. Egypt's Brigadier General Mohamed Samir said that during November 2015, the entrances of twenty cross-border tunnels had been destroyed in North Sinai.[80]

In September 2014, Saudi Arabia announced it was going to build a security barrier along its six-hundred-mile border with Iraq. Saudi officials have said that the barrier will include five layers of fencing and have watchtowers, night-vision cameras, and radar cameras.[81]

In 2014, Saudi authorities arrested three hundred thousand infiltrators who tried to illegally enter Saudi Arabia, mostly on its southern side, from Yemen. In response, Saudi Arabia is building a massive fence along its 1,060-mile border with Yemen.[82] In January 2015, it announced that it is widening the security buffer zone along its border with Yemen from seven miles to thirteen miles, and that no civilian presence or activity is allowed in the zone.[83]

In July 2015, the headline of an article in *Bloomberg* magazine by Salma El Wardany and Caroline Alexander read, "Fences Rise Across Middle East as Jihadi Threat Escalates." The authors wrote that "from Morocco to Saudi Arabia, boundaries are being fortified at a rate not seen since the months following the Sept. 11 attacks;"[84] and they quoted Said Saddiki, a professor of International Relations and International Law at Al-Ain University of Science and Technology in Abu Dhabi, who said, "The Middle East and North Africa is now the most walled region in the world . . . [Its divides range from] fences inside cities to anti-migrant walls and separation barriers to counter-insurgency [barricades].[85] The builders are spurred by a fear of the Islamic State.

The jihadist group has its own walls to fend off attackers and keep people from escaping, particularly around the Iraqi cities of Tal Afar and Mosul. Syria's embattled government has concrete shields around areas of regime support in Homs.[86]

ISIS

The name ISIS first appeared in Iraq in April 2013 as the new name of the al-Qaeda branch in Iraq previously known by different names like Jama'at al-Tawhid wal-Jihad and the al-Qaeda organization in the Land of Two Rivers (AQI). In February 2014, the leadership of al-Qaeda announced its official dissociation from ISIS.[87] The background for the split was an announcement in April 2013 by Abū Bakr al-Baghdadi, the leader of ISIS, that he intended to establish an Islamic emirate in Syria and Iraq and that, as such, al-Qaeda's branch in Syria, Jabhat al-Nusra (the Support Front for the People of ash-Sham; *ash-Sham* is the Arabic name that for centuries referred to a geographic area consisting of what is today Israel, Jordan, Lebanon, and Syria), was under his command. The leader of Jabhat al-Nusra, Abu Mohammad al-Joulani, who was appointed to that position by Baghdadi while ISIS was still part of al-Qaeda, argued that as the leader of Jabhat al-Nusra, al-Qaeda's branch in Syria, he was under the direct command of the leader of al-Qaeda, Ayman al-Zawahiri. Baghdadi argued that Joulani should be under *his* direct command. Zawahiri ruled in favor of Joulani, but Baghdadi refused to accept al-Zawahiri's decision. The al-Qaeda Supreme Council decided that Baghdadi's disobedience was unacceptable and decided to detach al-Qaeda from ISIS and its leader.[88]

There were also ideological differences. The al-Qaeda Supreme Council made it clear that they believed the time and conditions were not right for establishing a caliphate, adding that Baghdadi did not have the mandate or authority to make such an announcement.[89] And on the al-Qaeda website, al-Fajr (the Dawn) Center for Communication, it was hinted that its leadership—which is responsible for such heinous acts as the devastation inflicted on September 11, 2001, and the killing of many other innocent people around the world—is disturbed by ISIS's brutality.[90]

In June 2014 when ISIS's spokesman, Abū Muḥammad al-'Adnānī, announced the establishment of the Islamic State, he introduced Baghdadi as the "caliph of Islam."[91] Baghdadi—born Ibrahim Awad Ibrahim al-Badri al-Samarrai, but known as Abū Bakr al-Baghdadi or by a range of other names, Abū Bakr al-Baghdadi al-Husseini al-Qurashi, Ibrahim `Awwad Ibrahim al-Badri al-Samarrai, Dr. Ibrahim Awwad Ibrahim al-Samarra'I, and Caliph Ibrahim, for example—reportedly earned a PhD in Islamic studies from the Islamic University in Baghdad (today renamed the Iraqi University). According to various reports, he served as an *imam*, a Muslim religious leader, in the Ahmad Bin Hanbal mosque in Samarra, Iraq, and/or in a mosque in Diyala, Iraq.[92, 93, 94]

The caliph is the highest leader in the hierarchy of the caliphate. Some leaders of Salafi-Jihadi groups give themselves the title "emir"; the term is part of the title *amir al-mu'minin* (the ruler of the Muslim believers). The emirs are subdued to the caliph's orders and must pledge their allegiance to him through a *bay'ah* (oath of allegiance) ceremony. Some Salafi-Jihadi groups have proclaimed the areas they operate in, or have some or full control over, to be emirates or *wilaya*, governorates, which function mostly as administrative units within a framework that includes regions, districts, sub-districts, etc. The terms emir and *wilaya* date back to the historical Islamic caliphate, and it is common to see the names of Arab entities—often terrorist ones—with a version of "emir" or "*wilaya*" in them. The formal title of ISIS's arm in the Sinai Peninsula is Wilayat Sina.

In the caliphate, the governing authority of the emirates or the wilaya is subject to the authority of the caliph and the supreme legislative council, Majlis al-Shurah. The caliph is responsible for applying sharīʿah law side-by-side with the services it provides to the inhabitants of its districts. In today's terrorist-run entities, this leads to the imposition of a strict translation of sharīʿah into every aspect of life. This includes things such as making educational curriculums include only Islamic theology and sharīʿah, prohibiting the teaching of mathematics, science, foreign languages, sociology, and other disciplines.

In terrorist-run caliphates or emirates, violence is frequently embraced to make a statement. Terrorism used by ISIS is known for being particularly brutal. Videos document punishments imposed by ISIS, such as the cutting off the hands of people accused of being thieves, the whipping of people accused of using drugs or consuming alcohol, and the beheadings of kidnapped soldiers, non-Muslims, Westerners, and people accused of collaborating against them. It's also common for ISIS to persecute, abuse, and kill Christians and to enslave and sell Christian women and girls. In February 2015, ISIS beheaded twenty-one Egyptian Coptic Christians in Libya. And it indiscriminately destroys places and things such as archeological sites and artifacts, churches, libraries, museums, and non-Muslim symbols. According to a report published by the Syrian Observatory for Human Rights, as of May 2014—less than one year since ISIS declared the establishment of the Islamic State, on June 29, 2014—2,618 people, including twenty-three children and thirty-two women, had been executed by ISIS in the areas it controls in Syria.[95] The Syrian Observatory for Human Rights reported that between June 2014, when ISIS declared its Islamic caliphate, and December 2015, ISIS executed 3,591 people in Syria, more than half of them civilians.[96] The Iraqi Observatory for Human Rights reported that seventy-seven hundred people were executed in Iraq during that time period.[97]

Al-Qaeda and ISIS

There is a growing competition between al-Qaeda and ISIS to have the largest and strongest support group—and thus the most power and influence.

In Syria, al-Qaeda and ISIS are engaged in fierce battles raging throughout the country.[98, 99, 100, 101] In May 2015, the major coalition of Salafi-Jihadi groups in northern Syria, Jaish al-Fatah led by Jabhat al-Nusra, al-Qaeda's branch in Syria, announced the launching of a military campaign to root out ISIS's presence along the Syrian-Lebanese border.[102]

There is also a difference in the way they deal with the people under their jurisdiction. Jabhat al-Nusra, like ISIS, applies sharī'ah law in the areas it controls;[103, 104] but unlike ISIS, it does not enforce strict sharī'ah. Instead it focuses on providing social and municipal services and financial support.[105, 106, 107] This helps garner the support of the population in the areas it controls.

In Jordan, the growing tension between ISIS and al-Qaeda is resulting in tensions among the senior leaders of the Salafi-Jihadi movement in the kingdom. The spiritual mentor of the Salafi-Jihadi movement in Jordan, one of the most prominent Salafi figures and a central architect of global jihad, is Sheikh Muhammad Taher Isam al-Barqawi, who is known as Abu Muhammad al-Maqdisi. Maqdisi was the spiritual mentor of Abu Musab al-Zarqawi, al-Qaeda's leader in Iraq, and is also considered the "spiritual father of the Islamic State."[108] Maqdisi expressed his objection to ISIS and its Islamic State and urged Salafis to support the al-Qaeda arm in Syria, Jabhat al-Nusra.[109] His call was supported by Omar Mahmoud Othman, aka Abu Qatada, a senior leader of the Salafi-Jihadi movement and a senior al-Qaeda activist of Jordanian-Palestinian origin. Qatada described ISIS as "dogs of hell."[110]

Qatada went to the United Kingdom in 1993 by using forged passports and was granted asylum. He was among a group of Islamists who sought refuge there in the 1980s and the 1990s as they fled Arab regimes they had been seeking to overthrow. He was arrested on and off by British authorities, and Jordan demanded the UK deport him so that the Jordanian government could try him for his involvement in terror plots. Qatada attempted to appeal the ruling for this to the European Court of Human Rights, soliciting the court to block the deportation by arguing that he would face torture if deported. The court at first seemed to side with him, but then denied him from formally appealing. After a long process in which the Jordanian government promised that torture would not be used to gain evidence against him, he was deported to Jordan in July 2013. There, he was tried, but acquitted.

The announcements denouncing ISIS made by the leaders of the Salafi movement in Jordan took place at an interesting—and likely not by chance—conjunction. Maqdisi, who was sentenced to five years in Jordanian prison for recruiting fighters for al-Qaeda, was released in June 2014 before completing his term.[111] Shortly afterward, he issued a statement intensely criticizing the Islamic State, accusing it of killing Muslims who have different views and allegiances.[112] This played out in September 2014 and shortly after denouncing ISIS, he was acquitted of all charges that he had been deported to Jordan to face.[113] It's conceivable that the generosity of the Jordanian authorities toward Maqdisi and Qatada was not inspired by altruism but by the interests of the Jordanian government. The fact that two prominent Salafi leaders delegitimized ISIS served the Jordanian effort to limit the support of ISIS in Jordan.

There are, of course, Salafi leaders in Jordan who support ISIS. 'Abd Shehadeh, aka Sheikh Abu Muhammad al-Tahawi is among them. Tahawi is one of the major Salafi-Jihadi theologians in Jordan.[114]

In Yemen, reports indicate that the growing tension between al-Qaeda and ISIS is resulting in mounting tensions within al-Qaeda and a crisis among its leadership.[115, 116] It's thought by some that these tensions will inevitably result in a violent split within al-Qaeda in Yemen.[117]

In September 2014, two Salafi-Jihadi groups reportedly announced their disassociation from al-Qaeda and swore allegiance to Baghdadi: Algeria's Jund al-Khilafah (Soldiers of the Caliphate) and Libya's al-Mua'qi'oon Biddam (Those Who Sign with Blood Brigades)[118] led by former al-Qaeda military commander Mokhtar Belmokhtar.

The intensification of the tension between al-Qaeda and ISIS could potentially serve the Arab states that are threatened by militant Islam. At present, ISIS and al-Qaeda are on a track toward collision and ISIS seems to have the upper hand. It's had hearty achievements on the ground in Syria and Iraq. It's sophisticated in its use of social media and the Internet to recruit followers. The terrorist attacks in the heart of Europe have been either inspired by ISIS or guided by ISIS. And the area it governs in the heart of the Middle East is a stone's throw from Europe. Despite almost thirty years of activity, al-Qaeda is far less influential than

ISIS. Al-Qaeda is most active in remote areas of Afghanistan and Somalia and has failed to garner the enthusiasm and emotional identification among Muslims in Europe the way ISIS has. Many of its leaders are also in hiding.

In November 2015, in response to Russia's involvement in the war in Syria, al-Qaeda's leader, Ayman al-Zawahiri, published a message urging all Jihadi groups, including ISIS, to unite in the fight against Russia, Iran, and the United States, who are occupying Iraq and Syria.[119] Zawahiri's appeal could signal that al-Qaeda now acknowledges ISIS as a legitimate entity.

Militant Islam and the Israel Arena

All branches of militant Islam share a non-compromising animosity toward the State of Israel, which according to militant Islam must be erased. This is part of militant Islam's defining agenda and is also a method to gain support from the Arab public, even though the majority of its members are against its path, philosophy, and practices. Garnering support in this manner embraces slogans like "Liberate occupied Muslim land," a reference to Palestine and the Golan Heights, and "Liberate al-Quds" (the Arabic name for Jerusalem). Associating itself with the concept of "liberation" also increases militant Islam's attractiveness among audiences in the West who look at the militant Islam phenomenon with an admiration and romanticism.

To assess the threat to Israel that militant Islamist groups present, it helps to map them in the land bordering it: Jordan; the Palestinian arena—the West Bank under the jurisdiction of the Palestinian Authority—and the Gaza Strip; the Sinai Peninsula; the Syrian Golan Heights; and South Lebanon.

The Gaza Strip

Political and militant Islam creates the most instability in the Gaza Strip. In October 2005, after thirty-eight years of ruling the Gaza Strip, Israel withdrew and handed the governance of it to the Palestinian Authority. In June 2007, Ḥamās took control of the Gaza Strip in a bloody military coup, ousting the Palestinian Authority's rule. Today the Gaza Strip is ruled by Ḥamās, a Palestinian political Islamist organization and one of the Palestinians' two major political parties. (Fatah is the second.) Ḥamās, which defines itself as the arm of the Muslim Brotherhood in Palestine, was founded in the Gaza Strip in 1987 by Sheikh Ahmed Yassin. Its birth was during the outbreak of the first intifada (1987–1993), a Palestinian uprising against Israeli control of the West Bank, Gaza, and East Jerusalem.

The Gaza Strip is not a state, though it functions as a semi-state entity with Ḥamās acting as its sovereign. Ḥamās levies and collects taxes; provides government and municipal services; operates social welfare programs; develops and implements school curriculums; issues regulations and designs laws; imposes law and order through police, prisons, and courts; and maintains a military, security, and police force. It also uses violence toward Israel and calls for the elimination of the State of Israel and the killing of Jews. It's defined by the United States and the European Union as a terrorist organization.

In Ḥamās's charter, as well as in public statements and the speeches of its leaders, it freely and clearly says that it aspires to free Palestine through the way of *al-muqāwamah* (the resistance) and jihad; by this it means that it intends to destroy the State of Israel through violence.[120] In a July 2012 speech at a conference held by Nahḍah (the Muslim Brotherhood party in Tunisia), the keynote speaker, Khaled Mashal, the leader of Ḥamās, declared: "Palestine is our land and ours only. . . . There shall be no other people on that land other than us. . . . Our objective is the liberation of all of Palestine and it will be achieved only by the use of weapons."[121]

Under Ḥamās's control, the Gaza Strip has turned into an increasingly sizable military threat to Israel. Since 2007, there has been almost nonstop violence against Israel from within the Gaza Strip. The violence is perpetrated by Ḥamās and other Palestinian militant Islam organizations, such as the Palestinian Islamic Jihad and the Popular Resistance Committees. To a lesser extent, these Salafi-Jihadi groups threaten Egypt as well.

According to the Israeli Defense Forces, from 2001–2014, more than 15,200 rockets and mortars have targeted Israel.[122] Statistics indicate that the shooting of rockets from the Gaza Strip has substantially intensified since Ḥamās' military coup. According to the Shabak (the Israel Security Agency), from 2002–2007, 2,887 rockets were launched from the Gaza Strip.[123] More than 12,300 rockets have been launched at Israel from the Gaza Strip since Ḥamās took it over in June 2007. The growing threat is also manifested in the fact that the range, as well as the amount of explosives contained in the rockets, has become increasingly dangerous. As of 2015, Israel's two major metropolitan areas—Tel Aviv and Jerusalem—as well as many other Israeli cities and towns, are within the range of rockets launched from the Gaza Strip.

In between 2007, when Ḥamās took control, and 2014, there were three rounds of widespread military confrontations between Israel and Ḥamās: "Operation Cast Lead" in 2008, "Operation Pillar of Defense" in 2012, and "Operation Protective Edge" in 2014. During the 2014 round, Israel uncovered and destroyed some thirty tunnels dug by Ḥamās into Israeli communities located in Israeli territory next to the Gaza Strip. Ḥamās openly declares that the tunnels are intended to be used for occupying Israeli communities and killing and abducting Israeli civilians and soldiers. The tactic was infamously used to capture Israeli soldier Gilad Shalit in June 2006.[124, 125] In June 2015, Khalil al-Khayeh, a senior Ḥamās leader, announced that the tunnels crossing into Israeli territory are the most powerful weapon Ḥamās possesses, and that it will therefore continue to dig more tunnels.[126]

Like other areas bordering Israel, the Gaza Strip has a notable Salafi presence, which includes Salafi-Jihadi groups. It's estimated that in the Gaza Strip there are a few hundred Salafi-Jihadi militants and activists (activists are not necessarily active fighters—they can act in a support role or a management or administrative capacity).[127, 128] The major Salafi-Jihadi group in the Gaza Strip is Jaish al-Islam (the Army of Islam). It is affiliated with al-Qaeda and allegedly announced its allegiance to ISIS in September 2015.[129] Jaish al-Islam is the only Salafi-Jihadi group in a territory bordering Israel that shares some aspects of militant Islamist ideology with the ruling force on the ground. In this case it shares with Ḥamās the vision of a global caliphate and a commitment to destroy Israel through violence. Ḥamās and the Salafi-Jihadi groups cooperate toward this end. Therefore, the Gaza Strip serves as a base from which attacks on Israel are perpetrated both by the ruling factor, Ḥamās, as well as by Salafi-Jihadi groups. An example of this collaboration is how Jaish al-Islam and Ḥamās worked together in the operation that resulted in the kidnapping of the Israeli soldier Gilad Shalit in June 2006.

Egypt has said that the Gaza Strip serves as a base from which Salafi-Jihadi groups, mainly Jaish al-Islam, launch attacks on it, as well. In January 2015, an Egyptian court held Ḥamās accountable for these attacks because it controls the Gaza Strip and allows the terrorist activity. It has declared Ḥamās's military wing, the Ezzedeen al-Qassam Brigades, to be a terror organization.[130]

The cooperation between Ḥamās and the Salafi-Jihadi groups is controlled by Ḥamās. The Salafi-Jihadis in the Gaza Strip do not, however, have carte blanche to act as they wish. Ḥamās's policy stems from two major reasons: one reason is that while the Salafi-Jihadi groups in the Gaza Strip would like to constantly attack Israel, Ḥamās, as the governing body of the 1.8 million Palestinians in the Gaza Strip, must cautiously calculate its militant activity against Israel. It knows that attacking Israel serves it politically because it proves its commitment and dedication to fighting Israel in the name of "liberating Palestine"—thus affording it political dividends in the Palestinian arena—but it also cannot risk an overly aggressive Israeli retaliation that might jeopardize its rule in Gaza or cause such enormous devastation in Gaza that its people would direct their resulting fury at Ḥamās.

The second reason is that Ḥamās views the Salafi-Jihadi groups as potential competition. The tension stems from the fact that they have differing views on issues such as how strict the implementation of sharī'ah law should be and different ideologies on *tamkin* vs. *takwin*. Ḥamās adheres to the *tamkin* ideology of laying the groundwork, violently and nonviolently for the caliphate. The Salafi-Jihadi groups adhere to the *takwin* ideology of needing to create the caliphate now through the use of violence. They also have differing ideas of a separatist national identity vs. one global caliphate that erases separatist independent nationalism. Ḥamās can live, for now, with independent state entities. Salafi-Jihadi movements call for the immediate creation of a global caliphate with no independent entities.

Ḥamās has made it clear—mostly through violence—that it will not tolerate Salafi-Jihadi groups attempting to challenge its rule. In August 2009, Ḥamās violently crushed a Salafi-Jihadi group in the Gaza Strip named Jund Ansar Allah (Soldiers of Allah's Believers), following an announcement from its leader, Sheikh Abd al-Latif Musa , a.k.a. Abu Noor al-Maqdisi, of an Islamic emirate within the Gaza Strip. More than twenty Palestinians were killed in the fighting and dozens were injured.[131]

As a result of its policy of restricting Salafi-Jihadi activity, Ḥamās often arrests Salafi-Jihadi activists and leaders in the Gaza Strip.[132, 133, 134] In June 2015, Salafi-Jihadi sources in the Gaza Strip claimed that about one hundred Salafi supporters were imprisoned by Ḥamās.[135]

An agreement was reportedly signed between Ḥamās and the Salafi-Jihadi groups stating that the Salafi-Jihadi groups in Gaza are allowed to conduct political, military, and educational activities, but they are subject to Ḥamās's inspection and approval. The agreement prohibits Salafi-Jihadi groups from shooting rockets at Israel unless authorized by Ḥamās.[136]

Jordan

Jordan is a major target for the Salafi-Jihadi groups. Though their presence in Jordan is currently negligible, there is a significant presence of the Salafi movement in Jordan. This coupled with Jordan's substantial economic and societal challenges could provide militant Islamist groups a convenient environment in which to thrive.

The number of Salafi supporters in Jordan is estimated at twenty thousand,[137] with most based in the cities of Ma'an, al-Tafila, and al-Karak,[138] which suffer from severe poverty and unemployment. It is illegal for Jordanians to participate in the war in Syria, yet Salafi-Jihadi circles in Jordan claim that some two thousand Jordanian militants, inspired by the Salafi-Jihadi ideology, smuggled their way into Syria and are fighting within the ranks of ISIS or Jabhat al-Nusra.[139, 140, 141, 142, 143, 144] In this manner, Jordanian Salafi-Jihadis gain substantial combat experience that they can bring back to Jordan. Jordanian groups also operate in Iraq and the Sinai Peninsula.

The Salafi-Jihadi threat to Jordan could present a growing threat to Israel because Israel's longest border, about three hundred miles long, is with Jordan. The distance from the Israeli-Jordanian border to Jerusalem is a twenty-minute drive. Thus far, only a few rockets have been launched at Israel by Jordan's militant Islamist groups and they've proved harmless, but the threat is still there. Jordanian security agencies closely monitor the Salafi movement, and Salafi-Jihadi groups in particular, to prevent attacks. The Jordanian people are very concerned that the militant Islamists could increase instability in Jordan, and keeping them under control is of the upmost importance.

South Lebanon

The primary source of instability from Israel's northern border with Lebanon is not Sunni militant Islam, but Shiite militant Islam from Hezbollah (the Party of Allah). There are also a small number of Salafi-Jihadi groups in Lebanon. In south Lebanon, which borders Israel, it is estimated that there are a few hundred militants, mostly based in the Palestinian refugee camps in Tyre and Sidon.[145, 146] There have been a few rockets launched from there at Israel by the Abdullah Azzam Brigades, an offshoot of al-Qaeda, but there was no resulting damage.

The negligible activity of Salafi-Jihadi groups in this area stems from a variety of reasons: for one, the major power factors in South Lebanon—the Lebanese army; the Shiite Islamist militant group Hezbollah; the two major Palestinian organizations, Ḥamās and Fatah; and the United Nations combat units that are empowered to operate there (according to UN Security Council decision 1701, which created a buffer zone free of armed personnel other than UN ones after the 2006 Second Lebanon War)—have a shared interest in keeping the region calm and preventing attacks on Israel that might lead to a wide military confrontation.

The Salafi-Jihadi groups in Lebanon also have a limited military capacity in things such as arms, infrastructure, and manpower. This could change with the infiltration of Salafi-Jihadi activists from Syria into eastern and northern Lebanon as an outcome of the war in Syria. If it does, it will strengthen the Salafi-Jihadi groups in the Palestinian refugee camps in Lebanon, particularly in South Lebanon.[147, 148]

Sinai Peninsula

Of the territories bordering Israel, the Sinai Peninsula is the one from which the most severe attacks have been launched on Israel by Salafi-Jihadi groups.

In August 2011, a group of terrorists infiltrated Israeli territory next to the border, killing seven Israelis. The attackers were killed by the Israeli army.

The major Salafi-Jihadi group in Sinai is a branch of ISIS known as Wilāyat Saynā' (the Emirate of Sinai), previously known as Mujāhidīn Fī Aknāf Bayt al-Maqdis (the Jihad Warriors on the Outskirts of Jerusalem). Wilāyat Saynā' and other Salafi-Jihadi groups have been the target of an Egyptian military offensive that disrupts their ability to launch attacks on Israel. Their motivation to do so, however, has not diminished, and they view destroying Israel as a top priority. They also, despite the Egyptian military pressure, maintain high operational capabilities. Wilāyat Saynā' is armed with advanced weapons, such as anti-aircraft missiles, and enjoys a base of support from some of the Bedouin tribes in northern Sinai. Israeli intelligence estimates that the group is motivated and capable of launching attacks on Israel.[149]

Syria

Of all the arenas bordering Israel, the Salafi-Jihadi presence in Syria holds the greatest potential threat for three reasons:

First, Salafi-Jihadi groups reportedly control about 60 percent of Syria[150] and operate in all areas of it, including land close to the Israeli-Syrian ceasefire line in the Golan Heights. Syria also has the largest number of Salafi-Jihadi militants. There are so many Salafi-Jihadi groups in Syria that mapping them would be nearly impossible. Some groups comprise only a small number of militants and are not well known, and some are restructured, joined with one or more other groups, or split into subgroups.

At present there are two major Salafi-Jihadi groups in Syria. ISIS and Jaish al-Fatah mostly operates in northeast Syria, partially in central Syria, and to a lesser extent along the border of Syria and Lebanon. It has a limited presence in southern Syria and the Golan Heights.

In September 2014, ISIS forces in Iraq and Syria were estimated at about thirty-one thousand militants.[151] In June 2015, the number was the same despite the fact that, according to US Deputy Secretary of State Anthony Blinken, ten thousand ISIS militants had been killed.[152] The explanation for this provided by US intelligence officials was that "ISIS adequately replaces slain fighters through a combination of conscription and recruitment both inside and outside Syria and Iraq."[153]

Jaish al-Fatah is a coalition of a Salafi-Jihadi group led by Jabhat al-Nusra and operates mainly in central, northern, and northwestern Syria, including areas along the Syrian-Lebanese border and the Israeli-Syrian cease-fire line in the Golan Heights. The number of Jabhat al-Nusra militants is estimated as being between three thousand and fifteen thousand.[154, 155, 156]

Second, Salafi-Jihad groups in Syria have obtained a wealth of combat experience during the war in Syria, and many of their militants have also honed these skills in combat zones like Afghanistan, Chechnya, and Pakistan. They are heavily armed, including with advanced weapon systems,[157, 158] and are said to have chemical materials that were looted from Syrian army storages and can be used for the production of chemical weapons.[159]

Third, with the chaos currently raging in Syria, and the weakening and disintegration of Assad's regime, there is no longer a central authority that could impose its sovereignty to keep militant Islamist groups under control and prevent attacks on Israel from Syrian territory.

To date, in spite of the massive number of militants, their skills and resources, and their proximity to Israel, there have been a negligible number of attacks by Syria-based Salafi-Jihadi groups on Israel. There are three key reasons for this:

First, the Salafi-Jihadi groups have been focusing their energy on fighting Assad's regime and its allies: the Iranian military units, the Iranian-backed Shiite militias, and, most recently—the newest active player in the conflict—the Russians.

Second, the two major Salafi-Jihadi groups in Syria, Jabhat al-Nusra and ISIS, are busy fighting each other. Also, in spite of ISIS's limited presence in southern Syria and the Golan Heights, there have been skirmishes between Jabhat al-Nusra and ISIS in the area of the Golan Heights and the Syrian district of Quneitra.

Third, because of the balance of power in the southern part of Syria. The most influential powers there are al-Jaish al-Awal (the First Corps), which is not part of the Salafi-Jihadi camp, and al-Jabhah al-Islāmiyya as-Sūriyyah (the Syrian Islamic Front [SIF]), which leans more towards the Islamist pragmatic stream, two major Syrian rebel forces supported by Saudi Arabia, Jordan, and

Qatar. These groups have no interest in a military confrontation with Israel as they are focused on fighting the Assad regime and its allies.

West Bank—Palestinian Authority Territories

The Palestinian Authority Territories in the West Bank (al-Sulṭa al-Waṭanīya al-Filasṭīnīya)—also known as the Palestinian National Authority, PA, or PNA—formed in 1994. They were formed under an interim Palestinian self-governing body established as a result of the 1993 Oslo Accords, which were signed between the State of Israel and the Palestinian Liberation Organization. Their formation was intended to help resolve the Israeli-Palestinian conflict.

The major Salafi movement in the Palestinian National Authority areas in the West Bank is Ḥizb al-Taḥrīr (the Liberation Party), which presumably focuses on nonviolent political activities. Thus far, the Salafi-Jihadi presence and infrastructure in the PA territories has been limited and monitored by Israel's security agency, Shabak, and PA security services. Shabak has exposed and intercepted terror plots orchestrated by Salafi-Jihadi cells in the PA territories, including a terror cell inspired by ISIS.

Israel

The Salafi ideology is present in small circles of Israeli Muslim Arabs. The few attempts to establish Salafi-Jihadi terror cells in Israel have been intercepted by Shabak in their early stages.

At least forty Israeli citizens of Muslim Arab origin are known to have joined Salafi-Jihadi organizations in Syria. According to Israeli law, it is illegal to join these organizations, and individuals will face imprisonment if they are caught in the process of trying to join, or if they return to Israel. Though the number is small, Shabak estimates that more Israeli Arabs may join the Salafi-Jihadi movement, possibly even becoming militants.[160] This phenomenon is closely and seriously monitored. Policy is being developed and legal actions are being taken to deter others from joining militant Islamist groups.

The Arab View of ISIS

Western media and policymakers pay close attention to ISIS's activities, capacities, and threats. Arabs in their day-to-day are also heavily engaged in tracking it—they have to be. A close look at the Arab world's discourse on militant Islam reveals a shocking dimension of the discussion: Some Arab journalists claim that ISIS is a tool in the service of the United States and/or Israel and/or Iran.[161, 162] But these people are the minority. Most know and publicly discuss the unfortunate truth: that militant Islam emerged because of the Arab and Muslim world's failures.

Oraib al-Rantawi, the CEO of the al-Quds Center for Political Studies in Amman, Jordan, explained in an article titled "ISIS is a Quintessential Muslim-Arab Invention" how the poor quality of life in the Arab world led to its creation. He wrote:

> ISIS is the legitimate child of the failed attempt to establish a modern Arab state based on the values of citizenship, social justice, welfare, and development. ISIS is the offspring of the regimes of corruption. ISIS is the fruit of the stink of poverty, neglect, corruption, unemployment, and the lack on the horizon of a democratic future in which there is involvement in decision-making and the design of the future.[163]

In an article titled "September 11 Has Not Yet Happened," Syrian researcher and translator Hashem Saleh wrote:

> September 11 should have caused a "September 11" in the Arab and Muslim world as well, but that has not yet happened. The proof of this is the appearance of ISIS. . . . ISIS is a cancer that emerged from the depths of the Arab and Muslim world. . . . There are those in the Arab and Muslim world who attempt to minimize the seriousness of

> this phenomenon. . . . There are those who say it is a peripheral phenomenon, but surveys say otherwise. . . . There are surveys that have shown that 90 percent of Muslims support ISIS at certain times. . . . The extreme nature of ISIS reflects what many Muslims secretly believe in their heart of hearts. . . . ISIS and its path are the product of failing education, of books and school curricula covered by the dust of time that sanctify violence.[164]

A similar belief was presented by Ghassan Charbel, the editor-in chief of the pan-Arab daily newspaper *al-Hayat*, in an article titled "Small Flags." He wrote, "The Arab societies fell apart because of the gang mentality that was prevalent in them, one of neglect, irresponsible policies, and cruelty. The result is ISIS."[165]

Sawsan al-Abtah, a lecturer in Arabic literature and language at the Lebanese University, expressed in an article titled "Wake Up You ISIS Supporters" her belief that the Arab world needs to urgently get control of ISIS. She wrote:

> The ISIS organization revealed [the Arab world's] true face, without makeup and without shiny slogans. ISIS is a branch that grew out of the Arab world and is not cut off from it. It is Arabs' obligation to shake free and fight it, and those that resemble it, without compromises before it is too late.[166]

Abtah's words could not ring more true. It is the obligation of the Arab world to stand on the front lines and rid itself of militant Islam. But in this undertaking, it needs to understand that confronting militant Islam cannot only be a military effort. The Arab world needs to recognize, confront, and overcome the challenges of Arab society—the corruption, illiteracy, lack of civil and human rights, poverty, unemployment, violence, and other plagues—because this is the swamp that provides militant Islam an environment to thrive—and that swamp must be dried.

Iraqi journalist Aziz al-Hajj described this in his article "9/11 and the Global War on Terror." In it he wrote:

> It is mandatory to fight the factors and the circumstances that keep on deceiving the Muslims with ideas of Islamic extremism. . . . It is mandatory to fight the ignorance and to isolate the spiritual leaders of extremism. At the same time, it is mandatory to pursue relentlessly, constantly the terrorists, and the extremists without any reconciliation and without any legal concessions.[167]

Militant Islam and the West

It's critical to recognize and state simply and clearly, with no equivocation or room for misinterpretation, that militant Islam did not appear because of anything related to the West or Israel. Militant Islam appeared because of the immense hardships in the Arab world. Militant Islam retains a deep and uncompromising hostility toward the West, its culture, its way of life, and its values. Militant Islamist groups also retain a deep and uncompromising hostility toward Israel and Jews.

It is the obligation of the international community, particularly the West, to understand the true character of militant Islam, the essence of its threats, and the challenge it presents, and to join Muslim and Arab forces in their struggle against these groups.

The long-term objective as stated by President Barack Obama in September 2014 is to "degrade and ultimately destroy" ISIS.[168] In a press conference in December 2015, after the attack in San Bernardino, California, in which fourteen Americans were killed by ISIS supporters, President Obama said, "We will destroy ISIL and any other organization that tries to harm us."[169]

The necessary approach stems from recognizing that the threat militant Islam presents is global. Terrorists attacked New York, Pennsylvania, and Washington, DC, in September 2001; Boston in April 2013; Madrid in March 2004; London in July 2005; Ottowa in October 2014; Sydney in December 2014; Paris in January and November 2015; San Bernardino in December 2015; and many other places in the world over the years—and they'll continue to do so. These are painful reminders of its danger.

In a January 2015 article, Ghassan Charbel defined the battle with militant Islam as "the third world war."[170] Dr. Abd al-Hamid al-Ansari, the former dean of the faculty of law and Islamic law at Qatar University, described in a September 2015 article titled "The Absence of Democracy as an Excuse for the ISIS Phenomenon" the misunderstanding of the root of the development of ISIS. He wrote:

> There are those who claim that the source for the appearance of Islamic terror is in the absence of democracy, however this is a false statement. The fact is that many of those who join ISIS come from democratic Western societies. There are those who connect the ISIS phenomenon to the United States or Israel, but these are ideas that serve a narrow political agenda and they have no connection to reality. The explanation for the appearance of ISIS stems directly from a culture of hatred and dismissal of the other that was deeply implanted in the culture of Islam from its beginnings.[171]

Looking Forward

Militant Islam as showcased by Salafi-Jihadi groups like al-Qaeda, Boko Haram, Global Jihad, ISIS, and Jabhat al-Nusra, as well as groups inspired by the Muslim Brotherhood ideology, such as Ḥamās and al-Jama'ah al-Islamiya, present a growing threat.

The collapse or weakening of the state authority in parts of the Middle East and Africa, together with growing inner challenges and chronic instability in large parts of the region and the widening and escalating Iranian-Arab power struggle, creates a chaotic environment that militant Islamist groups exploit to expand their activities, operations, reach, and recruitment.

The threat of militant Islamist groups is growing exponentially due to: access to huge amounts of weapons; availability of advanced weapons and chemical materials that can be used to make weapons; the efficient use of the Internet and social media platforms for the recruitment and activation of activists and supporters; and a growing and widening global terror infrastructure, particularly in Europe, stemming from the massive influx of refugees fleeing the Middle East and Africa.

At present there is a T-shape axis of militant Islam in the Middle East: its horizontal corridor stretches from West Africa through Algeria, Tunisia, Libya, Egypt, the Gaza Strip, Jordan, and Iraq. Its vertical corridor stretches from North Africa south toward Mali, Niger, Nigeria, Somalia, and Yemen.

ISIS and al-Qaeda are competing for the same niche, and the collision between the two organizations is in full force in Syria and Afghanistan. The collision has also caused internal tensions, which have resulted in splits within Salafi-Jihadi groups in arenas like Libya, Jordan, and Yemen.

Not too long ago, many Westerners hadn't heard of ISIS. This changed on August 19, 2014 when ISIS published a video of the beheading of American journalist James Foley. The video was titled "A Message to America," and the message was received: ISIS wants to destroy the West. Today the dangers posed by ISIS are a focal point of the world's attention.

The readiness of the international community and the Arab states to take immediate action to stop ISIS is clear. In September 2014, the United Nations Security Council adopted Resolution 2178, and in the same month, President Obama announced the formation of a coalition of NATO states led by the United States to fight ISIS. President Obama expressed hope that Arab states would join the coalition and declared that its objective was to defeat ISIS. Jordan, Qatar, Saudi Arabia, and the United Arab Emirates joined the coalition and are participating in the aerial raids on ISIS targets in Iraq and Syria that have been conducted since September 2014.

The world has recognized that the rapid expansion of ISIS and the brutality it exhibits are a global threat. Similar to Afghanistan under the rule of the Taliban, the "Islamic State," proclaimed by ISIS in June 2014,[172] could become an attraction for thousands of young Muslims from all over the world and a hothouse of murderous terrorism. The idea of the Islamic State excites, inspires, and motivates militant Islamist groups throughout the Middle East.

In 2015 Western states significantly boosted their efforts to eliminate ISIS strongholds in Iraq and Syria and they continue to do so today. Following the terror attacks ISIS orchestrated in Paris in November 2015, in which 129 people were killed, France increased its aerial attacks on ISIS targets in Syria, the UK Parliament approved an aerial campaign against ISIS, and the United States sent elite forces to Iraq to conduct special operations on the ground targeting ISIS leaders and facilities.

Is the threat of militant Islam a passing episode? Will the "Islamic State" survive and continue to expand? Will the reigns of crime, fear, and terror—sometimes called "Islamic emirates"—that have been established in various regions of the Middle East wither? Or will they flourish? These questions are occupying the minds of both laymen and strategists, and opinions are varied. Some commentators and analysts believe that the reigns of militant Islam will disintegrate because its resources—income, manpower, military capacities, etc.—are limited, and without them its adherents will find themselves facing military powers they can't defeat.[173, 174, 175, 176]

ISIS is not invincible. It was defeated in the battle over the Kurdish city of Kobanî in northern Syria in January 2015 and was forced to retreat from the outskirts of the Syrian city of Aleppo in February 2015. Under Kurdish military pressure, ISIS was forced to withdraw from the Iraqi town if Sinjar in November 2015. It's had heavy losses and reports indicate that coalition attacks targeting the convoys of oil tankers and oil storage units are resulting in a decrease in its major income source, oil revenues.[177, 178] Reportedly, the accumulating pressure and difficulties are resulting in the defection of ISIS militants, including senior commanders.[179] It's also been said that Arab intelligence agencies have breached ISIS and, as a result, the organization's operational capacity has been substantially damaged.[180]

Still, at present, the reality on the ground is that ISIS is inflicting more and more terror. Despite the military pressure of the international coalition, ISIS has been able to keep its control over most of the "Islamic State." In May 2015, it occupied the city of Ramadi in central Iraq and the city of Palmyra in the center of Syria. It shows success in how it attracts Muslims from within the Arab and Muslim world, and also from the West.

It is possible to say with certainty the following things in the context of militant Islam:

> First, most Muslims are not extremists. Like most people, they aspire to have a life of dignity, a future, and satisfaction. Overall, however, Muslims are more involved in terrorism and violence than any other religious or ethnic group, with most of their victims being fellow Muslims. The majority of Muslims are not involved in terror. But Muslims, in the name of Islam, conduct the majority of terror attacks.
>
> Second, the responsibility for the emergence and development of militant Islam rests primarily on the shoulders of the Arab and Muslim world. Confronting and defeating militant Islam needs to be spearheaded by the Muslim and Arab world, but it demands a close and ongoing cooperation between it and the international community. And this cooperation should not be restricted to the military level: the international community must assist Arab societies in stabilizing and reducing the chaos within them. Their corruption, illiteracy, lack of civil rights, poverty, violence, and other challenges must be overcome. As long as they exist, militant Islam will be present.

The situation in Iraq exemplifies how political chaos enabled the emergence of ISIS, and how a lack of government in the northern part of Sinai allowed Salafi-Jihadi groups to take control. These processes are also allowing ISIS to gain power in countries such as Libya and Yemen. Stopping the chaos and stabilizing social and political systems will act as a restraining factor that could, in the distant future, lead to a significant reduction in the ability of militant Islam to influence the region.

The West fails to understand the context of the phenomenon of ISIS and its achievements in Syria and Iraq. The reports and terminology used in Western media and policy-making circles portray ISIS in a flat, one-dimensional way. The West needs to understand that ISIS is a card used by regional and global factors (for example, Russia justifies its involvement in the war in Syria by saying that it is "fighting ISIS," but the Russian bomber jets rarely do) and that ISIS takes advantage of how it is used.

ISIS's relationship to the Sunni-Shiite conflicts in Iraq and Syria exhibits its willingness to work with whatever party best supports it at any given time. Sunnis make up 80 percent of the population in Syria and about 35 percent of the population of Iraq. In both countries, the Sunnis are fixated on how the Shiites and the Iranian-Shiite axis are oppressing them. In central and western Iraq, Iranian-backed Iraqi Shiite militias kill and abuse Sunnis. In Syria, via the massive support of Iran, its Shiite militias, the Russian air force, and the Assad regime have butchered hundreds of thousands of Sunnis. As long as the Iranian-Shiite militias continue to oppress the Sunnis and chaos continues to reign, ISIS will continue to thrive. Arab journalist Abdulrahman al-Rashed wrote in an article titled "Syria and Iraq Are One State, One War" that "failing to address the Sunnis' concerns and discontent will result in a situation in which the Islamic State will become a real state that represents the majority of Sunnis in Syria and Iraq."[181]

ISIS's role in Syria has many dimensions. ISIS both fights the Assad regime and Iran and also collaborates with it. It both fights Syrian rebels and collaborates with them. But at some point, it will not be able to avoid a battle to the death with the Syrian rebel groups. The battle is inevitable and the ramifications will be significant for Syria and its Islamic State. In the fight between the two, al-Qaeda will support the Syrian rebels because it desires to overpower ISIS.

Turkey enables ISIS to operate in northeast Syria because it serves Turkey's interest in preventing the formation of an independent Kurdish entity in north Syria. Turkey claims to fight ISIS but enables ISIS activists to move freely through Turkey. Many Uighurs, members of a Turk ethnic group living in China, have passed through Turkey to join ISIS. In Iraq, ISIS is supported by some Sunni groups and fought by others.

Ideologically speaking, ISIS views the toppling of Arab regimes, particularly the Arab monarchies, as its most important mission on the path toward establishing the global caliphate. This said, it seems as if ISIS will continue, at least in the near future, to avoid confrontation with monarchial states such as Jordan and Saudi Arabia in which the balance of power would be to its disadvantage.

Militant Islam will not disappear in the foreseeable future, and the role it fills in the Middle East negatively influences the regional system. Arab states and monarchies that have not yet had the gloomy fate of Iraq, Libya, Syria, and Yemen see militant Islam as a significant threat to their sovereignty and stability. In their view, dismantling militant Islam is necessary to ensure stability within their borders and those of their neighboring states.

Militant Islam plays a more significant role in this second decade of the twenty-first century than it played in the past. This has required states to reprioritize their strategic interests and, accordingly, develop and apply adjusted policies. Redesigning and reprioritizing has generated some surprising alliances with a significant player in the region—Israel. An axis of stability exists between Israel, Egypt, and the Arab monarchies. The threat of militant Islam is one of the factors that has led to this axis, and it seems that it will endure for some time. The axis fashions a new regional political agenda, which could generate positive developments. One example is in the context of the Arab-Israeli conflict. Abd al-Mun'im Sa'id, chairman of the influential Egyptian newspaper *al-Youm* (*Today*) wrote about this in an article in August 2014 titled "The Upcoming War in the Gaza Strip." He wrote, "An Israeli–Palestinian agreement can be achieved only within the frame of a broader regional frame."[182] In the same month, the Saudi Arabian minister of foreign affairs declared in a conference of Sunni clergy that Saudi Arabia is willing to make compromises for the sake of peace and stability.[183] In June 2015, a meeting between Dore Gold, the director-general of the Israeli Ministry of Foreign Affairs and a previous Israeli ambassador to the United Nations, and Anwar Eshki, a retired Saudi general and former senior advisor to the Saudi government, took place in Washington, DC. The meeting was widely covered by the media and was a clear exhibit of the warming Israeli-Saudi relations and the formation of the axis of stability. In November 2015, Israel's foreign affairs office announced that it will open a diplomatic office in Abu Dhabi that will be attached to the UN Renewal Energy Delegation based in Abu Dhabi.

Expression of the forming Israeli-Arab stability axis emerged before the meeting in Washington and before the announcement about the Israeli office in Abu Dhabi. The precursor, which was little-known to most of the world at the time, was two-fold: the growing Israeli-Egyptian cooperation to fight terror groups in the Sinai Peninsula, and an Israeli-Arab cooperation that had been quietly brewing since 2011 regarding the now-unfolding war in Syria.

CHAPTER FIVE

THE IRANIAN-ARAB POWER STRUGGLE: THE PAST IS STILL PRESENT

The Sunni-Shia Split

TWO MAJOR HISTORIC STRUGGLES HAVE PLAYED a central role in shaping the Muslim world and the Middle East. One is the struggle between the Sunnis and the Shiites. The other is the struggle between the Arab civilization and the Persian civilization.

Let us look first at the background of the Sunni-Shiite struggle.

There are 1.6 billion Muslims in the world.[1] About 90 percent are Sunni and about 10 percent are Shiite.[2]

The history of the split began with the Prophet Muhammad, the founder of Islam, who died in 632 in al-Medina, at, it's said, the age of sixty-two. After his death, Abū Bakr, the prophet's father-in-law, was chosen to be caliph, the supreme religious and political leader of the Islamic caliphate. This marked the beginning of a divide within Islam. Some people believed that to be caliph, one needed to be a descendent of the Prophet Muhammad—others believed that the person should be chosen based on his skills and virtues and need not be a descendent of Muhammad.

The fact that the first three caliphs—Abū Bakr, Umar (another father-in-law of Muhammad), and Uthman (a member of a very powerful family, the Umayyads)—were not descendents of the Prophet Muhammad indicates that most Muslims at the time likely believed that leadership should be based on merit, not bloodline.

Muslims who argued that a direct relative of Prophet Muhammad should have been the next in line to the caliphate called for this to be ʿAlī ibn Abī

Ṭālib, Muhammad's cousin and son-in-law. Muhammad had no sons of his own who lived to adulthood, so by giving leadership of the Muslim world to ʿAlī and his heirs, a bloodline-based leadership would be instilled.

The believers in a merit-based rule became known as the *Sunnat al-Nabi* (the Path of the Prophet), or in short, *Sunnis*. The believers in a bloodline-based rule became known as *Shīʿatu ʿAlī*, meaning "Ali's faction," or in short, *Shīʿites* or *Shīʿī* (Shiites), members of the Shīʿah (Shia).

When Caliph Uthman was killed, ʿAlī proclaimed himself the fourth caliph. After just five years in power, in 661 CE, ʿAlī was assassinated. At the time of his death, he had twenty-one children from nine different women. Four of his children were with his first wife, Fāṭimah, the daughter of Prophet Muhammad: their eldest son, Hasan, their second-born son, al-Ḥusayn ibn ʿAlī, known as Ḥusayn, and their two daughters, Zaynab and Umm Kulthūm.

Hasan ruled for a short time but abdicated after six or seven months, at which time, his brother Ḥusayn demanded the throne. The caliphate at that time was ruled by the powerful Umayyad dynasty, and the caliph, Yazīd ibn Muʿāwiyah ibn Abī Sufyān, was not pleased with Ḥusayn's political aspirations, and so the struggle for control became violent. On the tenth day of the month of Muharram (the Forbidden), the first month in the Islamic calendar, in the year 680, soldiers of Yazīd killed Ḥusayn and his companions in a village named Karbalā, located in modern-day Iraq.

The slaughter at Karbalā is the cornerstone of the Shiite narrative. The killing of Ḥusayn, the son of Muhammad's daughter and the last direct male descendant of the prophet and, in the eyes of the Shiites, the next in line to rule the caliphate, caused debate between the bloodline camp, shīatu ʿAlī (ʿAli's faction), and the merit camp, the Sunnis, and led to an unbridgeable and irreconcilable hatred and animosity. The Shiites are deeply motivated by the notion that they were deprived of the right to lead the Muslim world.

Within the Shia faith, Ḥusayn has become a symbol of martyrdom and is considered by Shiites to be the *sayyid al-shuhada* (the master of martyrs). Shiites commemorate the day of his death every year—on the tenth day of the Muslim month of Muharram, an occasion known as the day of *Āshūrā* (ten). They curse Yazīd ibn Māwiyah, and some Shiites exhibit their solidarity with Ḥusayn by inflicting extreme suffering on themselves: they shave their heads and beat themselves with chains, knives, and swords until they bleed. The ceremony is called *ta'ziyah* (consolations).

Deep feelings of deprivation, grief, suffering, and being the victims of a profound injustice have become defining axioms of the Shiite narrative and existence, and there is a mystical dimension within Shia, which is expressed by an apocalyptic view of the world. A central figure in the Shia faith is the *mahdi*—the leader, the guide, the anointed one—who, it's believed, will lead the Shiites to victory over the Sunnis and put Islam on a path toward redemption.

Both the Sunnis and Shiites have *imams*; but while a Sunni *imam* is a cleric position acquired through study and theological education, a Shiite *imam* is a religious leader who is a descendant of 'Ali. According to the Shia belief, *imams* rule because of their divine genealogy, designated by Allah, and passed from father to son. The *imams* in Shia are said to be immune from sin and error and to have perfect talents and characteristics, and a sublime knowledge, whose source is in their forefathers' legacies and secret religious texts. A central principle in Shia is to have obedience, dedication, and loyalty to the *imams*. This is the basis for a political concept developed by the leader of the Islamic Revolution in Iran, Ayatollah Ruhollah Khomeini, known as *wilayat al-faqih*, the rule of the Shiite clergy and the demand for full obedience to his rule.

The largest branch in Shia Islam is *al-Ithnā 'Asharīyah,* also called *Ithnā Imāmiyāh,* Twelver Shia Islam. Adherents of this stream of thought, Twelvers, believe that there was a dynasty of twelve *imams* that began with 'Ali, who led the Shiites for generations. They believe the eleventh *imam* was Hasan ibn 'Ali Muhammad, known as al-Askari. After al-Askari's death in the year 874 CE, the role of *imam* is said to have passed to his son, Muhammad ibn Hasan al-Mahdī, who was only five-years-old at the time. Shiites believe that the boy, after being ordained, went into a cave where he spent sixty years, and from the cave sent his divine knowledge out into the world through his followers. This period of time is known in Shia as "the small absence." After sixty years, it is believed that Muhammad left the cave and disappeared—what is known in Shia as "the big absence." The Shiites, therefore, call him the "disappeared *imam*." They believe, however, that he did not die but is still alive and is choosing to not be seen and will appear again when he manifests himself as the messiah. (Another title for him is *al-muntazar*, the "One Expected to Appear.") It's said that when he reappears he will lead the Shiites to victory in a war in which most of the human race will be killed. And after the war, peace and divine justice will prevail and humanity will know only growth and prosperity. There will be an Islamic State and the law of Allah, as it was given to the Prophet Muhammad, will reign on earth.

The struggle between Sunni Islam and Shia Islam has resulted in an abyss of hostility, differing ideological and theological opinions, political clashes, and violence for more than thirteen hundred years.

Arab-Persian Rivalry

The second of the two most significant struggles to have shaped the Muslim world and the Middle East is the rivalry between the Arab civilization, which emerged from the Arab Peninsula and the Persian civilization.

In the year 651, the four-hundred-year-old Persian Sāsānian Empire was occupied and conquered by Sunni Arab Muslims, and the Persians, who were mostly Zoroastrians, converted to Islam. The rule of the Sunni Arab Muslims in Persia came to an end with the rise to power of the Shiite, non-Arab, Ṣafavid Dynasty (1501–1722). It was then that the Shiite twelver ideology was adopted as the dominant orthodoxy of the Persians.

Since 1500, the Persians have been ruled by non-Arab Shiite dynasties that compete with Sunni Arab and Sunni Turkish powers for political and territorial dominance. The tension and rivalry between the Shiite dynasties ruling Persia and the major Sunni political powers, both Arab and Turkish, intensified because the Shiite dynasties ruling Persia were of non-Arab origin. This is important because the Arabian Peninsula is the cradle of Islam, and in the eyes of the Arabs, pure Islamic values and traditions are Arab ones. The Arabs view Persians as pagans, which is incompliant with the essence of Islam—the total submission and unquestioning belief in monotheism and Allah's rule. An example of this is the ceremonies of the Persian holy day Nowruz, the first day of the year in the Persian calendar, which are rooted in Zoroastrianism.

The year 1979 marked a significant milestone in the Sunni-Shiite and Arab-Persian rivalries, because the last Persian dynasty, the Pahlavi Dynasty (1925–1979), was overthrown by the Shiite clergy. The *shah* at the time, Mohammad Reza Shah Pahlavi, was deposed in a popular coup—part of the Islamic Revolution of Iran, also known as the Islamic Revolution—and a group of Shiite clerics, spiritual religious priests called *mullahs*, rose to power under the leadership of Ruhollah Khomeini. When this happened, Persia, which had become known as Iran, became a Shiite Islamic theocracy and its name was changed to the "Islamic Republic of Iran."

During the nearly forty years that have passed since the Islamic Revolution, the Sunni-Shiite rivalry and Arab-Persian rivalry have intensified. In the second decade of the twenty-first century, the rivalry is manifested through wars between Sunnis, backed by Arab Sunni states and Turkey, and Shiites, backed by Iran.

The Islamic Revolution

Shiite mullahs function as part of a hierarchy. The highest rank is the *ayatollah 'uzma* (the great ayatollah), a position currently held by 'Alī al-Ḥusaynī al-Sīstānī, an Iranian-born Shiite who lives in Iraq. Ruhollah Khomeini, the leader of the Islamic Revolution, who died in 1989, had the rank of *ayatollah ruhollah* (translated as the sign of Allah).

The significance of the Islamic Revolution in the context of the Sunni-Shiite rivalry is that the mullahs, unlike the ousted shah, placed strict Shiite doctrine and narratives at the center of their regime's ideology. Stemming from this and motivated by the Shiite belief that they have been deprived of the right to lead the Muslim world, the Shiite mullah regime is determined to correct the historical injustice done to the Shiites and position the Islamic Republic of Iran, under its leadership, as the dominant regional superpower first and later as a global superpower. To this end, the regime applies a proactive, aggressive foreign policy intended to expand its influence and spread Shiite Islam throughout the world. This effort is known as "exporting the

Islamic Revolution." The Iranian mullah regime employs a sophisticated strategy to gain power and influence and spread its version of Islam. This involves putting tremendous energy and resources into developing a broad and intricate network of connections throughout Asia, Africa, and South America through activities such as arms and trades dealings, the offering of economic support and military assistance, and the development of cultural and diplomatic cooperation.

Under the leadership of Ali Khamenei, the second and current supreme leader (the most powerful figure in the mullah regime, who has control over the executive, legislative, and judicial branches of government, the military, and the media[3]) of Iran and the Muslim cleric who succeeded Ruhollah Khomeini, the regime has shown success in its mission. This success has contributed to the violent Sunni-Shiite clashes throughout the Middle East.

Iran and the Axis of Resistance

One of the most significant accomplishments of the Iranian mullah regime has been to develop the *mehwar al-muqāwamah* (the axis of resistance) and position itself as the leading factor of it, using the slogan, "Fighting Israel in the name of the resistance." The axis is a powerful web of allies and proxies that includes the Assad regime in Syria; Hezbollah in Lebanon; and Palestinian terror organizations in the Gaza Strip, including Ḥamās, Islamic Jihad, and the Popular Resistance Committees in Palestine. They work to help Iran in its goal of spreading the Islamic Revolution and positioning itself, under the control of its mullah regime, as a superpower.

Hezbollah in Lebanon

In Lebanon, in the beginning of the 1980s, the Iranians, through their elite al-Quds force (the paramilitary arm of the Iranian Revolutionary Guards Corps, founded after the Islamic Revolution and charged with defending the Islamic Republic against internal and external threats) established their most powerful proxy: the Shiite Lebanese militant Islam organization Hezbollah. The Iranians were particularly attracted to Lebanon because it borders Israel, and they capitalized on the fact that the Shiites are the biggest sect in Lebanon, more than a quarter of the population;[4] that Lebanon suffers from chronic political instability; and that Israel, much to the dismay of the Lebanese, occupied South Lebanon from 1982–2000. In the name of the resistance, Iran has been massively arming Hezbollah since its establishment. According to some estimations, Iran has supplied Lebanon's Hezbollah with more than one hundred thousand rockets and long-range missiles aimed at Israel.[5]

Following the Israeli withdrawal from Lebanon in the year 2000, the Lebanese government urged Hezbollah to disarm itself, saying that the only military force in Lebanon should be the Lebanese army. The leader of Hezbollah, Hassan Nasrallah, rejected the demand. He argued that the weapons of Hezbollah were necessary to defend Lebanon from Israel and announced that Lebanon's identity is based on three components: "*al-Jaish, al-sh'aab, walmukawamah*" (the [Lebanese] army, the people, and the resistance). Nasrallah proclaimed that "no voice is stronger than the voice of the resistance"[6] and "the weapon of the resistance is untouchable and we will cut any arm that stretches to touch it."[7] The message was aimed at Hezbollah's political opponents in Lebanon, and the Lebanese quickly learned that Nasrallah was serious.

In May 2008, with the weapons of the resistance supplied to Hezbollah by Iran, Hezbollah militants occupied the west side of Beirut, the capital of Lebanon, for seventy-two hours, killing dozens of Lebanese. The act was in response to the Lebanese government's objection to Iran funding a massive communication network that would exclusively serve Hezbollah. The Lebanese government had argued that the action undermined its sovereignty. The use of violence proved to be a successful strategy for Hezbollah. The aggressive and deadly strategy ended with a political agreement that allowed Hezbollah the right to nominate eleven ministers to the Lebanese parliament, a sufficient amount of representatives to be able to veto Lebanese government decisions.

Iran's enormous investments in Hezbollah, estimated to be in the billions of dollars,[8, 9, 10] have yielded important strategic dividends. In addition to establishing a convenient platform to ignite further violence against Israel in the name of the resistance, it gained a friendly base on the Mediterranean Sea.

Within Lebanon, Hezbollah executes the will of the Iranians through the Lebanese political system and its military might. It uses terror and assassinates political opponents.[11, 12] One of the most well-known examples of this is the 2005 assassination of Prime Minister Rafiq al-Hariri, a Sunni, ally of Saudi Arabia, and outspoken critic of Iran's aggressive regional policy, including its development, funding, and arming of proxies like Hezbollah. An international tribunal, the Special Tribunal for Lebanon (STL),[13] was empowered by UN Security Council Resolution 1757 to investigate the assassination. Based on its findings, the STL ordered a summons of four (in October 2013, a fifth person was added) Hezbollah senior commanders suspected to have been involved in the assassination.[14] The suspects did not come forward and Nasrallah claimed their whereabouts were unknown.

In 2012, Wissam al-Hassan, the intelligence chief of Lebanon's internal security forces, was assassinated in Beirut. Hassan was leading the investigation of the Hariri assassination and was a serious threat to Hezbollah.[15] Arab journalist Abdulrahman al-Rashed was one of many Arabs who expressed no doubt that Hezbollah was responsible for the assassination.[16, 17, 18] He wrote:

> More than twenty Lebanese figures have been assassinated, including former Prime Minister Rafiq al-Hariri, not to mention senior politicians, media figures, and military leaders. All of those assassinated have been affiliated with a single political movement . . . Following the assassination of Hariri, Hezbollah and [the Iranian proxy] the Syrian regime sought to promote the story that a youth, Abu Adas—a member of a terrorist Islamist organization—was responsible for Hariri's death as part of a suicide attack. They claimed that Abu Adas had recorded a video confession, which he left in a tree and was later discovered by the media. Only the stupid and ignorant would believe such a story! We knew from the first moment that the Syrian regime was behind the assassination of Hariri, and that its closest ally, Hezbollah, had carried out this operation. Of the estimated twenty people who have been killed in the past period, the conspirator and

> party responsible for the assassination have been one and the same. The latest assassination victim was Wissam al-Hassan, who was practically the only security official in Lebanon who was outside the authority of Hezbollah. This man, along with his team, succeeded in compiling a lot of the evidence that implicates the Syrian regime and Hezbollah. Only the stupid and ignorant are not aware that the conspirators and perpetrators were the Assad regime and Hezbollah."[19]

As of the end of 2015, the identities of the assassins of Prime Minister Hassan remain unknown. Through Hezbollah, the Iranian regime has become an influential player in Lebanon and has increased its power in the region. Arab journalists, leaders, and politicians—including prominent Lebanese Shiite clergy and intellectuals who oppose Hezbollah—say bluntly that Lebanon has been taken hostage by Hezbollah in the service of Iran. [20, 21, 22, 23, 24, 25, 26]

The clearest example of how Hezbollah acts in the service of Iran is the war in Syria. The Lebanese government announced a neutrality policy regarding the war in Syria. Yet Hezbollah—regardless of the fact that it is a member of the Lebanese government[27]—is, under the Iranian government's instructions, massively involved in the war in Syria.

Ḥamās and the Islamic Jihad in Palestine in the Gaza Strip

The Iranian mullah regime has duplicated its success in Lebanon in the Gaza Strip. Its goal is to use Gaza as another stage in the area that borders Israel to ignite violence against Israel in the name of the resistance.

In June 2007, the Islamist Palestinian movement, Ḥamās, ousted the Gaza Strip's Palestinian Authority in a violent coup led by Ḥamās's military wing, the Ezzedeen al-Qassam Brigades. The coup resulted in dozens of Palestinian fatalities and hundreds of people injured.[28]

Ḥamās, similar to Hezbollah, is supported financially and armed by Iran. Jawad Karimi Kadusi, a member of Iran's Parliament and a former commander in its Revolutionary Guards, said in 2012 that Ḥamās takes orders from Iran in return for weapons and financial support:

> The al-Qassam Brigades is moving under the direct orders of the military commanders in Iran. . . . The al-Qassam Brigades is not under the command of Ismail Haniyeh [a senior political leader of Ḥamās] or Khaled Mashal [the head of the political bureau of Ḥamās]. These forces are moving under Iranian orders.[29]

An illustration of the nature of the relations between Ḥamās and Iran was in 2012 when Ismail Haniyeh, then prime minister of Ḥamās's government in the Gaza Strip, visited the Islamic Republic. Haniyeh sat quietly while his host, Ali Khamenei, Iran's supreme leader, insulted the late Palestinian leader Yasser Arafat, the founder and leader of the Fatah political party, the chairman of the Palestine Liberation Organization, and the chairman of the Palestinian Authority. Arafat is perceived by most Palestinians as having been their greatest leader and is an icon of the Palestinian struggle. During the meeting, Khamenei described Arafat as a person who betrayed his people and neglected the way of the resistance.[30] For many Arab journalists, thinkers, and leaders, the episode displayed what they already knew, that in the name of the resistance, Ḥamās, like Hezbollah, was an agent in the service of Iran's interests, and that Iran's mullah regime couldn't care less about the Lebanese or Palestinian people.[31, 32, 33, 34, 35]

However, the Iranian mullah regime never puts all its eggs in one basket. Parallel to its generous support of Ḥamās, Iran also supports other militant groups in the Gaza Strip, particularly the Islamic Jihad in Palestine (IJIP), and this has proven wise. In the midst of the war in Syria, Ḥamās distanced itself from Iran. Iran retaliated by drastically cutting its support for Ḥamās and increasing its support of IJIP.

Syria and the Assad Regime, Iran's Strategic Partner

Syria under Assad's rule is a critical component of Iran's resistance axis. Damascus harbors and hosts senior Iranian Revolutionary Guards officers and leaders and militants from Ḥamās, Hezbollah, Islamic Jihad in Palestine, and other organizations. The militant groups strategize, coordinate activity, and share intelligence. The headquarters and offices of Palestinian organizations such as the IJIP and Ḥamās, until the beginning of 2012,[36, 37] were located in Damascus. Syria—particularly since Bashar al-Assad assumed office in 2000—has turned into a way station for the transfer of huge numbers of weapons from Iran to Hezbollah in Lebanon and a highway for thousands of militants going to military training camps in Iran.[38, 39]

The weapons supply route from Iran to the storehouses of Hezbollah is short and easy. Iranian planes loaded with weapons land in Damascus and unload their cargo, which is then sent by land to Hezbollah's storerooms and bunkers in Lebanon. The weapons supply route to the Gaza Strip is much more challenging because it is much longer and it has an Achilles' heel: the final part of the route is through the smuggling tunnels dug from Sinai to the Gaza Strip. These are the tunnels that were heavily destroyed by Egypt. In June 2015, the Israeli defense minister, Moshe Ya'alon, indicated that the destruction of most of the tunnels by Egypt has made it difficult for Ḥamās and the IJIP to arm and rearm with large amounts of advanced weapons.[40]

When events in Syria deteriorated in the summer and fall of 2011, red lights lit up in Tehran and the possibility of Assad's downfall alarmed the mullahs. Without Assad's regime, it would be hard for Iran to continue exerting its control over the resistance axis—and without Assad's rule, the land bridge that serves as a passage for weapons, ammunition, and military activists from Iran to Lebanon and Syria and back would be severed, the training bases and coordination headquarters of the resistance axis in Syria would be lost, and Hezbollah, Iran's main strategic asset in the Middle East, would lose its supply chain. Moreover, Iran would likely find itself facing a new rule in Syria that would be Sunni and would not forget that Hezbollah was Assad's close ally. In the view of the Iranian regime, the fall of Assad's government would be an enormous strategic blow; it would flush the enormous Iranian investments in building and developing the axis of resistance down the drain, and it would deprive Iran of one of its most significant strategic cards. This explains Iran's heavy involvement in the war in Syria.

With the axis of resistance, the Iranians shape political decisions on Israel's southern and northern borders—the Gaza Strip in the south and Lebanon in the north. For decades, the mullah regime has had its proxies kill Israelis, Lebanese, and Palestinians, while it sits securely in Tehran. And despite its contribution to the destruction of Lebanon and the Gaza Strip, it's earned high praise in the Arab world for its contribution to the resistance.

The rocket and missile capabilities developed by Iran are used by the mullah regime as a bargaining chip. Iran believes that the threat of attacking Israel with hundreds of thousands of rockets and missiles launched from Lebanon and the Gaza Strip, which would result in the devastating destruction of Israeli cities and strategic infrastructure, will deter an Israeli and/or US military attack on Iran's nuclear installations. It believes that Israel is the United States' most strategic asset in the Middle East and that a threat to Israel will improve its negotiating power in its talks with the West regarding its nuclear program. In the Iranian mindset, Israel is a hostage in the service of the Iranian military's nuclear project.

In 2004, Jordan's King Abdullah II warned that Iran's goal was to expand its influence through the creation of a "Shia crescent,"[41] and he was right in his prediction. Iran has established a crescent of influence stretching from the Mediterranean Sea (Lebanon and Syria) eastward through Iraq to the Arab (or, according to Iran, the *Persian*) Gulf (mostly in Bahrain, the only Arab monarchy whose population is predominately Shiite), and winding westward toward Yemen into Africa.

Iran views the Arab (Persian) Gulf and the land corridor from Iran through Iraq, Syria, and Lebanon to the Mediterranean Sea as areas of utmost importance to its strategic interests. In an interview that Mohammad 'Ali Jafari, the commander of the Iranian Revolutionary Guards, gave in December 2015, he said, "Iraq, Syria, and Lebanon are all part of the axis of resistance, thus there should be no borders between them."[42]

Iran: Exporting the Islamic Revolution and Iran's Goals

The Iranian mullah regime's geostrategic regional policy has three main goals: supporting Shiites and expanding Shiite orthodoxy, exporting its model of the Islamic Revolution, and positioning Iran as a dominant superpower.

Iran promotes its regional policy through diplomacy; setting up and financing social, economic, and cultural activities; arming and financing proxies; nurturing local factors in areas of Iranian interest—like the Shiites in Bahrain and southern Iraq, Hezbollah in Lebanon, Ḥamās and the Palestinian Islamic Jihad in the Gaza Strip, and the Houthis in Yemen; and the direct use of terror and military might. The aggressive Iranian regional policy results in an escalating and widening Iranian-Arab power struggle.

Two significant and unprecedented developments that have dramatically boosted the Iranian-Arab power struggle have taken place during the second decade of the twenty-first century. One is the involvement of Iranian military forces in Syria and Iraq. The second is the Joint Comprehensive Plan of Action of the Vienna Agreement, signed in July 2015, which marked the international community's formal recognition of the mullah regime as a legitimate factor and central player in the region. Many people argue that the inevitable outcome of the Vienna Agreement will be a nuclear arms race in the Middle East. At present, it's not on the verge of a nuclear arms race, but as a result of the Vienna Agreement, it is one step closer.

There are currently eight active arenas (of varying levels of intensity) of the Iranian-Arab power struggle in the Middle East: Bahrain, the Gaza Strip, Iraq, Lebanon, Syria, Yemen, three islands in the Gulf—Abu Musa, Greater Tunb, and Lesser Tunb, all occupied by Iran—and last, but not least—Iran's nuclear project.

Let's review each arena through the lens of the Iranian-Arab power struggle—aside from Syria, which we will explore deeper in the chapter "The War in Syria."

Eight Arenas of the Iranian-Arab Power Struggle

Bahrain

Bahrain is the only Arab Gulf state in which a Sunni minority, the al-Khalifah dynasty, rules over a population that is majority Shia, as well as a sizeable Persian community.[43] The result is a relationship that is increasingly tense, manifested in periodic flare-ups of unrest and sometimes violence. The major political opposition to the Shiites in Bahrain is a non-governmental organization known as the Al Wefaq National Islamic Society. Since the organization was founded in 2001, there have been efforts to negotiate the constitution and division of power within Bahrain's political system. Thus far it's yielded few results, but the channels for political dialogue exist, and both Al Wefaq and the monarchy work to contain the animosity between the Shiites and Sunnis.

The mullah regime claims ownership over Bahrain, arguing it was part of Persia during the rule of Shah 'Abbās I (1588–1629) and was taken away by the al-Khalifah family, with the support of the United Kingdom, in 1783. Following the withdrawal of British forces from the Arab Gulf in the beginning of the 1970s, Iran's shah demanded ownership of Bahrain. Yet, in a 1970 referendum conducted by the UN, the majority of Bahrainis expressed their desire to be independent. Bahrain's independence was formalized through UN Security Council resolution 278 and reaffirmed by the Iranian Parliament itself.

However, following the Islamic Revolution, the mullah regime renewed the claim for ownership over Bahrain. Thus, for example, in 1979, an advisor to Ayatollah Ruhollah Khomeini announced that Bahrain was the fourteenth district of Iran and since has strived to overthrow the al-Khalifah family's rule and establish an Islamic government in Bahrain.[44] In February 2009, Ali Akbar Nateq-Nouri, a former Iranian minister of interior and advisor to Iranian Supreme Leader Ayatollah Ali Khamenei, penned an inflammatory editorial claiming that, historically, "Bahrain was [Iran's] fourteenth province and had a representative at the parliament."[45]

Iran tries to enhance its influence in Bahrain by using the Shiites in Bahrain to increase unrest and instability. A peak in this drama unfolded in March 2011 when, in the face of violent Shia riots that threatened to topple the ruling family, Saudi Arabia sent soldiers into Bahrain to prevent a Shia takeover. The Saudi military involvement in Bahrain in March 2011 made it very clear they will not tolerate an Iranian takeover of Bahrain.

In April 2014, Bahrain revoked the citizenship of fourteen of its citizens accused of "carrying out acts harmful to the security of the country." One of them was a representative of the highest-ranking Shiite cleric, Ayatollah 'Uzma Ali Sistani, who lives in Iraq.[46]

In June 2015, Ali Salman, the leader of the Shiite opposition in Bahrain, was imprisoned for four years.

In July 2015, Iran's supreme leader, Ali Khamenei, committed that Iran would support the opposition in Bahrain.[47]

For now, the al-Khalifah family's reign is dependent on Saudi Arabia's support and patronage. Saudi Arabia will not tolerate an Iranian takeover of Bahrain, and the al-Khalifah family's rule will likely remain stable in the foreseeable future

The Gaza Strip

The Gaza Strip has a population of 1.8 million people, almost all of whom are Sunni.[48] Iran has two major channels of influence in the Gaza Strip: Ḥamās, which controls the Gaza Strip, and Islamic Jihad in Palestine. However, Iran's influence in the Gaza Strip has somewhat eroded for a number of reasons.

First, the weakening of the Assad-Iran axis in the war in Syria during the spring and summer of 2015 may have caused Ḥamās to reevaluate its attempts to rebuild relations with Iran—and today, it is reported that Ḥamās's major source of support is Turkey, whose current president and government are affiliated with the Muslim Brotherhood movement, the mother movement of Ḥamās.

Second, the repeated military rounds with Israel, and particularly the war in the summer of 2014 (July 8–August 26) caused Ḥamās, which rules the Gaza Strip, enormous damage. In addition, the human casualties and devastation caused to the infrastructure in the Gaza Strip has resulted in a growing anger among the people of Gaza and across the Arab world who criticize Ḥamās for its policy and hold it accountable for the disastrous outcomes of its militant path.

The third reason is the significant role of Egypt in the context of the Gaza Strip. The Palestinians in Gaza are desperately dependent on Egypt's goodwill because it is Egypt—not Iran—who holds the key to the Rafah crossing, Gaza's main gate to the world. Egypt's willingness to open the passage is conditional upon Ḥamās's good behavior.

Instability in the Gaza Strip is dangerous to Egypt because:

- It fuels militant Islamist groups operating in the Sinai Peninsula, which is a security threat to Egypt.
- Repeated military rounds between Ḥamās and Israel could play to the hands of the Islamists in Egypt who oppose the government, giving them an excuse to ignite the Egyptian street and challenge the government, which strives to maintain stability.
- Increased activity of militant Islamist groups in the Sinai Peninsula and/or repeated military rounds between Ḥamās and Israel could damage Egypt's ability to attract foreign investors and tourists, one of Egypt's major income sources.

The heavy campaign Egypt conducts to destroy the tunnel system between the Gaza strip and Egypt indicates Egypt's interest in stability. Egypt is sending a clear message to Iran to keep its hands off the Gaza Strip and to not continue to ignite violence by using the Gaza Strip as a platform for a military confrontation with Israel. Without the tunnels, Iran's ability to provide Ḥamās with weapons has substantially decreased, and its ability to fuel military rounds against Israel has been hampered.

The fourth reason is Ḥamās's dire financial situation and its growing dependence on Arab financial support. Just a few days after the signing of the Joint Comprehensive Plan of Action, on July 14, 2015 regarding Iran's nuclear program, the head of Ḥamās's political bureau, Khaled Mashal, was accepted for a short meeting with Saudi King Salman. The Saudi message to Ḥamās is clear and simple: keep Gaza calm, do not allow Iran to spark another fire, and you will be rewarded financially.

Reports also indicate the possibility that a primary beneficiary of Ḥamās's abandonment of Iran—and an increasingly important Iranian proxy—the Islamic Jihad in Palestine, which has maintained its loyalty to Iran thus far, is also considering a change of course. It seems that tension between IJIP and its Iranian patron began brewing in the beginning of 2015, following IJIP's refusal to support Iran and the Houthis in Yemen. In February 2015, Abdullah al-Shami, a spokesperson for the IJIP, was called upon to support Iran and its role in the Middle East.[49] And while a March 2015 report by Iran's state-run Radio Teheran claimed that a senior leader of IJIP expressed support for Iran and the Houthi tribe fighting against an Arab coalition in Yemen,[50] the report should be viewed cautiously since Radio Teheran serves as an official media platform for the Iranian mullah regime and no other source corroborates the story. In fact, IJIP leaders announced that the events in Yemen were "an inner-Arab affair,"[51] code for "Iran should stay out of Yemen." It was reported that in 2015, IJIP's leader, Ramadan Abdullah Shallah, moved from his home in Tehran, the Iranian capital, to Beirut.[52]

Iran reportedly retaliated against the IJIP by stopping salary payments to its personnel in the Gaza Strip and offering its support to another player in the Gaza Strip, Ḥarakat al-Sabirin (the Movement of Those Who Are Patient). Ḥarakat al-Sabirin was formed in 2014; it claims to be an offshoot of IJIP and to have formed when the Islamic Jihad in Palestine shifted its position toward Iran.[53, 54] Until the spring of 2015, Ḥarakat al-Sabirin was not well-known, but since March 2015, and parallel to reports about allegedly tensed Iran-IJIP relations, the group's name is frequently mentioned in the press; [55, 56] however, it is a negligible player in the Gaza Strip.

For now it seems that Ḥamās is looking for ways to get back into the arms of the Arab world, and that road goes through the Arab Gulf states and Saudi Arabia, because the Arab world, which is predominately Sunni, is, after all, the natural home for Ḥamās—a Palestinian, Arab, Sunni movement.

Iran may renew its financial support of Ḥamās; however, since the flow of Iranian weapons and ammunition to the Gaza Strip substantially diminished due the Egyptian campaign against the tunnels, that financial support will not guarantee its ability to trigger violence in the Gaza Strip as a platform to enhance its influence—the way it was accustomed to working. Given this, it is likely that Iran's ability to dictate its agenda in the Gaza Strip, which negatively impacts Israel and Egypt, will continue to be reduced.

Iraq

Iraq is a state of more than thirty-seven million people, of whom about 60–65 percent are Shiite and 30–35 percent are Sunni. Iraq is home to a significant amount of non-Arab ethnicities. The Kurds, who mostly reside in northern Iraq, make up about 15 percent of the population and Turkmen comprise about 5 percent. There has historically been a large Christian population, but its numbers have dramatically decreased following the violence in Iraq.[57] Two decades ago, Iraq was home to about one and a half million Christians; today it's home to less than three hundred thousand.[58]

From 1979–2003, Iraq was ruled by the brutal dictatorship of Saddam Hussein—a Sunni—who violently oppressed Iraqi Shiites and Kurds. Hussein's rule ended in the spring of 2003, following the invasion and eventual occupation of Iraq by the United States. Hussein faced trial in Iraq, was sentenced to death by an Iraqi court, and was executed in December 2006. Following his downfall, the balance of power in Iraq was altered and the Shiites gained control. Iran took advantage of the political shift in Iraq to increase its influence on the new, predominately Shiite, Iraqi government—and all subsequent Iraqi governments, which have also been predominately Shiite—and has increased its military and financial support for Iraqi Shiite militias.

Since 2003, Iraq has been an arena of an escalating bloody struggle between Iraqi Sunni and Shiite militias supported by Iran (and the struggle has worsened since the end of the US military presence in Iraq at the end of 2011). Iraqi Sunnis, discontent with the Shiite political dominance and the growing Iranian influence, argue that they are discriminated against and oppressed by the predominantly Shiite Iraqi government, strongly influenced by Iran. The growing discontent and bitterness caused the Iraqi Sunni tribes in western Iraq—who only a few years ago joined forces with the United States to fight al-Qaeda in Iraq—to make a drastic shift; since 2013 some of the same Sunni tribes have begun to provide the al-Qaeda branch in Iraq with a friendly environment to regain momentum and resume its operations in western Iraq. This resulted in the emergence of ISIS, as the branch of al-Qaeda in Iraq, in mid-2013, until the two organizations split in the beginning of 2014.

Iraq is a country of key strategic importance to Iran. Unlike many other arenas that Iran has significant influence in, it is physically next to Iraq, with a border between the two that is more than nine hundred miles long.[59] Turbulence in Iraq can easily spillover into Iran, and Iran is highly concerned about the reign of ISIS in central and western Iraq. Even though ISIS's reign in Syria in a way serves the interests of the Assad-Iran axis, ISIS, ideologically, is a bitter enemy of the Shiites and Iran. The name "Iran" does not appear on ISIS's map. Iran is named "Khorasan" on ISIS's map of the Middle East. Khorasan was the name of the area in central Asia that was occupied by the Arabs in the middle of the seventh century.[60]

The potential physical expansion of ISIS's presence in Iraq, combined with ISIS's hostile ideology toward Shiites and Iran and its growing capabilities achieved through the wealth derived from the takeover of Iraqi oil fields, presents a growing threat to Iran. Added to this is how ISIS's activity inspires and fuels expressions of uprising among minorities in Iran who are hostile to the mullah regime, groups like the Sunni Arabs in Iran, the Kurds, and the Shiite Arabs in the district of Khūzestān.

Khūzestān is located on the shore of the northern tip of the Arab Gulf and is one of Iran's significant districts. It has a population of 5.7 million people, the majority of whom are Shiite Arabs and about one million of whom are Sunni Arabs; they all are known as, and identify as, Ahwāzi Arabs, named after the capital of Khūzestān, Ahwāz.[61] Khūzestān is highly valuable territory, reportedly containing 85 percent of Iran's gas and oil and 45 percent of its water.[62, 63] Ahwāzi Arabs view themselves as part of the Arab Gulf area, want to be part of the Arab world, and are involved in an ongoing struggle to separate from Iran. The national, separatist aspirations generate ongoing tension accompanied by periodic eruptions of violence within the district. Iran uses force to suppress their separatist aspirations, which it fears could spur other separatist aspirations, and, most importantly, it doesn't want to risk losing Khūzestān.

Iran is also very concerned about protecting the two most sacred cities of Shiites, Karbalā and Najaf,[64] which are predominately populated by Shiites and located in southern Iraq. Karbalā is where ʿAli was killed, and his grave is located in Najaf. Both cities are the primary destination of Shiite pilgrims. ISIS, fueled by its animosity toward Iran and the Shiites, will not hesitate to destroy Shiite sacred sites if it has the opportunity to do so.

Basra, in southern Iraq, is the second largest city in Iraq and contains large oil fields and the largest harbor in Iraq, which is located on the banks of the Shaṭṭ Al-ʿArab river, which connects to the Arab (Persian) Gulf. Basra is viewed by Iran as an area of high importance to its national security interests, which explains the announcement attributed (though denied) to a senior advisor of the Iranian president who allegedly said that the "Iranian empire is back and Baghdad is its capital."[65]

If ISIS is not rooted out, its existing land corridor stretching from western Iraq to central Syria will endanger Iran's corridor of influence that stretches from Iran through Iraq to Syria and Lebanon.

Since August 2014,[66] Iranian military forces have been fighting side-by-side with Iraqi Shiite militias and the Iraqi army to destroy—albeit with limited success—ISIS's reign in central and western Iraq. The joint Iranian and Iraqi Shiite militia forces fighting in Iraq are estimated to be thirty to forty thousand strong, backed with artillery, tanks, and warplanes.[67, 68]

Similar to Syria and Lebanon, Iran's involvement in Iraq results in a growing dilemma for the Iranian mullah regime. Iraqi Sunnis, like their Syrian brothers, view Iran's involvement as occupation. Reports about massacres and ethnic cleansing by Iraqi Shiite militias against Sunni Iraqis,[69, 70, 71] as well as Iraqi reports indicating that nearly three million Sunnis have been dislocated because of the raging violence in central Iraq,[72] fuels Sunni rage. And the rage is translated into the increasing support among Iraqi Sunnis for ISIS,[73, 74, 75] support that Iran is desperate to put an end to.

Although the Iraqi foreign minister, Ibrahim al-Ja'afari, declared in September 2015 that Iraq is not an Iranian vassal and that Iran has no influence on Iraq's policy and domestic affairs, the reality is very different. Iran is deeply influencing Iraq. Iran views Iraq as a crucial component for its national security; therefore, Iran will continue—and perhaps increase—its involvement and influence in Iraq.

Lebanon

Lebanon has a population estimated to be between four-and-a-half and six million people, and similar to Syria, it is a tapestry of ethnicities and religions. Christians account for more than 40 percent of the population, yet they are not homogenous—but are divided between sects, like Maronite and Greek Orthodox. Shiites are 27 percent of the population, Sunnis are 25 percent, and Druze are 5 percent.

Iran through its proxy in Lebanon, Hezbollah, wields substantial influence there. Via Hezbollah, Iran has been able to establish a stronghold on the shores of the Mediterranean Sea and even dictates Lebanese foreign policy—most notably through instructing Hezbollah, a member of the Lebanese government, to join the war in Syria, ignoring Lebanon's official policy of neutrality in the conflict.

Also, since the end of the term of Lebanon's previous president, Michel Suleiman, in May 2014, Lebanese political parties have failed to agree on a new president. The failure stems from a stalemate between Lebanon's major political powers: Hezbollah (i.e. Iran) and the al-Mustaqbal (the Future) party, which enjoys wide Sunni Lebanese, as well as Druze and some Christian, support and is backed by Saudi Arabia. Given the worsening of the conflict in Syria and Iran's continued use of Hezbollah there, it's unclear whether a new president in Lebanon will be agreed upon soon.

For now it seems that Iran will continue to impact Lebanon and its politics, but that its hold on Lebanon has somewhat loosened. There are a number of reasons for this.

The first is Hezbollah's mounting difficulties. The growing number of Hezbollah militants killed in Syria is generating increasing rage and criticism among Hezbollah's core supporters, the Shiites in Lebanon. Also, Hezbollah's political opponents in Lebanon—Sunnis, Druze, and many Christians—criticize the organization for dragging Lebanon into the Syrian crisis. Hezbollah's tough image and its deterrent capacity has been damaged because of the daily funerals of Hezbollah militants killed in Syria, images of its militants held in captivity, and military failures, some of which have been very embarrassing. For example, in October 2014, al-Qaeda occupied one of Hezbollah's military posts. In July 2015, Hezbollah launched an attack on the town of al-Zabadani; however, while its militants were massively supported by Assad's air force and artillery, as well as by Iranian Revolutionary Guards officers, and in spite of the rebels' military inferiority, Hezbollah failed to complete the mission and take over the town. In August 2015, the failure forced the Assad-Iran axis to agree to a ceasefire in the battle. Hezbollah's failure was exacerbated by reports that during the attempt to conquer the town, Hezbollah sustained more than one hundred fatalities.[76]

Hezbollah and Iran's eroding influence in Lebanon was further showcased in August 2015 when it was reported that a joint operation of Saudi and Lebanese security services led to the arrest of Ahmad Ibrahim al-Mughassil, the leader of Hezbollah in the Arabian Peninsula. Following his arrest, Mughassil was turned over to Saudi Arabia. He was wanted by the Saudis and the United States for his involvement in a 1996 terror attack on the Khobar Towers in Saudi Arabia, which killed nineteen American soldiers. In 2006, the United States District Court in Washington, DC concluded that Iran had worked through a proxy, Hezbollah al-Hejaz, a Saudi militant group that is affiliated with the Lebanese Hezbollah, and was responsible for the attack. The court ordered Iran to pay $254 million to seventeen families of those killed in the bombing. Were Hezbollah and Iran in a stronger position, as they were in 2005 when, after the assassination of Prime Minister Rafiq al-Hariri, they refused to hand over suspected Hezbollah militants, Mughassil would have never been turned in by the Lebanese government. In 2005, before Hezbollah's involvement in the war in Syria, it was so powerful that it forced the Lebanese government to disobey the UN Security Council even though the Lebanese government was aware of the risk of sanctions being imposed on Lebanon for not complying with the UN Security Council, resolution. That is how strong Hezbollah's influence in Lebanon was. Today the tables have turned and the Lebanese, in conjunction with the Saudis, have arrested the leader of Hezbollah in the Arabian Peninsula.

The second reason is that Arab Gulf states have significant influence on Lebanon through financial support and investments in massive infrastructure and real estate projects. In addition, there are thousands of Lebanese—including Lebanese Shiites—working in the Arab Gulf states to provide for their families in Lebanon. The Lebanese government is well aware of the crucial role that the Arab Gulf states' investments play in the Lebanese economy and, therefore, are highly attuned to the Arab Gulf states' interests. This was evidenced by an announcement in October 2015 from the Lebanese Ministry of Justice that stated that Hezbollah's hostility toward Saudi Arabia is jeopardizing the income source of dozen of thousands of Lebanese.[77] In March 2015, dozens of Lebanese employed in the UAE were accused of being associated with Hezbollah and were deported by UAE authorities.

Another reason is the clear interest of international factors in helping Lebanon distance itself from Iran. Countries like the United States and France provide Lebanon with support to strengthen its armed forces and secure domestic stability, and Saudi Arabia reportedly gave Lebanon three billion USD for the same purpose.

Yemen

Yemen, a society primarily based on tribes, is an Arab state with a population of more than twenty-six million people. The majority of Yemenis, about 65 percent, are Sunni, primarily located in southern and central Yemen; Shiites of the Zaydīyah branch of Shia Islam make up the second largest group in Yemen, 35 percent,[78] and are mostly located in northern Yemen, which is poorer than the south.

The modern history of Yemen is a continuing saga of power struggles and violence. From 1967–1990, Yemen was divided into two states: the "Socialist Republic of Yemen" in South Yemen (which was the only communist Arab state) and the "Arab Republic of Yemen" in North Yemen. The period was not only characterized by hostility between the two states, but each suffered from violent domestic power struggles. In 1990 the states united, but the violence never ceased. Yemen's government has battled a separatist movement in South Yemen and Houthi tribes in North Yemen. The Houthis, a confederation of Zaydīyah Shiites, have controlled large areas of northern Yemen since the eleventh century and are the dominant factor on the ground. The Houthis's fight to retain their control has been constant throughout the twentieth century.

The Arab Awakening simply increased the preexisting violence in Yemen. Former President of Yemen ʿAlī ʿAbd Allāh Ṣāliḥ, a Shiite who ruled Yemen from 1978–2012, tried to suppress the public outcry by force, but this only resulted in a further deterioration. In the summer of 2011, Ṣāliḥ fled to Saudi Arabia after being badly injured in an assassination attempt. In November 2011, he transferred his authority to his vice president, ʿAbd Rabbuh Manṣūr Hadī, a Sunni; however, Ṣāliḥ kept his position as the leader of the General People's Congress party, Yemen's Arab nationalist party. Hadī was elected president of Yemen in February 2012, following an election that had been boycotted by the two major political factors in Yemen: the separatist movement in the south and the Houthis in the north. Over the following years, the crisis in Yemen escalated, and in September 2014, the military wing of the Houthis, Ansar Allah (Supporters of God), backed by Iran and cooperating with supporters of former President Ṣāliḥ, launched a military campaign resulting in the occupation of Yemen's capital, Sanaa, and the expansion of Houthi control in the majority of Yemen's districts. In January 2015, Hadī and his government resigned, and in February 2015, the Houthis abolished the Yemeni parliament and announced the establishment of a Revolutionary Council to rule Yemen. Hadī then fled to the city of Aden in South Yemen, and when Houthi forces approached the city, he fled to Saudi Arabia.

In March 2015, the Houthis reportedly signed an agreement with Iran to arrange for Iranian ships to have a base in the Yemeni port of al-Ḥudaydah, on the shores of the Red Sea. In return, Iran agreed to provide the Houthis with oil and logistical support, and likely also weapons.[79] Alarmed by growing Iranian involvement in Yemen, in March 2015, an Arab military coalition led by Saudi Arabia launched a military campaign, "Decisive Storm," to restore the rule of Hadī's government and put a stop to the Houthi-Iranian takeover of Yemen.

In April 2015, the United Nations Security Council adopted Resolution 2216, which demanded that all parties in Yemen, particularly the Houthis, immediately and unconditionally end their violence. It also called for the Houthis to withdraw from all areas seized during the latest conflict, relinquish arms seized from military and security institutions, and cease all actions falling exclusively within the authority of the legitimate government of Yemen. It also called on the Houthis to refrain from any provocations or threats to neighboring states, release the Yemeni minister of defense, Mahmoud al-Subaihi, who had been arrested in March 2015, as well as all other political prisoners and individuals under house arrest or arbitrarily detained, and end the recruitment of children.[80]

For now it seems that Iran will likely have to give up its ambitions to take over Yemen. Iranian involvement in Yemen, through the support Iran provides the Houthis, faces significant challenges. For one, the Arab coalition led by

Saudi Arabia in Yemen is gaining momentum in the fight against the Iranian-backed Shiite Houthis, and the coalition seems to be forceful enough to block Iran's continued attempts to control Yemen. Second, Iran is limited because of the international community's stance on Yemen.

Yemen is of the utmost strategic importance to the Arab Gulf monarchies and Egypt, who are determined to prevent an Iranian takeover of it. A diplomatic agreement could significantly reduce the prospects of this and is a viable option. Such an agreement could ensure the Arab Gulf monarchies and Egypt's two major strategic interests in Yemen. One is to prevent Iran from establishing enough influence that it could control maritime traffic on the Red Sea, the Indian Ocean, and the eastern shore of Africa. The second is to prevent the development of an ISIS base—similar to the one in Iraq and Syria—which could threaten the Arab Gulf monarchies and commerce.

The Gulf Islands

The Gulf Islands are Abu Musa, the Greater Tunb, and the Lesser Tunb. The only inhabited Island is Abu Musa, which has a population of about one thousand people. It is about thirty-five miles from the shore of the Emirate of Sharjah, one of the states of the United Arab Emirates, and about forty-three miles from the Iranian shore.

The islands are strategically valuable—located near the Strait of Hormuz and surrounded by deep water and huge oil reserves. They'd been ruled by the United Kingdom since 1819 when, in 1829, an agreement signed between the UK and the ruler of the Arab emirate al-Qawasim (today Sharjah) provided the emirate with UK protection in return for UK control in the naval Gulf.

In November 30, 1971, one day before the formal establishing of the United Arab Emirates (in which the emirate of Sharjah is a member) and the evacuation of British forces, Iran occupied the three islands. Though an agreement signed between the UAE and Iran regarding the co-managing of the Abu Musa was signed, Iran violated the agreement. In 1992 Iranian forces occupied the Island, ending the UAE's presence there. The Iranian takeover resulted in a formal complaint submitted by Abu Dhabi (a member of the UAE) to the

UN Security Council. In April 2012, Iranian former President Mahmoud Ahmadinejad announced during a visit to the island of Abu Musa that it was an Iranian territory.[81] In September 2012, an Iranian foreign affairs spokesperson announced that the islands would remain forever under Iran's sovereignty.[82] An Arab League resolution of its twenty-sixth summit, held in March 2015, urges Iran to commence negotiations regarding the islands' future or to agree to international arbitration, yet Iran thus far refuses to negotiate.

It appears that in the visible future, an arrangement to end the controversy is not viable. That said, it is unlikely that the controversy will further escalate.

The Vienna Agreement

On July 14, 2015, Iran and the "Five Plus One" states—China, France, Russia, the United Kingdom, the United States, and Germany—signed the Joint Comprehensive Plan of Action of the Vienna Agreement, regarding the Iranian nuclear program.

Opponents of the agreement argue that with the signing, the mullah regime marked three significant achievements:

First, the Iranian nuclear program was formally legitimized, and while this was presumably for peaceful purposes—according to the agreement—the regime retained the ability to switch its nuclear program to a military one in the future. The mechanisms and terms described in the Vienna Agreement to ensure that Iran will not develop nuclear military capacities all expire within ten to fifteen years, which means that in the not-too-distant future, Iran could develop its nuclear program completely undisturbed.

Second, the Iranian mullah regime became recognized by the major Western powers as a legitimate government and a legitimate regional superpower.

Third, the lifting of the sanctions on Iran arranged by the agreement set up a system that will result in the immediate flow of hundreds of billions of dollars into the crumbling Iranian economy and will open the doors for global companies who are eager to do business with Iran. The flow of money into the diminishing Iranian treasury could potentially enable Iran to continue to fund its proxies in the region, thereby maintaining and increasing Iran's regional influence in the different current arenas of struggle, and also to expand its influence to new ones.

As a result of these achievements, Iran's geostrategic policy is, for now, enjoying significant momentum and marking important achievements. The mullah regime seems to be on the path to securing its strategic interests and marking another milestone on its way to fulfilling its vision of being the leading Middle East superpower.

Iran's Domestic Struggles

Notwithstanding its successes, the Iranian mullah regime faces substantial challenges in the arenas in which it is massively involved and also on the home front. According to a May 2015 report from the United States Institute of Peace,[83] general unemployment in Iran exceeded 10 percent and youth unemployment reached nearly 27 percent. Some seven million Iranians, about 8 percent of Iran's population, are said by the Iranian government to be living in extreme poverty; it's likely that number is actually much higher.

Due to the overwhelming economic and social hardships suffered in Iran, discontent among most sectors of its society is mounting. If not addressed, this could present the Iranian regime with a serious challenge, likely an uprising.[84] The regime is struggling to be attuned to the growing economic and social challenges of the Iranians and is subsidizing basic commodities, but it knows that overcoming domestic challenges will require large long-term financial investments.

The Iranian government needs to focus on things like restoring its crumbling economy, building its transportation and communication infrastructure, restoring and maintaining its oil industry, and providing employment opportunities, particularly to its young people. Iran's major income source is oil, and that is its Achilles' heel because of the development of alternative energy sources and the low price of oil. In December 2014, Iranian President Hassan Rouhani presented a budget for 2015 based on an average oil price of only seventy USD per barrel, reduced from one hundred USD per barrel in the 2014 budget. The projected price was slashed to forty USD per barrel in

January 2015.[85] At the end of 2015, crude oil prices were about forty USD per barrel; according to some predictions, the price could be around fifty USD per barrel by the end of 2016,[86] yet it could be much lower. To maintain order and stability and ensure its rule and power, the regime will need to invest the majority of its income into ways of resolving its domestic challenges. It will need to prioritize its funds in this manner instead of pouring them into its support of Assad and groups like Ḥamās, Hezbollah, the Houthis, Islamic Jihad, and the Shiite Iraqi militias, and use them to fund its military operations in Iraq against ISIS.

Like the income it gets from oil, Iran must also use the lifting of international sanctions it enjoys as a result of the Vienna Agreement to immediately and tangibly improve the daily lives of its people—not to further aid its proxies outside Iran. If the Iranian regime continues to fail to meet its people's demands, it will further fuel their discontent and anger, and this could also present a serious challenge to the mullah regime. They know this, but it remains to be seen if they'll take preventive action.

Realigning Powers

The widening, intensifying Iranian-Arab power struggle, stemming from Iran's aggressive involvement in different parts of the Arab world, results in a growing call for an economic, military, and political regrouping of Arab resources and abilities, and for a proactive (and if needed aggressive) policy to counter Iran's ambitions to become the dominant power in the Middle East at the expense of the Arabs and Sunnis. Though that growing sentiment reemphasizes the old sentiments of Arab solidarity and mutual responsibility, it does not proclaim the return of a pan-Arab nationalism ideology, nor does it call for abolishing the concept of statehood and the existence of independent Arab states.

As a possible precursor to establishing a joint Arab task force, in December 2015, Saudi Arabia formally announced the establishment of an alliance of thirty-four Arab and non-Arab Muslim states (Iran, Syria, and Iraq are not included in the alliance) to fight terror. The alliance's headquarters will be in Saudi Arabia.[87]

Looking Forward

At present, it seems as if the Iranian-Arab confrontation is a zero sum game with neither side willing to allow the other to make real progress. Yet, the continuing power struggle exhausts both the Arab states and Iran and negatively impacts their ability to address their own inner challenges, which if left unaddressed may present both the mullah regime and the Arab governments and rulers with growing domestic instability.

It seems as if the Iranian-Arab power balance is entering an interim period of about a decade, during which both Iran and the Arabs will look for a mutually acceptable redefinition of the balance of power through new, likely unwritten, understandings and arrangements guided by compromises and concessions. The length of the time period matches the timeline of the Vienna Agreement.

The guidelines of such an understanding were laid out by the United States and are more in line with the desires of the Arab states than with Iran's. On September 4, 2015, President Obama and Saudi Arabian King Salman met in Washington, DC. A joint statement published by the White House following the meeting[88] included the following main points:

King Salman expressed his support for the Vienna Agreement between Iran and the "Five Plus One" countries, which once fully implemented will prevent Iran from obtaining a nuclear weapon and thereby enhance security in the region;

Fast-tracking the provision of certain military equipment to the kingdom, as well as heightened cooperation on counter-terrorism, maritime security, cyber security, and ballistic missile defense.

Concerning Yemen, the two parties stressed the urgent need to implement relevant United Nations Security Council resolutions, based upon UN Security Council resolution 2216, which demands that all parties in Yemen, particularly the Houthis, immediately and unconditionally end their violence in order to facilitate a political solution based on the Gulf Cooperation Council's Initiative and the outcomes of the National Dialogue.

Regarding the Palestinian-Israeli conflict, the two leaders underscored the enduring importance of the Saudi 2002 Arab Peace Initiative;

Both leaders stressed the importance of reaching a lasting solution to the Syrian conflict based on the principles of the June 2012 Geneva action group decision[89] (calling upon the transitional government body with full executive powers to end the suffering of the Syrian people) to maintain continuity of civilian and military government institutions, preserve the unity and territorial integrity of Syria, and ensure the emergence of a peaceful, pluralistic, and democratic state free of discrimination or sectarianism.

The two leaders reiterated that any meaningful political transition would have to include the departure of Bashar al-Assad, who has lost the legitimacy to lead Syria.

Securing Lebanon and its borders and resist extremist threats.

Finally, the two leaders discussed a new strategic partnership for the twenty-first century and how to significantly elevate the relationship between the two countries.[90]

CHAPTER SIX

THE WAR IN SYRIA

SYRIA IS A TAPESTRY OF COMMUNITIES and ethnic groups, with a population estimated to be between eighteen and almost twenty-three million.[1, 2] The majority of Syrians, an estimated 74 percent, are Sunnis, while Shiites in Syria—most of whom are ʿAlawites, also known as Nuṣayrīyah—only comprise about 13 percent of the population.[3] Shia ʿAlawites are considered by many Muslims to be heretics because their religion is secret and contains pagan symbols.[4] They are mainly concentrated in northwestern Syria, in central cities on the Mediterranean coast like Latakia, Qardaha, and Tartus, and in towns and villages in the mountainous region east of the Syrian coastline. There are also large ʿAlawite neighborhoods in Aleppo, Damascus, and Homs. The other major ethnic groups in Syria are Christians, which make up about 10 percent of the population;[5] Druze, which make up about 3 percent;[6] and Kurds, which make up 10–15 percent.[7, 8, 9]

Damascus, Syria's capital, was the center of the caliphate of the House of Umayyad (661–750), the first Muslim caliphate outside the Arabian Peninsula.[10] Damascus was the commercial, cultural, political, and social heart of ash-Sham—land that today includes Lebanon, Syria, Jordan, Israel, and the Palestinian territories in the West Bank and Gaza Strip.[11]

Following World War I (1914–1918) and the end of the Turkish Ottoman Empire in 1922, Syria was ruled by the French mandate. The French divided Syria into six semi-state entities: an ʿAlawite state along the Syrian coastline; a Druze state in southern Syria; the state of Damascus in central Syria; the state of Aleppo in northern Syria; the state of Alexandretta in northeastern Syria, also known by the name of *Hatay* (an area that later came under Turkish rule); and the state of Great Lebanon, which later became Lebanon. The entities were governed by local administrations and had symbols of sovereignty, such as their own flags and currency, but were ruled by the French mandate, with all decisions subject to the French government's approval. In 1935, the semi-state entities, aside from Great Lebanon, which had gained independence in 1943, were abolished by the French mandate and united within the framework of the Republic of Syria. Syria gained full independence in 1945 when it became a founding member of the United Nations, an act that formally ended the French mandate and caused French troops to withdraw in 1946.

In the twentieth century, Syria became known as *Qal'at al-'Uruba* (the Fortress of Arabism) and came to symbolize Arab nationalism. It introduced the concept in the late nineteenth century by calling for the establishment of independent Arab states, and it has used it many times over since then: during its revolt from 1925–1927 against the French mandate; during the establishment in 1947 of its Ba'ath Arab Socialist Party—a political party that envisioned the establishment of a pan-Arab entity unifying Arab societies based on spreading socialism; and during its union with Egypt that resulted in an entity known as the United Arab Republic (1958–1961). Syria has also been acclaimed for its central role in the wars with Israel. The cumulative result of all this is that it has played a key role in empowering the Arab world and thus positioned itself as a leader within it.

However, despite its vision and regional leadership, Syria has suffered from constant political power struggles since it declared its independence, and these have manifested in rapid changes of regimes, often through military coups. In 1971, Hafez al-Assad, the son of an 'Alawite family from the city of Qardaha and the commander of the Syrian Air Force, took control of Syria following a military coup. He served as the president of Syria and the leader of the Syrian Ba'ath party until his death in 2000, after which, he was succeeded by his son Bashar al-Assad. Bashar al-Assad was elected president of Syria in 2000, was reelected in May 2007—when, as the only candidate in the running, he "won" one-hundred percent of the "votes"—and was again reelected in June 2014, in the midst of the brutal war in Syria. Each of the elections is widely recognized as having been rigged. According to the Electoral Integrity Project run by Harvard University and the University of Sydney, "the [2014] Syrian election ranked as worst among all the contests held during 2014."[12] The rule of the two Assads has kept Syria under an ʿAlawite dictatorship, even though ʿAlawites are a minority of its population, for the last forty-five years.

The Syrian Uprising

The early signs in Syria of the approaching tsunami reached its shores in January 2011. Inspired by the outbreak of Arab Awakening events in Egypt, Libya, and Tunisia, a Facebook page was created titled "The Syrian uprising against Bashar al-Assad," and over the following weeks it became a platform to coordinate protests throughout the country. Syrians took to the streets chanting, "The Syrian people are not afraid [of the Assad regime]" and "*silmiya, silmiya*" (demonstrate peacefully, peacefully meaning not in a violent way). Assad's forces replied forcefully, and the demonstrations would be brutally dispersed—but they, nonetheless, gained momentum.

On March 17, 2011, messages on a Facebook page called on Syrians to go to the streets following the Friday prayers to protest and call for political reform—a means to end the authoritarian practices of the regime and improve day-to-day living conditions, regarding jobs, social services, education, etc. It was called the "Friday of Honor."[13] The next day, Syrian citizens were demonstrating in the streets of the cities of Homs, Banias, and Dara'a chanting, among other things, "*Allah, Suriya, hurryia—wabas,*" meaning "Allah, Syria, freedom—and that's it." The slogan spread like wildfire, and so much so that during the first few months of 2011, it was described as the anthem of the Syrian people in their struggle for freedom.[14]

That Friday in March signaled the beginning of one of the most dramatic events in the history of the Middle East: the war in Syria. It had started as a civilian, nonviolent uprising, but it turned, within a few months, into a war between the Sunnis and the Shiites and a proxy war between the axis of Sunni states—mainly Saudi Arabia, Qatar, Turkey, and Jordan—on the one side and the Assad rule, the Shia state of Iran, and its proxies on the other side.

By the summer of 2011, the popular uprising in Syria, spurred by economic stress and a demand for political reforms to empower the Syrian people and limit the brutal dictatorship of Bashar al-Assad, had dramatically expanded. It was further fueled by increasing reports of rape perpetrated by an Assad militia called *Shabiha* (Ghosts),[15, 16] as well as a growing number of protestors killed during anti-Assad demonstrations throughout the country.

As a response, many of Syria's Sunni soldiers and officers began to desert the Syrian army. In July 2011, they announced the establishment of a rebel group named al-Jaish as-Sūrī al-Ḥurr, the Free Syrian Army (FSA), under the leadership of a defecting Syrian colonel, Riad al-Asaad.[17] With the creation of the FSA, military clashes between the Sunni rebels and the Assad regime forces began widening and intensifying. By the summer of 2011, the popular uprising in Syria had turned into a civil war.

One of the immediate results of the conflict was the disintegration of the Syrian government's armed forces. Syria's army had always been a mosaic of ethnic groups; however, its senior officers and elite combat units were mostly 'Alawites. As Sunni, Druze, and Christian soldiers defected, the Syrian army disintegrated. The military units fighting in the service of the Assad-Iran axis were soon primarily 'Alawite.

In late 2011, some Arab analysts argued that Assad's days in power were numbered.[18] In February 2012, Israel's then secretary of defense, Ehud Barak, estimated that the Assad regime would collapse within a number of weeks.[19]

They were wrong. The Assad regime was of too great a strategic resource for the Iranian mullah regime to let it collapse. Syria is the central pillar in the axis of resistance and critical to its regional—and international—aspirations.

The Iranian Response

In the fall of 2011, when it seemed that the Assad government was on the verge of collapsing, alarm bells went off in Tehran and the Iranians hurried to prop it up before it could fall.

They accelerated and increased their assistance, hastily delivering ammunition, fuel, money, and weapons to Assad's army, as well as Iranian experts and military advisors, especially ones in the fields of intelligence and communication. Iran's annual support of the Assad regime was estimated to be six billion dollars a year and in 2012–2013 it spiked to fourteen or fifteen billion dollars.[20]

Iran also helped the Assad regime by increasing the number and boosting the activity of the Iranian Revolutionary Guards (IRG), the military backbone of the Iranian mullah regime in Syria. The IRG was founded by the late supreme leader Ayatollah Ruhollah Khomeini in the aftermath of the 1979 Islamic Revolution in Iran and was charged with defending the Islamic Republic against internal and external threats. IRG commander Mohammad 'Ali Jafari reports directly to Ali Khamenei, the supreme leader of the Islamic Republic of Iran, who is Iran's head of state, highest-ranking political figure, foremost religious authority, and uppermost decision-maker. The current IRG forces consist of naval, air, and ground regiments and total roughly 150,000 fighters who, if needed, could assist Iran's army, which has about 350,000 soldiers.[21] The elite unit and the spearhead of the IRG is the al-Quds force, estimated to have fifteen thousand soldiers, and is responsible for extra-territorial and clandestine missions, including terrorist operations.[22, 23] The commander of the al-Quds force is General Qasem Soleimani. According to accumulating reports by sources described as the "Iranian opposition," Soleimani was wounded in November 2105 in Syria; reports vary on the significance of this, with some saying he was wounded, other saying he was seriously injured, and others saying he was killed.[24, 25] Official Iranian government media platforms categorically deny all the reports.

In February 2012, the Syrian rebels' pressure on Assad's army increased. In response Iran sent more IRG advisers to assist Assad's officers in Syria,[26] and soon after, they sent in the Basij, a paramilitary volunteer militia under the command of the IRG that acts both as a semi-military force and as an internal Iranian police force. The Basij was responsible for the violent suppression of the mass demonstrations in Iran in the summer of 2009, following the scandal of forged elections results.

The Iranian regime also pulled out another card. It instructed its most powerful proxy, Hezbollah in Lebanon, to send its own elite forces into Syria to save the Assad regime from collapsing.

In the fall of 2011, reports began to surface regarding Hezbollah's involvement in the war in Syria. In the Hezbollah stronghold of al-Dahiya al-Janubiya

(Dahieh)—the southern quarter of Beirut—as well as the villages and towns in the Beqaa—the valley region in eastern Lebanon—and Shiite villages in southern Lebanon, posters appeared featuring pictures of killed Hezbollah fighters. The circumstances of their death were vaguely described as "killed on a military mission." In November 2011, rumors began to spread throughout Lebanon about funerals of Hezbollah fighters who had been killed in the war in Syria and buried secretly in the dead of night.[27, 28]

Hezbollah tried to hide its involvement in the war and the resulting casualties. In July 2012, for example, Hezbollah's deputy leader, Naim Qassem, denied that the organization was engaged in the fighting in Syria,[29] even though by that time it was already clear that it was.

Hezbollah denied its involvement for two major reasons: first, because Hezbollah's involvement in the war in Syria defied the neutrality policy formally declared by the Lebanese government in which Hezbollah is a member. And second, because Hezbollah understood that its involvement in the war in Syria could put it and the Shiites in Lebanon, Hezbollah's major political support-base in Lebanon, on a collision course with the Sunnis in Lebanon, who identify with their Sunni Syrian brothers and would not be very happy about their fellow Shiite Lebanese slaughtering Sunnis in Syria.

Yet, in spite of this, the decision was not in Hezbollah's hands; it was in Iran's. Iran demanded Hezbollah obey its orders—and Hezbollah obeyed.

Iran overtly inserting itself in the war in Syria via its proxy Hezbollah was an important turning point. Toward the end of 2011, the war in Syria was no longer an internal Syrian affair. It had evolved into both a Sunni-Shiite war and a war by proxies between the Assad-Iran axis and a Sunni states led by Saudi Arabia, Qatar, and Turkey.

Hezbollah is the largest Shiite militia fighting in Syria. Estimates are that five to seven thousand full-time, highly trained fighters from Hezbollah have been sent to fight in Syria,[30, 31, 32, 33] and as many as twenty to fifty thousand are part-time reservists.[34] Its most elite and qualified militants are among the fighters in Syria.[35]

In addition to the IRG, Basij, and Hezbollah, the Iranian regime also called in Shiite militias, mostly from Iraq, for backup. One Shiite militia sent to Syria by Iran was the Fatemiyon Brigade. Reports of it began to appear in February 2015, and accumulating information indicated that it primarily operated in southern Syria.[36, 37] Most of its militants were Afghan refugees who lived in Iran and were recruited by the Iranian Revolutionary Guards to join the war in Syria in exchange for a monthly salary of a couple hundred dollars.[38, 39] Syrian rebels report that during the fierce fighting in southern Syria in the spring of 2015, the Fatemiyon Brigade sustained heavy losses and disintegrated.[40]

According to a February 2015 report published by the Washington Institute for Near East Policy, Iraqi Shiite militias were deployed to support Hezbollah forces in multiple areas in Syria, with a high concentration along the Syrian-Lebanese border in the al-Qalamoun region.[41] Reports at the end of 2015 indicated that the number of Iraqi Shiite militants fighting in Syria varied from a couple of hundred to a few thousand, and that the troops were divided into six militias, with the largest being Liwa Abu al-Fadl al-Abbas and Liwa al-Haqq.[42, 43, 44, 45]

According to reports published during the second half of 2015, the total number of Iranian Revolutionary Guards, Basij forces, Hezbollah militants, and Iraqi Shiite militias fighting in Syria could be anywhere from eighteen to sixty thousand.[46, 47, 48, 49] The large gap in the estimated numbers of Iranian-affiliated forces might be partially explained by the participation of another militia that is part of the Assad-Iran axis, a Syrian militia known as al-Jaish al-Sh'abi (the People's Army).[50] It reportedly numbers fifty thousand militants[51] and is armed and funded by Iran and trained by IRG officers and Hezbollah.

In the spring of 2013, the Israeli head of military intelligence, Major General Aviv Kochavi, reported that Iran intended to double the size of this force to help prolong the life of the Assad regime and maintain Iran's influence after his fall.[52] However, as of December 2015, according to Western military sources, the picture is quite the opposite. As of the end of 2015, Iran's Revolutionary Guards in Syria are reportedly retreating. In October 2015, the *Wall Street Journal* reported that more than seven thousand Iranian Revolutionary Guard Corps members and other militia volunteers were aiding the Syrian regime.[53] In the same month, General Joseph Dunford, the chairman of the Joint Chiefs of Staff, testified that there were two thousand Iranian troops in Syria leading the fight to save Assad.[54] At the end of 2015, that number, according to the United States and other Western officials, has dwindled. An estimate by a source described as a "senior Western defense official" said there were only seven hundred Iranian Revolutionary Guard members now fighting in the Russian-led offensive, not including Iranian military advisers who have been embedded with the Syrian armed forces since 2012.[55]

Foreign Sunni Supporters

Sunnis in Syria and elsewhere viewed the presence of Iran and its proxies in Syria as an occupation and an Iranian-Shiite invasion.

As a response, Sunni Arabs from Algeria, Egypt, Iraq, Jordan, Lebanon, Libya, Yemen, and the Gaza Strip and non-Arab Sunnis from states like Afghanistan, Chechnya, China, Dagestan, and Pakistan began streaming into Syria for support.

Many of them join Sunni militant Islamist groups, such as ISIS, Jabhat al-Nusra, and other Salafi-Jihadi groups, and many of them bring prior military experience with them. Streams of Sunni Muslims, both born into the faith and converts, have also gone to Syria from Europe, particularly Austria, Belgium, France, and Germany, and a small number have gone from the Americas and Australia. In June 2014, about twenty-five hundred foreign fighters from Western countries had joined the war in Syria—mostly within the ranks of jihadi groups.[56] According to an August 2015 report, the number of Westerners who'd joined in support of the Sunnis was estimated to five thousand people.[57] In December 2015, it was reported that while the number of foreign fighters from western Europe had reached almost five thousand, the numbers from North America had remained flat and was estimated to be fewer than three hundred.[58]

The Syrian Civil War Becomes a Sunni-Shiite War

Throughout 2011, with Iran and Iranian-backed Shiite militias increasing their involvement and the resulting counter-reaction of the flow of Sunni fighters from beyond the borders of Syria, the Syrian civil war turned into a Sunni-Shiite war—and that is a war to the death.

Much of the rhetoric, symbols, and terminology of the war have been taken from the acrid history of the Sunni-Shiite conflict, as if more than thirteen hundred years had not passed since the death of ʿAlī. Shiite fighters wear headbands and armbands bearing slogans such as "We love you Ḥusayn" or "We love you Zaynab," a reference to his sister. Sunni fighters are organized into groups bearing the names of great Muslim military leaders or famous episodes from the history of early Islam. Rebel military operations are named after battles or other events from Islam's early history. Sunni rebels often refer to the Shiites as *Majūs*, the Arab name for Zoroastrians, who are loathed by Islam. Both Sunni and Shiite preachers in the Arab and Muslim world deliver speeches to stir incitement and enlist their followers as militants. The preachers employ rhetoric and symbols from a history overflowing with hostility.[59, 60, 61, 62]

Some Sunni and Shiite sites of symbolic and religious significance on Syrian soil have fallen victim to collateral damage from the war, and other times have been deliberately desecrated. The Umayyad mosques, also known as the Great Mosque in Aleppo and the Great Mosque in Damascus, with their iconic minarets, were an integral part of the skyline of both cities, but both have been nearly destroyed.[63] One of the greatest symbols of Sunni Islam in Syria, the Khālid ibn al-Walīd mosque, which was named for a celebrated seventh-century Muslim general, a leader in the early days of Islam,[64] and was built on his grave in the city of Homs in western Syria, has been badly damaged from the battles raging in its vicinity. On the Shiite side, the Sayyidah Zaynab mosque in the suburbs of Damascus, which is believed to house the grave of Zaynab,[65] has been a pilgrimage destination for generations—it is now a fortified compound controlled by Hezbollah and Iraqi Shiite militias and also has battles constantly raging in its vicinity. Reportedly, hundreds, if not thousands, of sacred Sunni and Shiite sites, as well as Christian churches, have been demolished in the war.[66, 67] According to a report attributed to the Syrian Network for Human Rights,[68] in 2013 more than 1,450 mosques had been damaged in the war.[69] In late 2014, a high-resolution satellite image analysis by the American Association for the Advancement of Science showed that five of the six World Heritage sites in Syria "exhibit significant damage" and some have even been "reduced to rubble."[70] Photographs of cities in Syria, such as Aleppo, Damascus, Daraa, Hama, Homs, and Idlib, are reminiscent of images of cities in Europe bombed during World War II. They also show that it's not only holy sites that are desecrated but also graves of the opposite sect. Sunnis desecrate Shiite graves and Shiites desecrate Sunni graves.[71, 72, 73] In the war in Syria, the living are dying and the dead are not at rest.

The al-Madina Souq (the town market) in Aleppo, which dates back to 3000 BCE and has been used by numerous civilizations, fell victim to mortar attacks and burned down on October 21, 2014.[74] In the historical city of Aleppo, the walls of the thirteenth-century Citadel of Aleppo have been used by Assad's forces in the three-year battle for the city and have been collapsing since a July 2015 explosion.[75]

In July 2015, Dr. Osama al-Qadi, president of the Syrian Economic Task Force,[76] estimated that the costs of the damage caused by the war was $300 billion, and that number is very likely to double.[77]

Competing Views for the Future of Syria

Beyond being a Sunni-Shiite war that has taken a toll on the lives and legacy of the Sunnis and Shiites, the growing involvement of non-Syrian Sunnis in the war, people who often identify with the Salafi-Jihadi ideology and join groups like Global Jihad, Jabhat al-Nusra, and ISIS, add another dimension to it. Though both Syrian and non-Syrian rebel groups share the same immediate objective, to crush the Assad regime and end the Iranian presence in Syria, on an ideological level, there is an unavoidable, built-in tension between the Sunni groups. This stems from the difference in their visions regarding Syria's future and identity.

The Human Toll

And then there is the heaviest loss: the death toll and the people made refugees.

The data regarding the death toll of the war varies greatly. According to figures published by the UN Humanitarian Affairs Mission, as of March 2015, more than 220,000 Syrians had been killed and 12.2 million people continue to require life-saving aid.[78] In April 2015, the Associated Press reported that the number of Syrians killed was 222,271, of which seventy thousand were civilians, including 11,000 children.[79] According to the Syrian Network for Human Rights, the death toll in Syria in April and May 2015 alone was 4,454 people.[80] According to a report published by the Syrian Observatory for Human Rights, as of October 2015, 251,124 Syrians have been killed, including 115,627 civilians of whom 12,517 were children and 8,062 were women over the age eighteen, and about two million have been wounded.[81]

Assad's forces have used chemical weapons on more than one occasion. In August 2013, the Syrian regime launched a chemical attack on an agricultural area named Ghouta, in the outskirts of Damascus. An announcement by the United States shortly after the attack reported that 1,429 people were killed, including at least 426 children. The United States' warning that it would attack Assad's chemical weapons storage and production sites, and an agreement between the US and Russia to do so, paved the way for the removal of the chemical weapons from Syria. According to a March 2015 report issued by the Syrian Network for Human Rights, Assad's forces had perpetrated seventy-one chlorine gas attacks since the regime vowed to give up its stockpile.[82] In April 2015, the United Nations Security Council held a session to hear a detailed report from Syrian doctors regarding the continued use of chemical weapons in the war in Syria. Samantha Power, the United States ambassador to the UN, said the UN Security Council would seek to identify those responsible for the attacks and ensure they face justice.

Though the majority of the chemical weapons have been removed, the mission is not yet complete. As of the end of 2015, the use of chemical weapons in the war in Syria seemed routine.[83]

It is estimated that between eleven and twelve million Syrians—more than half the country's population—have fled their homes.[84] Cities, villages, and neighborhoods throughout the country are the stage for fierce battles and street fighting—artillery, tanks, missiles, anti-tank missiles, mortar shells, aerial raids by Assad's air forces and Russia's air forces, and heavy machine guns are part of the daily existence of millions of Syrian men, women, and children. As of June 2015, according to the UN Refugee Agency, the number of Syrian refugees within Syria is 7.6 million[85] and the number of Syrian refugees outside Syria is more than 4.6 million.[86] In between April 2011 and November 2015, the official number of refugees in Jordan was said to be 632,762; in Lebanon 1,070,189; in Iraq, 244,527; in Turkey, 2,181,293; and in Egypt, 127,681.[87] In Europe, 775,291 Syrians have applied for asylum.[88]

Rebels

The rebel camps, supported by Jordan, Qatar, Saudi Arabia, and Turkey, can be categorized roughly speaking into three groups: the Free Syrian Army, the Salafi-Jihadi-oriented camp under the leadership of Jabhat al-Nusra, (al-Qaeda's branch in Syria), which formed Jaish al-Fath, and the coalition of rebel groups called al-Jabhah al-Islāmiyya as-Sūriyyah.

The Free Syrian Army envisions Syria becoming a modern state run as a parliamentary democracy to ensure that Syria has an independent national identity. It emphasizes the need to preserve the pluralistic, ethnic, and religious fabric of Syria through a legislative and political system that guarantees civil rights and gender equality, open and fair elections, freedom of worship, freedom of speech, and freedom of the press.

The Salafi-Jihadi ideology calls for abolishing the nation-state and, in its place, establishing an Islamist entity governed according the strictest translation of sharīʿah. Thus, the Salafi-Jihadi rebel groups want Syria to become an Islamic entity ruled by sharīʿah law. In their Syria, non-Muslims would be second-class citizens subdued to Islamic supremacy, with very little, if any, freedom of worship. It is worth noting that currently, Jabhat al-Nusra, currently the dominant factor in the Salafi-Jihadi camp, controlling areas in Syria that are more populated than the areas where ISIS has seized power, takes a somewhat softer approach than its mother movement ISIS (which until 2014 was al-Qaeda's branch in Iraq). In the areas that Jabhat al-Nusra controls in Syria, it does not implement strict sharīʿah like ISIS does in the territories under its jurisdiction. Rather, Jabhat al-Nusra focuses on providing social and municipal services, as well as financial support, to the civilians in the areas it dominates. Jabhat al-Nusra is ideologically no less radical than ISIS; its relatively softer approach stems from its political interest in continuing to accrue the support of the population in the areas it controls in Syria. Further differing from ISIS, whose militants are mostly non-Syrian,[89] Jabhat al-Nusra is mostly comprised of Syrian militants and is therefore less inclined to impose its rule as harshly as ISIS.[90]

The biggest rebel camp in Syria is the Syrian Islamic Front. It was established in November 2013 and is comprised of a wealth of Syrian rebel groups—reports suggest anywhere from forty to sixty thousand people.[91, 92, 93, 94, 95] The SIF is primarily supported by Saudi Arabia, Turkey, and Qatar, and its major leaders are considered to identify with the Salafi-Jihadi ideology. The SIF envisions Syria as an Islamic State in which the major source of legislation is sharīʿah law, but with a parliamentary system that protects the rights of minorities.[96] Its vision of what Syria's identity should become does not exactly match the vision of al-Qaeda, ISIS, or other extremist Salafi-Jihadi groups. In fact, statements made by leaders of SIF allude to the fact that its vision is different, even conflicting. For example, in an interview in November 2013, Zahran Alloush, then chief of staff of the Syrian Islamic Front and the supreme military commander of Jaish al-Islam, the major rebel body within SIF, admitted there were "ideological disputes" between SIF and Jabhat al-Nusra.[97] These differences may reflect a strategy on the part of senior SIF leaders to differentiate their vision, at least for now, from the more extreme Salafi-Jihadi camp, in order to gain support.

On the scale of the way that major Islamist-affiliated groups envision Syria's identity, ISIS, who belongs to the Salafi-Jihadi camp, stands on one end of the spectrum, pushing for a strict implementation of sharīʿah law in its most extreme version and as the only source for legislation. SIF stands on the other end, calling for a partial implementation of sharīʿah law in a moderate version, with sharīʿah as one, but not the only, source for legislation. And Jabhat al-Nusra is in between the two on the spectrum, calling for the implementation of sharīʿah law in a less strict version than ISIS, but with it as the only source for legislation.

The ideological differences between the Sunni rebels in Syria are significant because there will come a time when Syria will need to design its cultural, political, and social identity. When that happens, these ideological tensions will likely lead to a broad and open conflict between the rebel groups. In November 2014, for example, the leader of Jabhat al-Nusra, Abu Mohammad al-Joulani, announced the establishment of an Islamic emirate in the territory under its jurisdiction and vowed to "fight to the death against ISIS, the Free Syrian Army, or any other organization that attempts to challenge the emirate."[98] In March

2015, Hashim al-Sheikh, the senior leader of Ḥarakat Ahrar ash-Sham al-Islāmiyyah (Islamist Movement of the Free People of ash-Sham), a major rebel body within the Syrian Islamic Front, firmly denied reports that the Syrian city of Idlib, which was taken by the Syrian rebels, was to be announced as an emirate.[99]

A Shared Mission: The Fight against ISIS

For now, the shared goal of the Syrian and non-Syrian Sunni groups, to defeat Assad's rule and the Shiites, mostly pushes aside the tension between them—but there is one exception.

The tensions are neither concealed nor brushed away when it comes to ISIS. As far as the Syrian rebel groups—including Jabhat al-Nusra, the offspring of ISIS—are concerned, ISIS, with its extreme ideology and extreme vision regarding Syria's identity, is not, and could never be, a partner. ISIS, in their view, is a bitter enemy, and confronting it is both inevitable and necessary.

To that end, in March 2015, Jaish al-Islam, the major rebel body within the Syrian Islamic Front, announced the establishment of a military force called Jaish *'Alī ibn Abī Ṭālib* (the Army of *'Alī ibn Abī Ṭālib*), which was specifically created to fight ISIS in Syria.[100] In addition, in May 2015, Jaish al-Fath, a coalition of Salafi-Jihadi groups in Syria led by Jabhat al-Nusra, another offspring of ISIS, announced a war on ISIS, aimed to root out ISIS's presence in Syria.[101]

ISIS, as an adherent of Salafi-Jihadi ideology and an offspring of al-Qaeda, has a deep and uncompromising hatred of Shiites. The Syrian rebels fighting the Assad-Iran axis in Syria are motivated by their deep animosity toward Iran and its Shiite proxies. It would be reasonable to expect that ISIS would help the Syrian rebels in the war against Assad's rule and the Shiite forces that are assisting him, but this is not necessarily the case. Though, to some extent, ISIS is fighting the Assad regime and its Shiite allies in Syria, ISIS mostly fights the rebel groups in Syria, including its offspring Jabhat al-Nusra.

ISIS's priorities are not identical to those of the Syrian rebels. Whereas the rebels' primary goal is to topple Assad, end the Iranian occupation of Syria, and oust the Russians and other foreign factors, ISIS's primary interest is to gain more territory and control in order to expand the Islamic State.

Many Arab commentators, when they see what is actually happening on the ground, have expressed their belief that ISIS is acting under the direction of the Assad regime and the Iranians, or at least cooperating with them.[102, 103, 104] In noting this, Lebanese journalist 'Ali al-Amin pointed to the fact that ISIS took over the ancient city of Palmyra in Syria while crossing hundreds of miles of wide open desert totally undisturbed by the Assad regime army or his air force.[105] Jordan's king, Abdullah II, said in a May 2015 interview that "Assad is bombing everyone but ISIS strongholds."[106] A July 2015 video released by Jaish al-Islam documented alleged executions by ISIS militants and claimed that Assad's intelligence officers and ISIS have a close cooperation.[107]

Signs point to a collaboration, or at least an understanding, between ISIS and Assad, and both have incentives to cooperate. From Assad's perspective, the mutual bloodshed between the rebels and ISIS weakens the rebels, and this serves his regime. In addition, the struggle between the rebels and ISIS reinforces the propaganda of Assad's regime: that it is not fighting a Syrian popular uprising but rather militant Islamist terror groups, and that the purpose of his regime is to keep Syria stable. Syrian philosopher Dr. Sadiq Jalal al-Azm said that the stability Assad is looking to preserve is "a stability of graves."[108]

From ISIS's perspective, cooperating with Assad enables it to expand its control, even reaching it to major Syrian gas fields, which ensures a substantial income.[109] Information also points to economic cooperation between ISIS and Syrians associated with Assad in such fields as mobile phone companies, commodities trading, and transportation.[110, 111]

The Impact of the War on Iran and Its Proxies

When Iran inserted itself into the war in Syria, via its proxy Hezbollah, in the fall of 2011, it was an important turning point in the war. By the end of 2011, the war had become a central platform for the struggle between the axis of Sunni states, primarily Saudi Arabia, Jordan, Turkey, and Qatar, on one side, and the Iranian Shiite mullah regime and its allies on the other side.

For Iran, the war in Syria consumes much of its human and financial resources. Many dozens of Iranian soldiers, if not more, have been killed in the war, including high-ranking officers of the Iranian Revolutionary Guards.[112, 113] The war also places a heavy burden on the Iranian economy, which is already steeped in enormous difficulties. Iran's annual support of the Assad regime is estimated to be in the billions of dollars.[114]

The death toll paired with the growing burden on Iran's crumbling economy fuels the widespread feelings of discontent and anger inside Iran and boosts animosity among large sectors in Iran toward the mullah regime. Analysts argue that the growing discontent presents a serious threat to the endurance of the mullah regime.[115, 116, 117]

The cost of the war also negatively affects Iran's strongest proxy, Hezbollah, who is sinking in the Syrian mud. Iran, whose support for Hezbollah totals hundreds of millions of dollars per year, has had to drastically cut 25–40 percent of its financial support for the organization.[118, 119, 120] And Hezbollah is facing mounting criticism for its involvement in the war. There is growing anger among Lebanese Shiites, the major political base of Hezbollah, regarding the mounting number of Hezbollah's dead soldiers. Hezbollah adheres to a strict policy of ambiguity, severe censorship, and intentional distortion of statistics regarding the number of its dead or wounded soldiers. An example was showcased during a television interview (which is very rare) that Hezbollah's leader, Hassan Nasrallah, gave in December 2013. In the interview, conducted by a Lebanese television station, OTV, Nasrallah was asked how many Hezbollah fighters had been killed in the war in Syria. He gave an evasive and convoluted answer, at the end of which, he said, "There are those that say that 250 to 300 members of Hezbollah were killed, but we have not arrived at that number."[121] At the end 2015, according to cautious estimations, the number of Hezbollah militants killed in Syria was close to one thousand.[122, 123] Other sources argued that the number of Hezbollah militants killed in Syria was more than fifteen hundred.[124]

No amount of rhetoric and doubletalk can assuage the growing anger among the Lebanese Shiite community, the central political stronghold of Hezbollah. Sheikh Subhi al-Tufayli, the leader of Hezbollah from 1989–1991, has openly and harshly criticized the organization's involvement in the war and blames Nasrallah for dragging Hezbollah and Lebanon on a path toward destruction.[125] In March 2014, Fatima Abdullah, a Shiite Lebanese journalist, published an article eulogizing her brother, a Hezbollah fighter killed in Syria. Abdullah did not conceal her opinion that her brother was killed for no reason in a war that was not his.[126] The article fueled the fierce and growing debate in the Shiite community regarding Hezbollah's involvement in the war.[127, 128, 129]

In April 2015, critics of Hezbollah's involvement in the war in Syria allegedly launched a campaign named "The Coffins Revolution," whose title alludes to the fact Hezbollah fighters continually return from Syria in coffins.[130] In May 2015, a prominent Shiite cleric in Lebanon, Muhammad Ali al-Husseini, the secretary-general of the Arab Muslim Council, condemned Hezbollah's involvement in the war in Syria, arguing that it is dragging Lebanon toward catastrophe.[131]

The war is also causing fissures in the structure of other proxies nurtured by Iran. In February 2012, Ḥamās detached itself from the Assad-Iran axis. Its leaders locked their offices and left Damascus, breaking with the regime, the city, and the country that had comfortably harbored them for many years. Ḥamās's move stemmed from the fact that Ḥamās, a Sunni organization that formally defines itself as the "Arm of the Muslim Brotherhood in Palestine," could no longer afford for Sunnis to view it as part of a Shiite camp that butchers Sunnis in Syria, including the Palestinian brothers of Ḥamās.

In response to Ḥamās's abandonment of the Assad-Iran axis, the Assad regime confiscated Ḥamās property, including private property of its leadership. And more significantly, Iran drastically cut its financial support for Ḥamās. Some reports indicate that Iranian financial support for Ḥamās—which, in addition to huge amounts of weapons and military equipment, was estimated to have reached hundreds of millions of dollars[132, 133]—was reduced to fifty million dollars.[134] Other reports claim that Iran's support for Ḥamās almost entirely stopped.[135] As part of its retaliation, Iran diverted its support to Ḥamās's major competitor in the Gaza Strip, the Islamic Jihad in Palestine.

Ḥamās, struggling with a growing crisis in the Gaza Strip because of a reduction in Iranian funds[136, 137] and because of the overthrow in 2013 of

Ḥamās's natural ally, the Muslim Brotherhood in Egypt, tried to rehabilitate its relationship with Iran. But Iran made it clear that repairing the relationship had a price. Iran demanded that Ḥamās publicly apologize for leaving the Assad-Iran axis; detach itself from the Muslim Brotherhood; express its support for the Assad regime; and have Ḥamās's leader, Khaled Mashal, resign from his position as chairman of the political bureau of Ḥamās.[138, 139, 140] Following a Ḥamās delegation's visit to Iran in September 2014, reports followed that Mashal would also soon visit. But as of the end of 2015, Mashal was not known to have made the trip.

* * *

Salafi-Jihadi groups call for the ousting of existing Arab regimes, especially the Arab monarchies. The Sunni axis' support for the rebels in Syria provides Saudi Arabia, Jordan, Qatar, and Turkey with the opportunity to secure interests they view as being of high strategic importance.

At present, Salafi-Jihadi groups have a relatively small presence in southern Syria. They operate within a coalition established in June 2015 known as Jaish al-Fatah al-Manteqa al-Janubiya (Army of Triumph—the Southern Region), led by Jabhat al-Nusra.[141] A spokesman for al-Jaish al-Awal estimated in mid-2015 that al-Qaeda had two thousand militants in southern Syria.[142] In spite of their limited numbers, the presence of these groups is a threat to the Arab monarchies.

The southern part of Syria that borders northern Jordan is predominately controlled by two major Syrian rebel groups. One is the Free Syrian Army, which operates within a military coalition named al-Jabha al-Janubiya (the Southern Front). The Southern Front is formed out of forty-nine rebel groups, together numbering thirty to thirty-five thousand fighters.[143, 144] It includes military units such as al-Jaish al-Awal, al-Jaish al-Suri al-Muwahad (the United Syrian Army), and Tahalaf Suqour al-Janoub (the Hawks of the South). The second major Syrian rebel group is the Syrian Islamic Front.[145, 146] Both the Free Syrian Army and the Syrian Islamic Front are primarily funded by Saudi Arabia and Qatar. Jordan provides training, logistics, and medical support.[147]

The support of rebel groups in southern Syria by Saudi Arabia, Qatar, and Jordan reflects their interest in preventing—or at least limiting—the presence of ISIS and al-Qaeda in southern Syria, as well as Iranian forces and Iranian-backed Shiite militias close to Jordan's northern border.[148]

The War in Syria and the Sunni Axis

Jordan

The effects of the war in Syria on Jordan are internal and external challenges. Internally, the Syrian refugees in Jordan, numbering more than 630,000, has cost the already-suffering Jordanian economy more than six billion dollars.[149] Most of the refugees are living in refugee camps that the Jordanian government built for them in northern Jordan. The concentration of Syrian refugees is so great in northern Jordan that it has created a demographic shift. Jordan's Ministry of Interior announced in December 2013 that the number of Syrian refugees in the province of Mafraq, in northern Jordan, was higher than the number of Jordanians in the province.[150] To help alleviate the burden, the Saudi Arabian ambassador to Jordan announced in 2015 that the Saudis would cover the costs of Jordan's hosting the refugees.[151]

Another domestic challenge created for Jordan by the war in Syria is the Salafi-Jihadi Jordanians who go to Syria to fight and will return home after. Jordanian security services fear that when these militants return to Jordan they will create terrorist networks throughout the kingdom that could threaten domestic security and stability. The concern is exacerbated by the fact that Jordan is already dealing with the challenge of weapons, militants, criminals, and narcotics being smuggled into Jordan from Syria.

ISIS's "Islamic State," which touches Jordan's north and northeast borders, also presents a threat to the kingdom. One way of Jordan preemptively managing ISIS's threat is through the alliances it is building with the Bedouin tribes of southern Syria and western Iraq to create a security buffer zone. During the first half of 2015, reports indicated a growing military cooperation between Jordan and Iraq, which included Jordan's arming and training of Iraq's

Bedouin tribes.[152, 153, 154] In June 2015, the king of Jordan announced that Jordan was willing to arm the Bedouin tribes on both sides of the Jordanian-Syrian border and the Jordanian-Iraqi border.[155] The Bedouin population in Syria is estimated to be about one million people.[156]

Also in June 2015, the Jordanian minister of public diplomacy stated that Jordan would allow the Druze in southern Syria—mostly based in the city of Sweida—to find refuge in Jordan because Jordan is committed to providing the people of southern Syria with humanitarian aid.[157]

The Jordanian announcements were directed at the two most significant populations in southern Syria. It's estimated that the Druze number between seven and eight hundred thousand[158] people in Syria. In Jordan, there is an estimated twenty to thirty-two thousand Druze.[159, 160]

The June 2015 announcements took place at the same time that reports suggested ISIS was planning to storm the city of Sweida, which has a population of about 380,000 thousands inhabitants, most of them Druze.[161, 162, 163] ISIS has not yet stormed the city, but the Jordanian message continues to be important: it signals to the Druze that Jordan will not indifferently watch the fall of Sweida into ISIS's hands. Its policy on this was discussed in a meeting between the Jordanian king and the leader of the Druze of Lebanon, Walid Jumblatt, in which they reportedly "stressed the depth of the historic ties between Jordan and the Druze sect."[164]

Jordan's actions signal that it perceives the southern part of Syria and the western part of Iraq to be of great strategic significance to its national security interests.

The challenges Jordan faces because of the war in Syria have led to it embarking on a path in its regional policy that some Jordanian politicians and journalists call *al-Urdun al-Kabir*, Greater Jordan. The concept has ignited a political debate in Jordan. Some Jordanians argue that expanding Jordan's activity beyond its current borders is counter to its strategic interest because, in doing so, Jordan risks getting dragged into the war in Syria.[165] Supporters of the concept argue that Jordan must continue to proactively expand its control beyond its borders to preemptively confront the growing threat of ISIS and the Salafi-Jihadi groups.[166] The core of the debate is whether Jordan should shift its regional policy, which is traditionally characterized by a protective and reactionary approach, into a proactive and preemptive one. At present, the shift is unfolding in a carefully calculated and gradual process.

Saudi Arabia

Saudi Arabia's position regarding the crisis in Syria can generally be divided into two phases. During the first months of the events in Syria—from March 2011 through the fall of 2011—the kingdom urged Assad to reach out to the Syrians, to be attuned to their protests, and to respond to their calls for political reforms in order to bring an end to the crisis. In the fall of 2011, as the Iranian involvement in the war in Syria increased, Saudi Arabia's policy shifted and the Saudis demanded that Assad step down. Simultaneously, Saudi Arabia began to provide Syrian rebel groups—primarily the Free Syrian Army and the Syrian Islamic Front—with weapons, financing training, and logistical support.

There is a built-in paradox in the Saudi policy toward the Syrian rebel groups that is a perfect example of how in the Middle East one plus one does not equal two. Things don't always compute.

The late Zahran Alloush, the leader of the Syrian Islamic Front (who was killed in December 2015), studied Islamic studies in Saudi Arabia and was associated with Salafi-Jihadi thought. On the other hand, the Saudis view Salafi-Jihadi groups in Syria, like Jabhat al-Nusra and ISIS, as potential threats, primarily due to the presence of these groups in southern Jordan, which marks Saudi Arabia's northern border.

Egypt

Egypt's policy regarding the war in Syria is surprising. One could expect that Egypt, the most important and largest Arab-Sunni state, would be heavily involved in the war and would support the Syrian rebels. However, that is not the case. From the beginning of the crisis in Syria, Egypt distanced itself from the war. Egypt's official position has consistently called for a diplomatic solution to end the crisis. Contrary to expectations, Egyptian officials have not harshly criticized Iran's role in the war. Instead, Egypt has chosen a diplomatic position, that a solution to the crisis should be based upon the free will of the Syrians, politely hinting that Iran should halt its involvement in Syria.

Egypt's muted response toward Iran is also surprising given the fact that the Saudis—Egypt's major ally and supporter—have taken a hard-line policy with Iran.

Egyptian policy has largely stayed the same over the course of two president—Mohammed Morsi, who was the leader of Egypt when the Syrian crisis began, and its current president, Abdel Fattah al-Sisi. Of the two leaders' positions, Morsi's position is even more puzzling; as the leader of the Muslim Brotherhood and the president of Egypt, it's surprising that Morsi did not pursue an aggressive policy toward Iran. In fact, after being elected, Morsi visited Iran in August 2012. His visit, which was followed by a historic visit of then-Iranian President Mahmoud Ahmadinejad to Egypt in February 2013, ended thirty-two years of the absence of relations between the two states.

The Egyptian position toward the war in Syria, as well as its soft approach toward Iran, likely stems from two major factor: Egypt is preoccupied with its inner challenges, and it views Iran as a significant regional player and a significant economic counterpart in fields such as trade and Egypt's tourism industry, and therefore wants to keep the channels with Iran open.

Turkey

As southern Syria is becoming subject to a Jordanian-Saudi influence, northern Syria is the strategic interest of another major regional player, Turkey.

Prior to the war in Syria, Turkey and Syria had a strategic alliance. In 2009, Turkey's then-foreign minister, Ahmet Davutoğlu, and his Syrian counterpart, Walid Muallem, signed an accord named the "High-Level Strategic Cooperation Council Agreement." It had ended visa requirements for travelers between the countries and also included a bilateral cooperation accord, under which top ministers from the countries would meet annually.

Since the war, the relationship has turned into mutual animosity because Turkish President Recep Tayyip Erdoğan, who is Sunni, cannot not afford to be viewed as a friend of Assad's while Syrian Sunnis are being killed by the Assad-Iran axis.

As a result of the war in Syria, there is a Salafi-Jihadi corridor that stretches from Iraq, in the east, across northern Syria, parallel to the Turkish-Syrian border, and ends in the west on the shores of the Mediterranean Sea.

The eastern part of the corridor—the northeastern Syrian districts of al-Raqqah (ISIS's center of power and de-facto capital in Syria) and Deir ez-Zor—is a stage for constant clashes between ISIS and the Kurds in northern Syria. The two groups battle for control of the area because it contains more than 50 percent of Syria's oil fields—for which the potential annual income has been estimated at nine billion dollars—and more that 45 percent of Syria's agricultural crops—for which the potential annual income has been estimated at more than ten billion dollars.[167]

The central and western part of the corridor, including part of the city of Aleppo, the entire city of Idlib, and the Turkeman mountain ridge overlooking the Syrian coastline, where a majority of the 'Alawites in Syria live, is mostly dominated by Jaish al-Fath but is heavily influenced by Turkey.

In 2014, the prime minister of Turkey, Ahmet Davutoğlu, announced that three hundred armed Turkish soldiers were sent to secure the grave of Suleyman Shah, the grandfather of the founder of the Ottoman Empire. His grave is located in Syria, about twelve miles from the Turkish border. The action signaled that Turkey is willing to operate militarily in Syria to secure its interests.

The war in Syria stimulates a major concern for Turkey: the Kurdish aspiration for independence. There are approximately twenty-five million Kurds in the Middle East, and more that 40 percent of them are in Turkey; the rest are in Iran (eight million), Iraq (six million), and Syria (about three million).[168] Turkey's relations with both its own Kurdish population and Syria's Kurdish population are tense. The major Kurdish political power in northern Syria, the Kurdish Democratic Union Party (PYD), is associated with the Kurdish Workers Party (PKK), a bitter rival of Turkey that calls for the establishment of a Kurdish state within the current territory of Turkey. Dozens of thousands of Turks and Kurdish people were killed in the war between the sides during the 1980s, 1990s, and first decade of the twenty-first century. A truce signed between the sides in 2013 collapsed in the summer of 2015, against the background of Turkish aerial strikes on Kurdish strongholds in northern Syria and on the Turkish-Iraqi border. Each side holds the other responsible for the collapse of the truce.

The disintegration of Syria boosts Kurdish separatist national independence aspirations, a development that deeply concerns Turkey. In 1998, Turkey and Syria signed an understanding known as the Adana Protocol, in which Syria committed to stop its support for the PKK. Following the agreement, Syria closed PKK offices and bases in Syria and arrested hundreds of PKK militants. But with the war in Syria, the protocol has become meaningless. After Turkey positioned itself on the side of the rebels fighting the Assad-Iran axis, Iran retaliated by supporting the PKK. Reportedly, Iran now arms the PKK and allows it to have military bases in Iranian territory close to the Turkish border.[169] Iran has also warmed its relations with the PYD. In 2013, the leader of the PYD, Saleh Muslim, met with a senior Iranian official who promised Iranian support.[170] Shortly after, the Kurds in Syria approved a PYD initiative and announced the formation of a transitional autonomous government.[171] Turkey has been very concerned by these actions, and its concern deepened in June 2015 when in the elections to the Turkish Parliament, the Kurdish political party—the Peoples' Democratic Party—won 13 percent of the vote and garnered seventy-nine seats. It was the first time the Kurdish party in Turkey passed the 10 percent threshold required to receive seats in the government. The achievement boosted the Kurdish aspiration for independence.[172] In October 2015, Turkey's president announced that Turkey would not tolerate the establishment of a Kurdish autonomy in north Syria.[173] In new general elections held in Turkey in November 2015, the Kurdish party again passed the 10 percent threshold—though this time winning fewer than 13 percent of the votes.

Another interest of Turkey's in Syria is economically motivated. Reportedly, in July 2015 there was an initiative to replace the Syrian currency, its pound, in four "liberated areas" in northern Syria with the Turkish lira. The idea was discussed at a panel hosted by the Union for Media Professionals in Aleppo.[174] According to the presentation, a public marketing campaign was scheduled to begin in August 2015, which would last no more than six months, to promote the idea, inform citizens of the affected areas, and implement the plan on the ground.[175] The reasons presented for the change were the weakening of the Syrian currency and the fact that the use of Turkish currency is already common in northern Syria. The panel reported that "the effort is supported by rebel groups and local municipalities in northern Syria."[176] However, the exact identity of the supporters was not given.

The battle between ISIS and the Kurds in northeastern Syria increases the dependence of the north Syrian Kurds on Turkey. Turkey wants this and in turn quietly supports ISIS, doing such things as providing ISIS militants with medical care[177, 178] and allowing ISIS militants' passage to Syria and Iraq through Turkey. This has included the passage of hundreds of Uighurs, a policy that causes tension between Turkey and China.

Also by working with ISIS, Turkey has reportedly been allowed to purchase oil at a reduced price from the reservoirs under ISIS's control in Syria and Iraq, and is reaping a hefty profit from this.[179, 180]

In July 2014, thirty-two Turkish truck drivers arrested by ISIS were released after three months.[181] ISIS is not known for releasing hostages, and it's not believed that there was a ransom payment. Analysts argue that there was a secret deal made between Turkey and ISIS that in exchange for the release of the hostages,[182, 183] Turkey would turn a blind eye to ISIS taking over Syria's Kurdish city Kobanî, located on the Syrian-Turkish border. The city came under siege by ISIS in the beginning of July 2014 and from July–October 2014, Turkey refused to allow Kurdish fighters who lived in Turkish territory to go to the aid of their brothers in the besieged city.[184, 185] Only in October 2014 did Turkey change its policy and allow units of the Iraqi-Kurdish militia, Peshmerga, to cross the Turkish-Syrian border to help their Kurdish brothers in Kobanî.[186]

ISIS is also a valuable card for Turkey in the context of the delicate balance of power between Turkey and Iran. Iran uses the Kurds to put pressure on Turkey by enabling the PKK to have bases in northern Iran next to the border with Syria and through developing relations with PYD, the Kurds in northern Syria. Turkey counters Iran's threat by nurturing a relationship with ISIS. As long as Turkey does not go after ISIS in northeastern Syria, ISIS has a greater maneuvering capacity and can increase it actions in Iraq against Iran and the Iraqi Shiite militias backed by Iran.

Qatar

Far away from Iraq and Syria, on the other side of the Arabian Peninsula, the war in Syria also serves the interests of Qatar in many ways. Qatar aspires to be an influential player in the Middle East and, to that end, conducts a proactive foreign policy, making use of two major tools in its possession: its enormous wealth and its powerful Al Jazeera TV news network. The war in Syria provides Qatar with an excellent stage to promote its leadership ambitions, and to fuel this it provides significant financial support to different rebel groups in Syria, mostly Salafi-Jihadi groups.[187, 188, 189] The support is partly related to Qatar's objection to the expanding influence of Iran but also to its desire to use the war in Syria as an opportunity to position itself as an acceptable broker between the Arab world and Iran. Thus, Qatar does what seems to be the impossible: providing its services as an acceptable mediator while simultaneously supporting the rebels fighting the Assad-Iran axis.

Some Arab analysts believe that Qatar has come to the conclusion that Iran will achieve military nuclear capacity and is therefore looking for avenues to maintain good relations with Iran.[190, 191] Yet, as an Arab Sunni state, Qatar cannot line up with the Assad-Iran axis in Syria. So, Qatar has developed a sophisticated game. In a quintessential winding Middle Eastern way, the support it provides the rebel groups in Syria—who are fighting against the Assad-Iran axis—has also given it an opportunity to gain credibility in the eyes of none other than Iran.

In May 2012, a Syrian Salafi-Jihadi group, supported by Qatar, kidnapped, in Syrian territory, a group of eleven Lebanese Shiites believed to be members and senior military personnel of Hezbollah.[192] In November 2013, the abductees were released in exchange for the release of dozens of Syrian men and women who were imprisoned in Syria by the Assad regime. The kidnapped Shiites returned to Lebanon in a plane belonging to an airline owned by Qatar and were accompanied by Qatar's secretary of state. The release of the kidnapped people occurred because Qatar ordered the rebel group to release them (reportedly, Qatar generously compensated the kidnappers).[193]

The release of the abductees served Iranian interests because the kidnapping was very problematic for Hezbollah, Iran's proxy. The families of the kidnapped put heavy pressure on Hezbollah's leader, Hassan Nasrallah, to do whatever was necessary to release their relatives. Iran and Hezbollah were also concerned that the hostages would disclose information to their abductors. Therefore, Iran was very grateful to Qatar for its mediation services.[194]

In December 2015, Qatar was the broker for a swap between the Lebanese government and Jabhat al-Nusra in Syria. In it, sixteen Lebanese soldiers held by Jabhat al-Nusra were released in exchange for thirteen militant Islamist activists imprisoned in Lebanon, including the ex-wife of Abū Bakr al-Baghdadi, the leader of ISIS, who was detained in Lebanon.

Influence of the War in Syria on Syria's Other Neighbors

Saudi Arabia, Jordan, Turkey, and Qatar are proactive supporters of the rebels in Syria, but the war in Syria affects all of Syria's neighbors. One of the most affected states is Lebanon.

Lebanon

Lebanon has a population estimated to be between four-and-a-half and six million people,[195, 196] and similar to Syria, it is a tapestry of ethnicities and religions. Christians account for more than 40 percent of Lebanon's population, yet they are not homogenous—but are divided between sects, like Maronite and Greek Orthodox. Shiites are 27 percent of the population, Sunnis are 25 percent, and Druze are more than 5 percent.[197]

Lebanon became an independent country in 1943, and in its short history, it has had constant crises and political violence, including two civil wars, one in 1958 and the other 1975–1990. The chaos reflects the hostilities between its different sects, and clashes between sectarian militias and assassinations of journalists, politicians, and public officials are common.

Since the war broke out in Syria, it's estimated that more than one million Syrians have fled to Lebanon and become refugees there.[198] In October 2014, the Lebanese minister of labor said that Lebanon would not be able to absorb any more refugees from Syria,[199] but Syrians have still continued to flee there. At the end of 2015, one of four people in Lebanon was a refugee.[200]

The scale of this influx has shifted the demographic balance in Lebanon and made Sunnis its largest sect. The Lebanese government does not recognize the Syrian refugees as residents or citizens, but their presence has, nevertheless, put an enormous pressure on the weak Lebanese economy and is increasing social and political tensions.

Since October 2014, the Lebanese government has put restrictions on the movement of the refugees. The Lebanese army even seized areas in eastern Lebanon bordering Syria, trying to prevent the movement of Syrian refugees into the Lebanese heartland. The move was a response to the growing concern that Salafi-Jihadi militants disguised as refugees would scatter throughout Lebanon and establish terror cells, targeting Hezbollah's strongholds and Shiites. Lebanese Sunni opponents of Hezbollah view the Lebanese government's policy restricting the movement of the Syrian refugees as Hezbollah's policy, and this has generated a growing resentment among the Sunnis in Lebanon. Hezbollah's involvement in the war in Syria deepened resentments of Lebanese Sunnis toward Hezbollah, and the result has been a growing sectarian violence throughout Lebanon.

In and around the predominantly Sunni city of Tripoli—the largest city in northern Lebanon, with a population of about five hundred thousand people[201]—there have, since 2011, been armed clashes in the streets between Sunnis and the 'Alawite minority that lives there. The tension has required the Lebanese army to intervene, and Lebanese soldiers have been killed trying to restore order. The fighting has caused thousands of citizens to flee the city.[202]

The predominantly Sunni city of Sidon—the largest city in southern Lebanon, with a population estimated at nearly three hundred thousand inhabitants[203]—has experienced armed clashes between Lebanese Salafi-Jihadi militia and Hezbollah in June 2013. The clashes resulted in the widespread presence of the Lebanese army in the area, and tensions remain high.

Eastern Lebanon has also not been spared the ramifications of the Sunni-Shiite tensions. The Lebanese village of Arsal, also with a majority Sunni population, is located about eighty miles northeast of Beirut on the Syrian border and has become a focal point for the growing Sunni-Shiite tension in Lebanon. Thousands of Syrians fleeing Syria have found refuge in and around Arsal, but Hezbollah has claimed that it's also a base for the Salafi-Jihadi groups who are attacking Hezbollah posts and Shiite communities near the Lebanese-Syrian border. In 2014, Hezbollah forces and the Lebanese army attacked Arsal and battles raged between them and Jabhat al-Nusra, and possibly ISIS as well. In the clashes, dozens of Lebanese soldiers were killed and dozens more were captured, some subsequently executed.

In June 2015, Hezbollah's leader, Hassan Nasrallah, looking to thwart Hezbollah's skyrocketing difficulties in Syria, addressed the Lebanese people and urged them to join the fight to defend Lebanon. In his plea, he ignored the fact that he, as a member of the Lebanese government, had by taking part in the war in Syria violated the official neutrality policy of his government. He also ignored in his speech the fact that he had turned a deaf ear to the repeated calls of the majority of the Lebanese people that urged him to immediately withdraw his forces from Syria. Following Nasrallah's speech, Lebanese journalist 'Ali al-Amin wrote, "Nasrallah ignored all the demands of the Lebanese to withdraw from Syria; but now, as his militants are killed in Syria and he is in a desperate situation, all of the sudden he remembers the Lebanese."[204]

The fighting in Lebanon has fueled the rage of Sunnis, as well as factors like the Christians and Druze, against Hezbollah because they're angry that Hezbollah dragged the Lebanese army into the war in Syria, a war the Lebanese had no desire to be a part of. The tensions also impact another significant group in Lebanon and Syria: the Palestinians.

According to the United Nations Relief and Welfare Agency for Palestine Refugees in the Near East (UNRWA), there are 560,000 Palestinians in Syria.[205] Hundreds of thousands of Syrian Palestinians are displaced within Syria and eighty thousand are displaced in Egypt, Jordan, Lebanon, Turkey, and Europe.[206, 207] According to the Action Group for Palestinians of Syria,[208] as of October 2015, nearly three thousand Palestinians have been killed in the war in Syria.[209, 210]

The danger has caused more than forty-four thousand Palestinian refugees in Syria to flee from Syria to Lebanon,[211, 212] where they find shelter in Palestinian refugee camps. According to UNRWA, there are more than four hundred thousand Palestinians in twelve refugee camps in Lebanon.[213] The Palestinians are furious with Assad and his allies; but for now, the leading Palestinian organizations in Lebanon—Fatah, Ḥamās, and Islamic Jihad—are trying to keep the rage under control. They do not want to launch or be dragged into a military confrontation with Hezbollah in Lebanon.

However, the Palestinian Salafi-Jihadi groups who live in the Palestinian refugee camps in Lebanon are not afraid of attacking Hezbollah and the Iranians in Lebanon. And this has resulted in a number of high-profile attacks—suicide bombings and the launching of rockets. In November 2013, two suicide bombers attacked the Iranian embassy in Lebanon. In November 2015, two suicide bombers attacked Hezbollah's major stronghold in south Beirut, killing forty-five people and injuring hundreds. ISIS claimed responsibility, identifying the perpetrators of the attack as Palestinian and Syrian militants.

As the war in Syria continues, Palestinians in Lebanon grow increasingly frustrated by how Palestinians are butchered in Syria and how increasingly intolerable Palestinian refugee camps in Lebanon are. Tensions are escalating both between different Palestinian sects in Lebanon and also between Lebanon's Palestinians and Hezbollah. This process should be closely watched because the Palestinians in Lebanon are capable militants. Should clashes between Palestinian groups and Hezbollah in Lebanon flare up, the streets inside the camps and in surrounding areas could turn into a war zone.

Lebanon, like other arenas in the Middle East, is also a stage for the Saudi-Iranian power struggle. One expression of this is the battle over the position of the president of Lebanon—the highest executive role in the country. In May 2014, the term of Lebanese President Michel Suleiman, who had been in office since 2008, ended, and due to Saudi-Iranian disagreement, as of the end of 2015, Lebanese politicians have failed to agree on a candidate acceptable to all parties to become the next president.

There are two major political camps competing for power in Lebanon. One is Hezbollah and its political allies, the Amal Shiite movement and the Free Patriot Party, the latter led by former Lebanese Chief of Staff and Prime Minister Michel Aoun, who is a Maronite Christian, which is required according to the Lebanese constitution. The opposing camp is made up of a coalition of Sunnis represented mostly by the Istiqlal Party (the Independence Party) led by Saad al-Hariri, the son of the late Lebanese Prime Minister Rafiq al-Hariri; the Druze, led by Lebanese Druze leader Walid Jumblatt; and some Christian parties. This camp, supported by Saudi Arabia, is a bitter opponent of Hezbollah and Iran and so has vetoed Aoun's candidacy. Because of the disagreement, as of the end of 2015, for more than one year, Lebanon has had no president.

While Syria is an erupting volcano, Lebanon is a smoking one. Saudi Arabia and Iran, like the Lebanese, want to avoid a deterioration of the situation in Lebanon. But the continuation of the war in Syria and its increasing spillover into Lebanon is increasing the potential for a wide-scale conflagration.

Israel

Ironically and miraculously, the Syrian neighbor that has—at least as of the end of 2015—been least affected by the war in Syria is Israel, Syria's neighbor on its southwest side.

As a result of the fighting between rebels and Assad forces occasionally taking place in close proximity to the Israel-Syria cease, sporadic incidents of stray mortars and bullets accidentally crossing into the Israeli Golan Heights, as well as a small number of shooting incidents targeting Israeli military maneuvers along the separation fence between Syria and Israel, have occurred. These have resulted in a few injured Israeli soldiers and the death of one Israeli civilian—but the impact so far on Israel is in stark contrast with what Jordan, Lebanon, and Turkey are enduring. They have suffered deliberate attacks on their territory, including rockets and suicide bombings that have claimed the lives of hundreds of people.

Israel has allowed more than one thousand wounded Syrians into Israel for medical care, but there are very few Syrian refugees living there.[214] This, however, is subject to change. Israel could in time find itself dealing with an influx of Syrians looking for refuge or find itself under attack.

Since the signing of the Israel-Syria cease-fire agreement following the October 1973 Yom Kippur War, a three-week war launched by Egypt and

Syria on Israel, the Golan Heights has been Israel's calmest border, but the war in Syria has changed that. The presence of Salafi-Jihadi groups along the cease-fire line is a dramatic, negative change for Israel. The groups are currently busy fighting the Assad-Iran axis, but the elimination of Israel is still one of their core goals.

Hezbollah and Iran also might use the Syrian side of the Golan Heights as a base to attack Israeli communities in the Israeli Golan Heights and northern Israel.[215] It is already estimated that some of the attacks launched from the Syrian side of the Golan Heights at Israeli military forces were launched by Syrian militants backed by Hezbollah.[216] In January 2015, a group of senior Hezbollah military personnel and Iranian soldiers, including a general of the Iranian Revolutionary Guard, were killed in proximity to the Israeli-Syrian cease-fire line. [217] Israel was reported as being responsible for the attack.[218] Assuming Israel was responsible—though Israel never claimed responsibility—the act would represent an Israeli message to Iran and Hezbollah that the Golan Heights is off the table and that it will not allow Iran and Hezbollah to use the Syrian side of the Golan Heights as a base from which attacks against Israel can be launched.

The presence of Iranian Revolutionary Guard forces and Iran-backed militias in central and western Iraq and southern Syria could be used by Iran to establish a corridor stretching from Iraq to the Israeli-Syrian cease-fire line in the Golan Heights. One of the military missions of the IRG deployed in Iraq is, according to one report, to set the ground for missile attacks on Israel.[219] Another report claimed that Iran is seeking to create a corridor that stretches from Iraq through southern Syria to Lebanon.[220] In a December 2015 interview, Major General Mohammad 'Ali Jafari, the commander of the Iranian Revolutionary Guards, said, "Iraq, Syria, and Lebanon are all part of the axis of resistance thus there should be no borders between them."[221] The ramifications of such a development would be substantial, and it is unlikely that the Israeli government would watch such a development with indifference.

For Israel, the war in Syria has created a new reality in the Golan Heights. However, in spite of the changes and the growing military threats, Israel has so far weathered the war unscathed.

Israel's policy is to respond militarily to every shooting into its territory. Exceptions are made if the shooting is proven to have been a random accidental shooting that does not cause fatalities or damage. An escalation in attacks against Israel would lead to a parallel escalation in the Israeli military's reaction, with the goal of neutralizing the threat. If the presence of the groups along the Israeli-Syrian cease-fire line leads to military attacks on Israel, a fierce Israeli counter-operation will be inevitable.

Russia and the War in Syria

Russia provides the Assad regime with logistic, military, and diplomatic support but, until September 2015, was not directly in the war in Syria. In September 2015 this changed when Russian warplanes, in support of Assad, commenced attacks in northwest Syria. Since then, the Russian air force has been waging an air campaign that targets Syrian rebels in northwest Syria.

Russia's direct involvement in the war is a significant strategic development. Forty years after it lost its major stronghold in the Middle East, Egypt, Russia has found a way to return through the Syrian door. The Russian action in Syria is motivated by two major factors: one is that with the war, Russian President Vladimir Putin has identified a strategic opportunity to resume a long-term Russian presence in proximity to the massive gas reserves discovered in the eastern basin of the Mediterranean Sea. The second is Putin's desire for the establishment of a Russian stronghold in the Middle East that it could use as a card in its struggle with Western powers.

Arab analysts view Russian involvement in Syria in different ways. Some argue it marks the final disintegration of Syria and will lead to an 'Alawite protectorate in western Syria under a Russian-Iranian umbrella. Others argue that the Russian move is the outcome of an Iranian request due to the growing difficulties that the Assad-Iran axis is experiencing—Assad has lost control over most of Syria; the Assad-Hezbollah axis is cracking under the mounting pressure of the Syrian rebels; in the spring of 2015 a major offensive of the axis in southern Syria failed when rebels took over towns in northwest Syria, thereby controlling the major highway leading to the 'Alawite strongholds in the coast; and in August 2015, a major offensive of the axis on the city of al-Zabadani also failed.

Russia claims it's joined the war in order to fight ISIS, but this argument is questionable for three reasons. First, Russia has refused to participate in the international military coalition campaign against ISIS. Second, Russian jets are mostly operating in west, northwest, and south Syria, an area where ISIS is rarely present. Third, directly confronting ISIS may be counterproductive to Russian interests. Doing so could produce an influx of Islamist militants looking to fight Russian forces in Syria and also increase preexisting tension between Russia and its neighboring Muslim communities, in Chechnya or the Islamic republics of central Asia, which would also likely result in attacks by Islamist militants on Russia.

Russia's move in Syria has, however, had some repercussions. In October 2015, the Muslim Brotherhood movement in Syria announced armed jihad against Russians in Syria, urging every Syrian capable of holding a weapon to fight the Russian invasion.[222] Fifty-two Saudi clergy described Russian attacks in Syria as "a crusader invasion" and urged Muslims to thwart the attack by all means necessary.[223]

Some Arab analysts foresee the development of an "Afghan model" in Syria (i.e. a failing state whose territory harbors bases of terror) as an outcome of the deepening Russian involvement.[224] The possible duplication of the chaos and violence that characterizes Afghanistan should be an international concern. Syria, located in the heart of an area rich in energy sources, is a junction of major trade and transportation routes, and it is close to Europe. It's already become a comfortable base for militant Islamist groups—and the greater the chaos, the better it is for these groups. While the rule of the Taliban in Afghanistan—though extreme and brutal—did not pose a real threat to its neighbors, the rule of Salafi-Jihadi groups in Syria would be a constant and growing threat and a source of instability to nearby states like Israel, Jordan, Lebanon, and Turkey. Afghanistan, under Taliban rule, was the base from which 9/11, the biggest terrorist attack in history, was launched. If Syria turns into a base for militant Islamist groups, they could potentially unleash a terrorist attack like 9/11, or an even larger one. They likely will not hesitate to use chemical and biological weapons. In the summer of 2015, ISIS used mustard gas in its fights against Kurds.[225]

Russia is likely aware of the risk of another Afghanistan, and might accordingly avoid putting Russian boots on Syrian soil. A painful message was delivered to Russia with the crash of a Russian passenger jet in Sinai in November 2015, which resulted in the death of all 224 people on board. The plane crashed after it broke into pieces mid-air, apparently following the detonation of explosives planted on the aircraft by ISIS, which claimed responsibility.

At present, Russian aerial attacks seem to be blocking the rebels' momentum and giving Assad some breathing room. But if the Assad-Iran axis wants Russia's support to continue, it will have to comply with Russia's interests, which are not necessarily identical to Iran or Assad's goals. For example, some Arab analysts argue that Russia, unlike Iran, is not interested in the continued presence of Hezbollah in Syria, nor does it necessarily view the establishment of an 'Alawite protectorate as its ultimate objective. Russia is looking for the best platform to serve Russia, not Iran, Assad, or Hezbollah.[226, 227]

The Russian presence in the eastern Mediterranean has the potential to cause significant strategic ramifications. A Russian stronghold in proximity to major arenas of instability, like Iraq, Lebanon, and Syria, as well as the disputed gas fields between Israel and Lebanon in the Mediterranean Sea, which could spark a military confrontation between Israel and Hezbollah, enables Russia a position of influence, possibly a stabilizing one. Thus, for example, in a September 2015 meeting between Russian President Vladimir Putin and Israeli Prime Minister Benjamin Netanyahu, Putin acknowledged Israel's concerns regarding the risks of the spillover of the war in Syria into Israel. This expression showed support for Israel's strategic interest in preventing Iran from creating a military front against Israel in the Golan Heights. It was also a clear Russian message to Iran to stay away from the Israeli-Syrian cease-fire line in the Golan Heights.

ISIS and the War in Syria

The war in Syria manifests how the more chaotic the situation, the more ISIS and other militant Islamist groups thrive. ISIS benefits from the war in Syria in different ways, taking advantage of the unique, sometimes contradicting, interests of its major players.

In addition to the ways ISIS benefits from its relationship with Turkey, it benefits from its relationship with Assad. Even though ISIS is a bitter enemy of Assad and Iran, and engages in battles against the Assad-Iran axis in Syria, the two sides conduct relations based on mutual interests. Ironically, the more the Assad-Iran axis is weakened in Syria, the more the axis needs ISIS, who in turn takes advantage of this to gain momentum on the ground.

Assad benefits from ISIS's presence in Syria in a number of ways.

First, the current battle to the death between ISIS and the Syrian rebels eases the pressure on the Assad-Iran axis because it forces the rebels to fight ISIS, therefore diverting their attention and resources away from fighting the Assad-Iran axis. In May 2015, ISIS marched across the wide open Syrian desert completely undisturbed by Assad's force and occupied the city of Palmyra in central Syria.[228] Meanwhile, in southern Syria, ISIS began moving its forces toward the city of Sweida. Arab analysts argue that Assad hoped that ISIS's move in southern Syria would expand the battlefield between ISIS and the Syrian rebels, and in this way thwart the rebels' momentum following their military achievements in southern Syria during the spring of 2015.[229] ISIS made these advancements soon after the Assad-Iran axis suffered significant losses and lost some important tactical positions in southern Syria as well as the strategically important towns of Idlib and Jisr al-Shughur in northwestern Syria, which were occupied by the rebels in March 2015. The towns are strategically important because they are located on the highway that leads from the center of Syria to the coastline and the major 'Alawite cities of Latakia and Tartus, on the shore of the Mediterranean Sea.

Second, ISIS's presence in Syria serves Assad's argument that he is not facing an uprising of the Syrian people, but rather he is standing in the front line of war against brutal militant terror groups, thus not only protecting Syria but also the entire region and Europe.

ISIS, too, benefits in different ways.

First, the oil fields that ISIS occupies in Syria provide it with a significant income source. According to reports, Assad allowed ISIS to take over the fields in return for his regime's ability to buy the oil from ISIS at a low cost.[230] Reportedly, ISIS also conducts gains income from commercial relations it conducts with Syrian businesspeople affiliated with Assad's regime.[231]

Second, the war in Syria enables ISIS to expand its reign of terror, thus increasing its attractiveness for young Muslims, and some non-Muslims, from all over the world. Intelligence organizations and governments in the West are aware that this momentum presents security threats by Islamists militants returning to their own countries after terrorist training, joining ISIS and committing terrorist attacks from abroad, or never going abroad, but being inspired by ISIS and militant Islam's momentum from a distance. The terror attacks in Paris (January and November 2015) and San Bernardino, California (December 2015) prove the concern is justified and the process is already underway.

The Lost Generation

Syria today is a field of intense violence with no clear end in sight. The generation growing up in Syria is one for whom death and savage brutality are daily events. It remains to be seen what the psychological effects of this will be. The "lost generation" is, theoretically, an inexhaustible pool of future militants for organizations driven by extremism.

A June 2014 report by Human Rights Watch titled "Maybe We Live and Maybe We Die—Recruitment and Use of Children by Armed Groups in Syria" documented the recruitment of youth under the age of eighteen by all factors fighting in Syria. Part of this is the well-known phenomenon of Syrian child soldiers. The report stated:

> Human Rights Watch found that opposition armed groups used boys as young as 15 as fighters and children as young as 14 in support roles. Some children who participated were detained or killed in battle. Boys interviewed fought on the frontlines, spied on hostile forces, acted as snipers, treated the wounded on battlefields, and ferried ammunition and other supplies to battles while fighting raged. One doctor described treating a boy between 10 and 12 years old whose job it was to whip prisoners held in an ISIS detention facility, according to the adult fighter who brought him.[232]

The use of children by opposition armed groups has not been confined to one group, or to certain ideologies or ethnicities. Children interviewed by Human Rights Watch reported serving in brigades and battalions associated with the Free Syrian Army (FSA), extremist Islamist forces such as the Jabhat al-Nusra and the Islamic State of Iraq and Sham (ISIS), and Yekîneyên Parastina Gel (YPG) military and Asayish police forces in Kurdish-controlled parts of northern Syria.[233]

Children who wished to leave armed groups and resume a civilian life told Human Rights Watch they had few options to do so. Saleh, 17, said he fought with the Free Syrian Army at 15 after he was detained and tortured by government security forces. He later joined Ahrar al-Sham, then left to join the Jund al-Aqsa, an independent Islamist armed group. "*I thought of leaving [the fighting] a lot,*" he said. "*I lost my studies, I lost my future, I lost everything. I looked for work, but there's no work. This is the most difficult period for me.*"[234]

"*At first I was so scared. . . . then I got used to it,*" said Ayman, who began fighting with an FSA brigade in Salqin when he was 15 years old. Others interviewed echoed his words. [235]

Few had plans or real hopes for their future beyond the next battle. "*Maybe we'll live, and maybe we'll die,*" said Omar, who began fighting at age 14 with Jabhat al-Nusra.[236]

What Lies Ahead?

In the second decade of the twenty-first century, Syria, a major Arab state that has a unique place in Sunni Islam as well as in the Arab identity and history, is crumbling. What began as a popular uprising has turned into a stage for three different power struggles taking place at the same time: the Arab-Sunni axis vs. the Assad-Iran Shiite axis; the struggle between the Syrian rebels and ISIS; and Russia's aspirations vs. Western powers. No one considers defeat an option.

In the eyes of the majority of Syrians and Arabs, and the leaders of the United States and Europe, Assad had lost his legitimacy and must go—one way or another.

Following a series of Assad-Iran military defeats in the spring and summer of 2015, predictions are widespread that Assad will have to step down.[237, 238] But it's unclear when this will happen, as predications date back to Assad having to do this in 2011.

The majority of Syrians consider their land to be illegally occupied by Iran and its proxies. Syrian rebels will continue to fight to end the Iranian presence. Lebanese journalist and political analyst Abdul Wahab Badr Khan reflected on this sentiment in the title of his March 2015 article: "The Next War: Free Syria from the Iranian Occupation."[239]

For the Sunnis, a victory of the Assad-Iran axis in Syria would mean a defeat of historic proportions. It would signal the defeat of Sunni Islam in its struggle against the Shiites, and Iran would mark another takeover on its ambition to become the leading superpower in the Middle East. Therefore, for the Sunnis defeat is not an option.

For Assad and the ʿAlawites, defeat would be catastrophic. They would likely face the Syrian Sunnis' furious revenge, not only because of the war, but also because of decades of oppression by the ʿAlawite regime. So for them, too, defeat is not an option.

Increasing Challenges for Iran

In 2011, on the eve of the outbreak of the events in Syria that evolved into the war, the Assad-Iran axis was stable and Iran's ability to wield its influence in Syria and Lebanon was practically unchallenged. Today, Iran's dominance in Syria and Lebanon has substantially eroded. Assad has lost control over most of Syria, and the Assad-Hezbollah axis is cracking under the mounting pressure of the Syrian rebels.

Assad is no longer a "legitimate ruler" in the eyes of most Western powers and the Arab world. The consensus among the United States, European powers, Saudi Arabia, and Turkey is that Assad's rule needs to end.

The Assad-Iran axis is facing growing difficulties in Syria, and the continuation of the war has become increasingly counterproductive to Iranian interests. For one, it's expensive. Iran supports the Assad-Hezbollah camp in Syria with ammunition, money, oil, and weapons, and it's believed that the cost of this has reached one billion dollars per month. Yet, these resources are only meaningful to a point because the Assad-Hezbollah axis in Syria has limited human resources—a fact Assad admitted in July 2015 when he said in a press conference, "Everything is available [for the army], but there is a shortfall in human capacity."

For the Iranian mullah regime, a defeat of the Assad-Iran axis in Syria is liable to bring to naught not only the dream of hegemony that the regime has been cultivating, but its very existence as well. Defeat in Syria could bring the growing, deepening, and accelerating unrest in Iran against the regime. The Iranian people could hit their breaking point with regard to the economic and social hardships they face and begin to more fervently demand change—or new leadership. A defeat in Syria is liable to set a process in motion that will lead to a broad-based uprising in Iran, and the Iranian regime could likely find itself fighting for survival.[240] For the Iranian regime, a defeat in Syria is unacceptable. It is determined to maintain its influence. Yet as of December 2015, it seems as if Iran's maneuvering capacity in Syria has been substantially reduced. Assad's endurance is now primarily in Russia's hands—not Iran's.

The signing of the Vienna Agreement on July 14, 2015 between Iran and the "Five Plus One" states, China, France, Russia, the United Kingdom, the United States, plus Germany, regarding the Iranian nuclear program, presents the question of what the ramifications of the agreement on the Middle East, in general, and in the context of Syria, in particular, will be. Will the lifting of sanctions on Iran and the flow of hundreds of billions of dollars to it following the agreement be used by Iran to rehabilitate its own crumbling economy and address its massive domestic challenges? Or will they be used to increase the flow of weapons, ammunition, and funds to Iran's exhausted allies and proxies, first and foremost the Assad regime and Hezbollah?

Leading Arab columnists and analysts seem to doubt that Iran will pursue a more virtuous path. Saudi Prince Bandar bin Sultan, a former head of Saudi intelligence and senior advisor on Saudi national security who served as Saudi ambassador to the United States, asked, "Why was Obama determined to close the deal with Iran, knowing it will stream hundreds of billions of dollar to Iran thus increasing the chaos in the region?" His answer:

> President Obama made his decision to go ahead with the Iran nuclear deal fully aware that the strategic foreign policy analysis, the national intelligence information, and America's allies in the region's intelligence all predict not only the same outcome of the North Korean nuclear deal but worse, with the billions of dollars that Iran will have access to; because Obama is so sure that he is right and he dismisses the catastrophic outcomes as collateral damage.

In his short article expressing surprise and disappointment with Obama's regional policy, "which could be discussed at another time," bin Sultan wrote: "I am more convinced than ever that my dear friend, the old fox Henry Kissinger, was right when he said: 'The enemies of the United States should fear her—but her friends should fear her more.'" He ends his by noting that "this is heartbreaking, but the facts cannot be ignored." Bin Sultan named his article "*Tabq al-Asl Thanyia*," which can be translated in a positive context to mean "being true to yourself, holding on decisively to what you believe in" or, in a negative context, to "blind arrogance" or "dogmatism."[241]

Until recently, the war in Syria had mostly been a zero-sum game between the axis of Sunni states and the Assad-Iran axis. The outcome so far is a "mutual stranglehold" in both Syria and Lebanon, with no victors and no one definitively defeated. However, while there is no easy solution to end the war in Syria, there may be an opportunity for the opening of a path that could lead to an arrangement that would end the war.

This assessment is based on five major developments:

The first development is the Vienna Agreement. Paradoxically, the Vienna Agreement, which provides Iran legitimate membership in the club of "nuclear threshold states," at the same time takes away one of Iran's most significant cards—its nuclear program. A strong nuclear program is not Iran's ultimate goal, at least not today. The mullah regime's objective is to be a regional superpower and be recognized as such. In service of this, Iran skillfully uses two tools, its axis of resistance and its nuclear program, and both are intertwined and secure the other.

The axis of resistance is used by Iran to deter a possible attack on its nuclear facilities. Iran frequently threatens to retaliate if its strategic interests are jeopardized or its allies are attacked. For example, Iran threatened that a United States attack on Syria would result in "a military and terrorist reaction against US targets and allies."[242] The threat also applies to a military attack on Iran's nuclear facilities. The executor of the threats are Iranian proxies, like Hezbollah, Ḥamās, and IJIP, as well as terror cells Iran has deployed in the Arab Gulf states. An Iranian threat to set the Middle East afire by using its proxies is also always looming. In October 2011, Assad said that any threat to his rule "will unleash an earthquake that would burn the Middle East."[243] Iran used its nuclear program by threatening to walk away from talks over it and potential limitations of it if the international community did not give in to its requests. By using these tools, Iran was able to secure the continuation of Assad's rule, the strength of the axis of resistance, and the perpetuation of Hezbollah's involvement in the war in Syria.

The Vienna Agreement cuts the connection between the two tools, thus weakening Iran's maneuvering capabilities. Since Iran signed the agreement and pledged not to have a nuclear weapon, it can no longer threaten to walk away from the talks—because they are concluded.

The Vienna Agreement also reduces the effectiveness of the Iranian threat to use the axis of resistance as a way to deter a possible military attack on its nuclear facilities. Since the facilities were "legitimized" by the agreement, Iran cannot use the axis of resistance against the United States, Israel, or Saudi Arabia under the guise of deterring an attack on its nuclear facilities. Should Iran use the axis of resistance against the United States, Israel, or Saudi Arabia, it risks tough retaliations and sanctions and an attack on its nuclear program facilities. Thus, in a way, the signing of the Vienna Agreement narrowed Iran's maneuverability.

A possible indicator of Iran's narrowing maneuverability was shown in a speech given by Iran's supreme leader, Ali Khamenei, following the signing of the Vienna Agreement. In it he said, "Iran will keep supporting the people of Yemen, Iraq, and Syria, as well as the *mujahiddun* (the "warriors of holy war") in Palestine and Lebanon." Khamenei did not pledge to support Assad.

The second development is the weakening of the Assad-Iran axis in Syria.

The third development is that Arab states and Turkey, disturbed by the Vienna Agreement, will likely quickly intensify their efforts to block Iran's expansion. The day after the Vienna Agreement was signed, the Arab military coalition fighting the Iranian-backed Houthi militia in Yemen gained a significant achievement by retaking the port city of Aden. Under the growing pressure of the Arab military coalition in Yemen, it is likely that Houthis will turn to diplomatic channels to end the violence. In fact, following the defeat of the Houthis in Aden, the previous Yemeni president and current Houthi ally, ʿAlī ʿAbd Allāh Ṣāliḥ, called for an immediate end to the war in Yemen.[244]

The achievements of the Arab coalition in Yemen provided the Arab states with a momentum that is very relevant in the context of the war in Syria.[245, 246] Arab analysts indicate that the advanced military capacities of the Arab Gulf states demonstrated in Yemen—such as a modern and advanced air force, high-precision weapons, the ease of deployment and operation of mass ground forces, etc.—can be easily applied in Syria as well, since Iran and Assad's forces don't have the military capabilities to counter the Arab Gulf states' military advantage.[247]

In December 2015, Saudi Arabia announced the formation of a thirty-four-member Muslim and Arab state coalition to fight terror. Before this, immediately after the signing of the agreement, a delegation of senior Ḥamās leaders, including the chairman of its political bureau, Khalid Mashal, met the Saudi king during a visit to Saudi Arabia to celebrate the Muslim holyday 'Eid al-Fitr. The meeting had a few objectives for the Saudis:

First, to make sure that following the Vienna Agreement, Ḥamās would not rush back into Iran's arms. The Saudis know what Iran's price will be for resuming its support of Ḥamās—setting the Israel-Gaza strip on fire again in order to divert attention from the Syrian arena to allow Assad and Hezbollah to regroup. Saudi Arabia wants to avoid this.

Second, to make a gesture to Turkey, which supports the Muslim Brotherhood and its offspring Ḥamās. The gesture was intended to ease the tensions between Turkey and Saudi Arabia that stemmed from the fact that Saudis defines the Muslim Brotherhood as a terror organization and have given Ḥamās the cold shoulder. By inviting Ḥamās' leader to meet the king of Saudi Arabia, the Saudis intended to clear the air with Turkey and pave the way to improved cooperation between the two states in their mutual effort to prevent an Iranian takeover of Syria.

Third, to send a signal to Egypt, whose relationship with the Muslim Brotherhood and Ḥamās is very tense, to ease up its pressure on Ḥamās. This would encompass things like opening the passage to Egypt, allowing some tunnel traffic, etc., and would help diffuse the tension in the Gaza Strip.

Realizing these objectives is important to Saudi Arabia because they serve its strategic goal: to block Iran's aggressive expansion in the Middle East.

The fourth development is Russia's direct involvement in the war.

The fifth development is the growing understanding, mostly in Europe, that the repercussions of the war in Syria are not confined to its borders—that their dramatic ramifications exceed the region. The longer the war continues, the deeper and wider the repercussions become.

At present, almost five years after the outbreak of violence in Syria, the international community has totally failed to end the war. In June 2015, UN Secretary General Ban Ki-moon announced that the world should be "ashamed that three years after major powers approved a blueprint in Geneva to bring peace to Syria, the suffering of its people is reaching new depths and the country is on the brink of falling apart."[248]

The influx of dozens of thousands of Syrian fleeing to Europe in the summer of 2015 resulted in an emergency in some European states, which evolved into political crisis on the continent. Major European leaders realized that the war in Syria was very relevant to their own countries and the result was an increased feeling of urgency within European states to more proactively address the war in Syria. That understanding was further emphasized following the terror attacks in Paris in November 2015 and San Bernardino, California, in December 2015.

The tragedy in Syria necessitates an intensive international effort that will lead to the end of the war. Ending the war is conditional on international persistence and determination. Given the five aforementioned developments, an arrangement to end the war in Syria may be a visible option. But after the war, what will be the new face of Syria?

The war in Syria marks the end of forty-five years of a brutal 'Alawite dictatorship in Syria. The international community and Assad's opponents view free elections as the right and desirable way to end the crisis in Syria and start the path toward rehabilitating the ravaged country. Since the overwhelming majority of Syrians are Sunni, free and fair elections would inevitably result in a Sunni government—an intolerable outcome for Iran and the 'Alawites, and therefore these elections are unlikely.

A more probable scenario is the disintegration of Syria into protectorates. One protectorate, along the Syrian coastline, where most 'Alawites live, would be secured by Russia and Iran. The purpose of this territory would be to defend the 'Alawites and to secure and maintain Iran's access to the Mediterranean Sea and thereby ensure the supply line through which Iran supplies Hezbollah with weapons and ammunition, thus guaranteeing Iran's influence in Lebanon. Such a development may involve the transfer of 'Alawite communities who live in major cities like Damascus and Aleppo to the 'Alawite protectorate. This thought process could explain why Iran is considering sending massive military reinforcements into Syria as part of a defense pact with Syria,[250] and why a force of fifteen hundred Iranian troops recently arrived in the coastal city of Latakia.[251] It also potentially explains why the Iranian attaché in Iran's embassy in Syria is reported to have announced that Iran is interested in establishing a direct maritime line with Syria.[252]

However, the fate of an 'Alawite entity, as of the beginning of 2016, is to a large extent in Russia's hands. Iran's ability to send significant military reinforcement to Syria is doubtful, as showcased in December 2015 when, according to Western military sources, it began to substantially withdraw its forces from Syria. It's also doubtful that Hezbollah could secure the southern side of an 'Alawite entity. Hezbollah's limited manpower capacities do not allow it to stretch its forces along dozens of miles while at the same time thwarting the growing threats of revenge from Sunni Syrian and non-Syrian rebel groups already operating along the Lebanese-Syrian border. The area would be surrounded from the north, east, and southeast sides by hostile Sunni forces. 'Alawite communities along the Syrian coast are already exposed to daily rocket attacks by the rebels.[253] This 'Alawite "pocket" is vital to Iran's strategic interests. However, at the same time, it could be problematic for Iran. Surrounded by hostile Sunnis, this 'Alawite territory is very vulnerable. In the context of the Shiite-Iranian, Sunni-Arab conflict, Turkey and Saudi Arabia could easily hold this 'Alawite protectorate hostage.

A disintegration of Syria could also lead to ethnic and geographic–based protectorates: a Turkish protectorate in northeast Syria, mostly representing the Kurds; a Jordanian (and indirect Saudi and Israeli) protectorate in south Syria representing the Bedouin tribes and the Druze of south Syria; and a Russian-Iranian 'Alawite protectorate in northwest Syria representing the 'Alawites. These entities might operate within a political umbrella"—possibly a confederation or federation named "Syria"—but the political structure, the balance of power, and the authorities of such a body would be nothing like those of pre-war Syria.

At present, a scenario of understandings and a new balance of power between the major regional players involved in the war—Iran, Saudi Arabia, and Turkey—appears unachievable; the Sunnis and 'Alawites in Syria won't all of a sudden get along. But they might find ways to live side by side. After all, this is the Middle East—a region where yesterday's bitter enemies who brutally butchered one another are today's allies. For eight years, from 1980–1988, Iran and Iraq fought a vicious war in which one million people were killed, cities were bombed, and chemical weapons were used with gruesome results. But today, Iranian forces, invited by the Iraqi government, are fighting ISIS on Iraqi soil. 'Alī 'Abd Allāh Ṣāliḥ, Yemen's former president, fought Houthi tribes for years. In the war sparked in Yemen in 2014 between Houthi tribes backed by Iran and Arab military coalition, Ṣāliḥ is an ally of the Houthi tribes.

The road toward any peaceful arrangement for Syria is long and winding. Until one is made, Syria will continue bleeding and many more people will pay the price. In March 2015, the Lebanese journalist 'Ali al-Amin wrote an emotional article titled "In its Fifth Year, the Syrian Revolution Fights the International Community." In it he wrote:

> The Syrian revolution is an orphan. Yet, its will is invincible . . . and the Syrian revolution will win; it is inevitable. Four years ago, the children of Daraa [in southwest Syria] raised their fingers to mark the V sign. Assad cut off their fingers. Yet the blood from their cut fingers will give birth to a new Syria. A free Syria.[254]

CHAPTER SEVEN

LONG LIVE THE KING: THE MONARCHIC REGIMES

THE COUNTRIES IN THE ARAB WORLD that have monarchies are Bahrain, Jordan, Kuwait, Morocco, Oman, Qatar, Saudi Arabia, and the United Arab Emirates. Jordan, Morocco, and Saudi Arabia have a king; the rest are ruled by emirs or, in the case of Oman, a sultan.

The only monarchical Arab countries that have experienced activities inspired by the Arab Awakening—such as mass demonstrations, ongoing political violence, social unrest, political instability, or fierce public debates in their media or political or academic circles—have been Bahrain, Jordan, Kuwait, and Morocco; the unrest, however, was not sufficient in caliber to jeopardize the stability of their regimes.

But times have changed and today the regimes are very aware that the earthquake that has shaken the foundations of the Arab world is likely to reach them. To take preventative measures, most of the monarchies have been promoting reforms in a gradual manner. The monarchies in the Arab world, at present, are surviving the aftershocks of the earthquake—but this is by no means due to a lack of challenges. Significant social and economic distress prevails in most Arab monarchies. In fact, the precursor to the Arab Awakening took place in Jordan, where a monarchy has been in power since 1921. In the summer of 2010, a few months before Bouazizi set himself on fire, extravagant and ostentatious celebrations held to mark the fortieth birthday of Jordanian Queen Rania al-'Abdullah evoked furious reactions and led to violent demonstrations, chiefly in the southern cities of Jordan, which were suffering from high unemployment and poverty. King Abdullah II was forced to send in the Jordanian Army to subdue the riots.

So why are the monarchic regimes in the Arab world surviving at a time when some Arab countries are experiencing enormous upheavals and others are in the process of disintegration? It appears that three central factors are granting them—at least at this stage—"a certificate of immunity"—albeit one that's not unlimited.

One factor is that in the majority of the monarchical Arab Gulf or Persian Gulf states, and to a lesser extent in Jordan and Morocco, societies are made up of tribes. The tribes are represented in the government in such a way that they all share power, thus ensuring that the needs of their respective communities are met. Political and social leaders have an interest in preserving the stability of their country's socio-political-economic system—and the monarchies that guarantee them—to make sure their voices are heard. A good example of the perseverance of the monarchies took place in Saudi Arabia, with King Salman's ascent to the throne. Immediately after King Abdullah's funeral ended, a ceremony was held in the presidential palace and the entire leadership of the Saudi regime swore allegiance to the new king, Salman. The message inherent in a speedy, smooth, and supported transition of leadership in Saudi Arabia was clear: the monarchy must show the people that it will maintain power and will keep stability.

A second factor is the enormous wealth of the Arab Gulf monarchies, which enables them to provide their citizens with a high quality of life in areas like education and healthcare, as well as a guaranteed income. According to the Arab world's Gulf Cooperation Council (GCC),[1] the gross domestic product of the Arab Gulf States—all of which are monarchical except Iraq—is $1.60 trillion.[2] This constitutes approximately 40 percent of the $2.853 trillion gross domestic product of the Arab world in 2013.[3] Estimates from OPEC note that almost 66 percent of the world's proven oil reserves are located in its member countries in the Middle East: Iran, Iraq, Kuwait, Qatar, Saudi Arabia, and the United Arab Emirates.[4, 5]

A third factor in what seems like a "certificate of immunity" for the monarchies is the people's emotional solidarity with them that is based on three central components:

The first component is the perceived legitimacy of the royal dynasties on a religious basis. The monarchies in the Gulf, with Saudi Arabia's House of Saud monarchy as their leader, are located on the Arabian Peninsula, where the religion of Islam and Arab culture were born. The title of the Saudi king is Ḫādim al-Ḥaramayn aš-Šarīfayn, "Servant of the Two Noble Holy Sites," a reference to his leadership over the Saudi cities of Mecca and Medina, two of Islam's three holy sites. The third holy site is Jerusalem, or as it is called in Arabic, al-Quds, "the holy." One of the titles of the Jordanian king is Abid al-Quds, "Servant and Defender of al-Quds." (This title was bestowed upon the king of Jordan because between 1948–1967, Jordan ruled the east part of Jerusalem including the old city of Jerusalem and the al-Haram al-Sharif compound known also as the Temple Mount compound.)

The second component is the legitimacy of the royal dynasties based on familial lineage to Prophet Muhammad. The Hāshimite Dynasty of Jordan traces itself back to the grandfather of Muhammad the Prophet. The royal dynasty in Morocco traces itself to the daughter of Muhammad.

The third component is the people's affection for and admiration of their monarch. A video posted on YouTube in December 2013 exemplified the feelings of the Jordanian citizens toward King Abdullah II. In the video, a group of men is seen trying to free a car that was stuck in the snow in Amman, the capital of Jordan. Partway through the endeavor, it becomes clear that one of the men who have lent a helping hand is none other than the Jordanian king, who had passed by (by chance or not . . .), saw the men struggling, and joined the operation. When the identity of the anonymous man pushing the car is discovered, the men burst into spontaneous cries of support: "Long live the king, long live the king!"[6]

The importance of emotional connections in the Arab world should not be underestimated. Arab culture and society are tribal, and values of devotion, loyalty, and obedience to the leaders are deeply rooted. Ceremonies like the *bay'ah*, an oath of allegiance, are reflective of this devotion and are important traditions.

So what does the future hold for the Arab monarchies?

In the short and medium term, the stability of the monarchies will be preserved. For the monarchies, the need for their country's domestic stability is an existential interest; their survival depends on the support of their people—and their policies will therefore continue to be subordinated to this interest.

The desire for stability has also led the monarchies to develop initiatives between themselves, with the belief that if the Arab world's monarchical system can be strengthened across-the-board, it will support their survival. This process is playing out in the form of bilateral agreements and cooperative ventures between the Gulf monarchies—Bahrain, Kuwait, Qatar, Saudi Arabia, and Jordan—in areas such as the economy, security, and trade. An example of mutual cooperation is the participation of the Jordanian and Moroccan air forces in "Operation Decisive Storm," the Saudi-led effort in Yemen in April 2015 aimed at preventing Houthi Shiites in Yemen from succeeding in a violent takeover of the country, which is mostly Sunni. This led to an expanded strategic cooperation between the Gulf monarchies, Jordan, and Morocco. This alliance is in addition to the political and economic alliance known as the Gulf Cooperation Council, which was established in Abu Dhabi in 1981 between Bahrain, Kuwait, Oman, Qatar, Saudi Arabia, and the United Arab Emirates. The GCC is a regional intergovernmental political and economic union of the Arab Gulf states. It initiates, enhances, and coordinates regional policy, cooperation, and projects among its members on a plethora of issues and in a wide array of fields from education and technology to security and welfare; all designed to serve the member countries as well as the region.

Saudi Arabia

Saudi Arabia, the birthplace of Islam, will continue to stand at the head of the camp of monarchies and make great efforts to achieve stability. This was openly expressed by Saudi Prince bin Ṭalāl, one of the most influential people in the global economy, in a 2013 television interview when he said, "Reforms are indeed called for and critical, but they will be instituted according to the rhythm and scope that we determine to be correct and appropriate for us. We will not allow the Arab Spring to bring anarchy to our country." In his home country, these gradual reforms have included giving women the right to vote and to run for the Majlis al-Shura (a legislative body that advises the king of

Saudi Arabia); women were allowed to vote and be elected for the first time in municipal elections in December 2015. Saudi Arabia has also boosted its efforts to address its vast problems by broadening welfare programs and undertaking initiatives to diversify the economy and address the housing and unemployment crises, specifically among young people. The Saudi monarchy is intent on preventing protests and demonstrations that could lead to its downfall.

Bahrain

At this time, the largest potential for monarchical instability and unrest exists in Bahrain. One reason is Bahrain's demographic and political uniqueness. It is the only Arab monarchy in which a Sunni minority, its al-Khalifah dynasty, rules over a population that is majority Shia. The result is a relationship that is increasingly tense, manifested in periodic flare-ups of unrest and sometimes violence. The major political opposition to the Shiites in Bahrain is a non-governmental organization known as the Al Wefaq National Islamic Society. Since the organization was founded in 2001, there have been efforts to negotiate the constitution and division of power within Bahrain's political system. Thus far they've yielded few results, but the channels for political dialogue exist, and both Al Wefaq and the monarchy work to contain the animosity between the Shiites and Sunnis.

Bahrain, like Syria, Lebanon, and Yemen, has become a stage for the indirect, relatively low-intensity (at this stage) struggle between the two largest states in the Gulf: Saudi Arabia and Iran. Iran claims ownership over Bahrain, arguing it was part of Persia during the rule of Shah 'Abbās I (1588–1629) and was taken away by the al-Khalifah family with the support of the United Kingdom in 1783. Iran tries to enhance its influence in Bahrain by using the Shiites in Bahrain to increase unrest and instability. A peak in this drama unfolded in March 2011 when, in the face of violent Shia riots that threatened to topple the ruling family, Saudi Arabia sent soldiers into Bahrain to prevent a Shia takeover. The Saudi military involvement in Bahrain in March 2011 made it clear the Saudis will not tolerate an Iranian takeover of Bahrain. Today, the al-Khalifah family's reign is dependent on Saudi Arabia's support and patronage.

Jordan

At present and in the foreseeable future, the integrity of Jordan's Hāshimite monarchy seems intact. Nevertheless, Jordan faces significant economic, social, and political challenges and, concomitantly, is dealing with the repercussions of the war in Syria, its neighbor to the north, as well as the anarchy in Iraq, its neighbor to the east.

The enormous stream of refugees from Syria is a heavy burden on the already severely distressed Jordanian economy and is plunging the kingdom into debt.[7, 8] As of October 2015, the Zaatari refugee camp in northern Jordan, along the Syrian border, the biggest camp for Syrian refugees in Jordan, had a population of some eighty-one thousand people,[9] reportedly turning it into the fourth largest city in Jordan.[10] The United Nations High Commissioner for Refugees (UNHCR) stated that as of December 2015, there were more than 632,228 Syrian refugees in Jordan. The actual number is likely much higher. Jordanian officials estimate it to be double that number[11] because UNHCR numbers only reflect people who have registered as refugees with the United Nations. The Jordanian minister of planning and international cooperation, Imad Fakhoury, said in October 2015 that the cost of hosting the Syrian refugees in Jordan since the crisis began in 2011 is $6.6 billion.[12]

Militant Islamist organizations also constitute a potential threat to Jordan's monarchy. Groups such as ISIS in western Iraq and eastern Syria, and other militant Islamist groups in southern Syria, such as Jabhat al-Nusra, the arm of al-Qaeda in Syria, have established bases near the borders of Jordan. In accordance with militant Islam's ideology, these groups see the Jordanian royal house, like all other rulers and governments in the Muslim world, as an illegitimate entity because they don't believe it rules in accordance with the pure virtues and values established in the early days of Islam—and therefore that it should be overthrown. In a booklet allegedly published by ISIS in April 2015 and titled *The Allegiance to the Caliphate and Not to the National State*, the writer claimed that all Arab territory—other than the areas in Syria and Iraq controlled by ISIS—is ruled by *kāfirun*, infidels, who do not obey the rules of Allah—their God—and Islam.[13]

Because of its location, Jordan holds great strategic importance and its stability is a shared interest of its neighbors to the west, Israel and Egypt, and its neighbor to the south, Saudi Arabia. It also shares a longer border with Israel than any other country—a fact that attracts militant Islamist groups who call for the destruction of Israel. From their perspective, control over Jordan would provide a perfect base to achieve this goal. In June 2014, an Israeli news website, Ynet, reported that Israeli diplomats informed the United States that Israel would fight ISIS if militant Islamist organizations threatened Jordan.[14]

Militant Islamist groups pose an external as well as an internal threat to Jordan. Externally, in April 2014, the Jordanian air force destroyed combat vehicles in the Ruwaished area of eastern Jordan that belonged to either ISIS or smugglers who had infiltrated Jordan from Iraq or Syria. The incident highlighted the sensitive security issues that face Jordan on its borders with Iraq and Syria. For example, in April 2015, ISIS claimed responsibility for an attack on Jordan launched from the border crossing between Iraq and Jordan.

Internally, many hundreds of Jordanians,[15, 16] possibly as many as two thousand, have left the country to join militant Islamist groups in Iraq and Syria.[17, 18, 19] According to Jordanian law, any Jordanian caught joining or having joined a terrorist group faces up to five years in prison—yet this threat has not proved to be a significant deterrent, as the numbers are on the rise. In May 2014, al-Qaeda flags appeared in the streets of the city of Ma'an, in southern Jordan, during riots protesting the social and economic distress of the city's residents.

Morocco

Similar to the king of Jordan, the king of Morocco, King Mohammed VI, enjoys a high degree of popularity among the people in his country—but he too is facing substantial challenges outside of Morocco that could impact the monarchy's future. A potential threat to the stability of the monarchy in Morocco stems from a strip of terrorist activity in North Africa, extending from Algeria (Morocco's neighbor to the east) through Tunisia, Libya, Egypt, Gaza, Syria, and Iraq.[20] Due to tight security measures, Morocco has been successful in handling the threat—but it's now facing new dangers. Many of the fighters in the Sunni groups battling in Syria—estimates range from many hundreds to thousands—come from the countries of North Africa, specifically Algeria, Libya, and Tunisia.[21, 22] Of the estimated one hundred countries that have had citizens join the Islamic State and other violent extremist groups, Tunisia has had a higher number of people going to fight in the Syrian-Iraq arena than any country in the world, more than six thousand people.23 And once these fighters return to their home countries, they significantly strengthen their existing terrorist infrastructure. The Moroccan royal house is a tempting target for extreme Islamic groups, like ISIS, who would like to take control of the country. They see it as an illegitimate entity that should be brought down because its values do not align with theirs, and they consider Morocco an important base for the expansion of militant Islam into Europe.

Today, and in the foreseeable future, Morocco, like Jordan, has the intelligence, military, political, and security infrastructures to allow it to successfully deal with the potential threat presented by militant Islamist groups.

Looking Forward

Though the monarchies and the royal dynasties in the Arab Gulf will stay in power for the foreseeable future, a process is unfolding in Arab monarchies like Bahrain, Kuwait, Jordan, and Morocco, and, to a lesser extent, Oman, Qatar, Saudi Arabia, and the UAE, which will likely lead to the weakening of the political power of the monarchies as a result of the following trends:

1. Increased activity of organizations in the civil sector, along with the growing influence of the Internet and social media, are generating a process that increases the political power of individuals, civil society, and non-governmental organizations at the expense of the traditional centers of political power.

Both King Abdullah II of Jordan and King Muḥammad VI of Morocco have instituted political reforms, including broadening freedom of political and personal expression and improved civil rights, albeit in a gradual manner, while maintaining political and authoritative stability. The effect is that the countries' political parties are gaining strength, non-government organizations are taking on more responsibility, and individuals are increasingly making their voices heard. The relationships between the monarchies and their constituents are slowly, but surely, changing the character of these countries' societies and traditional internal balance of power.

2. A projected decrease in oil revenues, which may be exacerbated by Iran's entry into the oil market, will likely result in a decrease in most of the generous welfare policies of the Gulf monarchies, which was made possible until now by their wealth—money that is now becoming a double-edged sword. At the core of the welfare policies in the Arab Gulf states is the perception that in exchange for obedience to the ruler and minimal political involvement, citizens are entitled to that ruler's care for their welfare—particularly their economic wellbeing. The moment the ruler cannot take care of the economic needs of his citizens, this historical covenant will become invalid and an opening will be created for citizens to demand their rights by force.

A clear example of this occurred in Kuwait. Until a few years ago, Kuwait was synonymous with economic wealth. Because of its revenue from the oil industry, Kuwaiti citizens did not pay taxes and enjoyed free education, generous salaries, free health insurance, and affordable loans to purchase homes. Gasoline prices in Kuwait are only eighty cents a gallon and haven't changed much in a decade, and Kuwait's monarchy, under its emir, Sheikh Sabah IV al-Ahmad al-Jaber al-Sabah, subsidizes farmers, thus lowering the price of food (and reportedly resulting in an overconsumption of food and food wastage).[24]

Recently, however, demographic, economic, energy, and social changes have made Kuwait's welfare program an increasing burden on its state budget. Because of accelerated population growth, a sharp rise in the prices of raw materials and food, and the current and anticipated development of alternative energy sources that will lead to a sharp decline in the price of oil, and from there a sharp reduction in the main source of income for the Gulf states, Kuwait finds itself in growing distress. In October 2013, the prime minister of Kuwait, Sheikh Jaber al-Mubārak al-Hamad al-Sabah, announced that the generous welfare policy of the country could not linger on. The International Monetary Fund anticipates that in 2017 or 2018, the governmental expenses of Kuwait will exceed its revenues from oil.[25]

In an attempt to ensure their stability and power, it is likely that the monarchies will pursue policies to better manage their revenues and, at the same time, invest in infrastructure, housing, and jobs to improve the day-to-day lives of their citizens.

3. Transitions of power within the dynasties also have the potential for unrest, though generational transitions have so far been smooth.

In Saudi Arabia, according to Saudi law, the king must be a direct descendant of the founder of the Saudi Arabian kingdom, Muḥammad ibn Saʿūd. In January 2015, Salman ibn ʿAbd al-ʿAzīz Āl Saʿūd, the crown prince of the Saudi Arabian dynasty, was announced the seventh king, following the death of his half-brother, Abdullah bin Abdulaziz Āl Saʿūd. King Salman is eighty years old and reportedly not well. The next in line to be king after him is Prince Muqrin bin ʿAbdul-ʿAziz (born in 1945); he is the youngest surviving son of Abdullah bin Abdulaziz Āl Saʿūd and his rule will mark the last time that the king of Saudi Arabia will be a son of the founder of the kingdom. The next in line to the throne after Muqrin is Crown Prince Mohammed bin Nayef (born in 1959), the nephew of King Salman. He will be the first of Abdulaziz's grandsons to become king. The unavoidable question is if the shift of generations within the Saudi dynasty will be accompanied by a struggle over inheritance, and, if so, what the ramifications will be.

In Qatar, a "Velvet Revolution" took place in June 2013, in which its emir, Sheikh Tamim ibn Hamad al-Thāni, deposed his father. The exact circumstances of the coup and the son's motives were never publicly clear; however, it seems that the transition of power has not negatively affected its citizens, and has gone without any tangible or significant ramifications.

Qatar has consistently tried to position itself as a regional leader, but its ambitions and pursuit of independent policies often result in resentment from Saudi Arabia and other Gulf States. For example, because of Qatari support of the Muslim Brotherhood in Egypt and the dialogue Qatar conducted with Hezbollah, Saudi Arabia, Bahrain, and UAE, in March 2014, called their ambassadors back from Qatar. The crisis was solved in November

2014 following the signing of an agreement dictated to Qatar by the Gulf Cooperation Council and Saudi Arabia. This pattern of relations will likely continue, and the tense relations between the sides will experience escalations and lulls.

In the short and medium term, stability will likely be maintained by the Arab monarchies. Nevertheless, as both a result and a reflection of the events taking place in the region and throughout the world, there is a consistent process of change, albeit controlled, gradual, and moderate within the monarchies. Its essence is the reduction of the absolute political power of the royal families and dynasties and the strengthening of the parliamentary and non-parliamentary sources of power, including that of individual citizens, civil society, and non-governmental organizations and political parties.

In response to the growing chaos and instability in the region resulting from the Arab Awakening, the momentum of militant Islamist groups, and the growing Iranian aggressive regional policy, the Arab monarchies—particularly the Arab Gulf monarchies, led by Saudi Arabia—are liaising and developing regional policies using their wealth, political influence, and advanced military capabilities. This has been exemplified by the Arab military coalition against ISIS in Syria and the Houthis in Yemen, the massive support in funds and arms of rebel groups in Syria, and the substantial financial support that the Arab Gulf monarchies, especially Saudi Arabia, provide for Arab states like Egypt, Jordan, and Lebanon.

In the immediate and distant future, Arab monarchies are likely to not only outlast the Middle East turmoil but also to increasingly shape the Middle East.

CHAPTER EIGHT

THE FAILURES OF THE WEST

On June 4, 2009, President Barack Obama delivered a speech at Cairo University in Egypt titled "A New Beginning."[1] In it he called for the opening of a new page in the relationship of the West with the Muslim world. "I have come here," Obama said, "to seek a new beginning between the United States and Muslims around the world; one based upon mutual interest and mutual respect, and one based upon the truth that America and Islam are not exclusive, and need not be in competition. Instead, they overlap, and share common principles, principles of justice and progress, tolerance, and the dignity of all human beings."[2]

Obama's speech was viewed as a turning point and created expectations for a substantive change that would have a positive impact on the Middle East. Yet at the end of his second term in office, it seems that the only thing that exceeds the expectations of the Arab world following Obama's speech is the level of Arab disappointment in President Obama.

Today, to put it simply, many Arabs are convinced that his administration made a strategic shift by collaborating with Iran and throwing the Arab world under the bus.

Why do Arabs feel that way?

Let's quickly review some concepts we have explored in depth in other parts of this book. Two axes of a historic struggle have played—and continue to play—a central role in the history and the reality of the Middle East. One axis is the struggle between Sunnis and Shiites. An abyss of hostility, differing ideological and theological opinions, political clashes, and mutual violence has divided Sunni and Shiite Islam for more than thirteen hundred years. The other axis is the rivalry between two large regional civilizations: the Arab civilization of the Arabian Peninsula and the Persian civilization. Hundreds of years of political, military, and cultural rivalry have characterized the relations between these two civilizations.

Today as the wheels of history turn, the Sunni Arab world watches as its worst nightmare materializes. Four Arab states, Iraq, Lebanon, Syria, and Yemen, are today under the direct and indirect growing Iranian influence; the Iranian Revolutionary Guards, as well as Iranian-backed Shiite militias—Afghan Shiite militias, Hezbollah, and Iraqi Shiite militias—are fighting in Iraq and Syria; and in Yemen, the Iranian-backed Shiite Houthi tribe occupies central and northern Yemen, including its capital, Sana'a.

Iran is moving full steam ahead in occupying Arab states, either directly or indirectly, through proxies. A senior Iranian official announced that Baghdad, Iraq's capital, is the capital of the Persian Empire (though he later denied that he'd said this, arguing he was misunderstood).[3] Another Iranian official announced that Syria is the thirty-fifth district of the Iranian Empire.[4] Baghdad and Damascus are not only Arab state capitals; they were the center of the two biggest Arab Sunni dynasties that ruled the Muslim caliphate from 661–1250, and these dynasties were responsible for the creation of the Sunni-Arab domination over the Shiites and the Persian civilization. This helps explain why the Arab world is traumatized by the Iranian momentum.

And all of this seems to be accompanied by the silent blessing of the United States.

The signing of the Vienna Agreement in July 2015 between Iran and the "Five Plus One" states—China, France, Russia, the United Kingdom, the United States, plus Germany—regarding Iran's nuclear program fueled Arab concerns and anger and criticism toward Obama's policy. Arab states like Jordan, Kuwait, Saudi Arabia, and the United Arab Emirates formally gave their blessing to the agreement—yet it was mostly a diplomatic blessing. The statement often used in the Arab world regarding this agreement is, "We welcome the agreement because agreement is the right way." A "but . . ." or "however . . ." always follows, which reveals that the Arabs think that the agreement is dangerous.

Leading Arab analysts estimate that as a result of the agreement, the hundreds of billions of dollars that will flow into Iran will not be used to address its domestic hardships and alleviate the suffering of its people, but rather will be used by the mullah regime to increase its funding of its proxies in Iraq, Lebanon, Syria, Yemen, and the Gaza Strip. Arabs believe that the outcomes of the Vienna Agreement will bolster and increase Iran's aggressive regional policy, and that this will result in more violence and instability. They portrayed a gloomy future for the Middle East following the Vienna Agreement. At present, the Middle East is not on the verge of a nuclear arms race, but as a result to the Vienna Agreement, it is one step closer.

Today's Sunni world sees the Shiite Iranian mullah regime gaining momentum. Arab analysts are convinced that the momentum is taking place not only with the United States' silent consent, but as a joint US-Iran strategy aimed at making Iran the dominant superpower in the Middle East, ruling over the Arab Sunni world.[5, 6] They argue that the United States' dramatic shift toward Iran stems from the following reasons:

1. The US views the disintegrating Arab societies as a limping horse and believes Iran is focused, sharp, determined, and a source of strength.[7]

2. The US believes that Iran can generate and secure stability in the Middle East and can be useful in successfully fighting militant Islamist groups, like ISIS and al-Qaeda.[8, 9]

3. The US-Iranian alliance is part of an orchestrated deal aimed at supporting the interests of four partners: the United States, Iran, Turkey, and Israel—even at the expense of the crumbling Arab states and societies.[10]

4. The US has come to terms with the idea of a nuclear Iran, embracing a policy of containment and choosing to not confront Iran.[11] Part of the impetus for this stems from the fact that Iranian markets are desired by Western companies, and by signing a deal with Iran and lifting the sanctions, big money could be gained from the Iranian market.[12]

Some Arab analysts have called Obama's policies hesitant, inconsistent, directionless, and clumsy. According to that outlook, United States decision makers do not understand the Middle East at all, and as a result, the policies they create fail.

Khattar Abou Diab, a professor of Middle East studies at Paris University and the director of the Paris Center for Geopolitics, wrote in his article "The

Forbidden Love Affair between Obama and Iran," that "Obama's policy does not dialogue with the Middle East reality. . . . His hesitant policy increased Putin's ambitions."[13]

Saleh al-Kalab, the former Jordanian minister of information and culture and current member of the Jordanian senate, wrote in his article titled "These Are the Reasons Why Arabs Cannot Rely on the United States" that the "United States policy resulted in the rise of ISIS [and] the endurance of al-Assad regime . . . [and] it is the United States' policy that enabled Iran to expand its influence in the Middle East."[14]

On April 5, 2015, following the Lausanne interim agreements (the framework agreement by the five plus one states, the European Union, and Iran that outline the building blocks for reaching a full comprehensive agreement to resolve the Iranian nuclear crisis by the specified deadline),[15] Lebanese journalist Eyad Abu Shakra wrote in his article titled "What Is the Fate of Our [Arab] States Following the Lausanne Agreement?" that "the United States' Middle East policy is destructive."[16] Saudi journalist Mashari al-Zaidi wrote in an article titled "Lausanne Is Yours—Not Ours" that "the Obama administration has caused enormous damage to the Middle East; first by supporting the Muslim Brotherhood and then by supporting Iran."[17] Egyptian political analyst Adel Darwish wrote in an article titled "The Nuclear Agreement with Iran Threatens Peace" that "the gap between Obama's wishful thinking that the agreement seals the way for an Iranian nuclear bomb and the ambitions of the extreme Iranian regime is wider than the Atlantic Ocean, not the Arab Gulf."[18] Jamal Khashoggi, a Saudi columnist, wrote in an article titled "What Is Going to Kill Us Now: the Iranian Explosive Barrels or the Iranian Nuclear Bomb?" that "we [Arabs] do not have to subscribe to hallucinate Western policy makers who do not understand the Middle East reality nor care to do so."[19]

As a counterbalance to the criticism of the Obama administration, it is important to emphasize three things: First, in a way that is practically unavoidable, United States policy in the Middle East has always been subject to sharp criticism from factors in the Arab world and always will be, no matter the actions it takes or doesn't take. There will always be anger and criticism in the Arab world at the United States because of its support for Israel. Second, the Middle East is an extremely complex system, abounding with challenges, interests, changing-interests, counter-interests, inconsistent adversaries and alliances, and power struggles. It has a language and code of its own. Consolidating a policy for the Middle East labyrinth is a very challenging assignment. There is no uniform policy that would be appropriate for every situation nor is there one that will be satisfactory to all parties involved. Third, the fact that Middle East policy is criticized does not necessarily make the policy totally inaccurate or wrong. For example, the criticism in the Arab world of the United States' unwillingness to have boots on the ground in Syria does not necessarily attest to the fact that the United States policy on the issue was wrong or misguided.

There are people who argue, and with a measure of justice, that, in light of American interests, the decision not to send massive ground forces into Syria was a correct strategy. Some also argue in support of the United States' actions following the September 2013 ultimatum it issued to Assad after it was proven that the Syrian regime had used chemical weapons against Syrian civilians. The ultimatum demanded Assad hand over his entire stock of chemical weapons or face US military attack.[20] The fact that President Obama did not, in the end, act according to the ultimatum he had set, and decided instead to reach an agreement to eliminate the chemical weapons in Syria, was interpreted by some as a wise and advantageous policy that successfully achieved its goal without the use of military power.

Those more critical of US actions argue that Obama's unwillingness to fulfill the ultimatum contributed to the growing criticism of his policy in the Arab world. They argue that because the United States failed to follow through on its decisively stated threat, the American government was interpreted by Arabs to be weak and unreliable. As a result, not only did the United States not achieve its goal, it further eroded its image and influence.

Dr. Wahīd 'Abd al-Majīd, deputy director of the al-Ahram Center for Political and Strategic Studies, presented in his article titled "Who Will Defend Obama?" a long list of Arab criticisms of Obama's Middle East policy, including the episode of the fall 2013 ultimatum.[21] He concluded by expressing a concern that Obama, criticized for his policy and portrayed as a weak, hesitant leader will "make rash moves to correct the impression, thus resulting in more negative outcomes."[22]

This leads back to the West's misreading of the Middle East and a profound misunderstanding of the factors that shape it. A professor and writer on Middle East affairs, Dr. Walid Phares, an American of Lebanese descent, wrote is his 2014 book *The Lost Spring: U.S. Policy in the Middle East and Catastrophes to Avoid* that "the West failed to predict both cataclysmic seasons in world affairs and to meet their challenges." He wrote, "Washington is too hesitant to take action when necessary . . . [and] US foreign policy failed to see the explosions coming, didn't meet the challenges of political transformation where and with whom it should [have], and failed in isolating the Jihadi terrorists worldwide." He said, "Too many strategic errors were committed."[23] Dr. Phares's arguments reflect how the United States' faulty reading of the Middle East has led to negative results for both the region and the West. Andrew Green, the former British ambassador to Syria and Saudi Arabia, supported this thesis by writing that "the West's abject failure to understand the inner workings of these countries has had some disastrous effects."[24]

The West's Misunderstandings

One disturbing phenomenon of the inaccurate reading of the Middle East by the United States seems to stem from a fundamental lack of knowledge of basic terms. In 2011, General James Clapper, the director of the US Department of National Intelligence, appeared before a House Intelligence Committee hearing on Capitol Hill to discuss the Muslim Brotherhood. Clapper said, "The term 'Muslim Brotherhood' is an umbrella term for a variety of movements. In the case of Egypt, a very heterogeneous group, largely secular, which has eschewed violence and has decried al-Qaeda as a perversion of Islam."[25]

Clapper's statement reflected a disturbing misunderstanding of what the Muslim Brotherhood is, what it stands for, and what is aspires to accomplish. The Muslim Brotherhood eschews secularism, wanting instead for its extremist views on religion to thread through every aspect of life. Sayyid Qutb, who was one of the founding fathers of the Egyptian branch of the Muslim Brotherhood and who laid the ideological foundations of militant Islam in the second half of the twentieth century, stated categorically in his famous book

Ma'alim fi al-Tariq (*Milestones*) that secularism is the root of all evil. [26] Qutb used the Arabic word *ghartrasa,* which means defiance against Allah's rule, to describe secularism.

Clapper's inaccurate comment led, a few days later, to an official clarification statement by the Jamie Smith, a spokesperson for the Department of National Intelligence. Smith said: "To clarify Director Clapper's point, in Egypt the Muslim Brotherhood makes efforts to work through a political system that has been, under Mubārak's rule, one that is largely secular in its orientation. He is well aware that the Muslim Brotherhood is not a secular organization."[27]

In the West, the terms "truce" and "cease-fire" are used to set the ground for an agreement that will end conflict. In Arabic, there is a similar term, *hudna,* which describes a conflict mediation mechanism deeply rooted in Arab traditions. The term was first used during the time of Prophet Muhammad to describe a temporary truce, and over time it has become the standard term to describe a cessation of hostilities during jihad.[28] In 2008, Ḥamās's leader, Khaled Mashal, reportedly told former United States President Jimmy Carter that Ḥamās suggested ten years of *hudna* with Israel provided that Israel withdrew to the boundaries established following the Six-Day War in 1967. The suggested *hudna,* according to Mashal, was "proof of [Ḥamās's] recognition of the State of Israel."[29]

Following the meeting, in a public speech in Jerusalem, Carter called upon the United States and Israel to engage in direct negotiations with Ḥamās. He said that Ḥamās recognized Israel's right to exist and that "there's no doubt that both the Arab world and Ḥamās will accept Israel's right to exist in peace within 1967 borders." Carter could not have been more wrong in his analysis; the meaning of hudna, as interpreted by Ḥamās in the context of Israel, is contrary to this. Mashal did not mean that there would be a true truce or cease-fire, but simply "a lull." He later described this as "a tactic, a stage in the resistance, and nothing more." In May 2008, Mashal met the supreme leader of Iran, Ali Khamenei, and stated that "the Palestinian nation will continue its resistance despite all pressures and will not under any circumstances stop its jihad."[30]

Mashal's perspective has not veered from this. In 2012, as the guest speaker of the al-Nahda political party of the Muslim Brotherhood in Tunisia, he declared, "The negotiations with Israel must be stopped and ruled out eternally." He said, "The rifle is our only way. The core of the issue is the full liberation of all of

Palestine. That is our land and ours only—there should be no other people or foreigners on our land."[31] In the eyes of Jimmy Carter, a United States president, there had been a truce. In the eyes of Ḥamās, there had simply been a pause in order to regroup and wait for better circumstances to continue the conflict.

Another example of a disturbing lack of understanding and knowledge in the West is a broadcast made by a CNN security analyst. When interviewed about a July 2015 shooting in Tennessee that resulted in the death of five US marines, the analyst, Tom Fuentes, was unable or unwilling to conclude that the perpetrator was a Muslim even though information existed to support this. Fuentes said in the interview, "I know what the name sounds like, but we don't know that it's a Muslim name. We know it's an Arabic name."[32] The shooter had been identified as Muhammad Youssef Abdulazeez. Muhammad is the most common name for a male in the Muslim and the Arab world. Abdulazeez comes from Arab words. *Abdul* relates to the Arab word *'Abd*, which means "slave" or "servant," and *Aziz* means "the Dear One"—the Dear One being Allah. The name reflects a common Muslim name formation of *abdul* plus a reference to Allah. Other uses of it would be in combination with *Malik,* to lead to Servant of the *Ruler*; with *Rahman* to lead to Servant of the *Compassionate*; and *Jabbar* to lead to Servant of the Mighty One. The name is not just an Arabic name; it's also a Muslim name. The fact that the CNN analyst, a Western mediator of knowledge presented to the public as an "expert," did not know this is disturbing.

* * *

Let us look now at examples of missteps in the United States strategy regarding Middle East policy. To begin, at the height of the military clash between Ḥamās and Israel in the summer of 2014, the US secretary of state, John Kerry, presented a proposal for a cease-fire agreement between Ḥamās and Israel that was based on understandings that were reached between the United States and representatives of Qatar and Turkey—two major sponsors of the Muslim Brotherhood and its Palestinian offspring, Ḥamās.

Kerry's proposal came as a jolting shock to Egypt, Israel, the Palestinian Authority, Jordan, and Saudi Arabia—all of them US allies. The proposal included the opening of the Rafah crossing, which connects Egypt and Gaza, the promotion of the building and operation of a harbor in the Gaza Strip, and Israel's release of Ḥamās prisoners. It came across like a prize to be awarded to Ḥamās and its main attendants, Qatar and Turkey.

For Egypt, the proposed opening of the Rafah crossing was a terrible shock. Its president, Abdel Fattah al-Sisi, has a very tense relationship with Ḥamās and the Muslim Brotherhood. Since the second part of 2013, the relationship has deteriorated to the point that an Egyptian court defined Ḥamās as a terror organization, ordered that Ḥamās's properties in Egypt be frozen, and prohibited Ḥamās activity in Egypt. In December 2013, the Egyptian army announced the creation of a buffer zone, more than half a mile wide and seven miles long, on the Egyptian side of the border with Gaza.[33] It was part of Egypt's increasing efforts to destroy the massive tunnel system that connected the Gaza Strip and the Sinai Peninsula. By March 2014, it had reportedly destroyed more than thirteen hundred tunnels.[34] The Egyptian hard-line policy toward Ḥamās has resulted in strained relations between it and Turkey and Qatar because they're major sponsors of the Muslim Brotherhood and Ḥamās. It is hard to believe that the United States administration was not aware of this since it was an open and well-known rift.

Was this information not brought to Kerry's attention? If not—why? And if Kerry knew this then why did he, his staff, his analysts, and advisors pursue the Turkish-Qatari proposal, even though it was unrealistic to expect that Egypt—who physically holds the keys to the Rafah crossing, perceives Ḥamās as a threat to its national security, and was furious with Ḥamās and its sponsors, Turkey and Qatar—would agree to open the Rafah crossing? What made Kerry think that Egypt would adhere to agreements designed by Turkey, Qatar, and Ḥamās? Opening the crossing would reward Ḥamās and empower its sponsors. That was not going to happen.

If administration analysts and advisors were not aware what Egypt's take on the proposal would be, it is very disturbing. Equally disturbing is the possibility that Kerry was aware of this, yet ignored it. If that was the case, it is disturbing not because it was ignored, but because—as expected—the initiative failed and backfired on the United States. The fact that the US initiative was rejected intensified the United States' image as impotent instead of as a superpower capable of dictating its will. It also left a bitter aftertaste in the relationship of the United States with its allies in the Middle East—Egypt, Israel, Jordan, Saudi Arabia, and the Palestinian Authority.

On August 26, 2014, Ḥamās signed a cease-fire agreement brokered by Egypt. It was the exact agreement that was offered by Egypt when the 2014 war between Ḥamās and Israel, Operation Protective Edge, had started. The Turkish-Qatari offer brokered by the United States found itself in the garbage can.

There are a plethora of examples to support Dr. Phares's criticism of misguided American policies and beliefs—and a wealth of questions are the result. For example:

Why did the United States fail to foresee the Arab Awakening?

Why did American intelligence fail to see the looming crisis within the Muslim Brotherhood?

Why was the American administration surprised by the collapse of the US-backed government in Yemen?[35]

The answer could be that the United States consistently misreads the Middle East; it could be that American policy makers have been unable to identify the undercurrents in the Middle East and their impact. Since the mistakes can't possibly result from a lack of resources, capacity, or intelligent people, they must result from a built-in, systemic flaw.

Western policies are largely shaped by the narratives in and between five major circles: academics, large corporations, media, non-governmental and nonprofit organizations, and politicians. An examination of the process through which information and knowledge about the Middle East is conveyed and assimilated within these circles reveals two major weaknesses. One has to do with the mediating of information and the other has to do with the processing of information.

Language Barriers

A lack of fluency or at least some level of familiarity with Arabic has enormous ramifications. Without language skills, mediators of information about the Middle East are dependent on translated, sometimes deliberately manipulated, information. Not knowing Arabic impedes their ability to interact with a story and contextualize issues within a wider context. The complexity and layers of the story are hidden from the vast majority of Western mediators. They only see a partial image. In travels to the Arab world, they are exposed to limited voices and cannot understand the background noise. They can't understand the radio or TV news; can't hear what people talk about in coffee shops, barbershops, or academic settings; can't converse with cab drivers. They also can't read Arabic news, or things like graffiti, posters, and billboards. This compromises their ability to gain unguided and uncensored insight into society. It also limits their ability to acquire the tools they need to apply critical thinking regarding the information they are provided. As a result, what they intake and present to a Western audience, at best, reflects a small part of the picture.

Lack of language skills prevents them from having their finger on the pulse of the events and developments in the region. The commentaries, information, and opinions on the Middle East that they pass to their audiences, which form public opinion and impact policy, are fragmented and far from the true picture of what is actually taking place in the region. This is not to say that the reporters and journalists are unprofessional—they do their work professionally and passionately—and sometimes even put their own lives and safety at risk. They deserve admiration and appreciation, but not understanding Arabic limits their abilities, and this filter is something that most Westerners do not consider.

Interpretations through the Western Mindset

Western mediators of knowledge are also guided by a Western mindset and Western codes of thinking. They've been shaped by concepts regarding the Middle East that have been suffocated with Western terms like "colonialism," "democracy," "freedom," "human rights," "freedom fighters," and "pluralism," combined with a healthy dose of political correctness and relativism. These concepts, though resonating well with the like-minded hearts and heads of the Western audience, often do not dialogue with the Middle East reality.

A method of understanding this is through the book *Orientalism* published in 1978 by Edward Said. Said, who passed away in 2013, was a Palestinian educated in elite private schools in the Middle East and the United States who became a writer and professor of English literature and comparative literature at Columbia University. In *Orientalism*, Said argued that the West developed sophisticated mechanisms to justify and legitimize its rule over the people of the Orient in order to loot their wealth and procure their resources. The way the West did this, he reasoned, was with the development of the academic discipline of "Orientalism" and the fabrication of the so-called profession known as the "Middle East expert." The study of Orientalism and the Middle East expert, he argued, was created by the West to justify its domination and occupation of the East.

Said's theory sparked an intense debate within academic and intellectual circles. But in spite of the criticism and resulting debates, his concepts have become a cornerstone of the post-colonialism theory, which argues that although colonialism over Africa, Asia, and Latin America has ended and the people who were subdued to Western rule have gained their freedom, the nations of those continents are economically and militarily inferior to the West and thus remain subject to Western influence. Therefore, according to post-colonialism, the struggle against colonialism must continue.[36] This theory was popularized in intellectual circles in the West in the 1970s and in following years.[37] It exemplifies not only the percolation of narratives and theories but also the process of reading the processing of information. It shows how mediators of knowledge have created a "looping echo chamber" through talking among themselves and quoting themselves, and how this has percolated into the public consciousness. The concepts they created became "facts." The narratives they created became "reality." The theories they developed became "the truth."

In 2012, journalist Thomas Friedman wrote, "The Arab Awakening was driven not only by political and economic stresses, but, less visibly, by environmental, population, and climate stresses."[38] Friedman stated that "if we focus only on the former and not the latter, we will never be able to help stabilize these societies." Friedman is, like Said, a well-respected, influential writer with a powerful platform, but he too offered an observation that is not only not new, but also does not provide a better understanding of the Middle East's reality and instead misdirects. Nonetheless, his theory, like Orientalism, echoed.

In 2013, three American policy organizations, the Center for American Progress, the Center for Climate and Security, and the Stimson Center hosted an event for the release of a new volume on "Climate Change and the Arab Spring." Friedman was a panelist at the event.[39]

For perspective, it's helpful to recall some of the chaos that unfolded between the time of Friedman's article and the conference, April 2012–February 2013. In that period, Egypt struggled under growing political tension, instability, and disorder as its Muslim Brotherhood was on the brink of losing power; in Iraq, violence intensified and more than four thousand civilians were killed;[40] in Israel, it and Ḥamās were engaged in another intense military round; in Syria, the civil war had evolved into a full-blown and bloody Sunni-Shiite war. Throughout the region, militant Islamist groups expanded their presence and operation.

So while chaos, bloodshed, and turmoil were spinning out of control in the Middle East, Western academics, businessmen, journalists, non-governmental and nonprofit organizations, think tanks, and policy makers were spending energy, money, and time talking among themselves about things such as climate change and the Arab Awakening. A report by the Stimson Center titled "The Arab Spring and Climate Change" did not outrightly claim that climate change caused the Arab Spring, but it did cite it as a "threat multiplier."[41] Its self-description read:

> "The Arab Spring and Climate Change" does not argue that climate change caused the revolutions that have shaken the Arab world over the past two years. But the essays collected in this slim volume make a compelling case that the consequences of climate change are stressors that can ignite a volatile mix of underlying causes that erupt into revolution. The Arab Spring would likely have come one way or another, but the context in which it did is not inconsequential. Global warming may not have caused the Arab Spring, but it may have made it come earlier. Taken together, the phenomena they describe weave a complex web of conditions and interactions that help us understand the larger context for the Arab Awakening.[42]

In recent years, there has been a clear uptick in the amount of articles, cerebral capital, and resources that have gone into discussing the effects of climate change on the Arab Awakening. In May 2015, Obama said in reference to the war in Syria, "It's now believed that drought, crop failures, and high food prices helped fuel the early unrest in Syria, which descended into civil war in the heart of the Middle East."[43] An article from Sputnik International summed up a July 2015 report from the Department of Defense titled "National Security Implications of Climate Related Risks and a Changing Climate[44]" with the headline, "Pentagon Report Admits Disastrous Drought, Not Assad Caused Syrian Crisis."[45]

Before too long, the concept regarding the connection between global warming and the events in the Middle East was broadened by Western politicians to encompass another dimension: associating the rise of ISIS with global warming. Democratic candidate for the US presidency Bernie Sanders said, "Climate change is directly related to the growth of terrorism."[46] A similar opinion was expressed by another candidate, Martin O'Malley.[47] And Prince Charles, heir to the British throne, has echoed the concept. In an interview he gave in November 2015, he argued that "one of the major reasons for this horror in Syria is a years-long drought, which meant that huge numbers of people had to leave." He also said climate change had a "huge impact" on conflict and extremism.[48]

This dialogue, based on a domino effect of echoing reports and theories, distracts people and prevents scholars and policy makers from being able to see and address the core causes of the turmoil. The argument that "global warming may not have caused the Arab Spring, but it may have made it come earlier" led to a misdirection of resources that could have been used to cultivate and promote stability in a region grappling with chaos and violence. Neither drought nor climate change are responsible for the war in Syria or for the emergence of ISIS.

The United States and the Muslim Brotherhood

Another example of an arena in which Western concepts and erroneous narratives have resulted in poor US policy decisions is Egypt. Following the downfall of Mubārak in early 2011, Egypt entered a tense period with an escalating power struggle accompanied by violence and disorder. The first round of its parliamentary elections began in late November 2011, and final results weren't declared until January 2012. By early December 2011, the first round indicated that the Muslim Brotherhood and the Salafi movement were the big winners—and it was widely assumed that, in the end, the Muslim Brotherhood would emerge victorious. About a week after the first round, John Kerry, who was then serving as chairman of the United States Senate Committee on Foreign Relations, visited Egypt. While there, he and the US ambassador to Egypt, Anne Patterson, visited the headquarters of the Muslim Brotherhood's Freedom and Justice Party, in Cairo. The act gave a clear message: the United States recognized and legitimized the Muslim Brotherhood as the central political player in Egypt in the post-Mubārak era.

The meeting itself was not a wrong move—after all, the Muslim Brotherhood is a central political factor in the Arab world that cannot be ignored. What was wrong was the timing. The next round of elections, scheduled for December 14–15th and 21–22nd, was right around the corner, and yet the meeting was in advance of this. The result was perceived by political opponents of the Muslim Brotherhood as a rude US intervention into Egypt's internal affairs. Kerry's meeting was also insensitive given that, at the time, major allies of the United States, like the Arab Gulf states, Israel, and Jordan, were deeply concerned by the momentum of the Muslim Brotherhood.

It seemed that the US administration was oblivious to the 2010 speech given by Mohammed Badie, the Muslim Brotherhood's supreme guide, in which he said:

> Arab and Muslim regimes are betraying their people by failing to confront the Muslims' real enemies: not only Israel but also the United States. Waging jihad against both of these infidels is a commandment of Allah that cannot be disregarded. Governments have no right to stop their people from fighting the United States.[49]

It may also have been oblivious to the speech Badie gave in October 2011, not long before Kerry's visit, in which he proclaimed that "the improvement and change that the [Muslim] nation seeks can only be attained . . . by raising a jihadi generation that pursues death just as the enemies pursue life."[50]

Concerns among political opponents of the Muslim Brotherhood deepened throughout 2012, as it seemed that a United States romance with the Muslim Brotherhood was blooming. President Obama called Mohammad Morsi to congratulate him following his triumph in the presidential elections in 2012.[51]

The parliamentary elections were followed by a tense campaign to win the presidential elections that were scheduled for May and April 2012. In the midst of this, while Egypt was experiencing a tense presidential campaign, a delegation of the Freedom and Justice Party—the political party of the Muslim Brotherhood—arrived in the United States. The delegation's members had been carefully selected. All of them held advanced academic degrees and were fluent in English; it even included a woman—Sondos Asem Shalaby, the director of the English language website of the Muslim Brotherhood—who later served as the coordinator for foreign media relations in the Morsi administration.[52] Members of the delegation met with public officials and senior government personnel, including members of the White House staff,[53] and gave a plethora of media interviews. At times, members of the delegation were asked to discuss the non-democratic aspects of the Muslim Brotherhood's philosophy, such as its treatment of minorities and women. Yet, as accurately presented in a CNN report, "The delegation is really part of an international charm offensive, analysts and critics say, that is strategically unrepresentative of the deeply hierarchal Brotherhood."[54]

The friendly approach of the United States administration toward the Muslim Brotherhood at the time was guided by the mindset that the Muslim Brotherhood, in spite of its extreme ideology, could act as a pragmatic player if it was included in policy development and decision-making. That mindset has validity, but the American administration, blinded by that thinking, made a crucial error in being so swept away that it failed to identify the undercurrents that were flowing through Egyptian and Arab societies. Had it done so, it would have seen indications of the strong possibility that the Muslim Brotherhood's rule would not endure.

American policy makers did not accurately decode Egypt's politics. They misread the atmosphere on the Egyptian street, underestimated the significance of the groups opposing the Muslim Brotherhood, and failed to understand that the Muslim Brotherhood's largest political triumph would cause what became crises in Egypt, Tunisia, and Jordan. Its attempt to force its agenda on the Egyptian people practically brought Egypt to the verge of civil war, forcing the Egyptian army in July 2013 to end the Muslim Brotherhood's rule in order to return to stability.

In considering the visit of the delegation of the Muslim Brotherhood to the United States, Arab journalist Mohamed Elmenshawy, a former fellow of the Middle East Institute in Washington, DC, published an article in which he summarized the visit of the delegation to the United States as a successful one. The title of the article "*Ghazwah Najekha lilikhwan fi* Washington" translates to "A Successful Raid on Washington by the Muslim Brotherhood."[55] The word *ghazwah* has a clear connotation in Islamic historiography: it is used to describe the successful Islamic military campaigns of expansion in the seventh century, the century Islam was born.[56] It is also used by militant Islamist groups to reference a more recent event—September 11, 2001. Most Western mediators of knowledge about the Middle East or policy designers have likely never heard this term. It's also likely that American media that covered the visit of the Muslim Brotherhood delegation in a friendly manner, and the plethora of officials who met with the delegation, were unaware that in the internal vernacular of the Muslim Brotherhood, the visit was defined as ghazwah.[57] If Americans knew that the Muslim Brotherhood defined its visit to the United States the same way that al-Qaeda defined the terrorist event that caused the deaths of thousands of Americans, it might have aroused a rage and put pressure on decision-makers to reconsider reaching out to the Muslim Brotherhood. Had the US administration been familiar with the term, it might have avoided the unnecessary subsequent tension with Egypt and spared itself embarrassment connected to a January 2015 visit the Muslim Brotherhood made to the US Capital.

For the January 2015 visit, a delegation of Muslim Brotherhood members was invited to Washington, DC, by the Center for the Study of Islam and Democracy[58] to meet with top State Department officials. During the visit, one of the delegation's members, Judge Waleed Sharabi, the secretary general of the Egyptian Revolutionary Council,[59] whose goal is to topple the rule of Sisi, posted a picture of himself on his Facebook page,[60] in which he was posing under the US State Department's logo and a United States flag and holding up four fingers to make the *rabia* sign, a symbol named after Cairo's Rabia al-Adwiyya square. The square is named after an early Islamic female Saint, Raabi'ah al-'Adawiyyah, who was also called *Umm al-Kheir* (Mother of Goodness) and is a symbol of humble female worship in Islam.[61] Following the 2013 ousting of Mohammad Morsi, the square became the epicenter of protests by both supporters and detractors of the Muslim Brotherhood. The four finger sign used at the demonstrations spread throughout the Arab world. Its message protested the fact that through a military coup Sisi ousted the democratically elected President Morsi; it indicated the belief that because Morsi had been elected democratically, he should have stayed in office. This disregarded the fact that following the coup, Sisi, too, was elected in a democratic election.[62] Sharabi's photo did not improve US relations with Middle East regional powers like Egypt or Saudi Arabia.

The United States' displeasure over the ousting of the Muslim Brotherhood was exhibited by its withholding of military support for Egypt. This embargo lasted until April 2015. To have better determined how to proceed with Egypt and its Muslim Brotherhood, the American administration should have been watching the public discourse in Arab social media, cultural expressions of the political power struggle, the economic challenges and their domestic impact, and the impact on Egypt of other developments in the Arab world.

Western Views on the Israeli-Palestinian Conflict

Another example of the West's inaccurate reading of the Middle East was the assumption that solving the Israeli-Palestinian conflict would stabilize the region. In 2009, James L. Jones, then Obama's national-security adviser, stated:

> Of all the problems the administration faces globally, if there was one problem that I would recommend to the president that if he

> could do anything he wanted to solve—one problem—this [the Israeli-Palestinian conflict] would be it. Finding a solution to this problem has ripples that echo, that would run globally and affect many other problems that we face elsewhere in the globe. . . . This is the epicenter, and this is where we should focus our efforts. And I am delighted that this administration is doing so with such enthusiasm and commitment.[63]

Jones's belief that solving the Israeli-Palestinian conflict would "affect many other problems that we face elsewhere in the globe"[64] is a narrative that has caused many US administrations to put heavy efforts into trying to end the conflict. Michael Doran, a former US deputy assistant secretary of defense and a former senior director of the National Security Council, mirrored these sentiments in September 2014. He stated:

> Before anything else, American leaders need to repudiate, once and for all, what Elliott Abrams [who served in foreign policy positions for Presidents Ronald Reagan and George W. Bush] calls the "epicenter" theory: that is, the notion that the Israeli-Palestinian conflict is the central strategic question in the Middle East. While no American president has embraced this theory in any formal sense, almost every president since Jimmy Carter—and every secretary of state since Cyrus Vance—has taken it as axiomatic that to formulate a Middle East policy means initiating and presiding over a "peace process."[65]

The Israeli-Palestinian conflict is one of many conflicts in the region whose outcomes in terms of fatalities, human suffering, and destruction—as tragic as they are—are very small in comparison to the results of other conflicts in the Middle East. The Israeli-Palestinian conflict contributes to the instability in the Middle East, but solving it will not stabilize the region. The forces and undercurrents causing instability are far bigger and deeper, and most have nothing to do with the Israeli-Palestinian conflict. Solving the Israeli-Palestinian conflict will not end the war in Syria, thwart the chaos in Iraq, Libya, and Yemen, calm the turbulence in Egypt, Jordan, or Lebanon, make militant Islamist groups disappear, end the Iran-Arab power struggle, or address the underlying issues challenging Arab societies.

The centrality of the Israeli-Palestinian conflict in the public discourse and political arena in the West may appear in Western circles to be a reflection of the centrality of the conflict in the Arab discourse and media—but a review of Arab media platforms (aside from Palestinian ones) shows that on a daily basis, the Israeli-Palestinian conflict does not capture the headlines of Arab media. This is because most Arab societies have massive challenges of their own to address.

In 2011, Lebanese columnist Suleiman Taqi al-Din wrote in an article titled "We and Palestine and the Arab Revolutions" that "the Arab Spring pushes aside the issue of Palestine. Anyhow, that issue was mostly used (by Arab leaders) to win popularity nothing more."[66] In 2013, then Lebanese Prime Minister Najib Mikati said, "Against the background of events in the Arab world, and particularly in Syria, the Palestinian issue is not included in the priority list of top problems in the Arab world and the world in general."[67]

As the Israeli-Palestinian conflict increasingly shrinks in Arab media and public discourse, it seems to increasingly capture a central position in Western ones. An obstacle to truly grappling with the issues of the Israeli-Palestinian conflict and sewing the path toward a real understanding is the impact of narratives that are deeply embedded within Western elite circles.

Jerusalem, Israel's capital, is home to more than eight hundred thousand people. About 25 percent—most of them Jews—live in neighborhoods located in the part of the city known as East Jerusalem. East Jerusalem refers to the area east of the Green Line, the Israeli-Jordanian cease-fire line set by Israel, Egypt, Jordan, Lebanon, and Syria in the Armistice Agreements that ended the 1948 war. The area known today as East Jerusalem had, prior to the 1967 Six-Day War, been part of the West Bank controlled by Jordan. Most parts of the land were unpopulated under Jordanian rule. Between 1948 and 1967 Jerusalem was physically divided between Israel and Jordan, a division marked by barricades, fences, trenches, and walls, the "Seam Line." Following the war, the Seam Line was erased by Israel and the area known as East Jerusalem became included within the municipal boundaries of Jerusalem under Israeli rule and law.

In the eyes of many members of the international community, East Jerusalem is illegally occupied by Israel and its sovereignty over East Jerusalem should not be recognized. But in the Israeli mainstream political camp's view, the city after the 1967 war was not occupied, but rather reunified. Since 1967, Israeli governments have built neighborhoods—many of which have become medium or large towns—on those lands. These communities are illegal settlements according to those who believe Israel is illegally occupying the land.

The neighborhoods have apartments, houses, businesses, schools, malls, etc., and while an evacuation of these neighborhoods in the framework of an Israeli-Palestinian agreement is viable, it is unlikely. An Israeli evacuation of the neighborhood of Gilo, with its fifty thousand inhabitants, the neighborhood of Talpiot, with its thirty thousand inhabitants, or other East Jerusalem neighborhoods seems unrealistic. Practical conversations about events likely to happen are a better use of Westerners' time than ones that consider unlikely steps, like Israel agreeing to this. The West's time is better spent discussing more realistic scenarios and top-priority conflicts.

A Difference in Terminology

The difference between the Middle East mindset and Western mindset is often reflected in terminology. It can seem as if the Middle East's dictionary includes only language related to violence and nothing related to diplomacy and dialogue—but this is a misperception. The Middle East dictionary does contain diplomacy and dialogue; however, in the dictionary of the Middle East, violence is sometimes a kind of diplomacy. Understanding this mindset would enable Westerners to understand an interesting Middle East phenomenon: that many times throughout its history, "yesterday's enemies" became "today's friends." For example:

Iraq and Iran conducted a bloody war from 1980–1988, which included the use of chemical weapons and missiles, and resulting causalities have been estimated at being between five hundred thousand and one million people. In addition to this, millions of people were injured and millions of people became refugees.[68, 69] Despite this, Iranian military forces are today, at the request of the Iraqi government, fighting shoulder to shoulder with Iraqi forces, on Iraqi soil, against ISIS.

In Yemen, Houthi Shiite tribes are fighting against the Yemeni government. A Houthi ally in the war is Yemen's former President ʿAlī ʿAbd Allāh Ṣāliḥ, who during his term in office, 1978–2012, conducted a relentless war against the Houthis.

Al-Qaeda gave birth to ISIS then disassociated itself from ISIS in 2014. ISIS, as al-Qaeda's branch in Iraq, created Jabhat al-Nusra, which is now al-Qaeda's branch in Syria. And today in Syria, ISIS and Jabhat al-Nusra are in a battle to the death.

There is also the example of Ḥamās's on-again-off-again romance with the Iranians, the Egyptians, the Palestinian Authority, the Qataris, the Saudis, and the Turks—and the wheel for this continues to turn. A famous Arab phrase is, "Me and my brother against my cousin; me and my cousin against our neighbor." It shows the relevant, transitory nature of friends and enemies.

Looking Forward

It's popular in the West to mention things off-the-cuff such as, "Everybody knows there is a humanitarian crisis in Gaza." But this begs the question of why they think this to be true. Most people do not speak Arabic and have neither been nor have had access to information in Arabic from the Gaza Strip. Just because something is commonly said does not make it true. An article in *Al Arabiya* in October 2012 titled "Although Poverty . . . Gaza Residents Flock to iPhone 5" reported that the iPhone 5, which at the time of the article's printing was not yet available in Israel, was sold in the Gaza Strip for between $1100 and $1500, and demand was so huge that as soon as stores received a shipment, they immediately sold out. The article noted that the iPhone, available at malls and stores throughout the Gaza Strip, was just the latest luxury product to be smuggled into Gaza through the tunnels from Egypt (Mercedes Benz is another big seller).[70] Other articles related to the Gaza Strip cover its booming real estate prices or highlight beach resorts, luxury hotels, and shopping malls.

For the United States, the failure to accurately interpret the Middle East has led to failures of American policy. For Israel, it has resulted in the emergence of vocal critics within Western circles of influence including academia, labor unions, the media, and nonprofits, such as the Free Palestine Movement and Students for Justice in Palestine, as well as anti-Israel campaigns like the Boycott, Divestment, and Sanctions (BDS) campaign.

Improving the West's ability to have a more accurate reading of the Middle East requires revolutionizing the process through which information regarding the Middle East is gathered, processed, evaluated, and assimilated. Solutions to this include:

- Recognizing that the lack of knowledge of Arabic diminishes the capacity to accurately read the Middle East, and encouraging the study of Arabic.
- Making Middle East studies build a solid objective knowledge of the region based on culture, history, and language, with a strong emphasis on the current events, developments, and trends that mold the region today.
- Prioritizing media literacy and critical-thinking skills through teaching professional intelligence methodology as a way to gather and analyze information.
- Reducing dependence on Western news platforms as the sole source for information about the Middle East by encouraging the use of Middle Eastern media news platforms.

Revolutionizing the educational process in the West toward information and knowledge about the Middle East requires the abandonment of misguided narratives. It also requires looking at reality through the lens and language of the Middle East. Acquiring better knowledge and a better understanding of the Middle East requires a dedicated effort of information gathering, evaluating, processing, and reevaluating. It's impossible to have a crystal ball, but it's possible to make educated analyses and predictions of what's to come.

CHAPTER NINE

THE STRUGGLE FOR IDENTITY: SALSA DANCING AND THE NIQAB

THERE ARE MANY TO WHOM THE name Fāṭima 'Ibrāhīm al-Baltāǧī doesn't mean anything—including many in the Arab world. It is the birth name of the Egyptian singer and musician known by the stage name Umm Kulthūm (the Mother of all Mouths), who is one of the most prominent cultural symbols in the Muslim and Arab world.

"All Arabs agree," reads *The Rough Guide to World Music*, "Umm Kulthūm is indisputably the Arab world's greatest singer."[1]

"The Lady of Cairo" was included in a 2010 series by National Public Radio (NPR) on "50 Great Voices,"[2] a show that discovered and rediscovered awe-inspiring vocalists from around the world and across time.[3] NPR reporter Neda Ulaby said:

> Umm Kulthūm's legendary concerts were broadcast live from Cairo on the first Thursday of each month from the 1930s to the early '70s. The Arab world's buzz and bustle stopped from Medina to Marrakesh, from Jeddah to Jerusalem. Shops closed. Families gathered to listen for four, five, even six hours of rapture.[4]

Ulaby quoted her father, a Syrian, who she said swooned when she asked him about the iconic singer. "It's so hard to describe," he'd said. "[Her] words penetrate into your ears, into your psyche, into your brain when you're listening to her say things like '*inta omri*,' which means, 'You are my life, you are my world.'"[5]

Umm Kulthūm was the nightingale of the Arab world, an icon known affectionately by her fans as the "Star of the East" and a symbol of Arab nationalism. A *Harvard Magazine* article read: "Imagine a singer with the virtuosity of Joan Sutherland or Ella Fitzgerald, the public persona of Eleanor Roosevelt, and the audience of Elvis, and you have Umm Kulthūm, the most accomplished singer of her century in the Arab world."[6] Both children and adults can recite many of her songs verse by verse. When she passed away in February 1975, millions of people lined the streets of Cairo for her funeral and a heavy mourning engulfed the Arab world.[7]

Today there are public buildings, town squares, and statues throughout the Arab world that have been named after Umm Kulthūm to keep her memory alive. In February 2013, Egyptians discovered, to their great shock and surprise, that the statue of Umm Kulthūm in the al-Manṣūrah district of Egypt had been covered with a *niqab*—an opaque cloth, usually black, that covers the face except for the eyes and is worn by Muslim women who obey the strict, modest dress of fundamentalist Muslims.

Just as quickly as the niqab appeared, the cloth covering the Umm Kulthūm statue was replaced with an Egyptian flag.

The covering of the statue of Umm Kulthūm with a niqab and the replacement of it with a national flag symbolically illustrates the many layers of the new chapter in the ongoing struggle in the Arab world over identity, path, and direction. It's a struggle that the Arab Awakening is accelerating, enhancing, and intensifying, as well as a process in which infinite desires and needs collide with limitless differing and sometimes opposing identities. It's long, complicated, and difficult, fraught with challenges and dangers, but it also presents opportunities.

What are the origins of this struggle for identity that is taking place in the Arab world? What is its core? And how is it expressed?

Islam—the dominant religion in the Arab world—is a religion, like Judaism, which contains many laws that guide the believer in every aspect of life. Muslim religious sages who have acquired official Islamic theological training and higher education as religious legal authorities are called *mufti* in Arabic and are qualified to issue *fatwās. Fatwās* address a wide variety of subjects pertaining to the private life of the individual.

Muslim religious legal authorities hold the most central position in the shaping of the personal, political, cultural, and social norms of the Muslim world, and they directly affect the lives of hundreds of millions of Muslims.[8] Jordan, for example, has an official government authority responsible for issuing fatwās. It's known as Dār al-Iftā.[9] (*Dār* means house and *Iftā* is the name of the action associated with issuing a fatwā). Among other services, Dār al-Iftā provides online legal ruling services through a center staffed by religious legal authorities. It operates 365 days a year—and other countries have similar bodies. There are also Internet-based platforms in a wide variety of languages that offer advice and guidance, sites such as www.fatwa-online.com,[10] www.fatwaislam.com/fis,[11] and www.jamiabinoria.net.[12]

Arab and Muslim cultural, political, social, and religious codes of conservative thinking and behavior have been consolidated over hundreds of years. In the late nineteenth and beginning of the twentieth century, the increasing presence of the West in the Arab and Muslim world, coupled with Arab encounters with the West and Western culture, led to the appearance of a stream of Islamic thinkers known as the "Islamist modernists." They were endorsed by scholars such as Jamāl al-Dīn al-Afghānī (1838–1897),[13] Muḥammad ʿAbduh (1849–1905),[14] and Rashīd Riḍā (1865-1935).[15] The Islamist modernists believed that creating a society governed by the ideals and laws of pure early Islamic sharīʿah, which also embraced modernity, was the cure for the challenges of Muslim society. Though opposed to the West and its values, the modernists did not regard the Muslim society's encounter with the West and its culture to only be a source of threat; instead, they viewed the meeting of the two as an opportunity for cultural, economic, political, and social growth—progress for Arab societies and for the world of Islam. Muḥammad ʿAbduh, for example, who held very senior positions in the Muslim establishment in Egypt—including serving as the grand mufti of Egypt, called for the reformation of rigid Islamic theology and methodology and advocated for things such as women's rights and empowerment and the abolishment of rituals and ceremonies whose origins lay in superstitions or traditions not indigenous to Islam.

But there were also Muslims, Arabs and non-Arab, who strictly saw the West as a danger, and believed it to be a threat to the societal structure of

Islam, a moral threat to Islamic culture and its conservative values, and an existential threat to Islam itself. These sentiments were expressed by "Islamic conservatives," thinkers like Mawlana Abū'l-A'lā Mawdūdī, (1903–1979),[16] the founder of Jamaʿat-i Islami (Islamic Society) in southeast Asia and its leader until his retirement in 1972,[17] Sayyid Abul-Hasan Ali al-Hasani al-Nadawi (1914–1999), an Islamic scholar and author,[18] and Egyptian teacher Ḥasan al-Bannā' (1906–1949) who, at the end of the 1920s, founded the Muslim Brotherhood. People who adhere to the Islamic conservative philosophy are often described in Arabic as *Islāmiyyun*, Islamists.

The establishment of independent Arab and non-Arab Muslim states during the twentieth century, the increasing economic, political, and social distress within Arab and non-Arab Muslim societies, the growing and deepening encounters with the West, and the appearance and popularity of mass media generated the emergence of two opposing camps in the second half of the twentieth century: the Islamist fundamentalist camp and a civil society–oriented camp. The ideological and political gap between the model of fundamentalist Islam in its two branches, violent and nonviolent, and the model of a nation state that appeared in the Arab and Muslim world in the twentieth century is unbridgeable.

In the late 1960s, an additional radicalization took place within the Islamic militant ideology with the development of the concept of *takfir*. It was at this time that a group in Egypt appeared called al-Takfīr wa al-Hijrah (Excommunication and the Holy Flight or Excommunication and the Migration),[19] which was founded by Shukrī Muṣṭafā, who saw violence and terrorism as a necessary means for "purifying infected Islam" and as a step toward the realization of the caliphate.[20]

The extremism and violence in militant Islam's ideology gave birth to even more severe extremism and violence. In an article by Lebanese political analyst Huda al-Husseini titled "ISIS Confronts al-Qaeda and Taliban in Afghanistan" and published in 2015, she wrote, "ISIS attracts thousands with its vision of looting and raping. . . . The growing struggle between ISIS and al-Qaeda will result in more bloodshed and the murder of humanity. When will the world wake up?"[21]

This is the line that connects late nineteenth–century Islamist modernists, like Muḥammad ʿAbduh, to mid-twentieth-century conservative Islamists, like Mawdūdī Abū'l-Aʿlā or Ḥasan al-Bannāʾ, to fundamentalists, like Sayyid Quṭb and Shukrī Muṣṭafā, who added increasingly violent components, to Ayman al-Zawahiri, the leader of the Egyptian Islamic Jihad in the 1970s (and the successor of Osama bin Laden), to the late twentieth–century leader Osama bin Laden, the founder of al-Qaeda, and his spiritual mentor, Abdullah Yusuf Azzam, a radical militant Islamist scholar of Palestinian origin (1941–1989), to the twenty-first century's Abū Bakr al-Baghdadi, the leader of ISIS.

In the continually evolving debate within Muslim and Arab societies regarding identity, path, and direction, a third camp known as *ʿilmaniya* (which roughly translates to "scientific") has recently emerged. It was inspired by mid-nineteenth-century scientific concepts that appeared in Europe, and with the establishment of independent states in the Muslim and Arab world during the twentieth century and the deepening of Muslim—Arab and non-Arab—societies in the West, it has come to embrace a stream of thought known as *tanwiriya* (which translates to "enlighten"). *Tanwiriya* advocates for the implementation of a civil society with Western values, such as freedom of expression, gender equality, and accountable governments, declared and laid out by the state's legislative and executive systems.

While Islamist streams are exclusively focused on forming societies centered on Muslim elements, the tanwiriya stream enables the expression of non-Muslim elements. In Western eyes, tanwiriya is usually considered to be synonymous with "secularism," but this is not necessarily the case. Many Muslim followers of tanwiriya view Islam as their spiritual and ethical guide.

The 1940s and 1950s saw the emergence of two significant political ideologies in the Arab world: *baʿathism* (resurrection or renaissance) and Nasserism, named after Egypt's leader Gamal Abdel Nasser. Though both *baʿathism* and Nasserism emphasized concepts like socialism and "liberation" and diminished the religious component, they weren't promoting statehood or a civil society, like ʿilmaniya and tanwiriya. Baʿathism and Nasserism promoted a model of a regional entity based on the ideology of pan-Arabism, which diminishes the importance of a national identity. Brutal dictators like Saddam Hussein and Hafez al-Assad came to power under the flag of ba'athism and Nasserism.

The gap between adherents of fundamentalist militant Islam and advocates of nation states and civil societies is unbridgeable. The gap between fundamentalist militant Islam and conservative political Islam—though they have some common denominators—is substantial, as is the gap between conservative political Islam and the civil society–affiliated camp. The room for compromise necessary to build a basis of agreement is small.

We are currently witnessing and will continue to watch for a long time to come, an immeasurable amount of contradicting outlooks in the Arab world that are functioning in extremely chaotic environments with people facing great stressors in all factors of life. The vying factors and individual choices will determine the road ahead and shape the lives of hundreds of millions of people. This explains why Umm Kulthūm draped in a niqab, and then in an Egyptian flag, symbolizes the various aspects of this struggle for identity.

One aspect of the question of identity has to do with civil rights, particularly women's rights. Women in the Muslim and Arab world contend with discrimination, injustice, and oppression whose sources are rooted in traditions and social norms and sometimes even anchored in legislation. In Oman, for example, women only inherit 50 percent of what men do, and while a man can divorce his wife for any reason, a woman needs a good reason for requesting a divorce.[22] In the United Arab Emirates, a woman's testimony in court is half as significant as a man's testimony.[23]

Fundamental Islam views women as inferior and the suppression of women as an unquestionable religious imperative with no space for flexibility. Under the rule of the Taliban in Afghanistan, severe restrictions were imposed on women by law. Women were not allowed to work; were only allowed to leave the house if accompanied by their husband or brother; were not allowed to study; were not allowed to receive medical treatment by a male doctor without the presence of their husband; had no right to represent themselves in court; and could only be represented by a man.

The conservative Islamic camp also views women as inferior and the suppression of women as a religious imperative, but it leaves room for some flexibility. For example, it allows women to work and to study.

The statehood and civil society–affiliated groups strive for governmental legislation to ensure women's rights and gender equality.

There is a process underway—gradual, but consistent—that is strengthening the power of women in the Muslim and Arab world. Women are an important constituency and they are turning into a power that is increasingly politically courted.

After Egyptian President Abdel Fattah al-Sisi was elected in May 2014, he ordered the Egyptian minister of the interior to urgently institute legislation that would address the widespread sexual harassment and violence against women in Egypt. In response, the ministry established police departments to combat violent crimes against women and appointed female police officers.[24] According to Ambassador Mona Omar, former secretary general of the National Council for Women, "Women's rights under the rule of President Sisi improved compared to their situation during the reign of President Mohammed Morsi and the Muslim Brotherhood." Omar explained that the 2014 constitution enhanced the situation of Egyptian women, saying, "Egypt's new constitution contains articles in favor of Egyptian women."[25] According to article 11 of the revised constitution, Egypt "commits to achieving equality between women and men in all civil, political, economic, social, and cultural rights in accordance with the provisions of this constitution."[26] In December 2015, women in Saudi Arabia were, for the first time, allowed to vote and be elected in municipal elections.

As women's political power grows, more politicians will speak on behalf of achieving equality by improving things like education for women and their career opportunities. This said, in the second decade of the twenty-first century, women in Arab societies are not only discriminated against by law, they are also far from maximizing their political potential. According to a United Nations report from January 2015, the Middle East and North Africa ranked second to last in their percentage of women parliamentarians with just 16 percent (the Pacific was the lowest with just under 16 percent).[27]

The covering of the statue of Umm Kulthūm was a showcase of the struggle over the subjugation and independence of individuals, as well as the character and identity of Arab society as a cultural, social, and political system. It illustrated the difference between the worldview of the civil society–affiliated camp that wishes to encourage pluralism and openness, the worldview of the conservative Islamic camp that wishes to maintain its norms and way of life with little room for tolerance, and the worldview of the fundamentalist Islamic camp—both its militant and non-militant streams—that mandates the strict implementation of Islamic fundamentalism with an uncompromising intolerance for pluralism of any kind.

Another aspect of the covering of the Umm Kulthūm statue has to do with symbols of identity. Fundamentalist Islam aspires to negate all references to, and abolish all symbols of, identities in Arab society that are not Muslim. For instance, elements of the Salafi movement in Egypt seek to destroy the pyramids and the Sphinx—some of Egypt's most prominent symbols—because they are not Islamic symbols. ISIS and al-Qaeda have targeted and systematically destroyed archeological treasures and artifacts—ancient cities, temples, palaces, mosques, tombs, statues, museums, shrines, and other non-Islamic cultural symbols in the regions they have taken over in Iraq, Syria, and northern Africa. In the areas ISIS has conquered in Syria, it has ordered the blotting out of any mention of the official name of Syria—the Syrian Arab Republic—and requires the use of the "Islamic State" in its place.

The act of replacing the niqab with the Egyptian flag on the statue of Umm Kulthūm expressed the support for Arab nationalism, the idea of the independent nation state, the civil society–oriented camp's concept of statehood, and the identification with symbols that define national independence and the sovereignty of Arab states—things like a national flag, secure borders between states, a national currency, and a national anthem. It also expressed the civil society camp's identification with a pan-Arab cultural identity and symbols that are not necessarily Islamic. An example of this is the Christian Lebanese singer Fairuz, who is considered a cultural icon of the Arab world on the scale of Umm Kulthūm, or the Christian Lebanese movie star Sabah, whose funeral in 2014 was attended by delegations of artists and public figures from throughout the Arab world.

In August 2015, as Egypt prepared for celebrations marking the opening of the new Suez Canal, the streets of Cairo were decorated with national flags. Unfortunately (apparently there was a shortage of flags), they were not the flags of Egypt—they were the flags of Yemen. The flags have the same color, pattern, and shape, but the Egyptian flag has an eagle. An Egyptian television crew interviewed people on the street asking them if the flag was Egypt's flag and the answer ranged from a decisive "yes" to "the eagle is missing, but it is still the same flag."[28]

The struggle between the different movements over the identity, path, and direction of the individual and Arab society as a whole seeps into every nook and cranny of private and public life. Here are some examples:

At the end of 2010, the Saudi government announced its intention to block the surfing functions of BlackBerry devices. The reason given for doing so was because terrorist cells operating in Saudi Arabia were using these functions to initiate and coordinate domestic terrorist attacks. The real reason was completely different. Saudi Arabia is a very conservative society, and there are stringent laws within it regarding separation between women and men. Religious sages in Saudi Arabia were alarmed to discover that young men and women in Saudi Arabia were using BlackBerrys to arrange romantic dates, particularly in air-conditioned shopping malls, which is a serious breach of strict social norms and behaviors. The block was not, in the end, implemented. There was a fear of diplomatic complications with the government of Canada, the home of BlackBerry Ltd., and a fear that blocking the functions would prompt social protests, but the intention had been announced.

Fast forward to 2015 and Internet and mobile connectivity is ubiquitous in Saudi Arabia, particularly its use of social networking sites like Facebook, Twitter, and YouTube, and messaging apps like WhatsApp.[29] It even has popular dating websites. The dating website Topface explains itself by stating: "Topface is an easy and free dating service in Saudi Arabia and around the world. Meet guys and girls online, make friends, and find your love right now! Join us!!"[30] It claims to have connected more than ninety-nine million people.[31]

The dating website LoveHabibi has text that reads:

> At LoveHabibi, we've helped thousands of Muslim and Arab singles find true love and everlasting happiness. As one of the leading Muslim and Arab dating sites, we are committed to helping our

> members find the absolute best matches possible. There are plenty of dating sites to choose from, but what makes LoveHabibi unique is that we're one of the only dating sites that exclusively caters to Arabs and Muslims seeking friendship, dating, and marriage, while still adhering to your Islamic or Arab-Christian values and beliefs.[32]

Other popular sites and apps are Mingle2, Arab Lounge, and SinglesAroundMe, whose description reads: "The SinglesAroudMe (SAM) app is the new cool way to find singles and it is a must have app for singles on the go, like you."[33]

The flip side of this is that there is also a growing conservative presence in the digital realm. Conservative cleric Dr. Muhammad al-Arifi, for example, is ranked eighty-sixth[34] on twittercounter.com's list of most followed tweeters, with more than thirteen million followers. He is the only preacher or scholar in the top one hundred Twitter users in the world.

In 2011, the Iraq Civil Society Solidarity Initiative (ICSSI) was established to, in the words of its mission statement, "facilitate the process of building concrete links of solidarity between international civil society organizations and the growing Iraqi civil society, through practical projects that promote human rights and support the efforts against sectarian divisions, corruption, and violence."[35] Yet in Iraq in 2012, young boys and girls were murdered because they imitated the dress and behavior—through clothing, physical gestures, body language, symbols, etc.—prevalent in Western "heavy metal" or "emo" cultures. Reportedly, the murders were "approved" by the Iraqi government and the Iraqi authorities employed informers in universities to provide information on the teenagers to aid their arrest.[36] The Iraqi Ministry of Interior Affairs reportedly announced that it was "fully authorized to eliminate the emo phenomenon because it threatens Iraqi society."[37]

In an article titled "The 'Emo' Phenomenon and the Killing Sprees in Iraq," Iraqi-Kurdish journalist Girgis Gholizade wrote:

> The "Emo" phenomenon is a cry of distress from the youth in Iraq, who have grown up in a chaotic vacuum of values. It is the outcry of a young generation who has grown up in an atmosphere of terror,

> violence, neglect, corruption, and hopelessness. This is the youth of a society in which, every day, from twenty to seventy people are murdered against the background of ethnic animosities and crime.[38]

In 2014, ICSSI published an article titled "Youth of Iraq: Our Personal Freedoms Are Not Guaranteed and Government Authorities Are Responsible for Nearly Half of the Violations!"[39] In it, it cited a report from the organization al-Mesalla that promotes civil rights in Iraq. The article read:

> The Iraqi government and the authorities are the source of many of these violations. For example, the [al-Mesalla] report cites a decision of the General Secretariat of the Council of Ministers that stated, "The wearing or display of clothing and accessories that are contrary to traditions, and are considered an insult to public taste, is not permitted, and its promoters in local markets will be prosecuted." Such decisions and actions justify the targeting of young men and women by state authorities as well as by extremist groups.[40]

Another example of the struggle reflects the Muslim Brotherhood's short rule in Tunisia. The party was elected in October 2011, but it was defeated in the parliamentary elections in October 2014 and again in the presidential elections in December 2014. Both elections showed decisive wins for the national statehood and civil society–affiliated camp.

In March 2012, a Tunisian female student, Khaoula Rachidi, confronted Salafi-Jihadi activists who had replaced the Tunisian national flag located on the rooftop of a University of Manouba building with a Salafi-Jihadi black flag. Tunisian President Moncef Marzouki decorated Rachidi for her act. During the ceremony, Marzouki declared that "The [Tunisian] flag is the symbol of the country . . . the blood of martyrs . . . and the Arab-Islamic identity."[41]

In May 2012 (during the reign of the Muslim Brotherhood), a Tunisian court fined film executives who were involved in dubbing and broadcasting the animated film *Persepolis*, which was based on the graphic novels of the Iranian-born French novelist Marjane Satrapi, because they claimed the film "damages religious values."[42] Conservative Islamists called the punishment insufficient and called for the accused to be incarcerated. The accused and their supporters claimed that their freedom of expression and creativity had been violated by the fine, and the conservatives' demand was rejected.[43]

Today Tunisia's statehood and civil society–affiliated camp is the stronger political factor; yet, at the same time, Tunisia is reportedly the largest exporter of militant Islamists. In July 2015, the United Nations Human Rights Office of the High Commissioner for Human Rights released a report that stated:

> While the phenomenon of foreign fighters is not new, with a number of Tunisians joining conflict in Afghanistan, Iraq, Chechnya, and Bosnia, the current scope is unprecedented in term of the sheer scale. . . . Currently, it has been reported that the number of Tunisian foreign fighters is one of the highest among those travelling to join conflicts abroad such as in Syria and Iraq. We received information that there are some four thousand Tunisians in Syria, one thousand to fifteen hundred in Libya, two hundred in Iraq, sixty in Mali, and fifty in Yemen. Some 625 who have returned from conflict zones are being prosecuted. Most militants have reportedly joined takfiri or other extremist groups.[44]

A report by Al Jazeera quoted one of these Tunisian young people, Safouan Aichaoui, on Valentine's Day 2014, a bit more than a year after arriving in Syria. He'd posted on his Facebook page: "Many people think that jihad is the closest way to death. They don't realize that it actually prolongs life. I swear to God, you feel the pleasure of your existence. It's not a pointless existence. And every day you are born again." The report reviewed attempts to thwart this phenomenon, including closing mosques and arresting aspiring fighters, but also noted that the measures weren't sufficiently managing the problem. It read:

> The country's young people were raised under a dictatorship that suppressed critical thinking, rendering many of them at once hungry for religious identity and vulnerable to fundamentalist preaching. As Tunisia struggles with its democratic transition, they have fallen

prey to violent networks offering not only economic opportunity and social inclusion, but also a confident worldview.[45]

A young Egyptian blogger and women's rights activist named Aliaa Magda Elmahdy evoked an enormous media and political reaction when she published nude photographs of herself in red high heels and stockings on her blog and titled it, "Screams against a Society of Violence, Racism, Sexism, Sexual Harassment, and Hypocrisy."[46] The post was intended to be a political statement challenging the conservative values of Arab societies and the oppression of women in those societies. The photos, later posted on Twitter with the hashtag #nudephotorevolutionary, were viewed over a million times, and her followers quickly jumped from a few hundred to more than fourteen thousand, and they're now at more than forty-two thousand. In an interview with CNN in 2011, Elmahdy said, "I am not shy of being a woman in a society where women are nothing but sex objects harassed on a daily basis by men who know nothing about sex or the importance of a woman."[47] Responses on Arab social networks to her postings fluctuated along a spectrum from full support or support with some reservations to condemnation, and even calls to murder her.[48] In 2014, Elmahdy made an even more provocative move, which resulted in everything from wild support to even more extreme death threats, when she posted a nude picture of herself menstruating and next to her a woman in a hijab (a Muslim head scarf) defecating on an ISIS flag. Both women were flanked by what looks like machine guns and had the letters "IS" painted on their bare skin.[49] Elmahdy uses her blog, *A Rebel's Diary*, which has almost ten millions views, Twitter, and her Facebook page to advocate, boldly, brashly, and provocatively, for personal freedom.[50] But threatened and criticized for it, she had to seek asylum in Sweden.

In Egypt in 2014, the film *Noah* awakened a heated public debate. Al-Azhar University, considered the world's central religious leadership institution of Sunni Islam, demanded that the screening of the film be banned because it personified the prophet Noah.[51] In response, an Egyptian organization named the Egyptian Front for Creativity, a coalition of Egyptian artists and artistic entities, announced that banning the screening of the film violated individual freedom, specifically self-expression and creativity, and represented a medieval mindset.[52, 53, 54] In 2015, Egyptian censorship leaders authorized (after deleting thirteen scenes) the screening of a movie called *Family Secrets*, a movie whose main character, a young homosexual, is given advice on ways to "cure the disease."[55]

In 2015, the Egyptian Center for Women's Rights (ECWR) pressured the Ministry of Education to harshly prosecute a teacher who cut a young girl's hair, shoved her, and hit her hand because she did not wear a veil. According to ECWR's website:

> This crime raises concern over similar incidents taking place in Egyptian schools and escalations against female students. It also provides alarming indicator on the spread of extremist thinking in schools and the likelihood of other students adopting such behavior toward unveiled girls and Christians.

The website said that Nehad Abul Komsan, the chairperson of ECWR, "reiterates the necessity of countering this crime through administrative investigation and criminal prosecution, in addition to the importance of revising the regular teachers' evaluation and safety plans for all students."[56]

For many years, a struggle has been brewing in Egypt as some restaurants, beaches, and pools enforce a "no hijab" policy and some beaches and pools banned "Islamic swimsuits" that cover everything but a woman's feet, hands, and head. The "hijab-free zones" have sparked an ongoing debate on both sides of the issue regarding the legality of the measures. A veiled young woman was quoted as saying, "It feels degrading, we are in our own country and we are not happy. . . . No one has the right to deprive me of entering. This never happened to me anywhere else, even in the United States."[57] A woman who purchased an expensive chalet in an upscale resort about one hundred miles from Cairo was threatened that if she swam in the pool at the resort in her Islamic swimsuit, its owners would "throw excess chlorine in the water and shut off the fountains and the Jacuzzi."[58] An Egyptian Salafi cleric argued that the sea is "male," so if a woman is in the sea, she is conducting a sexual act—and therefore a woman should not enter the sea at all.[59]

In Jordan in November 2012, individuals identified with the Muslim Brotherhood and the Salafi movement tried to prevent—by force—a Halloween party from taking place at a coffee house in Amman, the capital of Jordan. They said that celebrating Halloween was "an activity that is not moral and not Islamic."[60]

Reportedly, in May 2015, the United States ambassador to Jordan attended a formal event organized by a Jordanian gay, lesbian, and transgender group.[61] Following the report, the political party of the Muslim Brotherhood movement in Jordan, the Islamic Action Front, published an announcement strongly condemning the event. It described it as a "provocation against Islamic virtues and values" and urged the Jordanian government to "crush the homosexual phenomenon with an iron fist."[62]

However, at the same time as the ongoing pressure for conservative ways in Jordan, more free-spirited groups have also been popping up. A Jordanian nonprofit known as the Jordan Open Source Association has been fighting for a "constitution" of the Internet that would provide more freedom on it. And there are now schools in Jordan that teach salsa dancing. The young men and women dancing together is in direct opposition to the call for total male-female segregation.[63]

In Lebanon, a nonprofit organization named HELEM (which translates to "wisdom" and is also the acronym in Arabic for the group's full name, Lebanese Protection for Lesbians, Gays, Bisexuals, and Transgenders) leads a peaceful push, through lobbying and marketing campaigns, for the freedom of these people and others with a non-conforming sexuality or gender identity. Its members work to abolish Law 534 of the Lebanese Penal Code, which states that "unnatural sexual intercourse" is punishable by an imprisonment up to one year. The organization has also launched an online initiative called the "Homophobia Meter," which collects information related to the homosexual community in the Arab world.[64]

ISIS and the Struggle over Identity

Looking to ISIS and its rule over the territories it calls the "Islamic State" provides a good way to evaluate features of the identity, path, and direction of the Arab and Muslim world. In June 2014, ISIS announced the establishment of its "Islamic State" in the territories it had conquered in Iraq and Syria. The leader of ISIS, Abū Bakr al-Baghdādi, was proclaimed the caliph and all subjects of the "Islamic State" were obligated to swear allegiance to him through a *bay'aa* ceremony. In the regions under ISIS's rule, it has developed and maintained a governance system that implements its extreme ideology, including forcing a severe dress code on women, performing female genital mutilation on women between the ages of twelve and forty-six, enforcing the growing of beards among men, obligating men to participate in prayer services, and implementing the punishment laws of ancient Islam, such as floggings, amputation of limbs, stonings, and beheadings.

In the city of al-Raqqah in northern Syria, which has become ISIS's de facto capital, ISIS imposes strict regulations on the city's Christian population, approximately one thousand people.[65] These regulations include laws obligating things such as the paying of a *jizya*, a heresy tax,[66] a ban on holding public Christian prayer services or publicly performing ritual ceremonies and customs, and a ban on drinking wine. Reportedly, in a workshop ISIS organized, educators were instructed to eliminate the sciences, history, civics, psychology, culture, and the study of religions from schools. ISIS also ordained that curriculums should only include subjects compatible with its ideology.[67]

Mariam al-Mansouri was a fighter pilot in the United Arab Emirates Air Force who participated in the international coalition that arose to fight ISIS in September 2014 and became a hero to many members of the Arab world. [68] In response to her achievements, Egyptian-born US professor and director of the London Global Strategy Institute, Mamoun Fandy, wrote an article titled "Mariam and al-Baghdadi—the Sky and the Ground." In it he wrote:

> Mariam al-Mansouri is a symbol of the movement that aspires to lead us into the future, to take off into the sky, while al-Baghdadi and his company are symbols of the movement aspiring to return us to the past, to moving backward. Mariam stands for good while al-Baghdadi stands for evil.[69]

Egyptian journalist Abdel Monem Said proclaimed Mariam al-Mansouri to be the symbol of a new generation of women in the Arab world that is taking off into the new skies of science, technology, and progress. He wrote:

> This is a new generation that completely rejects the attempt of groups that demand, in the name of religion, to deny half of the population all rights, and to enslave the other half in the name of the principle of blind obedience.[70]

The gap between salsa dancing in Jordan and the covering of the statue of Umm Kulthūm with a niqab symbolizes the dimensions of the struggle over identity, path, and direction in Arab and non-Arab Muslim societies. It is not a new struggle; however, in the second decade of the twenty-first century, a new, unprecedented, and very powerful player has appeared and fills an increasingly central role in the struggle. The new player is the Internet and social media.

CHAPTER TEN

THE INTERNET: THE PHANTOM EMPIRE

The controversial website WikiLeaks states that its mission is "to provide an innovative, secure, and anonymous way for sources to leak information to our journalists" and to publish "original source material."[1, 2] Its founder, Julian Assange, is a role model in the Arab world, and there is an Arab Twitter user who calls himself "Mujtahidd," an Arabic word that means "one who fights a holy war," who is known as the "Arab Julian Assange."[3] Mujtahidd has more than 1.4 million followers, and in his tweets, he focuses mostly on the Saudi Arabian royal house, often exposing alleged corruption and inefficiency of the authorities.[4, 5]

Today, the use of the Internet, Facebook, Twitter, and other social media platforms is widespread in the Arab world. In May 2015, a report titled "#Turn_Around_and_Go_Back"[6] was published by the Arabic Network for Human Rights Information and estimated that there were 157 million Internet users in the region stretching from the country of Mauritania, on the western coast of North Africa, to Yemen. This is about three times as many users as there were in 2009. About half—around seventy-eight million—had Facebook accounts (which is about six times as many as did in 2009). Seven million people use Twitter in Saudi Arabia, and four million people use it in Egypt. Saudi Prince al-Walīd ibn Ṭalāl, who invested three hundred million dollars in Twitter, is proud of this.[7]

The empire of the Internet and online social media networks is a phantom empire—it has no borders, no army, and no government; it also has no flag, no passport, and no citizenship, yet it has changed the face of human interactions. With the press of a button and at the speed of light, millions of people from different parts of the world communicate. They can exchange information and ideas, conduct commercial and business transactions, create personal connections, and initiate and coordinate cultural, economic, social, and political activities.

Everyone functioning in the Internet's phantom empire has as an easy method of self-expression—a power that is almost impossible to change, eliminate, limit, or negate. This empire grants the potential of equal power and influence to every person regardless of who the person is and what his or her beliefs are. And it's nearly impossible to destroy this phantom empire. Its army can't be defeated because it has no army. Its territory can't be conquered because it has no territory. Its flag can't be trampled because it has no flag. Attempts to block, limit, or neutralize its influence and those of its users usually fail and will ultimately be defeated.

The role of the Internet and related digital platforms is part and parcel to the current events of the Arab world. From connecting people from around the world to creating political initiatives to address economic and societal challenges to organizing demonstrations and protests to promoting ideologies and recruiting supporters, the Internet and digital platforms are shaping the face of modern Arab society. Through online networks, people can recruit thousands, tens of thousands, and sometimes hundreds of thousands of individuals in a very short time for immediate action that can generate substantial change. Media platforms have become not only a generator of change but also a catalyst—as a platform that can compress processes that previously might have taken generations into only a few years, or even just months or days.

The influence, speed, and immediate interactive capabilities of social media influenced the Egyptian Revolution, which began in January 2011 and led to the overthrow on February 11, 2011, of Ḥosnī Mubārak, who had ruled Egypt for thirty-years. Later, it led to the ousting of Mohammed Morsi, who ruled for a year, on July 3, 2013. It's also assisted in the ousting of the Muslim Brotherhood rule in Tunisia and spurred the Syrian people to take to the streets against their dictator, Bashar al-Assad. It's been an integral part of story of the Arab Awakening.

The mass demonstrations in Egypt became known by the nickname *malyuniah* (from the English word "million"), a reference to the large number of participants in the demonstrations, even though the demonstrations weren't actually at this scale. Malyuniah also became associated with other campaigns conducted through social media platforms throughout the Arab world, including such diverse ones as lobbying to boycott reality shows[8] and lobbying to boycott the wearing of the hijab.[9] One of the most successful and impactful online initiatives was called *tamarod* (rebellion),[10] which was an Egyptian grassroots action that collected signatures on a petition calling for President Morsi's resignation. Its proclaimed aim was to topple his rule and have new elections, and it spread like wildfire through social networking sites, collecting twenty-two million signatures of support.[11, 12] The Morsi Meter, which tracked and ultimately trumped Morsi and ended the rule of the Muslim Brotherhood in Egypt, offered a level of government transparency Egyptians had historically been deprived of.

Of course, media platforms are not a new phenomenon in the Arab world. Radio and television stations, cable and satellite channels, and a seemingly endless number of newspapers abound and have long offered—or at least claimed to offer—a platform for the expression of the individual voice. Yet, in reality, the majority of these platforms did not allow different voices a stage or dissenting voices to gain momentum.

Many—if not most—of the traditional mass media outlets in the Arab world serve as a mouthpiece for the government and, if not, are at least subject to government control and strict censorship. On a website that lists Arab news platforms from around the world,[13] there are more than fifty information platforms about Syria; a review of the links reveals that almost all of them echo the positions of the Assad regime. And it is not only local media, the two biggest Arab TV news networks, Al Jazeera and Al Arabiya, are owned and controlled by Qatar and Saudi Arabia, respectively. The leading Arab newspapers are also controlled or at least inclined to support the Arab governments they are affiliated with; these include *Asharq al-Awsat* (Saudi Arabia), *Al-Ahram* and *Al-Youm al-Sab'e* (Egypt), *Alghad* and *Al Rai* (Jordan), and more.

With the lack of significant media outlets that aired—or served as—a voice for public criticism and opposition to governments, dictators, and other power figures, public opinion was significantly influenced by a relatively small number of journalists with access to the highest level of decision making in the Arab world. This included people like Muhammad Hassanein Heikal, an Egyptian journalist and the former editor-in-chief of the Egyptian newspaper *Al-Ahram*; Anis Mansour, an Egyptian author and columnist who died in 2011; ʿAbd al-Bārī ʿAṭwān, the Palestinian-born former editor-in-chief of *Al-Quds Al-Arabi* and current editor-in-chief of the digital news site Ra ialyoum (Today's Opinion). Aṭwān has many fans in the Arab world, yet his detractors describe him as a "pen to hire" in the service of Arab rules and regimes,[14] and others dub him Abd "Dollar" Aṭwān.[15]

Because the majority of traditional media outlets in the Arab world have historically preferred to operate within the secure and comfortable arena of conforming to the ruling regime or their patron's political and social thinking, they have played into the limiting of self-expression by private citizens in Arab society. Now though, the phantom empire is mostly able to avoid censorship, and when attempts are made to block access to information, they are usually defeated.[16]

In the summer of 2011, Syrian citizens documented through photos and video the violence of the Syrian government against its citizens and distributed the images through digital platforms and text messages on their cell phones. The Syrian regime tried to block the distribution, but because southern Syria is covered by the Jordanian mobile network, the image distributors were able to bypass the Syrian systems.

In August 2012, the Jordanian government tried to institute censorship legislation that would have restricted access to pornography and websites it considered "immoral." In response, young Jordanians initiated a protest campaign under the banner "Freedom on the Network," in which thousands of Jordanians turned off their computer screens for one day.[17, 18] The campaign's message was that people had the ability to know and decide what was good and what was bad and that the government had no authority or right to make these decisions for them.[19] The campaign earned a significant supporter, former Jordanian Queen Noor al-Ḥussein, who tweeted, "Today the clouds in the skies over Jordan united according to the timing of the blackout."[20] The campaign was successful and Jordanian authorities retracted the measure.

In February 2014, Turkey passed a law that allowed authorities to unilaterally block websites. In March, a week before municipal elections, the government of Turkey blocked Twitter and President Tayyip Erdoğan threatened to indefinitely remove access to it.[21] Some people argued that the move of the Turkish government was intended to minimize damage to the ruling party following a report accusing President Erdoğan and his son of corruption.[22] The move evoked broad public protests and a wave of mass demonstrations in Turkey. In April 2014, the Constitutional Court of Turkey, the country's highest legal constitutional review body, ordered the government to remove the block. It declared the action to have violated Turkish citizens' freedom of expression and civil rights.

Many Arab journalists and other writers have often written—and usually with searing criticism—about the attempts of regimes in the Middle East to restrict the use of online social networks and to arrest bloggers. Lebanese journalist Sawsan al-Abtah wrote in an article titled "The Enslavement of Human Beings by Remote Control" that "it is ridiculous and laughable to see the governments in the Arab world still making use of the old means of control like arresting artists or outlawing broadcast, while technology today has such a sophisticated, powerful influence on our minds and needs."[23]

The phantom empire is a platform that reflects the different streams of thought within the Arab world and, at the same time, is a tool that shapes those forces. Rejecters of hard-line Islam use it, but so do members of terror groups, ones internationally known, like al-Qaeda and ISIS, and also ones less known in the West. Through digital means they influence and shape the identity of the Arab world and beyond. They sophisticatedly and effectively use the Internet and social media networks to promote their message, gain support, and empower their supporters to recruit others, and they even promote violence. On al-Qaeda's websites, one can learn how to make a homemade bomb in his kitchen.[24]

Militant Islamist groups recruit supporters and militants through social media platforms.[25, 26, 27, 28, 29] An article titled "Hashtag Terror: How ISIS Manipulates Social Media" published by the Anti-Defamation League,[30] an organization established in 1913 whose mission is "to stop the defamation of the Jewish people and to secure justice and fair treatment to all," described this phenomenon. It read, "As ISIS gains confidence and territory in the Middle East, its social media presence has expanded its influence well beyond the battlefields."[31]

James Phillips, the senior research fellow for Middle Eastern affairs at the Douglas and Sarah Allison Center for Foreign Policy Studies at the Heritage Foundation, wrote in an article titled "The Message ISIS Wants to Send to America, the World" that "the slickly-packaged jihadist propaganda seeks to stimulate and galvanize members of the movement, spur potential recruits to join in the carnage, and incite additional terrorist attacks against the United States."[32]

Phillips has said that "unlike [al-Qaeda], which saw itself as a revolutionary vanguard and focused its propaganda efforts on like-minded Islamist militants, ISIS is a mass movement led by a new generation of Islamist revolutionaries who have developed a much broader propaganda effort."[33]

J. M. Berger, a fellow with the Project on US Relations with the Islamic World at Brookings, and Jonathon Morgan, a technologist and data scientist, published a report titled "The ISIS Twitter Census: Defining and Describing the Population of ISIS Supporters on Twitter" for the Brookings Institute in March 2015. Highlights from the report include:[34]

- That from September–December 2014, an estimated forty-six thousand or more Twitter accounts were used by ISIS supporters, although not all of them were active at the same time.
- That the growth in ISIS-supporting accounts outstripped that of the overall Twitter user population. In 2013, Twitter's user base grew 30 percent while ISIS's user base nearly doubled. In 2014, Twitter's user base grew 20 percent while the number of ISIS supporters nearly tripled. [35]
- That ISIS-supporting accounts had an average of about one thousand followers, considerably higher than an ordinary Twitter user.
- That at least 151,617 Twitter hashtags included one of four most-common variations on the spelling of "Islamic State" in Arabic (all of the variations could not be fully accounted for), representing 2.8 percent of all tweets in

the report's sample. No other hashtags in the sample came close to that rate of usage.

- That ISIS-supporting accounts were considerably more active than other users. The mean number of followers of ISIS supporters was 1,004; for the average Twitter user, it was 208. The median for ISIS supporters was 177 followers; for the average Twitter user it was sixty-one.
- That much of ISIS's social media success can be attributed to a relatively small group of hyperactive users, referred to in ISIS social media strategy documents as the *mujtahidun* (industrious ones) and numbering between five hundred and two thousand accounts. And while the users might not tweet every day, they tweet in concentrated bursts of high volume, putting out a lot of content in a short time.

These bursts of activity cause hashtags to trend, resulting in third-party aggregation and the insertion of tweeted content into search results. The result is an effective promulgation of ISIS's messages on social media. And the strong presence of ISIS members online reflects anecdotal observations of increased adoption of social media by jihadist extremists starting in 2013.

Positive findings of the report noted that no overt ISIS supporter had more than fifty thousand followers; while some came close, it was few and far between. Even at their most popular levels, top ISIS influencers command an audience that is fractional compared to celebrities or prominent US government officials, such as President Obama (54.6 million followers), Vice President Joe Biden (735,000), and Secretary of State John Kerry (four hundred thousand). While highly active and committed, ISIS supporters are a speck in the overall sea of Twitter's active monthly user base of 284 million.[36]

Reportedly, in July 2015, Twitter shut down tens of thousands accounts of ISIS followers.[37]

There are also active hackers trolling the Internet on behalf of the extremists. In June 2015, hacker groups called "cyber caliphate" hacked and temporarily shut down the website of the Syrian Observatory for Human Rights.[38, 39] The same was done when Turkey blocked access to Islamic websites in June 2015 to "crack down on the Islamic State recruitment network."[40]

The Internet and social media also provide militant Islamist groups with a way to easily disseminate photos and videos. The dramatic, violent content of the footage and video pieces they produce, together with state of the art filming and editing, enables them to capture attention around the world and to convey their messages easily and efficiently. Some videos even use symbols, such as galloping horses and waving flags, which have romantic, adventurous connotations aimed at appealing to young people.[41] After ISIS's lead songwriter, Maher Meshaal, also known as Abu Hajar al-Hadrami, was killed in a drone strike on July 11, 2015, CBS News noted that, "Meshaal is the author of jihadi hymns such as 'Saleel al-Sawarem' and 'Halomoo Halomoo O' Lions of War,' which are regularly played as background music in combat and execution videos released by ISIS."[42] The melodic and spiritual *nasheed* (Islamic hymn or chant) that plays in the background of ISIS videos is a sophisticated and effective tool intended to draw in viewers. One song's lyrics translate to, "The banner has called us, to brighten the path of destiny, to wage war on the enemy, whosoever among us dies, in sacrifice for defense, will enjoy eternity in paradise."[43] The tune of one video encourages humming along as a young boy beheads a Syrian military officer.[44] In the words of Phillip Smyth, a researcher of Middle Eastern affairs at the University of Maryland, "If you are really trying to recruit and indoctrinate people, music is a fantastic way to do it. It's like Wagner being set to *Apocalypse Now*."[45]

This combination of slick marketing and barbaric violence disturbs people like Lebanese Arab journalist Diana Moukalled who accuses media, particularly Western media, of proactively playing to the hands of ISIS. In her 2014 article titled "ISIS and Hollywood Illusions," she wrote:

> Indeed ISIS was successfully terrifying us . . . but it is because media and mostly Western media, which is fascinated by ISIS, boosted and echoes ISIS atrocities. . . . There is a need to come up with a relevant media policy that will confront ISIS for what it is and not through lenses of Hollywood fiction because ISIS atrocities are for real.[46]

In July 2015, the United States and the United Arab Emirates announced the establishment of the Sawab Center (the "Correct" Center). The US State Department's press release read:

> The United States and the United Arab Emirates today launched the Sawab Center, the first-ever multinational online messaging and engagement program, in support of the Global Coalition Against *Daesh* (ISIS). . . . The Sawab Center will use direct online engagement to counter terrorist propaganda rapidly and effectively, including messages used to recruit foreign fighters, fundraise for illicit activities, and intimidate and terrorize local populations. The Sawab Center will increase the intensity of online debate by presenting moderate and tolerant voices from across the region and amplifying inclusive and constructive narratives.[47]

The Internet and social media generate social and cultural changes that are of no less importance than political changes when it comes to the struggle over the path, identity, and direction of Arab society. One of the best manifestations of this is in the context of the treatment of women.

In October 2011, four Arab women—two Lebanese, one Egyptian, and one Palestinian—created a nonprofit called the Uprising of the Women in the Arab World and described the group as being "together for fearless, free, and independent women in the Arab World."[48, 49] The initiative's Facebook page reads:

> The Uprising of the Women in the Arab World page is a page for all the women of the region from all religions and ethnicities: Arabs, Berbers, Nubians, Kurds, Assyrians, Arameans, Syrians, Armenians, Turks, Turkmen, Circassian, and others . . . This intifada is a free secular space for constructive dialogue and fearless listening about women's rights in the Arab world. It does not infringe on any religion or belief for any of the members. All members have the right and freedom to their beliefs as long as they are committed to the limits and do not try to impose his/her views on the others.[50]

The initiative was created to fight the exploitation of women and to tackle phenomena such as sexual harassment, forced marriages, discrimination, which is commonly anchored in custom or in law, and violence against women. With its website, blog, Facebook, Twitter, and Flickr accounts—which communicate through Arabic and English—it is capitalizing on social media to educate, protect, and empower.[51, 52, 53, 54]

A similar initiative was taken by a group of Egyptian women who in 2010 established a volunteer-based organization to counter *taharosh* (harassment), as sexual harassment and assault spread in Egypt and elsewhere in the Arab world. Dedicated to the mission of "engaging all of Egyptian society to create an environment that does not tolerate sexual harassment,"[55] it addresses these issues through a variety of initiatives, including digitally driven ones and others based on more traditional community building programs. Its flagship project, an online map based on crowdsourcing and real-time reports that document areas in Cairo and elsewhere in Egypt, alerts women of places with increased risk of sexual harassment. This warns women of places they should be particularly careful and also sets communities it wants to collaborate with to make systemic and permanent changes. [56]

Shortly after Egyptian President Sisi visited an Egyptian woman hospitalized following an attempted rape, the president ordered Egypt's minister of interior affairs to enhance Egypt's laws to better fight sexual harassment and rape.[57] The president's call likely reflects his awareness of the growing power of the female electorate.

In the Arab world, like in the West, there is an ongoing discussion regarding the negative and positive aspects of the Internet and social media. There are people in the Arab world who argue that they present a threat to the norms, values, and social fabrics of Arab societies. Jordanian sociologist Dr. Amal Salem al-Awawdeh argued that there had been a 25 percent increase in the rate of divorce in Jordan as a result of connections outside of marriage that have become more available because of the Internet.[58] Saudi journalist Mishari al-Zaidi wrote in an article titled "Virus of Social Media" that "it is because of social media that ISIS emerged and prostitution exists . . . [and] Twitter destroys the family cell."[59] A Palestinian youth group launched a campaign that called for blocking access to pornography websites, arguing that they are the reason people are marrying less in Palestinian society.[60]

There are also people who believe social media will have no long-term impact in the shaping of the Arab world. In 2012, Lebanese journalist and political analyst Samir Atallah wrote that "Twitter is a phenomenon that will not endure because it cannot answer all of the various needs, and even if the use of Twitter expands, that fact will have no influence on writing or television or journalism."[61]

But evidence shows that the use of the Internet and social media in the Arab world is expanding—and growing fast. There is a consensus among Arab intellectuals and public opinion that social networks play—and will increasingly continue to play—a central role, perhaps the most central role, in molding the face of the Arab world.

In 2014, Sheikh Mohammed bin Rashid al-Maktoum, vice president and prime minister of the United Arab Emirates and the emir of Dubai, who is among the top ten most followed world leaders on social media—with almost six million followers across his various social media platforms—and was the first world leader to announce a cabinet change on Twitter,[62] launched the Arab Social Media Influencers Summit and the creation of the "Arab Social Media Awards." The event was described as "the first of its kind in the region for social media channels influencers honoring innovations by both individuals and institutions who have made a positive impact on the development and prosperity of their communities, while contributing to the progress and development of the people."[63]

Stated objectives were to "boost engagement and encourage communication across social media channels, encourage creative thinking and contribute to the development of people and communities, and increase awareness for issues of concern to the Arab community in a responsible and positive manner."[64] The summit and awards ceremony, intended as an annual event, offers awards to organizations and individuals. Social media initiatives in a variety of categories are eligible: government entities, private sector, blogs, media, sports, tolerance, social service, education, youth, technology, entrepreneurship, economy, politics, health, arts, security and safety, shopping, environment, tourism, and entertainment.[65]

Mohammed al-Gergawi, Egypt's minister of cabinet affairs and chairman of the Organizing Committee for the Arab Social Media Influencers Summit, said, "We will honor individuals and organizations who are active and successful on social media platforms, and in doing so we will shed light on the social media initiatives that make the most powerful positive impact in the Arab world."[66] Sheikh Mohammed bin Rashid al-Maktoum said he launched the program because he believes that "combining the productive energy of youth with the vast capabilities of social media platforms can effect real positive change in the Arab world."[67] More than fifteen hundred social media experts from around the world attended the 2015 summit and there were thirty-seven winners.[68] In the awards ceremony, the sheikh commended their outstanding achievements and their valuable contribution to increase awareness of issues of concern in the Arab region. He said:

> The efforts of the winners have helped spread the best methods in the use of social networks and encouraged optimal and responsible use of these platforms to contribute to the development of Arab societies toward a brighter future. . . . You are the pride of the Arab nation, because you sensed the needs of your community and you searched for the optimal usage of social media platforms to fulfill your noble purposes. We are proud of you, and this recognition you won today is a tribute for the Arab people, who do get deterred by challenges but look through them for prospects of excellence, achievement, and innovation.[69]

There is an opportunity to build a civil society in which people can discuss political, social, economic, and cultural issues openly: the Internet and social media can ease communication and allow collaboration; amplify the voice of the individual; enable the generation of mass demonstrations; ease the initiation of public campaigns; encourage open, honest debates; offer a platform for ideological pluralism; politically empower sectors that are discriminated against; and narrow and minimize rulers' capacities to suffocate criticism. The possibility of open public discourse offers people the opportunity to discuss the kind of government they want, and that conversation has the potential to be a solid building block in the path toward a healthy and vibrant civil society.

Looking Forward

With the ability for the open dialogue they allow, the Internet and social media can offer Arab societies a cure for the diseases that plague them, but they can also be used by its corrupt leaders as a way to spread their propaganda. So what does the future hold? It seems that the impact of the phantom empire in the context of the struggle over identity, path, and direction is more beneficial than detrimental. The Internet and social media platforms are laying the foundations for the appearance of a true civil society in the Arab world, without which the Arab world will not be able to heal, grow, and thrive. Still, the road to health is long and winding. In some Western media and political circles of influence, people have mistakenly rushed to conclude that the growing impact of the Internet and social media, as well as the emergence of budding civil societies and democratic values in Arab societies, indicate that Arab societies are adopting Western-style democracy. That is not the case.

Western-style democracy is far from being absorbed by the majority of Arab societies. Arab monarchs are not elected democratically and still hold most of the political power in the Arab world. In Egypt, a democratically elected president and government were overthrown in a coup, and though replaced by a new president and government, also democratically elected, the power primarily resides in the hands of the army. Lebanon has a parliament, free elections, political parties, and armed forces that are subdued to the authority of the government; yet, one member of that government—Hezbollah—keeps its own separate armed force, and continually uses this force to impose its political will and the interests of its master, Iran, on the Lebanese people. This included initiating a war with Israel in 2006, the occupation of West Beirut in 2008, and fighting in the wars in Syria and Iraq. Iraq, too, has a parliament, elections, and political parties, but its army is supported by an Iranian-backed Iraqi Shiite militia, al-Hashd al-Shaabi (the Popular Congregation), in the fight against ISIS.

Unfortunately, freedom of the press and freedom of self-expression through spoken word, writing, and digital communication are still restricted and subject to sanctions. Qatari poet Mohammed al-Ajami was jailed in 2011 after he wrote a poem titled "Tunisian Jasmine" that supported the uprisings in the Arab world. In it he wrote, "We are all Tunisia in the face of repressive elites!"[70] For this he was given a life sentence, which in 2013 was reduced to fifteen years in prison. His act was defined by the court as "offensive to the state symbols and calling for ousting of the ruler."[71] In April 2015, Reporters Without Borders stated, "the frequency with which bloggers and social network users are arrested and convicted in the Oman reflects the appalling state of online freedom of information and expression there."[72]

Also throughout the Arab world, laws sanction and punish homosexual and transgender individuals, and women are legally and institutionally discriminated against. According to Article 340 of the Jordanian Penal Code, for example, when there is a murder that is related to "dishonoring the family" or a spouse's infidelity, both men and women are, theoretically, entitled to plea for a decreased sentence under "unique circumstances." The article, however, discriminates against women in two ways: first, a man who killed his sister in an "honor killing" is entitled to plea for a decreased sentence under unique circumstances; yet a woman who kills a female family member for the same reason is not; second, if a man kills his wife for infidelity, he is entitled to plea for a decreased sentence under unique circumstances regardless of the location in which the infidelity occurred. But if a woman killed her husband for the same reason, she is only entitled to plea for a decreased sentence given the circumstances if the infidelity took place at home.[73]

Given that Western-style democracy is not embedded within the Arab political and cultural structure, it's hard to envision Arab societies adopting a true Western-style democracy. They may increasingly embrace ones more similar than they have now, but these could easily encompass values that the West does not condone.

CHAPTER ELEVEN

THE CRITICISM OF ISRAEL: THE KNIGHT AND THE DRAGON

THIS CHAPTER IS DIFFERENT FROM THE other chapters in this book. It is largely my personal and political statement as a Jew, an Israeli, and a Zionist.

As a private Israeli citizen, I am highly critical of the governments of Israel in a number of arenas—including its conduct with regard to the Israeli-Palestinian conflict. To the same extent, I am also critical of the Palestinians and their conduct. In my view, Israel and the Palestinians are equally responsible for the failure to put an end to the conflict between them. I identify with the suffering of the Palestinians just as I identify with the suffering of the Israelis. I do not think that suffering is the lot of only one of them. I also do not see Palestinians as "the enemy"; however, there are Palestinians who—by their own choice—are my enemy.

The focal point of criticism toward Israel, which is legitimate—though, of course, highly debatable—within Western circles such as academic, government, media, and nonprofit ones has mostly centered around three issues: the Israeli occupation of the West Bank, Israeli settlements in the West Bank and East Jerusalem, and the Israeli closure of the Gaza Strip. In the last decade a new topic has been added, a claim that Israel has used excessive force and committed war crimes during the recent violent military rounds between Israel and Palestinian armed groups in the Gaza Strip: Operation Cast Lead (December 2008–January 2009), Operation Pillar of Defense (November 2012), and Operation Protective Edge (July–August 2014).

I believe that the harsh critique leveled against Israel regarding the Gaza Strip emanates from a distorted view of reality. Let's explore the emotional and cultural environment within Western circles of influence gave birth to, but first let's review a brief history of events related to the Gaza Strip over the past decade.

In December 2003, late Israeli Prime Minister Ariel Sharon proposed the evacuation of the seventy-five hundred settlers and twenty-one settlements in the Gaza Strip. In February 2005, the Israeli parliament approved the law. By the end of September 2005, Israel's presence in the Gaza Strip came to an end. In a unilateral act known as "the disengagement," Israel dismantled all Israeli settlements and military facilities, and all Israeli settlers were evacuated from the Gaza Strip. Some of them were relocated inside Israel, others moved to Israeli settlements in the West Bank. Four Israeli settlements in the northern part of the West Bank were also dismantled and the settlers who lived there were also relocated.

Following the Israeli disengagement, control and rule over the Gaza Strip was given to the Palestinian Authority, while Israel continued to maintain control along the land and sea borders of the Gaza Strip and Israel.

In November 2005, shortly after the Israeli withdrawal from the Gaza Strip, an agreement regarding the Rafah crossing, which connects the Gaza Strip with Egypt, was brokered by the United States and the European Union and signed by Israel and the Palestinian Authority. The main points of the agreement were:

- The Rafah crossing was formally recognized as an international border crossing.
- The Palestinian Authority and Egypt would jointly operate the Rafah crossing—the Palestinian Authority from the Gaza side and Egypt from the Egyptian side.
- Israel would manage the safe passage of people and goods between the Gaza Strip and the West Bank.
- A seaport, operating under terms similar to those developed for the Rafah crossing, would be built in the Gaza Strip, and Israel would be willing to discuss the building of an airport in the Gaza Strip.

Following the agreement, the European Union assembled a border assistance mission known as EU BAM Rafah (the European Union Border Assistance Mission for the Rafah crossing). It was intended to provide a third party presence at the Rafah crossing to contribute to the opening of the crossing point and build confidence between Israel and the Palestinian Authority. Its responsibilities included actively monitoring, verifying, and evaluating the Palestinian Authority's performance with regard to the implementation of the framework, security, and customs agreements made between the parties on the operation of the Rafah terminal; contributing through mentoring to the Palestinian Authority's set-up of its border management system at Rafah; and contributing to the liaison between the Palestinian, Israeli, and Egyptian authorities in all aspects regarding the management of the Rafah crossing.[1]

In June 2007, about a year and a half after the Israeli disengagement, Ḥamās conducted a violent coup in the Gaza Strip against the rule of the Palestinian Authority. Dozens of Palestinians were killed and hundreds were injured during the fighting between Ḥamās's military force—the Ezzedeen al-Qassam Brigades—and Palestinian Authority security forces. Ḥamās won, took over the Gaza Strip, and established its rule.

Following Ḥamās's takeover, the Rafah crossing was closed and EU BAM Rafah suspended its operation at the crossing point. However, EU BAM Rafah continued to formally exist, and in June 2015, the EU council extended the mandate of EU BAM Rafah until June 30, 2016.[2]

Since 2007, violence between Israel and Ḥamās, as well as other Palestinian armed groups in the Gaza Strip, like the Islamic Jihad in Palestine, the Palestinian Resistance Committees, and Salafi-Jihadi groups, has resulted in the deaths of thousands of Palestinian militants and civilians, the injury of many more, and the massive destruction of residential areas and infrastructure in the Gaza Strip.

On the Israeli side, the results of its battle with Ḥamās have been tragic; hundreds of Israelis have been killed or injured, both soldiers and civilians, and the conflict has caused damage to residential areas and infrastructure.

In September 2007, the Israeli government declared the Gaza Strip under Ḥamās's rule to be a hostile entity and imposed a closure on it. Today the entry of people from Gaza to Israel is limited. Entrance visas are primarily given to business people in the import-export field, students studying abroad, people older than sixty visiting their families in the West bank, and people who need special medical treatment not available in Gaza hospitals. Israel does, however, support the people living in the Gaza Strip by continually providing them with a wide range of commodities, such as food, fuel, and medicine. Israeli companies sell their products in the Gaza Strip and Gaza farmers and manufactures are permitted to export their products—flowers, fruit, furniture, textiles, vegetables, etc.—through Israel to destinations like Europe, Jordan, Saudi Arabia, and the Arab Gulf states.

The Gaza Strip, with a population of 1.8 million people, is about twenty-five miles long and ranges from three to seven miles wide. On a day-to-day basis, life in the Gaza Strip for an overwhelming majority of its people is very difficult. According to a World Bank report from May 2015, the rate of unemployment in the Gaza Strip was 44 percent; more than 60 percent of youth between fifteen and twenty-nine were unemployed; and 40 percent of Gazans lived below the poverty line.[3] According to the United Nations Office for the Coordination of Humanitarian Affairs, as of July 2015 nearly 80 percent of Gaza's population receives some form of international aid, the bulk of which is food assistance.[4] In 2013, the World Bank ranked the Gaza Strip the third poorest area in the Middle East, behind only the Sudan and Yemen. According to a September 2015 report presented by the United Nations Conference on Trade and Development, the Gaza Strip could become unlivable within just five years.[5] The situation inside the Gaza Strip during and following military rounds is even worse.

Without negating the suffering and hardships of people in the Gaza Strip, I have often wondered why the situation there is frequently referred to as a "humanitarian crisis caused by the Israeli siege." This language, widely used in Western circles and frequently accepted to be factually accurate, fuels criticism of Israel. It promotes the propaganda on Ḥamās's website and other pro-Palestinian websites, most of which address foreign audiences.

Even if we recognize that Western mediators of knowledge often do not provide their audiences with accurate information, there is an overwhelming amount of information shared digitally or through spoken word or print from the public and organizations around the world that is communicated in almost every language and provides accurate details on the amount of goods supplied by Israel to inhabitants of the Gaza Strip. The facts are not hard to come by.[6] There are an increasing number of articles, videos, television programs, etc. that show how the multilayered reality in the Gaza Strip is far different from the one-dimensional Western narrative that is promoted by Ḥamās. The reality of the Gaza Strip is that within it, poverty, scarcity, and unemployment exist side-by-side with coffee shops, gyms, hospitals, hotels, resorts, fancy restaurants, schools, sport arenas, malls, and universities.[7, 8, 9, 10, 11, 12, 13, 14]

Across the globe, different dimensions of the reality in the Gaza Strip can be found, and if one describes the situation in the Gaza Strip as a humanitarian crisis, one should wonder how to define the situation of millions and millions of people who live in poor conditions in the Middle East, Southeast Asia, Africa, and South America.

In the summer of 2015, the United Nations Office for the Coordination of Humanitarian Affairs released a number of reports that presented colossal human tragedies that were caused by brutal rulers like Bashar al-Assad and the Iranian mullahs' regime, as well as their brutal and violent off-springs and proxies.

In Syria, as it nears the fifth year of its war, more than 251,124 Syrians have been killed, including 115,627 civilians of whom 12,517 were children and 8,062 were women (over eighteen years old). About two million people have been wounded and millions have been displaced. There are shortages of every commodity, and schools and hospitals are barely functioning, as are other basic services. Life expectancy has decreased by twenty years, and people are sinking into severe poverty. Human rights violations and abuses are rampant, as are relentless violence and indiscriminate attacks on civilians.[15, 16] An article published in the *Washington Post* in September 2015 stated:

> The Syrian refugees are making Syria the biggest single source of refugees in the world and the worst humanitarian emergency in more than four decades . . . presenting the international community with a long-term crisis that it is ill-equipped to address and that could prove deeply destabilizing, for the region and the wider world. . . . The United Nations has received less than half the amount it said

> was needed to care for the refugees over the past four years. Aid is being cut and programs are being suspended at the very moment when those who left Syria in haste, expecting they soon would go home, are running out of savings and wearing out the welcome they initially received.

In Iraq—said to be experiencing "one of the most brutal insurgencies in the world,"[17]—more than eight million Iraqis, nearly 25 percent of its population, require some form of humanitarian assistance. Millions of its people have been forcefully displaced, and millions of its children are without access to education. Adults and children are subjected to booby-trapped buildings, roads contaminated with improvised explosive devices (IEDs), mass executions, systematic rape, and horrendous acts of violence. Children are abused, traumatized by violence and destitution, and used as suicide bombers and human shields. Women and girls have been enslaved and subjected to terrible sexual violence.[18]

In Libya, almost twenty-four hundred people have been killed, almost half a million have been displaced, two million are in need of humanitarian assistance, and two and a half million need health services. Education in eastern Libya has been suspended, with most children no longer attending school. Landmines and other unexploded ordnances are widespread.[19]

In Yemen, more than half a million people have been displaced, critical infrastructure has been damaged, there is an absence of basic services, and commodities and medical supplies are in short supply.[20]

With all this in mind, then why, against the background of evolving crises and suffering throughout the Middle East, is the Western conversation regarding the Middle East so frequently focused on the Gaza Strip—and how Israel should be blamed for the crisis there? "The humanitarian crisis in the Gaza Strip caused by the Israeli siege" is a common Western narrative and a frequent theme of conversation at colleges and universities and as part of rallies and other events. Would time not be better spent by spreading the truth about the dictators, militant organizations, and brutal regimes responsible for the epic, heart-wrenching tragedy that has befallen millions of Syrian, Iraqis, and others? To quote Palestinian human rights activist Bassem Eid, "I wonder why those same people remain silent when Palestinians are slaughtered in the Yarmouk refugee camp in Syria."[21]

And why is Israel blamed for the crisis, and not the Palestinian leadership, Ḥamās?

Part of the answer may be related to the challenges of information mediation and processing, the limited ability of Western audiences to evaluate the information, and the phenomenon of the "echo chamber." Another possible explanation is that Westerners may believe their efforts could affect decisions made by the Israeli government—but not by Assad, the Iranian mullahs, or other perpetrators of violence and destroyers of basic human rights.

But even with these answers, it's hard to understand how those so critical of Israel can make their claims in light of the evidence of what has actually unfolded between Israel and the Palestinians. During and following military confrontations between Israel and Ḥamās, there has been visual evidence documenting the Palestinians' launching of rockets from civilian areas inside the Gaza Strip—including residential streets and schools—that proved that weapons were stored in residential areas and mosques, and that thousands of rockets—an imprecise, non-controllable weapon once launched—were shot at cities in Israel. The evidence proves that Palestinian armed groups were deliberately targeting Israeli civilians and using their Palestinian civilian brothers as shields. These are clear war crimes and the evidence is undisputable.

Judge Richard Goldstone, head of the United Nations Fact Finding Mission on the Gaza Conflict, was sent to investigate suspicions of war crimes during the December 2008–January 2009 military confrontation between Israel and Ḥamās. He wrote, "That the crimes allegedly committed by Ḥamās were intentional goes without saying—its rockets were purposefully and indiscriminately aimed at civilian targets."[22]

In response to a United Nations inquiry into the 2014 Gaza war that confirmed that at least three UN schools were used by Palestinian terrorists to hide weapons and fire rockets, United Nations Secretary General Ban Ki-moon said, "I am dismayed that Palestinian militant groups would put United Nations schools at risk by using them to hide their arms."[23]

Unlike Ḥamās and its counterparts, Israel has provided video footage as evidence that its military operations target legitimate military bases and related effects, such as rocket launchers, ammunition bunkers, etc., and provides facts and documentation showing that its operations are conducted with the utmost attempt to avoid collateral damage. Israel has shown that it uses high-precision remote-controlled weapons and gives early warning to civilians to evacuate areas prior to an attack. Israel's efforts have been recognized and lauded by the United States' highest-ranking military body, the Department of Defense's Joint Chiefs of Staff. Its chairman, General Martin Dempsey, said that Israel "went to extraordinary lengths to limit collateral damage and civilian casualties" during its war with Ḥamās in the summer of 2014.[24]

Despite all this, Israel is unabashedly accused of committing war crimes.

In April 2009, following Operation Cast Lead, the United Nations Fact Finding Mission on the Gaza Conflict, headed by South African judge Richard Goldstone, was established to investigate accusations of war crimes in the Gaza Strip. Israel refused to cooperate with the commission's work, arguing that the mission's mandate was biased. The final report, known as the "Goldstone Report," was published in September 2009 and ruled that there was evidence that both sides had potentially committed war crimes and crimes against humanity. It called for Ḥamās and Israel to investigate their own actions. However, in April 2011, Judge Goldstone published an article in the *Washington Post* titled "Reconsidering the Goldstone Report on Israel and War Crimes," and in it he explained that he had erred in his opinion. He wrote:

> If I had known then what I know now, the Goldstone Report would have been a different document. The allegations of intentionality by Israel were based on the deaths of and injuries to civilians in situations where our fact-finding mission had no evidence on which to draw any other reasonable conclusion. While the investigations published by the Israeli military and recognized in the U.N. committee's report have established the validity of some incidents that we investigated in cases involving individual soldiers, they also indicate that civilians were not intentionally targeted as a matter of policy.[25]

It's respectable that Judge Goldstone realized his mistake and publicly acknowledged it, but it was too little too late. It's doubtful that his 2011 statements contributed to a more fair and balanced approach toward Israel within Western circles or diplomatic international forums, such as the United Nations Human Rights Council and the United Nations General Assembly, who are known for their biased approach toward Israel.[26, 27] What we do know is that this is an all-too-common situation.

After the 2008–2009 conflict, Ḥamās continued to attack Israeli cities and continued to use the people of the Gaza Strip as human shields—committing clear and horrifying war crimes[28]—and Israel has continued to provide evidence proving its efforts to avoid collateral damage and mitigate the chance of harming civilians by taking preventative measures.[29]

Why then do some Western circles squarely point the finger of blame at Israel, while Ḥamās, which rules the Gaza Strip and formally call for the destruction of Israel through jihad and is formally defined by United States and the European Union as a terror reorganization, is frequently exempted from responsibility? Why is Islamic Jihad in Palestine, another Palestinian organization defined as a terror organization, also frequently exempted from responsibility?

The Council for Foreign Relations stated:

> The Islamic Jihad in Palestine [IJIP] wants to reestablish a sovereign, Islamic Palestinian state with the geographic borders of the pre-1948 mandate Palestine. The PIJ advocates the destruction of Israel through violent means; it approaches the Arab-Israeli conflict as an ideological war, not a territorial dispute. PIJ members see violence as the only way to remove Israel from the Middle East map and reject any two-state arrangement in which Israel and Palestine coexist. The PIJ, unlike other Palestinian separatist groups, refuses to negotiate or engage in the diplomatic process.[30]

Ḥamās's charter follows the ideology of Ḥasan al-Bannā', the founder of the Muslim Brotherhood, who proclaimed:

> Israel will rise and will remain erect until Islam eliminates it as it had eliminated its predecessors. Our struggle against the Jews is extremely

> wide-ranging and grave, so much so that it will need all the loyal efforts we can wield, to be followed by further steps and reinforced by successive battalions from the multifarious Arab and Islamic world, until the enemies are defeated and Allah's victory prevails. . . . Ḥamās is one of the links in the chain of jihad in the confrontation with the Zionist invasion. . . . There is no solution to the Palestinian problem except by jihad.[31]

Ḥamās and Islamic Jihad in Palestine are not looking for reconciliation—they are not calling for a peaceful solution to the Israeli-Palestinian conflict.[32, 33] For Ḥamās and IJIP, the use of violence is the only means for them to achieve their objectives. They shoot rockets at Israeli cities and dig tunnels into Israeli communities not because they have a disagreement with Israel about issues like borders or the use of natural resources, but because they want to destroy Israel by any means necessary. In the eyes of Ḥamās and IJIP, the presence of Jews in any part of Israel—or "Palestine" in their terminology—is an act of occupation. They believe that Jerusalem and Tel Aviv are Israeli settlements and that all Jews in Israel are colonialists and foreigners who have no right to be there and must be forced out. These views are stated brazenly and publicly and yet frequently go unheard by Westerners who believe the violence is about Israel's "occupation," "human rights," and the "humanitarian crisis in the Gaza Strip caused by Israel."

Throughout my career as an advisor, in policy design, as a strategic intelligence analyst, and in my capacity as the fellow of Intelligence and Middle East Affairs at the Eisenhower Institute in Washington, DC, and Gettysburg, Pennsylvania, I have had the honor of addressing and meeting a wide variety of Western audiences—thousands of people of all ages and backgrounds. In this capacity, I have frequently heard the wrong, all-too-common Western narrative. Over the years, I've tried to get to the root of it, but for a long time, my encounters did not help me answer these questions, and sometimes they added to my confusion. However, in recent years, a number of incidents have begun to shed light on the puzzling phenomenon and the mindset and motivation behind it.

One encounter took place on a hot summer day at the end of 2009. I was in the Israeli border town of Sderot, located just over half a mile from the northern border of the Gaza Strip, and was briefing a group of journalists from Europe about the security situation in the area surrounding the Gaza Strip, including the ramifications of the rockets and mortar shells launched from the Gaza Strip at Sderot, a city of twenty-five thousand people. The briefing took place at the Sderot police station, where there were dozens of these rockets and mortar shells on display.

I frequently encounter people, particularly foreign journalists and students, who refer to rockets and mortar shells as "primitive weapons." This is an exceedingly deceptive label. These weapons are lethal—they destroy and kill. They are only "primitive" in the sense that they are relatively easy and inexpensive to produce. Once launched, their flight paths cannot be controlled and there is no way to know where they will land. However, when they are aimed at cities, the probability that they will hit some target—a bus, a coffee shop, a home, a restaurant, a school, a shopping mall—is high. Where exactly is a game of Russian roulette.

The first rocket launched at Israel from the Gaza Strip was in 2001. The launching of mortars and rockets has intensified since Ḥamās took over the Gaza Strip in 2007. During the last two violent rounds between Israel and Ḥamās, Operation Pillar of Defense in November 2012 and Operation Protective Edge from July–August 2014, rockets fired from Gaza reached Tel Aviv and Jerusalem, the two largest metropolitan areas in Israel.

To date, tens of thousands of rockets and mortar shells have been fired from the Gaza Strip at towns and cities in Israel. The rockets and mortars have caused more than forty Israeli deaths of both soldiers and civilians. Over time, the range of the rockets has been extended. The warheads contain increasing amounts of explosives.

It is thanks to the Israeli rocket defense system, Iron Dome—which intercepts short-range rockets and 155 mm artillery shell threats with ranges of up to forty-three miles[34]—that the scale of death and destruction in Israeli cities has not been bigger. Had Israel not developed the Iron Dome system, the toll would not only have been higher on the Israeli side, it would have been enormously higher on the Palestinian side, since if thousands of rockets and mortar shells were raining down on Israeli civilians, Israel would have had no choice other than to use much more severe military capacities in the Gaza Strip to end the shooting, as well as to end Ḥamās's rule. The outcome could have been catastrophic for the people of the Gaza Strip. Ironically, Ḥamās and the people of Gaza should thank Israel for developing Iron Dome.

In my briefing with the journalists, as we stood beside the display of rockets, I explained that because of the rockets and mortar shells, it's easy to understand the Israeli position and the self-defense steps it has had to take against Ḥamās and other Palestinian organizations in the Gaza Strip. But as soon as the words came out of my mouth, a journalist was quick to jump in, "It's true that it's possible to understand the Israeli claim of self-defense, but . . ."

There was that familiar "*but.*" I have heard that "*but*" over and over from various Western journalists, academics, politicians, social activists, students, and others. It's true that Israel has the right to defend its citizens, "but that does not justify the terrible price that the residents of Gaza are paying"; "but the struggle isn't fair because Israel is much stronger than Ḥamās"; "but the Israeli military reaction is disproportional."

On one level, the "but" reflects feelings of upset, anger, and compassion stemming from the impact of disturbing and heart-wrenching pictures on the Internet and television. While Israel conducts a policy of self-restraint when it comes to broadcasting pictures of Israeli fatalities, Arab news networks and platforms—particularly Qatar's Al Jazeera News Network—share as many graphic scenes as possible from—or ostensibly from—the Gaza Strip. Photos of lifeless children and distraught people sitting in the rubble of their homes are always powerful and heartbreaking. It's easy to understand why people are so upset when they see these pictures.

On another level, the "but" reflects and reinforces the accumulating and damaging impact of statements and streams of thought that already echo within Western circles—statements like "the crisis caused by Israel in the Gaza Strip"; "Israel is the mighty aggressor"; and "the Israeli siege on the Gaza Strip."

The combination of being upset, angry, and compassionate together with deeply embedded narratives is so powerful that it creates a cognitive dissonance. On one hand, the people who use the "but" know that Ḥamās is shooting rockets that kill, that shooting rockets at Israelis must be stopped, and that Israel has the right to defend itself. They morally identify with the Israeli arguments, acknowledging their ethical and practical validity. They know that it is Ḥamās, not Israel, who controls the Gaza Strip. They know that Ḥamās shoots rockets from civilian areas and that it uses human shields. They know that Ḥamās diverts resources that could be used for reconstruction to procure weapons and build tunnels. They know that Ḥamās is committed to the destruction of Israel. These are facts that these people are well are of; however, at the same time, they are emotionally impacted by the pictures coming from the Gaza Strip and are overwhelmed by narratives. To makes sense of their feelings, the narratives, and reality, they feel the need to "balance" their outlook—and that is the role of the "but . . ." It is a tool to bridge an inner confusion and conflict. In their mindset, if they don't add the word "but," they wouldn't be identifying with the Gazan people.

It was an important insight, but led to another question: why is it important for these people to identify with the Gazan people? At the time I didn't have an answer.

The next link in my chain of questioning happened on a hilltop at the height of the fighting between Israel and Ḥamās in the summer of 2014. I was briefing a group of students studying at leading universities in the United States, Europe, and Southeast Asia—all members of an elite leadership development program. We stood on a hill overlooking the coastal plain of Israel and the city of Tel Aviv. The runways of Ben Gurion Airport, the international airport of the State of Israel, were spread out in front of us. Every few minutes, a passenger plane flew over us on its way to land. I pointed out to the students that the planes were taking a different route than usual because there was increased danger that a rocket or missile might be fired at the aircraft from the Gaza Strip. The fact was that rockets were being deliberately fired in the general direction of the airport with the goal of leading to a full or partial paralysis of the airport. During the war the airport shut down for almost forty-eight hours.

One of the students, a young Jewish man from the States said, "The scope of the destruction that has been caused as a result of the Israeli military operation in Gaza is not at all proportional to the threat of the rockets. The threat of the rockets is not so serious, in the end. So what if rockets land in open areas here and there?"

I was dumbfounded. I said, "We are at the height of fighting. You can see the destruction, death, and terror that have been caused in Israeli cities and communities as a result of the shooting of rockets and mortar shells. You can see right here, with your own eyes, how the threat of rockets impacts Israel's airspace and you can understand the catastrophic ramifications of rockets launched from Gaza striking a passenger plane. Why are you dismissing such a serious threat?"

He didn't answer.

This episode bothered me for a long time. I wondered why he made his statement. It completely contradicted the reality playing out in front of him. I felt that his reaction reflected an inner dissonance between an element of his worldview that was not compatible with reality, and his way of dealing with this was by denying reality. It also seemed that his statement was an attempt to placate some inner need—I just couldn't figure out what the need was. What was so important to this Jewish, educated, Western young man, who lives thousands of miles away from the conflict, that he needed to guard and preserve? What motivated him to airbrush the reality that does not match some preconceived perception of his on what is actually unfolding?

My recurring encounter with this phenomenon led me to believe that there was something deep within people at play. I intuitively felt that emotional and psychological factors, rather than intellectual and academic considerations, were operating. This insight was a first clue for me, and I realized that I had to focus on understanding the essence and origins of this mindset.

But there was still something missing, a central piece of the puzzle. My answer to what this was came from a surprising place.

I was watching a documentary film called *In the Dark Room*,[35] a movie about Magdalena Kopp, who was an active member of the Revolutionary Cells, a left-wing German terrorist group active from the 1970s until the mid-1990s, and the former wife of Ilich Ramírez Sánchez. Sánchez, known as "Carlos the Jackal," was born in Venezuela and, now in prison, was considered an epic terrorist—a "bin Laden of the West"—during the 1970s and 1980s. He worked with terror organizations like the Baader-Meinhof group, a German militant group that became the Red Army Faction,[36] and the Popular Front for the Liberation of Palestine, run by Palestinian radical Wadie Haddad,[37] which was associated with terror attacks that shocked the world. Among them were the massacre of Israeli athletes at the Munich Olympics in 1972, the kidnapping of OPEC oil ministers in 1975 when Sánchez led a takeover of OPEC's headquarters in Vienna, the hijacking of an Air France plane to Entebbe, Uganda, in 1976, and a half-dozen attacks on French targets. Sánchez was sentenced to life in prison by a French court in December 1997.[38]

The documentary introduced Carlos and Kopp's daughter, Rosa, a young woman in her late twenties, who was exploring the personal history of her father. Along her journey, she met Bassam Abu Sharif, who had been an advisor to former Palestinian President Yasser Arafat and had known her father well. When I saw Sharif on the screen, memories of the personal meetings I had with him in the 1990s in his swanky apartment in Amman, the capital of Jordan, flooded my mind. Sharif and I had talked late into the night. He was a fascinating conversationalist, charismatic and cordial, and an exemplary host. It was not a unique discovery for either one of us to learn that the enemy had a face, a history, a name, and a life story. In one of our conversations he said to me with a smile, "You [Israel] took an ear and an eye from me,"—his hearing had been badly damaged and he had lost an eye in an attempted assassination of him in 1972, which was attributed to the Israeli Intelligence and Special Operations Agency, Mossad[39]—"but I don't hate you. I believe it is possible to find a solution."

In Rosa's meeting with him, as documented in the film, Sharif presented the Palestinian narrative to her and then, when he finished speaking, took out a *keffiyeh*—the traditional head covering worn by many men in the Arab world—and wrapped it around her shoulders. The camera focused on Rosa's eyes and captured her expression as he did this. The emotion offered me another important piece of the puzzle. Rosa's awe made it clear that she was emotionally caught up in her father's history, but I intuitively felt that there was a deeper level to the scene.

This related to the act taking place—all the elements of a ceremony were present in it: the story (the Palestinian narrative), the idealistic mission ("liberation" and "fighting against injustice"), the authoritative mentor (Bassam Abu Sharif), the symbol (the *keffiyeh*), and the act itself (the placing of the *keffiyeh* around Rosa's shoulders).

It was then that the wheels of my understanding really began to turn . . .

A lot of young people from the West have an international multicultural value system. They are environmentally aware and are drawn to social activism.

Their worldview is a universe that is an integrated human-ecological system, a world in which romantic idealism in the form of missions to protect animals, save the environment, help the underprivileged, and volunteer for organizations engaged in humanitarian assistance make an important personal statement and provide a mission that offers self-fulfillment. Their world is one of relativism, in which it isn't always clear who is right and who is wrong because there are many sides and narratives to every issue and these are steeped in cultural, economic, historical, political, normative, and social backgrounds—and the goal is to accept and understand the *other*. These young people have learned to agree to disagree—respectfully. Yet, curiously, in this world of colors, there is one place where the rainbow becomes black and white, where their world becomes a dual narrative, a two-colored world. This place is the zone of the Israeli-Palestinian conflict. The white, legitimate narrative often belongs to the Palestinians, and the black, illegitimate one often belongs to Israel.

As I understood this, I began to assemble all the pieces of the puzzle into a whole picture: The various characters—the journalist in Sderot, the student on the hilltop overlooking Tel Aviv, and Rosa, the daughter of Sánchez—merged into a single, three-dimensional image. I thought about what they had in common: they were approximately the same age, in their mid- to late twenties; they grew up in a Western culture, in the United States or Europe; and they belonged to Western elites, in this case academia or media. Their generation, described as Generation "Y" or millennials, is educated, liberal, technologically sophisticated—the "hero generation"[40, 41] whose strength is in collective civic action and who are supposed to rebuild institutions.[42] They are driven by romantic idealism—to aid, to protect, to respond, to save.

The ideals of this generation are laudable, noble, respectable, and valuable. They express positive values, such as awareness, compassion, initiative, commitment, and responsibility. It is my thesis that these Western-bred millennials see themselves as knights, with *just* and *noble* goals. Western culture is suffocated with the concept of the knight who saves the day. It is present in countless Western fantasy movies and video games and is often powerful in the lives of children growing up in the West. But the knight cannot only function in a rainbow of relativism, multiculturalism, and a sea of narratives. A knight—from the essence of his being—also needs the ideal of a world of black-and-white, good and evil. He must resolutely protect the weak, pursue what is noble and just, and stand up to the dragon. The Israeli-Palestinian conflict has become an arena in which some of the young Western elites believe they must protect the "weak Palestinians," pursue the "justice" of there being a Palestinian state, and fight Israel, the "dragon." The set-up has led to the active, enthusiastic involvement of Western youth in organizations like the "Free Palestine Movement," "Students for Justice in Palestine," and the Boycott, Divestment, and Sanctions movement (BDS).

The developers of the Boycott, Divestment, and Sanctions campaign claim that it allows "people of conscience" to play an effective role in the "Palestinian struggle for justice."[43] The mission statements of the Free Palestine Movement and Students for Justice in Palestine express similar virtuous-sounding intentions. The mission statement of the Free Palestine Movement reads:

> The purpose of Free Palestine Movement is to defend and advocate for the human rights of all Palestinians. We propose to support these rights by defying barriers imposed by Israeli and international authorities upon travel and trade to, from and within Palestine for Palestinians and persons invited by Palestinians, such as visitors, human rights observers, humanitarian aid workers, journalists, merchants or others, and to impose pressure and sanctions upon any parties that deny such rights.[44]

The mission statement of Students for Justice in Palestine reads:

> We believe that our mission as students living in a free democracy is to promote the cause of justice and speak out against oppression. Students for Justice in Palestine envisions a world where humans are treated equally with respect and dignity; where people live without the oppression of foreign occupation. We envision a world where justice and the rule of law bind humans together. We envision that one day, Palestinians will be free from occupation, free from fear, free from poverty, and will be able to determine their own fate as an independent nation living peacefully with its neighbors. Fully cognizant

> of the realities on the ground, we will nonetheless continue our work and keep in mind what Elie Wiesel once said, "There may be times when we are powerless to prevent injustice, but there must never be a time when we fail to protest."[45]

Advocate, defend, defy, free, support in the pursuit of freedom, independence, justice, and the rule of law—these are the actions the knight takes to counter the injustice, oppression, lack of human rights, imposed barriers, and limitation of freedom of movement it perceives.

History teaches that a cultural, emotional, intellectual, and political atmosphere that gives birth to romantic idealism can sometimes produce fanaticism. Communism is one example. The Free Palestine Movement, Students for Justice in Palestine, and the Boycott, Divestment, and Sanctions movement are other examples.

The fanatic is motivated by the perception that he knows the ultimate truth. The fanatic is inspired by an ideal or vision that in his view embraces the highest moral grounds. The fanatic views his ideal or vision to be pure and whole—and therefore immune to criticism, questioning, and doubts. Facts or aspects of reality that do not comply with the fanatic's ideal or vision are seen as irrelevant or simply ignored. The fanatic must be passionately dedicated to the ideal or vision as a way to counter uncomfortable facts or aspects of reality that compromise or cast doubt on the validity of the ideal or vision.

In the Palestinian-Israeli conversation, the knights' romantic idealism turns them into fanatics. Facts, sequences of events, actions and reactions, and causes and outcomes are minimized or irrelevant, sometimes brushed away, other times deliberately and fully ignored. Thus, for example, the fact that following a bloody coup by Ḥamās in 2007, the Gaza Strip, at the choice of the Palestinian people, has been governed by Ḥamās, a terrorist organization, is airbrushed. It does not comply with the narrative "occupation" of the Gaza Strip by Israel. The fact that Ḥamās has armed forces numbering dozens of thousands of militants[46] and these militants proudly display their weapons and shoot thousands of rockets at Israeli cities is also airbrushed. It does not comply with the narrative that the Palestinians are helpless, defenseless people who need to be rescued. In fact, many of the Ḥamās charters are altogether ignored: Articles six and seven of its charter read:

> The Islamic Resistance Movement is a distinct Palestinian Movement that owes its loyalty to Allah, derives from Islam its way of life, and strives to raise the banner of Allah over every inch of Palestine. . . . Ḥamās has been looking forward to implementing Allah's promise and will take however long is necessary to do so. The prophet, prayer and peace be upon him, said, "The time will not come until Muslims will fight the Jews and kill them; until the Jews hide behind rocks and trees, which will cry, 'O Muslim! There is a Jew hiding behind me, come on and kill him!'"

Article thirteen of the Ḥamās charter reads:

> The so-called peaceful solutions and the international conferences to resolve the Palestinian problem are all contrary to the beliefs of the Islamic Resistance Movement because renouncing any part of Palestine means renouncing part of the religion. The nationalism of the Islamic Resistance Movement is part of its faith. The movement educates its members to adhere to its principles and to raise the banner of Allah over their homeland as they fight their jihad. . . . There is no solution to the Palestinian problem except by jihad.[47]

The charters are overlooked because they do not comply with the narratives that "Israel is the aggressor," "the problem is the settlements," "defending the powerless," or "it's about justice and freedom." The Gaza Strip is viewed through the romantic lenses of the need to act in order to defend "occupied people," "defenseless people," and for the noble cause of "justice." In the passion of romantic knighthood, no questions regarding Ḥamās's responsibility for the situation in the Gaza Strip are presented. The people of Gaza are not held accountable for holding their leaders accountable. Reality is ignored.

The student who stood on the hilltop is a fanatic because he subdued reality to an ideal he stands for. This explains his statement, "So what if a few rockets land in open areas?" The fact that the rockets were launched is irrelevant as far as he is concerned since he believes that "the Palestinian side is the weak side" and to attain justice, he must defend the weak.

But reality *is* relevant—and here is the reality:

Since 2007, Ḥamās has controlled the Gaza Strip with an iron fist. Ḥamās collects taxes, conducts foreign policy, maintains a government, legislates and enforces laws, and employs dozens of thousands of workers—doctors, government officials, municipal workers, preachers, street cleaners, tax collectors, teachers, etc.

Ḥamās has a military force, a police force, and security services made up of dozens of thousands of people.

Ḥamās does not come from the moon. Ḥamās is from the Gaza Strip—its leadership grew up there and still lives there. Their family and friends live there too.

Hundreds of thousands of people in the Gaza Strip directly and indirectly benefit from Ḥamās' rule.[48, 49]

Many people in the Arab word—including from inside the Gaza Strip—accuse the Ḥamās leadership and officials of corruption.[50, 51, 52, 53]

In the summer of 2014, Ḥamās initiated a new military round against Israel. The war lasted fifty days. More than two thousand Palestinians were killed, many of them civilians, and thousands of people were injured. Residential areas and infrastructure in the Gaza Strip were destroyed. On the Israeli side, dozens of people—most of them soldiers—were killed, hundreds were injured, and residential areas and infrastructure were damaged.

In August 2014, in the midst of the war, Dr. David Palumbo-Liu, a professor of comparative literature at Stanford University who has a very impressive curriculum vitae[54]—but is not a Middle East scholar—published an article titled "Millennials Are Over Israel: A New Generation, Outraged Over Gaza, Rejects Washington's Reflexive Support." In it he quoted an article in the *Washington Post* that presented statistics gathered by the Pew Research Center:

> A new Pew Research Center poll is the second in the past week to show a huge generational split on the current conflict in Gaza. While all age groups north of 30 years old clearly blame Ḥamās

> more than Israel for the current violence, young adults buck the trend in a big way. Among 18 to 29-year olds, 29 percent blame Israel more for the current wave of violence, while 21 percent blame Ḥamās.[55]

Palumbo-Liu wrote, "More and more younger Americans, growing up well past the postwar era, find the Holocaust narrative to be less than absolutely and unquestionably a good reason to support the horrible killings in Gaza."[56] He wrote that while anti-Semitism raised its ugly head against the background of the war, the criticism of Israel is mostly "because of the actions of the state of Israel in staging a brutal, prolonged attack on the Palestinian people that is replete with violations of human rights and international law. That Ḥamās has also committed attacks on civilians does not erase the fact that Israel's violence violates basic international humanitarian laws."[57]

In considering how what was going on in Gaza was shared with a Western audience, Palumbo-Liu wrote that "the massive attack on Gaza and its obscene civilian death toll is now delivered to a global audience via a variety of media forms that far exceed the mainstream media. Contemporary forms of social media deliver images from Gaza and opinions on the invasion as it takes place."[58]

Toward the end of his article, Palumbo-Liu expressed clear sympathy for the Boycott, Divestment, and Sanctions movement:

> The fact that more and more younger Americans are increasingly skeptical of supporting Israel's military efforts is encouraging in the long run. But we should not lose sight of the tremendous humanitarian crisis we are witnessing today. Change might be coming, but for now action is needed.[59]

Palumbo-Liu comes across as both a knight who wants to slay the dragon and a Western mediator of knowledge who—while very esteemed and highly educated—has no background in the Middle East and yet has become a self-styled Middle East expert with a long list of published anti-Israel, pro-Palestinian, pro-BDS articles. In this article, he presented the findings of the

Pew Poll regarding the spread of criticism among millennials and a litany of concepts to explain the results. However, he did not provide an analysis or explanation of the circumstances that led to the war, and the language he used was suffocated with the knight vs. dragon mindset, that Israel is staging a brutal, prolonged attack on Gaza and the Palestinian people that is replete with violations of human rights and international law, and is causing an obscene civilian death toll.

Like a typical knight, Palumbo-Liu airbrushed away Ḥamās's responsibility for the war. Ḥamās's role was summed up in two sentences. One is the vague sentence, "Ḥamās is shooting rockets," in which he failed to mention that thousands of rockets have been launched at Israeli cities. The other sentence argued, "The fact that Ḥamās has also committed attacks on civilians does not erase the fact that Israel's violence violates basic international humanitarian laws regarding proportionality." Not only did he create a distorted analogy between Israel and Ḥamās (writing that Ḥamās *also* committed attacks on civilians), but, amazingly, he also did not write one word about the suffering of Israelis caused by the shooting of rockets.

Palumbo-Liu dismissed the sequence of events, actions and reactions, and causes and outcomes as being irrelevant. "Armed," like a knight, with the conviction that he knew the noncontroversial truth, Palumbo-Liu, like his comrades, subdued reality to concepts, rhetoric, slogans, and terminology, ignoring it when it contradicted or did not comply with his argument, rather than embarking on a path of investigation, questioning, and critical thinking.

Another assertion of his was, "Notwithstanding Netanyahu's ghoulish assertion that Ḥamās was opportunistically using 'telegenic' corpses to garner sympathy and political points . . . one cannot help but ask back, 'Who created those corpses in the first place?'" This is a strong statement and a question that deserves a real answer.

Ḥamās did not initiate the 2014 war because of romantic ideals. It was not about "fighting occupation," "freedom," or any of the other slogans and concepts embedded within Western circles. The truth is much less glorious and noble. Ḥamās launched a war against Israel because of its own financial and political crisis. Let's look at the facts and not the narratives.

In the summer of 2014, Ḥamās was desperate. It was drowning in a financial and political crisis following two major developments, both of which occurred in 2012 and 2013. One development was its loss of Iranian funds. Under increasing pressure from the Sunni world due to the slaughtering of Sunnis by the Assad-Iran alliance, Ḥamās had left Damascus and detached itself from the axis. Throughout 2013 and the first few months of 2014, Ḥamās tried to rehabilitate its relations with Iran, hoping that Iran would resume its financial support, but the attempts failed.[60, 61, 62] Ḥamās did receive funds from Qatar and Turkey, but they were too small to ease its growing financial crisis.[63, 64] The other development was the downfall of the Muslim Brotherhood in Egypt—a government very friendly to Ḥamās—in July 2013. Ḥamās formally defines itself as the branch of the Muslim Brotherhood in Palestine—and the rise of a new government in Egypt that was hostile to Ḥamās and its mother movement, the Muslim Brotherhood, was not good news for Ḥamās. The Egyptian government, under President Sisi, launched a massive campaign aimed at demolishing Ḥamās's major income source: the thousands of tunnels dug from the Sinai Peninsula into the Gaza Strip. In April 2015, Egyptian Major General Khalid Okasha said:[65]

> [The] tunnels are gates for terrorism and external support of terrorism from Gaza to Sinai. . . . Expanding the buffer zone, maximizing tunnel digging, and using sanctions will restore stability to Sinai and decrease the amount of terrorist attacks that often enter into Egypt from the Gaza border.

Ḥamās has long used a massive tunnel industry to smuggle things like ammunition, cars, cash, fuel, militants, narcotics, and weapons into the Gaza Strip from the Sinai Peninsula.

A detailed report made by the Institute for Palestine Studies shed light on the scale, operation, and funding of the tunnels industry in the Gaza Strip under Ḥamās's control.[66] It noted that tunnels, which cost between eighty thousand and two hundred thousand dollars to build, were funded by mosques who promoted the project as part of "the resistance," as well as by money raised by public and private institutions and investors.

As the industry progressed and more and more tunnels were built, there was an increasing profit reaped from it. A report from the Institute for Palestinian Studies explained:

> Private investors, including Ḥamās members who raised capital through their mosque networks, partnered with families straddling the border. Lawyers drafted contracts for cooperatives to build and operate commercial tunnels. The contracts detailed the number of partners (generally four to fifteen), the value of the respective shares, and the mechanism for distributing shareholder profits. A typical partnership encompassed a cross-section of Gazan society, including, for example, a porter at the Rafah land crossing, a security officer in the former PA administration, agricultural workers, university graduates, nongovernmental organization (NGO) employees, and diggers.[67]

The tunnels also offered direct employment; and for a time, tunnel workers were the best-paid workers in Gaza and the tunnel trade was also the largest overall employer of youth.[68]

The Ḥamās government formalized the smuggling economy through the creation of the Tunnel Affairs Commission—which in 2015 evolved into the Border and Crossings Authority. The entity was overseen by the Palestinian Ministry of Interior, which introduced a tunnel application and licensing system and regulations regarding what was allowed to be imported by whom and for how much, and also acted as a mediator between suppliers, operators, and merchants. It developed a more sophisticated customs, revenue collection, and taxation system and also increased fees for things such as getting permits, building, and connecting to electricity. By 2009, it was reported that Ḥamās annually earned one hundred and fifty to two hundred million dollars in revenue.

By late 2010, some five thousand tunnel owners and twenty-five thousand workers, supporting about one hundred and fifty thousand dependents, 10 percent of Gaza's population,[69] were working on between one thousand and two thousand sophisticated, well-built tunnels. Trade was brisk, prices were low, and shortages were non-existent. The elite, as well as tourists, flocked to swanky resorts and glitzy cafes. Real estate prices were booming and luxury cars were plentiful and cheap.

Ḥamās was intent on one thing, staying in power, and built a kingdom of crime through corruption and cartel-style business practices to ensure it maintained control over resources, and therefore total control, over the Gaza Strip. The tunnels became a chicken laying golden eggs for Ḥamās officials and their families and friends.[70, 71, 72, 73]

During the rule of Mubārak, Egypt, from time to time, conducted campaigns during which parts of the tunnels were destroyed. However, following the downfall of the Muslim Brotherhood's rule in Egypt in July 2013 and the rise to power of a government hostile to the Muslim Brotherhood, Egypt began an increasingly intense, systematic, and sometimes brutal military campaign, which it accelerated after two attacks on October 24, 2014, killed more than thirty Egyptian soldiers. The military campaign intended to destroy the massive underground infrastructure[74] and included the use of tear gas and explosives, the plugging of tunnel entrances with solid waste, and the flooding of tunnels with sewage. The Egyptians' shift to this hard-line policy stemmed from the fact that the tunnels were used for the smuggling of ammunition, money, terrorists, and weapons to fuel terror attacks on Egyptian targets in the Sinai Peninsula.

As part of its efforts, Egypt also created a buffer zone along the Egyptian-Gaza border. In the buffer zone, residents were evacuated, and buildings, businesses, farms, greenhouses, homes, shops, etc. located in its path were bulldozed and razed. Many tunnels were found under them.

Without money coming in through the tunnels, Ḥamās could not pay the salaries of its more than fifty thousand employees—which totaled almost forty million dollars a month.[75]

During the first half of 2014, with limited patronage and Ḥamās's main income source strangled by Egypt, its financial crisis was deepening fast. It had become unable to offer the people of the Gaza Strip with a practical way out of their difficult situation, a situation that no one other than Ḥamās, who has governed the Gaza Strip since 2007, was responsible for.

Then, in March 2014, Ḥamās sustained another blow. In the concluding announcement of an Arab League summit held in Kuwait, no reference was made to the closure of the Gaza Strip. This was a major disappointment for Ḥamās. It had thought it was on the road to becoming a recognized player in the Arab world and would elicit sympathy at the summit because of the impact the closing had on it. Yet it had again been overlooked.[76]

Desperate, unable to pay salaries, with nowhere to turn, ignored—or harshly criticized—by major factors in the Arab world, Ḥamās decided to initiate a war. The logic beyond its decision was that by initiating a war, Ḥamās could divert Gazans' attention away from their dire situation. A war would enable Ḥamās to present demands—like the opening of the Rafah crossing, the building of a seaport, etc.—that would alleviate the growing economic stresses. In its calculation, a war would earn Ḥamās political points over its political rival, the Palestinian Authority, and would position Ḥamās as the defender of the Palestinians—committed to the idea of defeating Israel by force, thereby fulfilling the ultimate Palestinian goal. Most importantly, they thought it would bring money. It thought that Iran and the Muslim Brotherhood would support its mission to destroy Israel and revert to financially supporting it.

Iranian journalist Amir Taheri summed up the plan in an article titled "Gaza Strip and the Curse of Never-Ending Wars." In it he wrote:

> What are the reasons for the war? One is the downfall of the Muslim Brotherhood. The other is the cut of Iranian support to Ḥamās, and the growing discontent among the people of Gaza against the background of economic challenge. Ḥamās needed to look for an exit from his its situation and the way to do that was by launching rockets on Israel.[77]

The war had nothing to do with Israel—yet Israel had to pay the price.

Indeed, many Arab journalists pointed the finger of blame at Ḥamās, arguing that it sacrificed the people of Gaza in the service of "foreign powers"—i.e. Iran and the Muslim Brotherhood—and for political calculations. Saudi journalist Abdullah al-Obaidi wrote that "spring will arrive in the Gaza Strip once its people realize that Ḥamās sacrifices them in the service of foreign states' interests."[78] In an article titled "Decision at the Service of the

Muslim Brotherhood and Iran," former Jordanian Minister of Information Saleh al-Qalab wrote:

> Ḥamās initiated the war in the service of Iran and the Muslim Brotherhood. The Palestinians should demand Ḥamās take accountability for the destruction and suffering it caused them. For how long will the Palestinians continue to pay the price of the Arab world's inner politics?[79]

The war had nothing to do with romantic idealism, nothing to do with "occupation," "the humanitarian crisis," "freedom," "human rights," or anything of that nature. It was a cynical calculation whose aim was to pull Ḥamās out of the muddy reality that it was responsible for and to ensure its continued power and rule.

Dozens of Israelis and thousands of Palestinians paid for this with their lives.

Despite the fact, the Ḥamās took over the Gaza Strip in a military coup; rules the Gaza Strip; has massively armed military and security forces; employs thousands of people; calls for the elimination of the State of Israel and the killing of Jews; and time and time again initiates military confrontations, the Western knights do not hold Ḥamās accountable for the situation in the Gaza Strip. According to this mindset, Ḥamās is qualified to rule and launch violence, yet it is exempt from accountability and responsibility.

During 2015, Egypt boosted its activity and destroyed the tunnels leading into Sinai. It dug thirty forty-six thousand feet deep and thirty feet wide land ditches about one mile from the border with Gaza.[80] For this it moved hundreds of families, paid millions of dollars in compensation, and now, reportedly, plans to fill the tunnels with water and create fish farms.[81] The activity is so impactful that the mayor of Rafah, Subhi Radwan, said: "We appeal to our brothers in Egypt to stop the work that endangers the people of Gaza. We have enough problems: wars, siege, and a difficult economic situation."[82]

The tough Egyptian policy toward Ḥamās, which impacts the lives of the almost two million residents of the Gaza Strip, is met with silence from Western circles who actively and vocally fully blame Israel for the dire situation in the Gaza Strip. They don't speak of how Egypt's actions are affecting the Palestinian people because this does not jive with their thesis and where they like to place the blame. Palestinian journalist Khaled Abu Toameh described this well when he wrote:

> Egyptian President Abdel Fattah el-Sisi's uncompromising war on terrorism, especially along the border with the Gaza Strip, seems to be bearing fruit. It is a war that is being waged away from the spotlight and with almost no reaction from the international community. This situation is a perfect example of how the international community and the United Nations do not care about the "plight" of the Palestinians as long as Israel is not involved.[83]

Time and time again the finger is pointed solely at Israel. And that brings me back to Professor Palumbo-Liu. Given his biography, I will allow myself to assume that he probably did not have the professional skills to investigate the events that led to the war between Ḥamās and Israel in 2014, and also that he was unaware of the growing criticism in the Arab world of Ḥamās and its responsibility for the tragedy of the Gaza Strip. Yet a lack of knowledge did not prevent him from throwing accusations at Israel. It is easy to write articles against Israel using buzz words and propaganda. Whether or not they dialogue with reality is not always of concern.

Professor Palumbo-Liu blamed Israel's behavior and actions for the declining support of young Americans. Perhaps the real reason for the declining support is because people like him are given a central stage to percolate and assimilate the concept of Israel as a dragon. Palumbo-Liu's articles are published by media such as Salon.com, which has an audience of 17.6 million unique viewers a month;[84] Truthout, an investigative website that claims it "works to spark action by revealing systemic injustice;[85] Al Jazeera; the *Huffington Post*; and the *Nation*.

In order for the truth to be heard louder than the rants of Palumbo-Liu and others like him, people who want to improve the discourse, to contribute to a better, more accurate understanding of the Middle East, need to fine-tune their critical thinking and analytical capacities. Informed advocates for

Israel can counter the sad atmosphere that gives stage to intellectuals who—although they lack the knowledge and tools to interpret the reality of the Middle East—assimilate and percolate a moral judgment of Israel, portraying Israel as the dragon, and avoid accountability for their inaccurate statements and misguided accusations.

Intellectuals who are educating, informing, teaching, and molding young minds are expected to be professionals and knowledgeable. They should be confronted with the demand to explain to what extent their moral judgment is dialoguing with reality. Lack of knowledge should make one more humble in his or her professional outlook and moral judgments. Airbrushing facts is inexcusable.

There are different kinds of fanaticism. There is a tolerant, nonviolent fanaticism—not all fanatics wish to impose themselves on others. And there is a violent, intolerant fanaticism—like that of ISIS—that strives to create a world subdued not only to its ideology but also to a distorted value system and moral codes of behavior.

Many people argue that the Boycott, Divestment, and Sanctions campaign was a mask for anti-Semitism. I do not agree with that outlook. Some of Israel's harshest critics are motivated by blind hatred toward Israel and Jews, but I do not believe that most of the Western supporters of the BDS campaign are. I believe that most of them genuinely believe that BDS is the right way to bring peace. Yet, the BDS campaign is a form of fanaticism, striving to impose its vision, even through the use of violence.

Boycotts, divestments, and sanctions are proactive moves. The BDS campaign is justified by the belief that the policies Israel uses in response to its conflict with the Palestinians are immoral and therefore the measures are undertaken so that Westerners are not idly watching injustice unfold. One could argue that the campaign is nonviolent pressure and therefore a legitimate method of protest—but that's an inaccurate characterization. The BDS movement demands that Israel comply with what it perceives as the morally correct ideal, while dismissing Israel's right to present its arguments. That's not a legitimate way of functioning. Israel should have its argument heard. On the website of the BDS movement, it defines itself as "the global movement for a campaign of Boycott, Divestment and Sanctions (BDS) against Israel until it complies with international law and Palestinian rights . . ."[86] It is BDS's way or the highway.

Part of the refusal to represent Israel's argument is the suffocation of the voices of its supporters. Israeli speakers are interrupted on Western campuses with well-orchestrated shouting and protests.[87, 88] This attempt to suffocate Israel's voice even goes so far as to suffocate Israeli voices when they're not speaking about the conflict. In September 2011, for example, a performance in London by the Israeli Philharmonic Orchestra was repeatedly disrupted by solidarity activists inside and outside of the venue, the Royal Albert Hall.[89]

The violent, intolerant feature of BDS fanaticism is exemplified by an incident involving Palestinian human rights activist Bassam Eid. Eid accuses BDS and pro-Palestinian activists of being ignorant, anti-Palestinian, and the all-time champions in dehumanizing Palestinians. He says the movement exploits the death of Palestinians for propaganda purposes and is a form of economic terrorism because it thrives on the unemployment of Palestinians—believing that the loss of jobs by Palestinians and damage to their society is a reasonable price to pay for the greater goal of weakening Israel.[90] In March—human rights month—2015, during a speech he gave at South Africa's University of Johannesburg for the eleventh International Apartheid Week, students wearing BDS and University of Johannesburg Palestine Solidarity Forum T-shirts barged into the venue and proceeded to interrupt Eid, refusing to allow him to continue his address and calling him "a liar and a sell-out."[91] Intolerant fanaticism suffocates any voice or opinion that does not comply with its outlook.

The underlying goal of the BDS movement is to end any kind of Israeli presence, particularly Israeli settlements, in Palestinian territory or what it perceives to be Palestinian territory. It claims its methods are peaceful and that the Israeli settlements are the obstacle to peace.

However, many people in Israel argue that rockets launched on Israeli cities by armed Palestinian groups like Ḥamās and Islamic Jihad, who regard Tel Aviv and Jerusalem as illegitimate settlements, or the tunnels dug across the Israeli-Gaza border to enable militants to infiltrate Israeli communities inside Israel and murder its inhabitants, are the obstacle to peace. Settlements are a controversial issue that should be discussed in the framework of negotiations—and settlements do not kill, rockets kill. BDS supporters argue that sanctions are to be applied because of an issue that does not kill (settlements), yet make no call for sanctions to be applied against what does kill (rockets). The BDS movement, inspired by a dogmatic vision and outlook, seems to view the value of life as being relative.

As mentioned, the intention of this evaluation is not to counter the arguments of the BDS movement or other anti-Israel groups; rather, to explain why I consider the BDS movement, the Free Palestine Movement, the Palestine Solidarity Campaign, Students for Justice in Palestine, and other groups like them to be fanatics inspired by a romantic ideal of the knight and the dragon. They claim to have the moral superiority of fighting for "freedom, justice, and peace," and claim to support the one and only truth. In the process they delegitimize the moral ground of any counterargument; they ignore or negate facts and reality that do not comply with their moral argument; and they proactively and forcefully attempt to impose their outlook both by dictating a solution, the BDS campaign, and by suffocating the voices of those who disagree with them. These are classic characteristics of fanaticism.

Understanding the drive and motivation of the BDS movement and similar groups of fanatics is essential for those who want to counter anti-Israel activity and bring a true resolution to the conflict and stability to the region.

A word of advice and warning to those who believe that efforts like the BDS campaign will lead to peace and improve the lives of Palestinians: while you may think you're well-intentioned, you are actually placing obstacles in the path toward reconciliation and hope for both Israelis and Palestinians, and you are making the chance for positive progress even more difficult and unlikely.

Why?

First and foremost, because exempting Palestinians from any responsibility for their future perpetuates their vision of themselves as the victim and does not empower them to take responsibility for creating a better future as individuals or a nation.

People who ask, "What is Israel doing for the Palestinians?" as opposed to asking, "What are the Palestinians doing for the Palestinians?" contribute to the atmosphere in which Palestinians perceive themselves—and the world in turn perceives them—as "victims." And this provides Palestinians with an excuse to avoid confronting substantial questions when it comes to the conflict with Israel.

Palestinians need to ask themselves if they are going to subscribe to the path of Ḥamās and Islamic Jihad in Palestine, which has no intention of resolving the conflict peacefully through negotiations and compromises, or if they will reject that path and choose a path that can lead to a better future for themselves and the generations to come.

People in the West who truly want a better future for the Palestinians should dedicate their efforts to empower and strengthen the evolution and development of processes designed to strengthen Palestinian society from within, as opposed to vilifying and holding only one side—Israel—accountable. Such endeavors would better serve the Palestinians than things like boycotts, flotillas, and pressuring artists to cancel concerts in Tel Aviv. An arrangement that may lead to a peaceful solution of the Israeli-Palestinian conflict will not be achieved through boycotts, divestments, sanctions, or the de-legitimization of either side.

CHAPTER TWELVE

WHAT LIES AHEAD: REIGNS OF FEAR, EMPIRE OF HOPE

In the second decade of the twenty-first century, the Middle East is changing dramatically. Some Arab states are coming apart in a violent manner. Regimes, rulers, and all-powerful tyrants who have been an inseparable part of the Middle East for dozens of years have disappeared from sight. Militant Islamist groups are broadening their influence and control throughout the region. Political Islamist groups are at a crossroad and engaged in a process of reorganization and a renewed examination of their paths and future. And a new empire has appeared on the stage of the Middle East—the phantom empire of the Internet and social media.

The massive turbulence has created a Middle East that is, paradoxically, both "new" and "old." It is "new" in the sense that some Arab states established during the twentieth century have disintegrated, and borders between states like Egypt and Libya, Syria and Lebanon, and Iraq and Syria, which were merely lines on maps with no actual barriers on the ground, have become even less relevant. It is "old" in the sense that two ideological, political, and social models, which existed in the Middle East prior to the establishment of the Arab states in the twentieth century, have returned to center stage with a vengeance.

One model is the Islamic caliphate, the central power entity in the Middle East from the emergence of Islam in the seventh century until the end of the first world war and the disintegration of the Turkish Ottoman Empire. It would be inaccurate to say that the Islamic caliphate disappeared with the fall of the Ottoman Empire; instead, the vision and goals of the caliphate continued to exist both as an ideology and as a political outlook among segments of Muslim and Arab societies. However, with the emergence of the modern nation state in the Middle East in the twentieth century, the concept of the caliphate lost its dominancy and was excluded from the centers of political power and policy-making in the Arab and Muslim world. In the second decade of the twenty-first century, the concept of the caliphate is evolving in its most extreme interpretation with the creation of the "Islamic State," which is controlled by ISIS.

ISIS's model of the caliphate aims to realize the ideological, political, and normative characteristics that resemble those that existed in the ancient caliphate. The brutal face of the caliphate that ISIS has developed in the twenty-first century—murderous behavior, female slavery, barbaric destruction of the cultural and archeological legacy of ancient civilizations, an absolute disregard for human life, and the cruel trampling of all acceptable humane norms—bears witness to the intensified extremism and the distortion of human values that has evolved in the Arab and Muslim world.

In the second decade of the twenty-first century, in the shadow of its black flags and in the name of the vision of the Islamic caliphate, militant Islam is establishing reigns of dread, fear, and terror. They stretch from the western part of Africa across the northern Sahara, eastward toward Egypt and the Sinai Peninsula, through the Gaza Strip, northeast to Syria, and eastward through Iraq to central Asia—while increasing its presence in central and southern Africa. Those reigns constitute a growing threat on a regional and global level.

The other phenomenon we see returning to the forefront of the Middle Eastern stage is the model of independent or semi-independent political entities based on ethnic, religious, social, and tribal homogeneity (or clear dominance), usually within a defined territorial space, similar to the example of the independent ethnic entities that existed in Mount Lebanon and Syria during the 1920s. For example, we already see that the disintegration of Syria has led to the formation of a Kurdish semi-autonomy in northeastern Syria. It is also possible that the war in Syria will result in the recreation of an 'Alawite entity on the northwestern coastline of Syria, similar to the one that existed during the 1920s. And in September 2015 there were calls for the establishment of a Druze autonomy in southern Syria.[1]

In a June 2015 article titled "The Middle East and the End of Ideology," Egyptian-born political scientist and the director of the London Global Strategy Institute, Dr. Mamoun Fandy, argued that despite ongoing events, the ideology of groups like ISIS will be overcome. He wrote:

> With the crumbling of the concept of the modern state in the Middle East and the rise of ISIS, the Middle East, which was subdued to ideologies like pan-Arabism or a caliphate that can be defined as above statehood ideologies, is now moving through the phase of beneath statehood, as tribes and ethnic groups fight against ideology. History teaches us that tribes are always the winning side; thus, in my view, regardless of the phenomenon of ISIS, the end of ideology is the next phase in the Middle East.[2]

Dr. Fandy's observation of the historic struggle of tribes and ethnic groups against oppressive ideologies accurately reflects what is unfolding in the Kurdish areas of northern Syria and parts of the Sunni tribal areas of western Iraq where they are battling ISIS. However, I believe his projection is flawed because while the concept of statehood has collapsed in some places, the Middle East is not in a phase of being beneath statehood, and most Arab states—though struggling with serious challenges—have not disintegrated. The struggles of Algeria, Egypt, Jordan, Lebanon, and Tunisia against the ideology of ISIS and political Islam is even being waged by the state itself as opposed to sub-entities, like ethnic groups or tribes.

It also seems highly unlikely that the end of ideologies is the next phase in the Middle East. Beyond extremist ideologies, the emergence and strengthening of civil society in Arab societies represents its own ideology, a civil society–oriented ideology, and it will play a central role in the next phase of the Middle East.

Still, at present, the concept of statehood has collapsed in Iraq, Libya, Syria, and Yemen, where the state—either totally or to a large extent—no longer functions as a state. Other Arab countries, like Algeria, Bahrain, Egypt, Jordan, Kuwait, Lebanon, the Sudan, and Tunisia suffer, with fluctuating degrees of intensity, from political and social upheaval.

The Arab monarchies have so far managed to outlast the tsunami of the Arab Awakening. In response to the growing chaos and instability in the region, the momentum of militant Islamist groups, and the growing Iranian aggressive regional policy, the Arab monarchies—particularly the Arab Gulf monarchies, led by Saudi Arabia—are liaising and developing regional policies using their wealth, political influence, and advanced military capabilities. This has been exhibited by the creation of the Arab military coalition against ISIS in Syria and against the Houthis in Yemen, as well as in the growing financial support they provide other Arab states like Egypt and Jordan. In the immediate and foreseeable future, Arab monarchies will outlast the Middle Eastern turmoil. Their role in shaping the Middle East will likely grow and may even generate new geostrategic alliances and frameworks of cooperation—even surprising ones.

A Restructured Middle East

In my evaluation, the disintegration of some Arab states; the substantial domestic challenges countries in the region are facing today and will in the future; the momentum of militant Islamist groups; and the likely shaping of the Iranian-Arab balance of power, in which both sides make compromises, will contribute to the emergence of new regional frameworks and surprising geostrategic alliances.

A NATO-Style Arab Coalition

Iran's expansionist policies, particularly in Yemen, were met with a Sunni response in the shape of an Arab-Sunni military coalition led by Saudi Arabia that has been operating in Yemen since March 2015. Also in March 2015, the Arab League called for the creation of a joint military force to counter extremism and political instability across the Middle East.[3]

Following these events, in April 2015, chiefs of staff and army officials from twenty Arab countries (with the absence of Syria) attended a summit in Cairo to discuss a potential framework for a joint Arab military force.[4] At the conference, the Egyptian army's chief of staff, Major-General Mahmoud Hijazi, announced that the joint Arab force's tasks were to "confront the threat of terror and to defend Arab national security"—though he emphasized that each Arab state is responsible for its own security and that the taskforce's actions are subject to a specific request of the relevant state and must comply with the charter of the Arab League and the resolutions of the United Nations.[5]

Following the meeting of President Obama and the king of Saudi Arabia in September 2015, the Saudi minister of foreign affairs announced that his country supported the establishment of the joint Arab task force and that Saudi Arabia was in talks with other Arab states on the matter.[6] In December 2015, Saudi Arabia announced the establishment of a coalition of thirty-four Arab and Muslim non-Arab states to fight terror; the coalition's headquarters will be in Saudi Arabia. In the same month, Saudi Arabia and Turkey signed an agreement to establish a joint strategic council.

In my estimation, the coalition will evolve into an Arab NATO-model military alliance whose core will be the Gulf Cooperation Council, Egypt, and Jordan.

In the context of the struggle over identity, path, and direction in Arab societies, the formation of an Arab NATO-model military coalition, though reemphasizing old sentiments of Arab solidarity and mutual responsibility, would not proclaim the return of the pan-Arab nationalism ideology (which called for the unification of Arab states), nor would it call for abolishing the concept of statehood and the existence of independent Arab states.

Greater Jordan

Jordan borders two disintegrating Arab states, Syria and Iraq. The chaos, the presence of Iranian military forces in Syria and Iraq, the stream of Syrian refuges, and the scores of Salafi-Jihadi groups, including ISIS in Syria and in Iraq, present a serious threat to Jordan, Egypt, the Arab Gulf states, and Israel.

Because of its location, Jordan is evolving into a critical buffer zone. It is the northern gatekeeper for the Arab monarchies in the Arabian Peninsula and the eastern gatekeeper for Israel and Egypt, as it is located at the heart of the horizontal corridor of the militant Islam T-shape structure. The horizontal corridor of that infrastructure stretches from West Africa through Algeria, Tunisia, Libya, Egypt, the Gaza Strip, Jordan, and Iraq. The vertical corridor stretches from North Africa south toward Mali, Niger, and Nigeria, and continues toward Somalia.

In response to the threats and as a way to secure the Jordanian kingdom, a concept referred to as "Greater Jordan"[7, 8] has emerged within Jordanian political discourse. The concept centers around Jordan extending its influence into southern Syria and western Iraq through the building and nurturing of alliances—or at least strong cooperation—with Bedouin tribes in those areas, as well as the Druze in southern Syria, to create security buffer zones based on new and old goals and alliances.[9, 10, 11] The Bedouin tribes in southern Syria are blood relatives of the Bedouin tribes of northern Jordan; and from 1921–1958, Iraq was ruled by the Hāshimite dynasty, the same dynasty that today rules Jordan. Some Iraqi Bedouin tribes have been engaged in a long battle against al-Qaeda and ISIS in Iraq, and because Jordan and the Bedouin tribes share the same culture, heritage, and values, Jordan considers a Bedouin identity past as part of its defining identity.

The concept of "Greater Jordan" generates controversy in Jordan.[12, 13] Opponents argue that it will backfire and cause the country to fall into the disaster that is Syria and Iraq. Proponents say the alliance would be solid because it would be based on substantial common denominators and that it will add security to the kingdom because a buffer zone would protect Jordan from ISIS and other militant Islamist groups.

In the restructuring of the Middle East, Jordan's stability is crucial for the stability of Arab states. This was evident in a joint Jordanian-Saudi statement in July 2015 following a meeting between the king of Jordan and the Saudi Arabian minister of defense that emphasized that the two states' national securities are "intertwined and inseparable."[14]

Israeli-Arab Geostrategic Alliance

In the second decade of the twenty-first century, a quiet Israeli-Arab axis has been created. It is based on mutual long-term strategic interests—primarily to thwart Salafi-Jihadi and Iranian expansion. The axis includes Israel, Egypt, Jordan, and the Arab monarchies. Undertakings of it include:

- Israel and Egypt cooperating tactically and sharing intelligence in their fight against militant Islamist groups in the Sinai Peninsula.
- Israel, Egypt, and Saudi Arabia collaborating on policies to restrain Ḥamās in the Gaza Strip.
- Israel, Jordan, and Saudi Arabia collaborating on policies to thwart the ISIS and Iranian threats to Jordan's borders. It is likely, due to the severity of the threat, that Israel and the GCC will operate on very quiet channels of communication to exchange intelligence.

It is my prediction that the axis will play a significant role in reshaping the Middle East. One example of its potential influence relates to the Israeli-Palestinian conflict.

Solutions to the Israeli-Palestinian Conflict: Thinking Out of the Box

Almost a generation has passed since the signing of the Oslo Accords between Israel and the Palestinians. The Oslo Accords, signed in Washington, DC, in 1993 and in Taba, Egypt, in 1995, were guided by the concept that the two-state solution was the preferable and achievable solution to the conflict. At the time of the signings, it seemed that the conflict could be solved through negotiations, compromises, and concessions—but a generation later, the reality is gloomy. The expectations and hopes crashed violently, and both sides are right in blaming each other for the bleak reality. Both sides have failed to fulfill their commitments.

Since the signing of the Oslo Accords, the Palestinians have failed to consolidate a consensus that supports and nurtures the agreements' guidelines that were set as the roadmap to end the conflict and achieve peace through diplomacy, compromise, and concessions. Ḥamās, who rejects dialogue, compromise, and concessions, and calls for the continuation of violence until

Israel is eliminated, won the Palestinian parliamentary elections in 2006 and enjoys the support of most of the people in the Gaza Strip. Its ideology and that of other Palestinian militant groups led to the violence against Israel and the resulting diminished willingness of Israelis to move forward in pursuit of a two-state solution.

Israel, for its part, has also failed to nurture, support, and encourage a pragmatic Palestinian camp. The Israeli government's policy has been a dichotomy. On one hand, Israel fully withdrew from the Gaza Strip; but on the other hand, Israeli settlements in the West Bank have expanded. There's been a "one step forward, two steps backward" implementation of the Oslo Accords. The Israeli security measures—the building of the anti-terror fence, the checkpoints, the restrictions on Palestinian activities, and the closure of Gaza Strip—though justifiable in light of the Palestinian suicide bombers who have killed and maimed thousands of Israelis, most of them civilians, in addition to the rocket attacks launched from Gaza—have still increased the frustration of the Palestinians. Many Palestinians believe that Israel does not want to pursue the two-state solution, and this sentiment fuels Palestinian support for Ḥamās and the Islamic Jihad in Palestine.

Israelis and Palestinians are caught in a sad, frustrating—some say hopeless—and vicious loop. And a new round of violence, sparked in October 2015, is taking place, resulting in dozens of fatalities on both sides.

Counter to the narrative that became common in Western circles that argued that the Israeli-Palestinian conflict shapes the Middle East, the reality is the other way around. The Middle East reality shapes the Israeli-Palestinian conflict.

The bad news is that a sustainable Israeli-Palestinian peace agreement is not likely to happen anytime soon. The good news is that the changing Middle East has generated the preliminary conditions necessary for a positive breakthrough of the cycle of conflict.

For the Palestinians, the combination of the growing and polarizing struggle within Arab societies over their path, identity, and direction; the escalating and widening Iranian-Arab power struggle; and the momentum of militant Islamist groups brings new dimensions to the internal Palestinian discussions of what the future should bring. One of the outcomes of the events in the

Middle East is that the Palestinian agenda is pushed aside in the political and cultural agenda of the Arab world which is engaged with its own challenges and hardships. In previous generations, the Palestinian issue was perceived in the Arab world as an important *Arab* task that it needed to take on. It was known as *al-qadiya al-Filastiniya* (the Palestinian cause). This is no longer the case. The Arab world today sends a clear message to the Palestinians: the Palestinian cause is now first and foremost a *Palestinian* task.

The second dimension is the growing debate within Palestinian society regarding the use of violence, *al-muqāwamah* (the resistance), against Israel as a means to achieve its political objectives and enhance the Palestinian cause. Against the growing violence in the region, the momentum of militant Islamist groups, and the catastrophy caused in the Gaza Strip as an outcome of the military rounds between Ḥamās and Israel—which have produced no tangible political achievements to further the Palestinian cause—the Palestinians are going through a process similar to the one that the Israelis have been going through over the last generation.

It is a process of understanding that the use of military might to obtain political visions and objectives has limited effectiveness. This realization explains the statements made by Palestinian President Mahmoud Abbas in October 2014 when he said:

> The armed struggle is counter-productive. . . . What were the results of the recent violence? Let me be honest and say to my people the truth: the way of an armed struggle did not win . . . I will never allow presence of an armed resistance movement in the West Bank.[15]

The evolving Palestinian discussion of its path, identity, and direction is a process that holds positive potential because it forces the Palestinians to confront major issues they have bypassed until now, such as of the appropriateness of an armed struggle and what can be done for the Palestinian refugees—defined in the Palestinian narrative by the term *haq al-awdah* ("the right of return"). There are approximately 472,000 Arabs, according to a report by the United Nations Mediator on Palestine,[16] who lived in mixed Arab and Jewish villages or cities in Palestine/Israel and fled them during the 1948–1949 war between Israel and the Arab states, whose militants included the Palestinian armed forces. Palestinians argue that the number was between eight hundred thousand and one million. One of the Palestinian requirements to end the conflict with Israel is that Israel allow those who fled, and their descendants—according to the Palestinians, three million people—to return to where they lived in 1948. The demand is flatly rejected by Israel because the practical outcome of complying with it would be the end of Israel as the homeland of the Jewish people.

Israel argues that an independent Palestinian state, which could be established next to Israel in the framework of a two-state solution, should be the entity that absorbs every Palestinian who wants to live in the Palestinian homeland. This would be the same way Israel welcomes every Jew who wants to live in the Jewish homeland.

A breakthrough in the cycle of conflict is unlikely if discussing these issues remains taboo in the Palestinian political discourse. For Israel to work with the Palestinians, it needs them to abandon the violent struggle and their demand that Palestinian descendants of refugees can live in Israel—what the Palestinians view as an entitlement and call "the right of return."

A possible manifestation of the impact of the recent events in the Arab world on the Palestinian discussion of the Palestinian refugees can be found in an interview Mahmoud Abbas gave to Israeli TV Channel 2 in November 2012. In it he said:

> I was born in Safed [a mixed Israeli-Arab city] in what since 1948 has been northern Israel and I have visited the town and would like to see it again, but not to make my home there. It's my right to see it, but not to live there.[17]

One can view this statement as an innocent observation or as a message Abbas wanted to send to his people, hinting they might have to compromise their demands. In light of the fact that this issue is still taboo within the Palestinian discourse and given the fact that Ḥamās argues that the right of return is an individual right that no Palestinian government can negotiate or compromise on, Abbas's statement was bold and completely unprecedented.

That said, the path to a substantial change in the Palestinian discussion regarding the Palestinian refugees is, at best, in its most preliminary phase.

Israel and the Palestinians would also ultimately need to compromise on controversial matters, such as: aerial sovereignty; the borders of Israel in the West Bank; the status of Jerusalem; the future of settlements; the use of water, airspace, and natural resources; environmental issues like energy supply sources; waste management; and trade and taxation.

A realistic observation of the Israeli-Palestinian conflict leads to the conclusion that a sustainable Israeli-Palestinian peace agreement is not likely to happen anytime soon. Israelis and Palestinians have a long road to take on the path toward reconciliation. But the Arab Awakening has brought hope of changes throughout the region. The key for progress in the Israeli-Palestinian arena is the proactive involvement of Arab states—and this is in their interest too.

The evolution of an Israeli-Arab axis might incentivize an Israeli-Arab discussion regarding a possible arrangement between Israel and the Palestinians. Such an arrangement would be motivated by the assumption that an Israeli-Palestinian agreement would contribute to regional stability—a primary goal of the axis.

Together the Israeli-Arab axis along with the proactive involvement of Arab states in the Israeli-Palestinian arena could develop a creative out-of-the-box strategy and apparatus to tackle the Israeli-Palestinian issue and achieve tangible results, which would enable all sides to move down a path of stability toward an eventual agreement.

Arab states can guarantee or at least bolster Israel's security by eliminating or decreasing attacks. Arab states can financially and politically encourage and support a pragmatic Palestinian camp, and restrain extremist Palestinian destabilizing and threatening factors, like Ḥamās.

I suggest the creation of an interim triangular Palestinian-Egyptian-Jordanian confederation that would be a temporary member of the Gulf Cooperation Council and have a seat in the Arab League. The confederation, in conjunction with the GCC, would authorize a representative body to negotiate with Israel.

Their first goal should be to pursue an interim agreement consisting of tangible and measurable confidence-building measures, including: the total cessation of hostilities from Gaza; the deployment of an armed GCC force, and perhaps a joint force with the Egyptians, in the Gaza Strip; the opening of the Rafah crossing; the building of a harbor in the Gaza Strip; the cessation of Israeli construction in the West Bank; and the broadening of Palestinian control in other areas in the West Bank.

Sub task forces would negotiate all the controversial issues—borders, Jerusalem, settlements, etc.—and draw the guidelines for an agreement acceptable by both sides and guaranteed by the GCC, Egypt, Jordan, the United States, Russia, and the European Union. The agreements would be affirmed by the Arab League and the UN Security Council.

Once a solid foundation of trust and stability is achieved on the ground and agreements are signed and affirmed, the Palestinian-Egyptian-Jordanian confederation would be dismantled and a Palestinian government committed to the agreements could take over.

* * *

The Middle East is like a global weather system; events and developments in one place impact other areas. Its turbulent nature is restrained by a complicated system of checks and balances.

In this book we explored a few examples of how this happens. We saw how events and developments in Egypt, Iran, and Syria generated a process that led to the inevitable war between Ḥamās and Israel in the summer of 2014. We saw how the fate of the "Islamic State" is directly connected to political developments in Iraq, Syria, and Turkey. We saw how the course and outcomes of the war in Yemen, one stage of the Iranian-Arab power struggle, impact the course and outcomes of the war in Syria, another stage of the Iranian-Arab power struggle. And we saw how the Iranian-Arab power struggle impacts Syria and Yemen.

Understanding that events and developments in the Middle East have a spiral effect and impact many other parties than the one they were originally related to helps understand the big picture and can enable us to predict possible developments, outcomes, and ramifications.

Another skill needed to dialogue with the Middle East is the ability to simultaneously "zoom in" and "zoom out." We need to be able to interpret both the micro and the macro—to understand individuals, but also movements, society, the region, and international politics—and their interconnections. This enables us to assemble the very complicated puzzle.

By employing these strategies, I was able to foresee many developments in the Middle East. It's how in 2008 I was able to "predict" the Arab Awakening; in 2010 I was able to "predict" the war in Syria; in 2012 I was able to "predict" the crisis within the Muslim Brotherhood as well as Hezbollah sinking in the Syrian mud; in 2013 I was able to "predict" Ḥamās's crisis; and mid-2014 I was able to "predict" the violence in Yemen.

Beyond navigating the region, the ability to "zoom in" and "zoom out" helps us understand more specific events, even ones related to single, "oridinary" people. Gilad Shalit, for example, was kidnapped by Ḥamās in 2006 and held in captivity in the Gaza Strip. Attempts to broker a deal between Israel and Ḥamās for his release failed repeatedly.

On the surface the situation looked hopeless, but I was optimistic a deal could be reached. My optimism stemmed from events and developments that took place in a different arena with a different player, and both on the surface had nothing to do with the story of the Israeli soldier.

The arena was Egypt and the player was the Muslim Brotherhood. Following the downfall of Mubārak in Egypt in early 2011, the Muslim Brotherhood in Egypt knew it had a unique opportunity to rise to power. The Muslim Brotherhood was eager to gain international recognition as a legitimate political player, to gain credibility for itself with the United States and the European Union, and to prove that it could be a constructive factor and contribute to regional stability. To that end, Gilad Shalit was a valuable card. The Muslim Brotherhood could put pressure on Ḥamās (the branch of the Muslim Brotherhood in Palestine) to make a deal.

On October 18, 2011, after 1,941 days in captivity, Gilad Shalit was released in return for 1,027 Palestinians imprisoned in Israel. Egypt, in a hush-hush alliance with the Muslim Brotherhood had brokered the deal.

The Struggle for Identity, Path, and Direction in Muslim and Arab Societies

In the second decade of the twenty-first century, a new chapter in the history of the struggle for identity, path, and direction in the Muslim and Arab world begins. This chapter is unique because of the unprecedented chaos and power of two opposing types of people. One is the violent type who in the name of a distorted ideology orchestrates the slaughtering and beheading of innocent people as he seeks to recreate a past that has disappeared in the sands of time. The other type fights for a future of hope; for modern and virtuous education; for responsible and uncorrupted rule; for housing solutions; for economic equality; for healthcare; for employment; for individual rights, such as the rights of women, minorities, and underprivileged groups; and for enlightenment and progress.

The chance for the Arab world to recover, to set out on a route that will lead to a future of hope, growth, enlightenment, and progress is contingent on the ability of the Arab world to look in the mirror and take responsibility. Only by doing this can the Arab world encourage real and open conversations on every subject; absorb the norms and values of tolerance and acceptance of differences; encourage and endorse pluralism and diversity; and nurture and develop productive and constructive mechanisms of compromise and the bridging of differences.

The world must assist Arab states in this process, but the assistance must be conducted from a position that makes it clear that the central responsibility for the challenges and hardships of the Arab world—as well as the central responsibility to deal with them—fall first and foremost on the Arab world and its leaders. This is a necessary condition for the Arab world to recover and take the road to progress and enlightenment.

At present, skepticism that the Arab world will be able to heal is common in the political and cultural discourse of Arab societies, and a number of Arab writers have described this. Lebanese journalist Samir Atallah wrote of this in a September 2015 article, stating,

> Iran aspires to reestablish the Persian Empire; Turkey aspires to reestablish the Ottoman Empire; militant Islam aspires to return to the Stone Age, while the Arab nations, beaten down by violence and suffering, leave their countries.[18]

Arab journalist Randa Taqi a-Din wrote in her September 2015 article "Dark Future Awaits Middle East Youth" that "the next generations in the

Middle East are facing a future threatened by extremism, violence, and the absence of science and culture."[19]

Egyptian poet Farouk Goweda wrote in October 2015, "I will write on the epitaph this is a nation who disappeared without a trace."[20]

Yet at the height of the seismic shake-up that is engulfing the Arab world, the overwhelming challenges of Arab societies, and the intensifying inner struggle over identity, path, and direction, there is the possibility to develop a process that will lead to growth and recovery. But it will be long, complicated, and difficult, accompanied by intense upheavals and more bloodshed.

I am often asked how I see the future of the Middle East. Most often, people express deep skepticism regarding the ability of Arab societies to heal and take a positive direction. My answer is that one should remember the current model of democracy and civil society, as known in the West, did not appeared overnight. It involved a long, agonizing, and bloody process.

At the time this book is written, I believe that the future of Arab societies and the Middle East must be examined from a cold and sober view that is painfully real and has no illusions. The challenges that the Middle East and Arab societies are facing, the enormous earthquakes that are rocking the region, and the aftershocks—big and small—are deep and real. But I believe there is room for a cautious optimism and that optimism is integral to our analysis.

There is an acute and important need in the West, particularly in academia, governments, and the media, to fundamentally change the methods of gathering and processing information about the Middle East. Preconceived and often misguided concepts, narratives, and theories must be cast aside and in their place an accurate dialogue with the Middle East reality must begin.

A comprehensive understanding of the Middle East obtained through efforts such as the cultivation of critical thinking and the ongoing engagement with Arab media are crucial to the future relationship between the West and Arab and Muslim societies and the pursuit of global security. People should not be told what to think—they should be taught how to think. To that end, they should be provided with simple, yet efficient tools and skills.

It is time to revolutionize the Western approach to understanding the Middle East, and this methodology must be based on four major pillars:

1. **A**ssimilating simple yet efficient skills and tools for professional gathering, analyzing, processing accurate information.
2. **B**reaking dependence on Western mediators of knowledge through using Middle Eastern platforms to emphasize and enhance the importance of media literacy.
3. **C**ultivating a culture of critical thinking by creating minds that interrogate, probe, and question.
4. **D**eveloping a new discourse by demanding that concepts and narratives be replaced with facts and reality.

At this point in my life, after a very long career in intelligence, policy development, entrepreneurship, and education, I refuse to be a bystander and let misconceptions continue to spread. My hope is that this volume offered you the tools necessary to make sense of the Middle East. As I said in the preface, the goal of this book was not to provide you with an all-encompassing study of the Middle East; it was to help build your basic knowledge—as well get as an insider's perspective that most Westerners do not have access to—about the processes, bring awareness, and deepen your understanding of the streams of thought and major players that have made the region what it is today. I hope your new understandings are helpful and will allow you to make sense of the unfolding events in the region and navigate what's to come.

GLOSSARY

A

‘Abd Shcahdah aka *Muhammad at-Ṭaḥāwī*: Major Salafi-Jihadi theologian in Jordan who reportedly expressed his support for ISIS

‘Abduh, Muḥammad ‘Abduh: Islamist modernist thinker

Abī Ṭālib, ‘Alī ibn Abī Ṭālib: Prophet Muhammad's cousin and son-in-law, whose followers, known as shīatu ‘Alī (Ali's faction), later Shiites, believe that Islamic caliphs should have a bloodline tie to Prophet Muhammad

Abu al-Fadl al-Abbas Brigade: Iraqi Shiite militia backed by Iran

Al Wefaq National Islamic Society: Political Shiite opposition in Bahrain, a non-governmental organization

Al-Abadi, Haider al-Abadi: Iraqi prime minister since 2014, of Shiite origin

Al-‘Adnānī, Abū Muḥammad al-‘Adnānī: A senior ISIS leader and the official ISIS spokesperson

Al-Afghānī, Jamāl al-Dīn al-Afghānī: Islamist modernist thinker

Al-Assad, Bashar al-Assad: President of Syria since 2000, son of Ḥafiz al-Assad

Al-Assad, Ḥafiz al-Assad: President of Syria from 1970–2000

Al-Asaad, Riad al-Asaad: Defecting Syrian colonel and the leader of al-Jaish as-Sūrī al-Ḥurr (the Free Syrian Army), a Syrian rebel group

Al-Azhar University: Considered the world's central religious leadership institution of Sunni Islam, located in Cairo

Al-Baghdadi, Abū Bakr al-Baghdadi: Leader of ISIS since 2013

Al-Bannā', Ḥasan al-Bannā: Founder of the Muslim Brotherhood movement

Al-Barqawi, 'Isam al-Barqawi, known as *Abu Muhammad al-Maqdisi*: Spiritual mentor of the Salafi-Jihadist movement in Jordan

Al-Hariri, Rafiq al-Hariri: Lebanese Sunni prime minister, assassinated in 2005

Al-Hariri, Saad al-Hariri: Lebanese Sunni politician and the leader of Istiqlal (the Independence Party); the son of Lebanese Prime Minister Rafiq al-Hariri

Al-Hashd al-Shaabi (the Popular Congregation): Iranian-backed Iraqi Shiite militia involved in the fight against ISIS in Iraq

Al-Ḥusayn ibn 'Alī, known as *Ḥusayn*: Son of Prophet Muhammad's daughter Fāṭimah, killed by Caliph Yazīd ibn Muʿāwiyah ibn Abī Sufyān in the year 680 at Karbala; referred to as *sayyid al-shuhada*, (master of martyrs) by Shiites

Al-Husseini, Muhammad Ali al-Husseini: Senior Lebanese Shiite clergy and the secretary-general of the Arab Muslim Council; condemned Hezbollah's involvement in the war in Syria

Al-Ikhwān al-Muslimūn: See Muslim Brotherhood

Al-Islam Hu al-Hal (Islam is the solution): The Muslim Brotherhood's slogan

Al-Jabha al-Janubiya (the Southern Front): Coalition of Syrian rebel groups operating in southern Syria; thought to include military units such as al-Jaish al-Awal (the First Corps), al-Jaish al-Suri al-Muwahad (the United Syrian Army), and Tahalaf Suqour al-Janoub (the Hawks of the South)

Al-Jabhah al-Islāmiyya as-Sūriyyah (the Syrian Islamic Front): Coalition of Islamist Syrian rebels groups

Al-Jaish as-Sūrī al-Ḥurr, (the Free Syrian Army): Rebel group in Syria

Al-Jama'ah al-Islāmiyyah (the Islamic Group): Islamist militant group, offspring of the Muslim Brotherhood

Al-Joulani, Abu Mohammad al-Joulani: Leader of Jabhat al-Nusra (al-Qaeda's branch in Syria)

Al-Khalifah family: Sunni rulers of Bahrain

Al-khulafā'u ar-rāshidūn (the righteous caliphs who lead the path): The first four successors of Prophet Muhammad, admired by Sunnis as role models for Islamic leadership

Al-Madīnah (the City): See Medina

Al-Maktoum, Mohammed bin Rashid al-Maktoum: Vice president and prime minister of the United Arab Emirates and the emir of Dubai

Al-Mālikī, Nūrī al-Mālikī: Iraqi prime minister from 2006–2014, of Shiite origin

Al-Mansouri, Mariam al-Mansouri: Female fighter pilot in the UAE air force

Al-Maqdisi, Abu Muhammad al-Maqdisi: See al-Barqawi, 'Isam al-Barqawi

Al-muamira (the conspiracy): The perception by Arab Muslims that they are victims of plots against them

Al-Mua'qi'oon Biddam (Those who Sign with Blood Brigade): Salafi-Jihadi group in Libya

Al-Mughassil, Ahmad Ibrahim al-Mughassil: Leader of Hezbollah's branch in the Arabian Peninsula

Al-muqāwamah (the resistance): Ideology developed in the Arab world following World War II; perceives following its hard-line interpretation of Islam as necessary for the uprising and rehabilitation of Muslim and Arab societies; today synonymous with the violent desires of terror groups, including to eliminate Israel

Al-Nahda (Awakening or Renaissance): Muslim Brotherhood political party in Tunisia

Al-Nizam al-Khass (the Special Apparatus): Confidential terror arm of the Muslim Brotherhood in Egypt

Al-Nuqrāshī, Maḥmūd Fahmī al-Nuqrāshī: Egyptian prime minister from 1945–1946 and 1946–1948, assassinated by Muslim Brotherhood activists

Al-Qaddafi, Muammar al-Qaddafi: Ruler of Libya from 1969–2011

Al-Qaeda (the base, the foundation): Islamist militant organization inspired by Salafi-Jihadi and Wahhābī ideologies

Al-Quds: The Arabic name for Jerusalem

Al-Quds Force: Paramilitary arm of the Iranian Revolutionary Guards Corps

Al-Shami, Abdullah al-Shami: Spokesperson for Islamic Jihad in Palestine

Al-Shabaab: See Ḥarakat al-Shabāb al-Mujāhidīn

Al-Sheikh, Hashim al-Sheikh: Senior leader of Ḥarakat Ahrar ash-Sham al-Islāmiyyah (the Islamist Movement of the Free People of ash-Sham), a major rebel group within al-Jabhah al-Islāmiyya (the Syrian Islamic Front)

Al-Sisi, Abdel Fattah al-Sisi: President of Egypt since June 2014

Al-Sulṭa al-Waṭanīya al-Filasṭīnīya (the Palestinian Authority Territories in the West Bank also known as *the Palestinian National Authority)*: Formed in 1994 following the signing of the Oslo Accords, part of an interim self-governing Palestinian body

Al-Takfīr wa al-Hijrah (Excommunication and the Holy Flight or Excommunication and the Migration): Militant Islamist group founded by Shukrī Muṣṭafā

Al-Thani, Tamim ibn Hamad al-Thāni: Emir of Qatar since 2013

Al-Tufayli, Subhi al-Tufayli: Secretary-general of Lebanese Hezbollah from 1989–1991

Al-Wahhāb, Muḥammad ibn 'Abd al-Wahhāb: Eighteenth-century Muslim theologian and founder of the Wahhābī movement, which attempted a return to the "true" principles of Islam

Al-Zawahiri, Ayman al-Zawahiri: The leader of al-Qaeda since 1998

Al-Zawahiri, Muhammad al-Zawahiri: Senior leader of the Salafi-Jihadi movement in Egypt and brother of Ayman al-Zawahiri, the leader of al-Qaeda

'Alawites, also known as *Nuṣayrīyah*: A distant branch of Shia Islam, considered by many Muslims to be heretics because their religion is secret and contains pagan symbols

Alhomayed, Tariq Alhomayed: Senior journalist in the Arab world and former editor-in-chief of *Asharq al-Awsat*

Allah or *Allāh*: The one and only God in Islam

Alloush, Zahran Alloush: Supreme military commander of Jaish al-Islam (the Army of Islam) and chief of staff of al-Jabhah al-Islāmiyya (the Syrian Islamic Front); killed in December 2015

An-Nour (the Light): Salafi political party in Egypt

Ansar Allah (Supporters of God): The military wing of the Houthi tribe in Yemen

Aoun, Michel Aoun: Lebanese politician and leader of the Free Patriot Party, an ally of Hezbollah

Ash-Sham: Arabic name that for centuries referred to a geographic area consisting of what is today Israel, Jordan, Lebanon, and Syria

Āshūrā (ten): The tenth day of the Muslim month of Muharram, when Shiites commemorate the day of Ḥusayn's murder

At-Ṭaḥāwī, Muhammad at-Ṭaḥāwī: See 'Abd Shcahdah

Awlaki, Anwar al-Awlaki: American-born leader of al-Qaeda, killed by a US drone strike in September 2011

Azzam, Abdullah Yusuf Azzam: Senior theologian and militant leader of Palestinian origin; considered the founder of Global Jihad and credited with creating what Osama bin Laden evolved into al-Qaeda

B

Ba'ath (Mission): Arab Socialist political party, appeared in Iraq and Syria during the second part of the twentieth century

Badie, Mohammed Badie: Supreme guide of the Muslim Brotherhood

Bakri, Mohammad Bakri: Controversial Israeli-Arab film director and actor

Barak, Ehud Barak: Israeli prime minister from 1999–2001

Basij: Paramilitary force acting mostly inside Iran, responsible for the brutal oppression of Iranian protesters following the scandal of the 2009 elections

Bay'ah: Oath of allegiance, important Arab tradition

Ben Ali, Zine al-Abidine Ben Ali: President of Tunisia from 1987–2011

Bin Laden, Osama bin Laden: Founder of al-Qaeda, killed by a US military unit in 2011

Bin Ṭalāl, Prince Al-Walīd ibn Ṭalāl ibn 'Abd al-'Azīz Āl Sa'ūd': Saudi prince and influential businessman

Boko Haram (Western Values Are Forbidden), the name for *Jamā'at Ahl al-Sunna lil-Da'awah wa al-Jihād (the Sunni Group of Indoctrination and Jihad)*: A violent Islamist movement founded in 2002 in northeast Nigeria, pledged its allegiance to ISIS in March 2015

Bouazizi, Tarek al-Tayeb Mohamed Bouazizi: Tunisian peddler who set himself on fire, protesting a fine he was given; his death in 2011 sparked mass demonstrations in the Arab world

D

Da'wa (call or invitation): The preaching, indoctrination, and proselytization of the masses

E

Egyptian Jihad: Egyptian Islamist militant group, offspring of the Muslim Brotherhood

Elmahdy, Aliaa Magda: Egyptian blogger and women's rights activist

Emir (prince or lord): Title used to refer to an administrative position or Islamic leader

Emirate or *wilaya*: Terms used by the historical Islamic caliphate to refer to districts under its administration

Ezzedeen al-Qassam Brigades: Armed, militant wing of Ḥamās

F

Fatemiyon Brigade: Afghan Shiite militia backed by Iran, fights in Syria

Fatwā: A Muslim religious legal ruling, can address a wide variety of subjects pertaining to the private life of the individual

G

Ghazwah (raid): The successful Islamic military campaigns of expansion in the seventh century, the century Islam was born; the term is also used by militant Islamist groups to refer to the September 11, 2001, terror attack

Global Jihad: Militant Islamist Salafi-Jihadi organization founded by Abdullah Yusuf Azzam

H

Haddad, Wadie Haddad: Former leader of the Popular Front for the Liberation of Palestine, responsible for several airplane hijackings in the 1960s and 1970s.

Hadī, 'Abd Rabbuh Manṣūr Hadī: Shiite president of Yemen since 2012

Ḥamās: Palestinian political Islamist organization that defines itself as the arm of the Muslim Brotherhood in Palestine; Ḥamās means "enthusiasm" and is an acronym for Ḥarakat al-Muqāwamah al-'Islāmiyyah (the Islamic Resistance Movement)

Haniyeh, Ismail Haniyeh: Senior political leader of Ḥamās and prime minister of its government in the Gaza Strip from 2006–2014

Ḥarakat Ahrar ash-Sham al-Islāmiyyah (Islamist Movement of the Free People of ash-Sham): Major Islamist Syrian rebel body within al-Jabhah al-Islāmiyya (the Syrian Islamic Front)

Ḥarakat al-Sabirin (the Movement of Those Who are Patient): Shiite militant group in the Gaza Strip

Ḥarakat al-Shabāb al-Mujāhidīn (the Movement of the Young Jihadists), known *as al-Shabaab*: Al-Qaeda's branch in Somalia, also operates in Kenya

Ḥarakat al-Muqāwamah al-'Islāmiyyah: See Ḥamās

Hezbollah: Shia militia group and militant body that first emerged in Lebanon, known for its forceful attacks on Israel

Hijra (the migration): Term used to mark the year Prophet Muhammad fled Mecca, 622 CE or year 0 in the Muslim calendar (the *hijri* or *hijra* calendar)

Ḥizb al-Ḥurriya Wal-'Adala (the Freedom and Justice Party): The political party of the Muslim Brotherhood in Egypt, established in March 2011

Ḥizb al-Islah (the Reform Party): Jordanian political party, established in March 2015 following the formal split of the Muslim Brotherhood in Jordan

Ḥizb al-Tahrir (the Liberation Party): The major Salafi movement in the Palestinian National Authority areas in the West Bank

Ḥizb al-Wasat al-Jadid (the Party of the New Center): Egyptian political party established in 2011 by resigned young members of the Muslim Brotherhood

Houthis: Shiite tribe in Yemen

Hudna: Temporary truce

Hussein, Saddam Hussein: President of Iraq from 1979–2003, executed in 2006

I

Imam: A Muslim religious leader; for Shiites an *imam* is a descendant of ʿAli and should rule because of Allah's will, his divine genealogy, and his perfect talents

ISIS, acronym for the *Islamic State of Iraq and Syria* or the *Islamic State of Iraq and ash-Sham,* also called *ISIL* or the *Islamic State*: A brutal Salafi-Jihadi Islamist militant group, proclaimed its "Islamic State" to be a caliphate ruled by Abū Bakr al-Baghdadi

Islamic Jihad in Palestine: Militant Islamist Palestinian organization, heavily supported by Iran

Istiqlal (Independence Party): A Sunni political party in Lebanon, led by Saad al-Hariri

J

Jabhat al-'Amal al-Islami (the Islamic Action Front): The Muslim Brotherhood's political party in Jordan, developed in 1992

Jabhat Al-Nusra (the Support for the People of ash-Sham): Al-Qaeda's branch in Syria

Jaish al-Fatah (the Army of Triumph): A coalition of Salafi-Jihadi groups operating mainly in south, central, north, and northwestern areas of Syria

Jaish al-Islam (the Arm of Islam): The major Salafi-Jihadi group in the Gaza Strip, affiliated with al-Qaeda

Jamāʿat Ahl al-Sunna lil-Daʿawah wa al-Jihād (the Sunni Group of Indoctrination and Jihad): See Boko Haram

Jihad (struggle or battle): Term for waging a "holy war" in response to what some Muslims consider a religious duty

Jihad fi Sabil Allah (an effort to implement Allah's way): A concept that relates to the early phases of Islam when jihad was considered an intensive spiritual journey to reach a higher degree of inner purity in one's worship of Allah

Jumblatt, Walid Jumblatt: Leader of the Druze of Lebanon

Jund al-Khilafah (the Soldiers of the Caliphate): Salafi-Jihadi group in Algeria, denounced its association from al-Qaeda and swore allegiance to Baghdadi

Jund Ansar Allah (the Soldiers of Allah's Believers): Salafi-Jihadi group in the Gaza Strip, violently crushed by Ḥamās in 2009 after announcing an Islamic emirate

K

Kāfir (infidel): A non-Muslim, one who doesn't believe in the holiness of Allah, Prophet Muhammad, or the Koran

Karbalā: The city in south Iraq where ʿAlī ibn Abī Ṭālib was killed, sacred for Shiites

Khalifa (caliphate): A global Islamic cultural, political, and religious entity in which no independent or sovereign state exists

Khamenei, Ali Khamenei: The supreme leader of Iran

King Abdullah II: The King of Jordan since 1999

King Abdullah ibn ʿAbd al-ʿAziz Al Saʿud: Former king of Saudi Arabia, died in January 2015

King Mohammed VI: The King of Morocco since 1999

King Salman ibn ʿAbd al-ʿAziz Al Saʿud: King of Saudi Arabia since January 2015

Koran or *Qurʾān*: The sacred scripture of Islam, perceived by Muslims as the word of God

Kurdish Democratic Union Party (PYD): A major Kurdish political power in north Syria

Kurdish Workers Party (PKK): A major Kurdish political power, calls for the establishment of a Kurdish state within the current territory of Turkey

L

Liwa Abu al-Fadl al-Abbas: A major Iraqi Shiite militia backed by Iran

Liwa al-Haqq: A major Iraqi Shiite militia backed by Iran

M

Mahdi (the leader, the guide, the anointed one): A central figure in the Shiite faith who it's believed will lead the Shiites to victory over the Sunnis and the rest of the world, and on the path to redemption; considered the descendant of Prophet Mohammed and ʿAlī ibn Abī Ṭālib

Mashal, Khalid Mashal: Chairman of Ḥamās's political bureau

Mecca: The birthplace of Prophet Muhammad, considered Islam's holiest city

Medina (al-Madīnah): The burial place of Prophet Muhammad, considered the second holiest city in Islam

Mikati, Najib Mikati: Prime minister of Lebanon from April 2005–July 2005 and June 2011–February 2014

Militant Islam: Radical, violent, and uncompromising fundamentalist Islamist organizations, compromised of parties such as ISIS, al-Qaeda, Global Jihad, Islamic Jihad, and Jabhat al-Nusra, embraces takwin (the immediate need for a global caliphate)

Modernist Islam: An ideology whose followers believe that creating a society governed by the ideals and laws of pure early Islamic sharīʿah, which embraced modernity, is the cure for the challenges of Muslim society

Morsi, Mohammed Morsi: The senior leader of the Muslim Brotherhood, president of Egypt from 2012–2013

Mubārak, Ḥosnī Mubārak: President of Egypt from 1981–2011, forced to step down because of popular unrest

Muslim Brotherhood (al-Ikhwān al-Muslimūn): The biggest mass movement in the Muslim Sunni world, views Islamic religion and culture as the only right way of life for all mankind; established in Egypt in 1929

Muṣṭafā, Shukrī Muṣṭafā: Militant Islamist founder of al-Takfīr wa al-Hijrah (Excommunication and the Holy Flight or Excommunication and the Migration)

N

Nahḍah (Awakening or Renaissance) Party: The Muslim Brotherhood's political party in Tunisia

Najaf: The city in southern Iraq where ʿAlī ibn Abī Tālib is buried, sacred for Shiites

Nasrallah, Hassan Nasrallah: Secretary-general of Lebanon's Hezbollah

Nasser, Gamal Abdel Nasser: Egyptian prime minister from 1954–1956 and president from 1956–1970

Netanyahu, Benjamin Netanyahu: Prime minister of Israel since 2009

Nidā' Tūnis (Call of Tunisia): National/civil society–affiliated camp in Tunisia, came to power in 2014

Nuṣayrīyah: See ʿAlawites

P

Political Islam: A conservative Islamist movement whose goal is to create a global Islamic cultural, political, and religious entity; comprised of organizations such as the Muslim Brotherhood and Salafi groups who embrace sabr (patience)

Popular Front for the Liberation of Palestine: Palestinian terrorist organization formerly run by Wadie Haddad

Prince Bandar bin Sultan: Former head of Saudi Intelligence and senior advisor on Saudi national security, served as Saudi ambassador to the United States

Prince Mohammed bin Nayef: Saudi crown prince, in line to the throne after Prince Muqrin

Prince Muqrin bin ʿAbdul-ʿAziz: Saudi crown prince, next in line to the throne

Prince Salman ibn ʿAbd al-ʿAzīz Āl Saʿūd: Crown prince of the Saudi Arabian dynasty

Q

Qassem, Naim Qassem: Lebanese Hezbollah deputy leader

Queen Rania al-ʿAbdullah: Queen of Jordan

Quṭb, Sayyid Quṭb: A leader of the Muslim Brotherhood in the 1950s and 1960s, laid the foundations for contemporary militant Islam; executed by Egyptian authorities in 1966

R

Riḍā, Rashīd Riḍā: Islamic modernist thinker
Rouhani, Hassan Rouhani: President of Iran since 1948

S

Sabr (patience): One of political Islam's core values, reflective of its mission to establish a global caliphate
Salaf (the past of something, its origin, its roots, its primal source): Term that led to what is known as the Salafi movement, reflects the desire to return to the original codes of Islam
Salafi-Jihadi: An ideology that calls for proactively and violently spreading and implementing the Salafi ideology
Salafi movement: A movement of people who believe that Islam will flourish again once it applies Islamic codes as they were in the early days of Islam
Ṣāliḥ, 'Alī 'Abd Allāh Ṣāliḥ: President of Yemen from 1978–2011
Shabak: Israel's security agency
Shabiha (ghosts): Syrian paramilitary militia ruled by Bashar al-Assad
Shahid (martyr): Term used to glorify those who die in service of jihad
Shalit, Gilad Shalit: Israeli soldier kidnapped by Ḥamās and held in captivity in the Gaza Strip from 2006–2011
Sharī'ah or *sharia (the path)*: Islam's moral and religious code
Shia or Shī'ah: The sect of Islam that believes all leaders of Islam should be descendants of 'Alī ibn Abī Ṭālib, Muhammad's cousin and son-in-law
Shī'ite or *Shī'ī*: A Muslim who is a member of the Shia branch of Islam
Soleimani, Qasem Soleimani: Commander of the Iranian elite force al-Quds
Sultan (ruler): Title of the head of the Turkish Ottoman Empire, title of the ruler of Oman
Sunni: The sect of Islam or a member of the sect of Islam that believes that the leaders of Islam should chosen by their merit, not by bloodline

T

Takfir (infidel): A term used by Muslims to refer to people they consider to be "corrupting" or "contaminating" Islam from within

Takwin (the immediate establishment): Core value of militant Islam that demands the immediate establishment of a global caliphate based on the implementation of strict sharīʿah law into all aspects of life

Talb a-shahada (the quest for martyrdom): Reference to militant Islam's belief in the importance of the pursuit of jihad and being a shahid

Tamkin (to make possible): A core value of political Islam related to its belief in focusing today on laying the foundations for a future—undefined in time—in which it will be possible to actualize a global caliphate based on the implementation of sharīʿah into all aspects of life

U

UAE: United Arab Emirates

Umm Kulthūm: Stage name of the Egyptian singer Fāṭima ʾIbrāhīm al-Baltāǧī, one of the most prominent cultural symbols in the Muslim and Arab world

W

Wahhābī movement: Muslim puritan movement founded by Muḥammad ibn ʿAbd al-Wahhāb, inspires militant Islamist organizations

Wilaya: See emirate

Wilāyat Saynāʾ (the Emirate of Sinai): ISIS's official branch in the Sinai Peninsula, previously known as Mujāhidīn Fī Aknāf Bayt al-Maqdis (the Jihad Warriors on the Outskirts of Jerusalem)

CENTRAL PLAYERS AND QUICK FACTS

People's Democratic Republic of Algeria

Prime Minister	Abdelmalek Sellal (since April 28, 1999)
President	Abdelaziz Bouteflika (since April 28, 2014)
Population	39,542,166 (July 2015 est.)
Ethnic Groups	Arab-Berber 99%, European < 1%
Religions	Muslim 99%, other (includes Christian and Jewish) less than 1% Predominately Sunni

Bahrain

Prime Minister	Khalīfah ibn Sulmān Āl Khalīfah (since March 6, 1999)
King	Ḥamad ibn ʿIsā Āl Khalīfah (since 1971)
Population	1,346,613 Note: immigrants make up almost 55% of the total population, according to UN data (2013) (July 2015 est.)
Ethnic Groups	Bahraini 46%, Asian 45.5%, other Arabs 4.7%, African 1.6%, other 1.2% (includes Gulf Co-operative country nationals, North and South Americans, and Oceanians)

Religions	Muslim 70.3%, Christian 14.5%, Hindu 9.8%, Buddhist 2.5%, Jewish 0.6%, folk religion <.1, unaffiliated 1.9%, other 0.2% (2010 est.) Exact numbers are unclear, but Shiites are the majority.

Arab Republic of Egypt

President	Abdel Fattah al-Sisi (since June 8, 2014)
Prime Minister	Sherif Ismail (since September 12, 2015)
Population	90,167, 947
Ethnic Groups	Egyptian 99.6%, other 0.4%
Religions	Muslim 90%, Christian (majority Coptic Orthodox, other Christians include Armenian Apostolic, Catholic, Maronite, Orthodox, and Anglican) 10% (2012 est.) Predominantly Sunni

Islamic Republic of Iran

Head of State	Supreme Leader Ali Khamenei, (since June 4, 1989)
President	Hassan Rouhani (since August 3, 2013)
Population	81,824,270 (July 2015 est.)
Ethnic Groups	Persian, Azeri, Kurd, Lur, Baloch, Arab, Turkmen and Turkic tribes
Religions	Muslim (official) 99.4%, other (includes Zoroastrian, Jewish, and Christian) 0.3%, unspecified 0.4% (2011 est.) Shiite 90–95%, Sunni 5–10%

Republic of Iraq

President	Fuad Masum (since July 24, 2014)
Prime Minister	Haider al-Abadi (since September 8, 2014)
Population	37,056,169 (July 2015 est.)
Ethnic Groups	Arab 75%, Kurdish 15%–20%, Turkoman, Assyrian, or other 5%
Religions	Muslim (official) 99%, Christian 0.8%, Hindu <.1, Buddhist <.1, Jewish <.1, folk religion <.1, unafilliated .1, other <.1 Shiite 60%–65%, Sunni 32%-37%

Israel

President	Reuven Rivlin (July 27, 2014)
Prime Minister	Benjamin Netanyahu (since March 31, 2009)
Population	8,462,000 6,335,000 Jews (includes populations of the Golan Heights annexed to Israel by a law in 1981 and East Jerusalem, which was annexed by Israel after 1967) (July 2014 est.) Note: approximately 19,400 Israeli settlers live in the Golan Heights; approximately 200,000 Israeli settlers live in East Jerusalem (2013) (July 2015 est.)
Ethnic Groups	1,757,000 Arabs Jewish 75% (of which Israel-born 74.4%, Europe/America/Oceania-born 17.4%, Africa-born 5.1%, Asia-born 3.1%), non-Jewish 25% (mostly Arab) (2013 est.)
Religions	Jewish 75%, Muslim 17.5% (predominantly Sunni), Christian 2%, Druze 1.6%, other 3.9% (2013 est.)

Hāshimite Kingdom of Jordan

King	Abdullah II (since February 7, 1999)
Prime Minister	Abdullah Ensour (since October 11, 2012)
Population	8,117,564 Note: increased estimate reflects revised assumptions about the net migration rate due to the increased flow of Syrian refugees (July 2015 est.)
Ethnic Groups	Arab 98%, Circassian 1%, Armenian 1%
Religions	Muslim 97.2% (official), Christian 2.2% (majority Greek Orthodox, but some Greek and Roman Catholics, Syrian Orthodox, Coptic Orthodox, Armenian Orthodox, and Protestant denominations), Buddhist 0.4%, Hindu 0.1%, Jewish <.1, folk religion <.1, unaffiliated <.1, other <.1 (2010 est.) Predominantly Sunni

Kuwait

Emir	Sheikh Sabah al-Ahmad al-Jabir al-Sabah (since January 29, 2006)
Prime Minister	Sheikh Jabir al-Mubarak al-Hamad al-Sabah (since November 30, 2011)
Population	2,788,534 Note: Kuwait's Public Authority for Civil Information estimates the country's total population to be 3,996,899 for 2014, with immigrants accounting for almost 69% (July 2015 est.)
Ethnic Groups	Kuwaiti 31.3%, other Arab 27.9%, Asian 37.8%, African 1.9%, other 1.1% (includes European, North American, South American, and Australian) (2013 est.) Note: represents the total population; about 69% of the population consists of immigrants (2013 est.)

Religions	Muslim (official) 76.7%, Christian 17.3%, other and unspecified 5.9% Majority Sunni, minority Shiite exact numbers unclear

Lebanese Republic

President (vacant)	President Michel Suleiman's term expired on May 25, 2014; the prime minister and his cabinet are temporarily assuming the duties of the president; as of December 2015, the National Assembly had failed to elect a president
Prime Minister	Tammam Salam (since April 6, 2013)
Population	6,184,701(July 2015 est.)
Ethnic Groups	Arab 95%, Armenian 4%, other 1%
Religions	Muslim 54%, Christian 40.5% (includes 21% Maronite Catholic, 8% Greek Orthodox, 5% Greek Catholic, 6.5% other Christian), Druze 5.6%, very small numbers of Jews, Baha'is, Buddhists, Hindus, and Mormons 27% Sunni, 27% Shiite

Libya

Head of State	President of the House of Representatives Akila Saleh Issa (since August 5, 2014)
Prime Minister	Abdullah al-Thani (since March 11, 2014)
Population	6,411,776
	Berber and Arab 97%, other 3% (includes Greeks, Maltese, Italians, Egyptians, Pakistanis, Turks, Indians, and Tunisians)
Religions	Muslim (official) 96.6%, Christian 2.7%, Buddhist 0.3%, Hindu <.1, Jewish <.1, folk religion <.1, unaffiliated 0.2%, other <.1 Virtually all Sunni

Kingdom of Morocco

King	Muhammad VI (since July 30, 1999)
Prime Minister	Abdelilah Benkirane (since November 29, 2011)
Population	33,322,699 (July 2015 est.)
Ethnic Groups	Arab-Berber 99%, other 1%
Religions	Muslim 99% (official), other 1% (includes Christian, Jewish, and Baha'i), Jewish about 6,000 Virtually all Sunni, <0.1 Shiite

Sultanate of Oman

Sultan	Qaboos bin Said (sultan since July 23, 1970 and prime minister since July 23, 1972)
Prime Minister	Qaboos bin Said (sultan since July 23, 1970 and prime minister since July 23, 1972)
Population	3,286,936
Ethnic Groups	Arab, Baluchi, South Asian (Indian, Pakistani, Sri Lankan, Bangladeshi), African
Religions	Muslim (official) 85.9%, Christian 6.5%, Hindu 5.5%, Buddhist 0.8%, Jewish <.1, other 1%, unaffiliated 0.2% Majority are Ibadhi, lesser numbers of Sunni and Shiite

Gaza Strip*

President	Mahmoud Abbas (since January 15, 2005)
Population	1,869,055
Ethnic Groups	Palestinian Arab
	Muslim 98–99%, Christian <1%, other, unaffiliated, unspecified <1%
Religion	Predominantly Sunni

West Bank*

Prime Minister	Rami Hamdallah (since June 2, 2014)
President	Mahmoud Abbas (since January 15, 2005)
Population	2,785,366 Palestinians; approximately 356,000 Israeli settlers live in the West Bank; approximately 200,000 Israeli settlers live in East Jerusalem (2013) (July 2015 est.)
Ethnic Groups	Palestinian Arab and other 83%, Jewish 17%
Religions	Muslim 80–85%; Jewish 12–14%, Christian 1–2.5% (mainly Greek Orthodox), other, unaffiliated, unspecified <1.0% Predominantly Sunni

Qatar

Emir	Sheikh Tamim ibn Hamad al-Thāni (since June 25, 2013)
Prime Minister	Sheikh Abdullah ibn Nasser ibn Khalifah al-Thāni (since June 26, 2013)
Population	2,194,817 (July 2015 est.)
Ethnic Groups	Arab 40%, Indian 18%, Pakistani 18%, Iranian 10%, other 14%
Religions	Muslim 77.5%, Christian 8.5%, other (includes mainly Hindu and other Indian religions) 14% Majority Sunni, estimated between 10–20% Shiite

Kingdom of Saudi Arabia

King	Salman ibn ʿAbd al-ʿAziz Al Saʿud (since January 23, 2015)
Prime Minister	Salman ibn ʿAbd al-ʿAziz Al Saʿud (since January 23, 2015)
Population	27,752,316

	Note: immigrants make up more than 30% of the total population, according to UN data (2013) (July 2015 est.)
Ethnic Groups	Arab 90%, Afro-Asian 10%
Religions	Muslim (official), other (includes Eastern Orthodox, Protestant, Roman Catholic, Jewish, Hindu, Buddhist, and Sikh) (2012 est.) Sunni 85–90%, Shiite 10–15%

Somalia

President	Hassan Sheikh Mohamud (since September 10, 2012)
Prime Minister	Omar Abdirashid Ali Sharmarke (since December 24, 2014)
Population	10,616,380
Ethnic Groups	Somali 85%, Bantu and other non-Somali 15% (including 30,000 Arabs)
Religion	Sunni Muslim

Republic of the Sudan

President	Omar Hassan Ahmad al-Bashir (since October 16, 1993)
Population	36,108,853
Ethnic Groups	Sudanese Arab (approximately 70%), Fur, Beja, Nuba, Fallata
Religions	Sunni Muslim, small Christian minority

Republic of South Sudan

President	Salva Kiir Mayardit (since July 9, 2011)
Population	12,042.912 (July 2015 est.)

Ethnic Groups	Dinka 35.8%, Nuer 15.6%, Shilluk, Azande, Bari, Kakwa, Kuku, Murle, Mandari, Didinga, Ndogo, Bviri, Lndi, Anuak, Bongo, Lango, Dungotona, Acholi (2011 est.)
Religions	Animist, Christian

Syrian Arab Republic

President	Bashar al-Assad (since July 17, 2000)
Prime Minister	Wael al-Halqi (since August 9, 2012)
Population	17,064,854 (July 2014 est.)
Ethnic Groups	Arab 90.3%, Kurds, Armenians, and other 9.7%
Religions	Muslim 87% (official), Christian (includes Orthodox, Uniate, and Nestorian) 10%, Druze 3%, Jewish (few remaining in Damascus and Aleppo) Sunni 74% and Alawi, Ismaili, and Shiite 13%

United Arab Emirates

President	Sheikh Khalīfah ibn Zāyid Āl Nahyān (since November 3, 2004)
Prime Minister	Sheikh Muḥammad ibn Rashīd Āl Maktūm (since January 5, 2006)
Population	5,779,760 Note: the UN estimates the country's total population to be 9,445,624 as of mid-year 2014; immigrants make up more than 80% of the total population, according to 2013 UN data (2014) (July 2015 est.)
Ethnic Groups	Emirati 19%, other Arab and Iranian 23%, South Asian 50%, other expatriates (includes Westerners and East Asians) 8% (1982)

Religions	Muslim (official) 76%, Christian 9%, other (primarily Hindu and Buddhist, less than 5% of the population consists of Parsi, Baha'i, Druze, Sikh, Ahmadi, Ismaili, Dawoodi Bohra Muslim, and Jewish) 15% Approximately 85% Sunni; 15% Shi'ite

Turkey

President	Recep Tayyip Erdoğan (since August 10, 2014)
Prime Minister	Ahmet Davutoğlu (since August 28, 2014)
Population	79,414,269 (July 2015 est.)
Ethnic Groups	Turkish 70–75%, Kurdish 18%, other minorities 7–12% (2008 est.)
Religions	Muslim 99.8%, other 0.2% (mostly Christians and Jews) Predominantly Sunni

The Republic of Yemen

President	ʿAbd Rabbuh Manṣūr Hadī (since February 21, 2012); Note President Hadī submitted his resignation in late January 2015, but Parliament did not convene to accept it; he later rescinded his resignation and remains the internationally recognized President of Yemen; he fled to Saudi Arabia in late March 2015 but returned in September after government loyalist forces aided by a Saudi-led coalition regained control of Aden from Huthi rebels in July.

Prime Minister	Khaled Bahah; Note: Bahah submitted his resignation in late January 2015, but Parliament did not convene to accept it; Bahah later rescinded his resignation and remains prime minister; on April 13 2015, he was named vice president but continues to be the prime minister; he returned to Yemen from weeks of exile in Saudi Arabia on September 16, 2015.
Population	26,737,317 (July 2015 est.)
Ethnic Groups	Predominantly Arab; but also Afro-Arab, South Asians, Europeans
Religions	Muslim 99.1% (official; virtually all are citizens), other 0.9% (includes Jewish, Baha'i, Hindu, and Christian; many are refugees or temporary foreign residents) An estimated 65% are Sunni and 35% are Shiite

*The Gaza Strip and the West Bank are not states.

References

Forbes.com
Encyclopedia Britannica
CIA World Fact Book
Central Agency for Public Mobilization and Statistics, Egypt

Notes

Head of state is listed first
Head of government is listed second

The Middle East

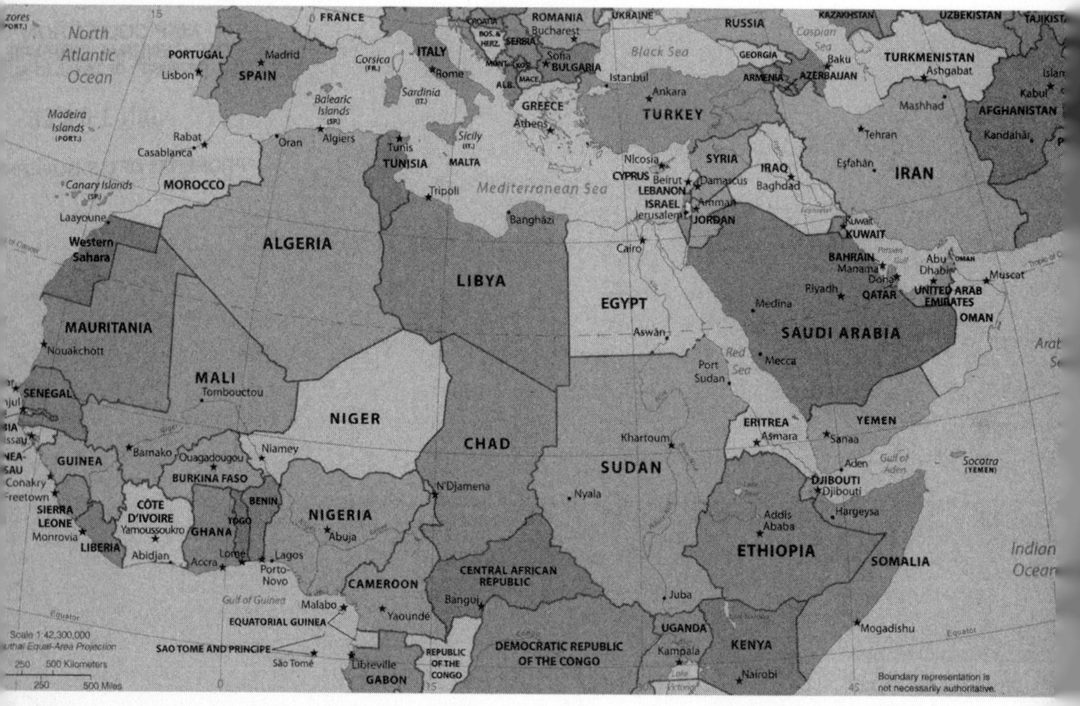

ISIS's Map of the Middle East

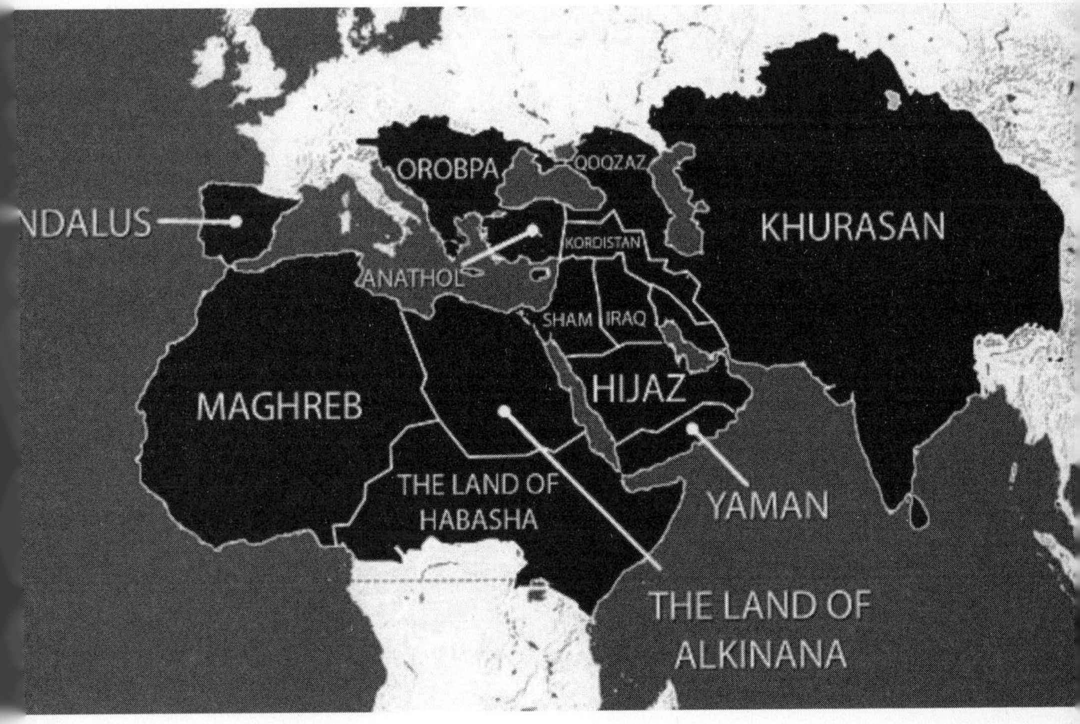

NOTES

Chapter One: The Distorted Compass

1. Salman Mahalha, "The Crazy Person Speaks and the Wise Person Listens," M E Transparent, 2014, http://www.metransparent.com/spip.php?page=article&id_article=26450&lang=ar
2. Ibid.
3. Ibid.
4. Ibid.
5. Ibid.
6. http://www.alaraby.co.uk/opinion/2015/3/3/
7. http://www.addustour.com, https://goo.gl/rY0rOJ
8. Abdulrahman al-Rashed, "The Theory of the Plot—The Theory that Will Never Die," *Alwatan Voice*, 2014, http://www.alwatanvoice.com/arabic/news/2014/02/23/499487.html
9. Maria Golovnina, "Gaddafi blames Qaeda, says conspiracy over Libya oil," *Reuters*, 2011, http://www.reuters.com/article/2011/03/02/us-libya-Qaddafi-idUSTRE7212UE20110302
10. Marisol Seibold, "Syria's Assad blames unrest on Israeli plot," *Jihad Watch*, 2011, http://www.jihadwatch.org/2011/03/syrias-assad-blames-unrest-on-israeli-plot
11. George Baghdadi, "Assad blames 'conspiracy' for Syria unrest," *CBS News*, 2012, http://www.cbsnews.com/news/assad-blames-conspiracy-for-syria-unrest/
12. *Al Arabiya*, 2012, http://www.alarabiya.net/articles/2012/06/19/221602.html
13. *Al Quds*, 2012, http://www.alquds.co.uk/index.asp?fname=today\06qpt999.htm&arc=data\2012\08\08-06\06qpt999.htm
14. *Al Jazeera*, http://www.aljazeera.net/news/pages/b5321a1b-a5dd-418f-8dc5-0d023bb8eb25?GoogleStatID=21
15. *Elaph*, 2012, http://www.elaph.com/Web/NewsPapers/2012/8/754929.html?entry=todays article
16. Wassim Syrian, YouTube, 2013, https://www.YouTube.com/watch?v=-YbqY4NPUpk
17. *El-Dorar al-Shamia*, http://eldorar.com/node/40204

18. Basim al-Jisr, "The Conspiracy of the Arabs Against Themselves," *Asharq Al-Awsat*, 2014, http://aawsat.com/home/article/146761
19. Ibid.
20. Saddam Hussein, Radio broadcast, 1991, http://www.cryan.com/war/quotes.html
21. Saddam Hussein, Baghdad Radio, 1991, http://www.au.af.mil/au/awc/awcgate/iraq/sadquots.htm
22. Saddam Hussein, Baghdad Radio, 1991, http://www.au.af.mil/au/awc/awcgate/iraq/sadquots.htm
23. "Arafat's costly Gulf War choice," *Al Jazeera*, 2009, http://www.aljazeera.com/programmes/plohistoryofrevolution/2009/2009/08/200981294137853350.html
24. http://www.ahewar.org/debat/show.art.asp?aid=23404
25. *Al Jazeera*, 2009, http://www.aljazeera.com/programmes/plohistoryofrevolution/2009/2009/08/200981294137853350.htm
26. "Abbas apology to Kuwait over Iraq," *BBC News*, 2004, http://news.bbc.co.uk/2/hi/middle_east/4089961.stm
27. http://goo.gl/ROj1V1
28. 'Abd al-Salam Wa'il, "Israel, the Everlasting Arab Treasure," *Al Sharq*, 2013, http://www.alsharq.net.sa/2013/06/15/867307
29. Samir Atallah, *Asharq Al-Awsat*, 2014, http://aawsat.com/home/article/192186
30. Muntazer al-Zaidi, "Why I threw the shoe," *The Guardian*, 2009, http://www.theguardian.com/commentisfree/2009/sep/17/why-i-threw-shoe-bush
31. Abdulateef al-Mulhim, "Arab Spring: Mirror, Mirror on the Wall," *Arab News*, 2013, http://www.arabnews.com/news/457444
32. Ibid.
33. *Alwatan Voice*, 2013, http://www.alwatanvoice.com/arabic/news/2013/10/04/443565.html
34. http://goo.gl/0OE3ET
35. Action Group for Palestinians of Syria, 2015, http://www.actionpal.org.uk/en/press-release.html
36. "Starving 20,000 at Damascus camp eating dogs, cat," *Arab News*, 2014, http://www.arabnews.com/news/517771
37. "'People are eating cats': Starvation, deaths plague Syria camp," NBC News, 2014, http://worldnews.nbcnews.com/_news/2014/02/03/22526114-people-are-eating-cats-starvation-deaths-plague-syria-camp?lite
38. IUMS, http://iumsonline.org/portal/en-US/Home/28/
39. *JBC News*, 2015, http://www.jbcnews.net/article/112768
40. *Al-Quds Al-Arabi*, 2014, http://www.alquds.co.uk/?p=142514
41. *Alhadass*, 2015, http://www.alhadass.com/DA.aspx?AID=22672
42. Mohammad Bakri, *Yarmouk*, 2014, http://www.all4syria.info/Archive/138333—*AUTHOR NOTE: While the film was taken off of YouTube, it's viewable here, https://www.facebook.com/video.php?v=277051432471121

43. Ibid.
44. Ibid.
45. *Alwatan Voice*, 2013, http://www.alwatanvoice.com/arabic/news/2013/08/17/425365.html
46. http://www.mwarid.com/i/lebanon.html?http://www.alkalimaonline.com
47. http://www.beirutobserver.com/2013/11/88419/
48. *Alwatan Voice*, 2014, http://www.alwatanvoice.com/arabic/news/2014/04/25/528044.html
49. James Bennet, "U.N. Report Rejects Claims of a Massacre of Refugees," *The New York Times*, 2002, http://www.nytimes.com/2002/08/02/international/middleeast/02JENI.html
50. *Ynet*, 2003, http://www.ynet.co.il/articles/0,7340,L-2815880,00.html
51. Abdel Monem Said, "Concerning Defeat and Victory," *Asharq Al-Awsat*, 2014, http://aaw-sat.com/home/article/178351
52. Abdulateef al-Mulhim, "The Arab Spring and the Israeli Enemy," *Arab News*, 2012, http://www.arabnews.com/arab-spring-and-israeli-enemy
53. Abdel Bari Atwan, "Sinai Is the Nightmare of Israel," *Yemen Press*, 2012, http://www.yemen-press1.com/article4152.html
54. "Abdel Bari Atwan on Islamic State in Iraq and Sham (ISIS)," BBC News, 2014, https://www.YouTube.com/watch?v=P0WvIBLR7zU
55. *BBC Watch*, 2015, http://bbcwatch.org/tag/abdel-bari-atwan/
56. "Abdel Bari Atwan: If Iranian Missiles Hit Israel, I Will Dance in Trafalgar Square," ANB, 2007, https://www.YouTube.com/watch?v=BDYS7JuOcC0
57. "Al Arabi Editor Abd Al Bari Atwan Jihad against Israel Is the Only Thing We Arabs Have in common," Al Mayadeen, 2015, https://www.YouTube.com/watch?v=5OoJHDz_iS4
58. *Asharq Al-Awsat,* http://aawsat.com/details.asp?section=4&article=671288&issueno=12182
59. http://www.aljazeera.net/news/pages/2ef3e5f8-cb6d-4488-9420-7af432dc8516?GoogleS-tatID=24
60. http://www.alwatanvoice.com/arabic/news/2012/12/26/346008.html
61. *Elaph*, 2011, http://www.elaph.com/Web/opinion/2011/8/676729.html?entry=homepage writers
62. *Asharq Al-Awsat,* http://www.aawsat.com/leader.asp?section=3&article=687400&issueno=12289
63. *Asharq Al-Awsat,* http://www.aawsat.com/leader.asp?section=3&article=718934&issueno=12510
64. *Middle East Transparent,* http://www.metransparent.com/spip.php?page=article&id_article=21991&lang=ar
65. http://www.mwarid.com/i/lebanon.html?http://www.alkalimaonline.com/
66. http://www.soryoon.com/?p=6445
67. Dr. Fateen al-Baddad, *JBC News*, 2014, http://goo.gl/wG0jaL
68. "Nasrallah: Road to Jerusalem passes through Syria," *NOW*, 2015, https://now.mmedia.me/lb/en/NewsReports/565573-nasrallah-road-to-jerusalem-passes-through-syria
69. http://goo.gl/HY3BnL

70. https://goo.gl/fKQXLE
71. Muna Fayad, "What Nasrallah Has to Hear," *Middle East Transparent*, http://www.middleeasttransparent.com/spip.php?page=article&id_article=21849&lang=ar
72. Ibid.
73. Hadir Taher, "It is Because of My Admiration for Israel that I Had to Cut Relationships with My Friends," *Elaph*, 2010, http://www.elaph.com/Web/opinion/2010/11/611177.html?entry=homepagearaa
74. *Alwatan Voice*, 2014, http://www.alwatanvoice.com/arabic/news/2014/04/25/528078.html
75. Ibid.

Chapter Two: The Arab Awakening: Screams of Anger

1. http://data.worldbank.org/region/AR
2. *Freedom in the World 2015: Freedom Declines for Ninth Year*, Freedom House, 2015, https://freedomhouse.org/article/freedom-world-2015-freedom-declines-ninth-year#.VUjsa_lViko
3. Ibid.
4. "ALECSO report: 97 million illiterates in Arab countries" *Middle East Monitor*, 2014, https://www.middleeastmonitor.com/news/middle-east/9152-alecso-report-97-million-illiterates-in-arab-countries.
5. *Toward New Horizons Arab Economic Transformation Amid Political Transitions*, IMF, 2014, http://www.imf.org/external/pubs/ft/dp/2014/1401mcd.pdf, published by staff in the International Monetary Fund, Middle East and Central Asia Department.
6. Inger Andersen, "Arab Forum for Development and Employment," The World Bank, 2014, http://www.worldbank.org/en/news/speech/2014/02/26/arab-forum-for-development-and-employment.
7. Mina al-Oraibi, "World Bank Vice-President: Half of region's population living on less than $4 a day," *Asharq Al-Awsat*, 2014, http://www.aawsat.net/2014/10/article55337518/world-bank-mena-vice-president-half-of-regions-population-living-on-less-than-4-a-day
8. "Saudi Arabia," U.S. Energy Information Administration, 2014, http://www.eia.gov/countries/analysisbriefs/Saudi_Arabia/saudi_arabia.pdf
9. "Saudi Arabia Facts and Figures," OPEC, 2015, http://www.opec.org/opec_web/en/about_us/169.htm
10. Alwatan Voice, 2013, http://www.alwatanvoice.com/arabic/news/2013/05/01/388449.html
11. *The World Fact Book*, Central Intelligence Agency, 2016, https://www.cia.gov/library/publications/the-world-factbook/geos/sa.html

12. *Saudi Gazette*, 2014, http://www.saudigazette.com.sa/index.cfm?method=home.regcon&contentid=20141106223548
13. *Asharq Al-Awsat*, 2015, http://goo.gl/l9lXj4
14. *The World Fact Book*, Central Intelligence Agency, 2016, https://www.cia.gov/Library/publications/the-world-factbook/fields/2129.ht
15. "Women constitute 13% of Saudi workforce: stats agency," *Al Arabiya*, 2015, http://english.alarabiya.net/en/News/middle-east/2015/02/10/Women-constitute-13-of-Saudi-workforce-stats-agency.html
16. *The World Fact Book*, Central Intelligence Agency, 2016, https://www.cia.gov/library/publications/the-world-factbook/geos/sa.html
17. Ibid.
18. "Inability of the Government to the housing crisis in Saudi Arabia," *Al-Araby al-Jadeed*, 2015, http://www.alaraby.co.uk/economy/2015/1/17/عجز حكومي- أمام- أزمة- السكن- في- السعودية
19. *Al-Youm al-Sab*, 2015, http://goo.gl/JTfXBz
20. CAPMAS, 2015, http://goo.gl/xInBT9
21. "The World's Billionaires," *Forbes*, 2015, http://www.forbes.com/billionaires/list/#version:static_search:egypt
22. "Total Petroleum and Other Liquids Production," US Energy Information and Administration, http://www.eia.gov/countries/analysisbriefs/Egypt/egypt.pdf
23. "Egypt's Illiteracy rates increase in 2013: CAPMAS report," *Ahram Online*, 2014, http://english.ahram.org.eg/NewsContent/1/64/110142/Egypt/Politics-/Egypts-Illiteracy-rates-increase-in--CAPMAS-report.aspx
24. Ibid.
25. "Growth Slowdown Heightens the Need for Reforms," *MENA Quarterly Economic Brief, Issue 2*, Office of the Chief Economist, The World Bank, 2014, http://www.worldbank.org/content/dam/Worldbank/document/MNA/QEBissue2January2014FINAL.pdf
26. Ibid.
27. http://www.capmas.gov.eg/pdf/poor15%20_e.pdf
28. *Masr Al Arabiya*, 2015, http://goo.gl/CUyCAi *Masr Al Arabiya.*
29. Khalil Ali Haidar, "Did the Fall of Baghdad Dismantle Arab Unity?" *Elaph*, 2013, http://www.elaph.com/Web/NewsPapers/2013/5/809353.html?entry=todaysarticle
30. Dr. Hussein Amar Toka, "Satellites—A Campaign in Which the Arabs Suffered Defeat: The Jamraya Center in Syria and the Israeli Assault," *Alwatan Voice*, 2013, http://www.alwatanvoice.com/arabic/news/2013/05/16/394018.html
31. Dr. Amal al-Hazzani, "A Study of the Shanghai Ranking Chart—Israel Knows What It Wants," *Asharq Al-Awsat*, 2011, http://archive.aawsat.com/leader.asp?section=3&article=643994&issueno=12002#.VU8dOPCbpqw
32. Rudy Khalil, *Al Jazeera*, 2012, http://goo.gl/CINuMU

Chapter Three: Political Islam: Belly Dancing in the Driver's Seat

1. *Asharq Al-Awsat,* http://www.aawsat.com//details.asp?section=4&article=662023&issueno=12121
2. *Asharq Al-Awsat,* http://www.aawsat.com/details.asp?section=4&article=726281&issueno=12569
3. *Al Arabiya*, 2013, http://www.alarabiya.net/articles/2013/02/21/267515.html
4. *Al Arabiya*, 2012, http://www.alarabiya.net/articles/2012/11/13/249406.html
5. http://www.khaleejonline.com/news/view/7110
6. Asma Ghribi, "Tunisians Erupt in Anger Over Desecration of Flag," *Tunisia Live*, 2012, http://www.tunisia-live.net/2012/03/09/tunisians-erupt-in-anger-over-desecration-of-flag/
7. http://www.alquds.co.uk/index.asp?fname=today\15qpt966.htm&arc=data\2013\02\02-15\15qpt966.htm
8. http://alnaharjo.com/index.php?option=com_content&view=article&id=8132:2012-11-01-21-54-28&catid=54:2011-09-22-10-14-28&Itemid=234
9. Patrick Kingsley, "Muslin Brotherhood Backlash Against UN Declaration on Women's Rights," *The Guardian*, 2013, http://www.theguardian.com/world/2013/mar/15/muslim-brotherhood-backlash-un-womens-rights
10. http://www.khaleejonline.com/news/view/4310
11. *Elaph*, 2012, http://www.elaph.com/Web/ElaphWriter/2012/4/727757.htm?entry=homepage writers
12. *Asharq Al-Awsat*, http://www.aawsat.com/leader.asp?section=3&article=718261&issueno=12505
13. *Asharq Al-Awsat*, http://aawsat.com/details.asp?section=4&article=670989&issueno=12180
14. *Al Arabiya*, 2012, http://www.alarabiya.net/articles/2012/06/12/220276.html
15. http://www.alquds.co.uk/index.asp?fname=today\22qpt970.htm&arc=data\2012\08\08-22\22qpt970.htm
16. *Morsi Meter!*, http://morsimeter.com/en
17 *Elaph*, 2014, http://www.elaph.com/Web/opinion/2014/9/944787.html
18. Khairallah Khairallah, *Elaph*, 2014, http://www.elaph.com/Web/opinion/2014/9/944787.html
19. *Asharq Al-Awsat*, 2013, http://archive.aawsat.com/details.asp?section=4&article=755269&issueno=12812#.VmFjvr-WHIU
20. *Middle East Transparent*, 2013, http://www.metransparent.com/spip.php?page=article&id_article=22697&lang=ar
21. *Al-Hayat*, http://international.daralhayat.com/internationalarticle/322438
22. *Elaph*, 2011, http://www.elaph.com/Web/news/2011/10/692890.html
23. *Alwatan Voice*, 2012, http://www.alwatanvoice.com/arabic/news/2012/11/27/338435.html
24. *Alwatan Voice*, 2012, http://www.alwatanvoice.com/arabic/news/2012/12/20/344713.html

25. *Asharq Al-Awsat*, http://aawsat.com/home/article/280511
26. *Elaph*, 2015, http://elaph.com/Web/NewsPapers/2015/11/1055873.html
27. *Asharq Al-Awsat*, http://aawsat.com/leader.asp?section=3&article=700316&issueno=12378
28. *Elaph*, 2012, http://www.elaph.com/Web/NewsPapers/2012/10/767009.html?entry=todaysarticle
29. *Alwatan Voice*, 2012, http://www.alwatanvoice.com/arabic/news/2012/09/10/315583.html
30. Ikwan Wiki, http://www.ikhwanwiki.com/index.php
31. "Innocence of Muslin," *Archive*, 2012, https://archive.org/details/Innocence.of.Muslims
32. Janine di Giovanni and Fredrik Ellisson, "Egypt is Trying to Crush the Muslim Brotherhood. Can it Survive?" *Newsweek*, 2015, http://www.newsweek.com/2015/08/21/egypt-muslim-brotherhood-fate-361663.html

Chapter Four: Militant Islam: Bin Laden is Both Dead and Alive

1. Diana Moukalled, "The bin Laden Movie," *Asharq Al-Awsat*, 2012, http://archive.aawsat.com/leader.asp?section=3&issueno=12371&article=699232#.VVB0io2JjIU
2. Ibid.
3. Hussein al-Shabakshy, *Asharq Al-Awsat*, 2011, http://archive.aawsat.com/leader.asp?section=3&issueno=11844&article=619892#.VWweBY2JjIU
4. "Al-Takfir wa al-Hijrah," *Encyclopedia Britannica*, http://www.britannica.com/topic/al-Takfir-wa-al-Hijrah
5. Bruce Livesey, "The Salafist Movement," *Frontline*, 2005, http://www.pbs.org/wgbh/pages/frontline/shows/front/special/sala.html
6. Ruth Alexander and Hannah Moore, "Are Most Victims of Terrorism Muslim?" *BBC News*, 2015, http://www.bbc.com/news/magazine-30883058
7. *Middle East Transparent*, http://www.middleeasttransparent.com/spip.php?page=article&id_article=23274&lang=ar
8. Huda al-Husseini, *Asharq Al-Awsat*, 2013, http://www.aawsat.com/leader.asp?section=3&article=739996&issueno=12679#.Ugx056wU6So
9. *Asharq Al-Awsat*, 2012, http://aawsat.com/details.asp?section=4&article=675687&issueno=12211
10. Tariq al-Humaid, *Asharq Al-Awsat*, http://aawsat.com/home/article/366781
11. *The World Fact Book*, Central Intelligence Agency, 2016, https://www.cia.gov/library/publications/the-world-factbook/geos/iz.html
12. "Iraq Religions," *Index Mundi*, 2015, http://www.indexmundi.com/iraq/religions.html
13. *Asharq Al-Awsat*, 2013, http://www.aawsat.com/details.asp?section=4&article=726055&issueno=12567

14. *Einelhelweh*, 2013, http://www.einelhelweh.net/shownews.php?full=news&id_topic=3637
15. *Elaph*, 2015, http://www.elaph.com/Web/NewsPapers/2013/5/809354.html?entry=todays article
16. *Beirut Observer*, http://beirutobserver.com/index.php?option=com_content&view=article &id=93366:20
17. *Alwatan Voice*, 2014, http://www.alwatanvoice.com/arabic/news/2014/06/29/560008.html
18. *The World Fact Book*, Central Intelligence Agency, 2016, https://www.cia.gov/library/publications/the-world-factbook/geos/ly.html
19. John Lee, "Unemployment Rate Passes 25%," *Iraq-Business News*, 2015, http://www.iraq-businessnews.com/2015/03/04/unemployment-rate-passes-25/
20. "1/4 Iraqi Population Below Poverty Line, Planning Ministry," *Iraqi Tradelink News Agency*, 2015, http://www.iraqtradelinknews.com/2015/03/14-iraqi-population-below-poverty-line.html
21. *The World Fact Book*, Central Intelligence Agency, 2016, https://www.cia.gov/library/publications/the-world-factbook/fields/2103.html
22. Daryl Grisgraber, "Displaced in Iraq: Little Aid and Few Options," *Refugees International*, 2015, http://static1.squarespace.com/static/506c8e1e4b01d9450dd53f5/t/5633c6bfe4b03216f-d2ea132/1446233807064/Displaced+in+Iraq%3A+Little+Aid+and+Few+Options
23. "Iraq," UN, OCHA, http://www.unocha.org/iraq
24. Ibid.
25. *Asharq Al-Awsat*, 2011, http://www.aawsat.com//leader.asp?section=3&article=639751& issueno=11975
26. Ibid.
27. *Elaph*, 2013, http://elaph.com/Web/news/2013/5/809426.html?entry=articleTaggedArticles
28. *Asharq Al-Awsat*, 2013, http://www.aawsat.com/details.asp?section=4&article=739364&is-sueno=12673#.UgSJ4qwU6So
29. *Al Arabiya*, 2013, http://goo.gl/SQANZA
30. http://www.youkal.net/2012-12-02-14-05-23/24-27/34507
31. Mustafa al-Kadhimi, "Death in Iraq Has Become Just a Statistic," *Elaph*, 2013, http://www.elaph.com/Web/NewsPapers/2013/9/839024.html?entry=todaysarticle
32. "National Consortium for the Study of Terrorism and Responses to Terrorism: Annex of Statistical Informtation," US Department of State, Bureau of Counterterrorism, 2014 http://www.state.gov/j/ct/rls/crt/2014/239416.htm
33. Ibid.
34. UN Assistance Mission for Iraq, "Briefing of SRSG for Iraq Ján Kubiš to the 7443rd Meeting of the UN Security Council," *Relief Web*, 2015, http://reliefweb.int/report/iraq/briefing-srsg-iraq-jan-kubi-7443rd-meeting-un-security-council-new-york-14-may-2015

35. UN Assistance Mission for Iraq, "Briefing of SRSG for Iraq Jan Kubis to the UN Security Council," *Relief Web*, 2015, http://reliefweb.int/report/iraq/briefing-srsg-iraq-jan-kubi-un-security-council-new-york-22-july-2015-enar
36. "Iraq—Complex Emergency," USAID, 2015, https://www.usaid.gov/sites/default/files/documents/1866/iraq_ce_fs08_09-30-2015.pdf
37. Ibid.
38. "500 Iraqi Children Killed, Injured in 2015: UN," *Press TV*, 2015, http://www.presstv.ir/Detail/2015/12/04/440274/Iraqi-children-UN-report
39. Ibid.
40. *JBC News*, 2015, http://www.jbcnews.net/article/136235
41. Kawthar al-Arbash, "How Do You Produce an ISIS Member Before the Age of 20?" *Elaph*, 2015, http://elaph.com/Web/NewsPapers/2015/10/1044679.html
42. http://www.rosaelyoussef.com/news/117012
43. *Al-Monitor*, 2015, http://www.al-monitor.com/pulse/ar/contents/articles/originals/2015/04/lebanon-islamic-state-child-soldiers-syria-iraq-hrw-afp.html
44. *Al-Monitor*, 2015, http://www.al-monitor.com/pulse/ar/contents/articles/origials/2015/06/iraq-isis-children-recruits-army-qaeda-execution.html
45. J. Dana Stuster, "Humanitarian Crisis in Yemen, One-Third of Fighters Children," *Foreign Policy*, 2015, http://foreignpolicy.com/2015/04/10/humanitarian-crisis-in-yemen-one-third-of-fighters-children/
46. *Al-Monitor*, 2013, http://www.al-monitor.com/pulse/ar/contents/articles/originals/2013/11/al-qaeda-zawahri-baghdadi-split.html
47. http://time.com/3340662/cia-isis-isil/
48. *AsharqAl-Awsat, 2013,* http://www.aawsat.com/leader.asp?section=3&article=716325&issueno=12490
49. *JBC News*, 2013, http://www.jbcnews.net/article/3523
50. http://soufangroup.com/wp-content/uploads/2015/12/TSG_ForeignFightersUpdate1.pd
51. "Security Council Unanimously Adopts Resolution Condemning Violent Extremism, Underscoring Need to Prevent Travel, Support for Foreign Terrorist Fighters," Security Council, United Nations, 2014, http://www.un.org/press/en/2014/sc11580.doc.htm
52. *Middle East Panorama*, 2015, http://goo.gl/alx8yx
53. Robert Windrem, "ISIS by the Numbers: Foreign Fighter Total Keeps Growing," *NBC News*, 2015, http://www.nbcnews.com/storyline/isis-terror/isis-numbers-foreign-fighter-total-keeps-growing-n314731
54. *Reuters*, "Former British Spy Chief: Militant in Syria Attract 31,000 Foreign Fighters," *Voice of America*, 2015, http://www.voanews.com/content/former-british-spy-chief-militants-in-syria-attract-thousands-foreign-fighters/3093323.html
55. *Egypt News*, http://www.egynews.net

56. "Egypt Tourism Numbers Jump 70 Percent in Third Quarter Despite Sinai Insurgency," *Reuters*, 2014, http://www.reuters.com/article/2014/12/02/us-egypt-tourism-idUSKCN0JG1WF20141202
57. *Al Arabiya*, 2011, http://www.alarabiya.net/articles/2011/12/09/181700.html
58. *JBC News*, 2014, http://www.jbcnews.net/article/90801
59. "Egypt Bails Jordan Out with Gas Worth $2 Billion—Despite Own Energy and Financial Crisis," *Platform*, 2013, http://platformlondon.org/2013/04/01/egypt-to-keep-exporting-gas-to-jordan-despite-energy-crisis-searching-for-imports/
60. *JBC News*, 2014, http://www.jbcnews.net/article/90
61. *Asharq Al-Awsat*, 2015, http://goo.gl/G6p3CR
62. *Elaph*, 2012, http://www.elaph.com/Web/news/2012/8/753974.html?entry=Israel
63. Ibid.
64. *Asharq Al-Awsat,* 2012, http://www.aawsat.com/details.asp?section=4&article=689966&issueno=12307
65. *Asharq Al-Awsat*, 2012, http://www.aawsat.com/details.asp?section=4&article=688650&issueno=12298
66. *Asharq Al-Awsat*, 2012, http://www.aawsat.com/details.asp?section=4&article=689966&issueno=12307
67. *Elaph*, 2012, http://www.elaph.com/Web/news/2012/8/753974.html?entry=Israel
68. http://www.YouTube.com/watch?v=05-h8J9lgZg
69. "Arish Gasline Explodes for the 30th Time," *The Cairo Post*, 2015, http://www.thecairopost.com/news/153307/news/arish-gas-line-explodes-for-30th-time
70. "Egypt's Tourism Industry Counts the Cost of Terrorism Fears," *Financial Times*, 2015, http://www.ft.com/cms/s/0/b519e56e-83bd-11e5-8095-ed1a37d1e096.html#axzz3tvJ0flLS
71. http://www.ammanads.com/i.html?http://www.ahram.org.eg/
72. *Al Arabiya*, 2013, http://www.alarabiya.net/ar/alhadath/2013/10/29/%D8%A7%D9%8
73. http://www.middleeasttransparent.com/spip.php?page=article&id_article=22221&lang=ar
74. Frederic Wehrey, David Bishop, and Ala' Alrababa'h, "Backdrop to Intervention: Sources of Egyptian-Libyan Border Tension," Carnegie Endowment for International Peace, 2014, http://carnegieendowment.org/2014/08/27/backdrop-to-intervention-sources-of-egyptian-libyan-border-tension
75. *Alwatan Voice*, 2014, http://www.alwatanvoice.com/arabic/news/2014/02/17/497346.html
76. *Ma'an News Agency*, 2014, http://www.maannews.net/arb/ViewDetails.aspx?ID=749921
77. *JBC News*, 2014, http://www.jbcnews.net/article/92576--يبدأ-المرحلة-الثانية-من-تفجير-المنازل-في-سيناء-الجيش-المصري
78. *JBC News*, 2015, http://www.jbcnews.net/article/121058-من-الأنفاق-على-الحدود-مع-غزة-السيسي-دمرنا
79. "Sisi Says Gaza Tunnels Flooded in Coordination with PA," *Middle East Monitor*, 2015, https://www.middleeastmonitor.com/news/africa/21303-sisi-says-gaza-tunnels-flooded-in-coordination-with-pa

80. "Eyptian Army Says It Destroyed 20 Gaza Tunnels in November," *Middle East Monitor*, 2015, https://www.middleeastmonitor.com/news/africa/22687-egyptian-army-says-it-destroyed-20-gaza-tunnels-in-november
81. Richard Spenser, "Saudia Arabia is Building a 600-mile 'Great Wall' to Shield Itself from Isis," *Business Insider*, 2015, http://www.businessinsider.com/saudi-arabia-is-building-a-600-mile-great-wall-to-shield-from-isis-2015-1
82. "Saudi Arabia's New Yemen Strategy: Get Behind a Fence," *Reuters*, 2015, http://www.reuters.com/article/2015/01/22/us-yemen-security-saudi-idUSKBN0KV1VH20150122
83. *JBC News*, 2015, http://www.jbcnews.net/article/99791
84. Salma El Wardeny and Caroline Alexander, "Fences Rise Across Middle East as Jihadi Threat Escalates," *Bloomberg Business*, 2015, http://www.bloomberg.com/news/articles/2015-07-22/fences-rise-across-middle-east-as-jihadi-threat-rattles-leaders
85. Ibid.
86. Ibid.
87. http://azelin.files.wordpress.com/2014/02/al-qc481_idah-22on-the-relationship-of-qc481idat-al-jihc481d-and-the-islamic-state-of-iraq-and-al-shc481m22.pdf
88. Ibid.
89. http://azelin.files.wordpress.com/2014/02/al-qc481_idah-22on-the-relationship-of-qc481idat-al-jihc481d-and-the-islamic-state-of-iraq-and-al-shc481m22.pdf
90. https://azelin.files.wordpress.com/2014/02/al-qc481_idah-22on-the-relationship-of-qc481idat-al-jihc481d-and-the-islamic-state-of-iraq-and-al-shc481m22.pdf
91. *Alwatan Voice*, 2014, http://www.alwatanvoice.com/arabic/news/2014/06/29/560008.html
92. Raya Post, 2013, http://rayapost.com/index.php/2013-09-26-00-42-07/917-2014-01-10-11-05-51
93. *Orient Net*, 2014, http://orient-news.net/?page=news_show&id=7192
94. *Voice of Iraq*, http://www.sotaliraq.com/mobile-news.php?id=153788#axzz34r1pI7SP10/13
95. https://www.syriahr.com/en/2015/05/is-executes-2618-since-the-declaration-of-its-alleged-caliphate-including-464-in-one-month/
96. *Syrian Observatory for Human Rights*, http://www.syriahr.com/en/
97. http://goo.gl/BLEUVQ
98. *Al Arabiya*, 2013, http://www.alarabiya.net/ar/alhadath/2013/07/25/
99. *El-Dorar al-Shamia*, 2014, http://eldorar.com/node/40210
100. http://www.youkal.net/2012-12-02-14-05-23/24-26/41821-
101. http://www.ammanads.com/i.html?http://www.dampress.net/
102. *JBC News*, 2015, http://www.jbcnews.net/article/121316
103. http://www.mepanorama.com/197569
104. *Alhadath News*, 2013, http://goo.gl/WLTZGN
105. *Elaph*, 2013, http://www.elaph.com/Web/NewsPapers/2013/3/802589.html?entry=todaysarticle

106. *Alwatan Voice*, 2013, http://www.alwatanvoice.com/arabic/news/2013/05/03/389127.html
107. https://www.YouTube.com/watch?v=78gX1Nz8-30&feature=YouTube_gdata_player
108. *Al-Monitor*, 2015, http://www.al-monitor.com/pulse/originals/2015/04/jordan-amman-is-nusra-militants-salafi-jihadists.html#
109. *Soryoon Net*, http://www.soryoon.com/?p=8421
110. *Asharq Al-Awsat*, 2014, http://www.aawsat.com/home/article/176971
111. *Asharq Al-Awsat*, 2014, http://www.aawsat.com/details.asp?section=4&article=775933&issueno=12985#.U5-eKii9bx8
112. "Interview and Translation: Shayk Abu Muhammad al-Maqdisi," *pietervanostaeyen*, 2015, https://pietervanostaeyen.wordpress.com/2015/02/09/interview-and-translation-shaykh-abu-muhammad-al-maqdisi-dd-february-6-2015/
113. *JBC News*, 2015, http://www.jbcnews.net/article/79024-
114. *JBC News*, 2014, http://www.jbcnews.net/article/70900
115. *Asharq Al-Awsat*, 2014, http://www.aawsat.com/home/article/160681
116. *Asharq Al-Awsat*, 2014, http://aawsat.com/home/article/340981
117. *Asharq Al-Awsat*, 2014, http://www.aawsat.com/home/article/199751
118. *JBC News*, 2014, http://www.jbcnews.net/article/80139
119. *JBC News*, 2015, http://jbcnews.net/article/160326-
120. Ibid.
121. https://www.facebook.com/soukournahda/videos/156449444491219
122. "Rocket Attacks on Israel from Gaza," Israel Defense Forces, http://web.archive.org/web/20141230070356/http://www.idfblog.com/facts-figures/rocket-attacks-toward-israel/
123. "Rocket Launching," Israel Security Agency, 2013, http://www.shabak.gov.il/English/EnTerrorData/decade/Rocket/Pages/
124. *BBC News*, 2015, http://www.bbc.co.uk/arabic/middleeast/2015/02/150228_gaza_tunnels_feature
125. *Al-Monitor*, 2013, http://www.al-monitor.com/pulse/iw/originals/2013/10/gaza-tunnel-israel-shift-Ḥamās-war.html#
126. *Islam Times*, 2015, http://www.islamtimes.org/ar/doc/news/465246/print/
127. *Middle East Transparent*, http://www.metransparent.com/spip.php?page=article&id_article=19987&lang=ar
128. http://www.einelhelweh.net/shownews.php?full=news&id_topic=4028
129. Morgan Winsor, "Gaza's Jaish Al-Islam ISIS Allegiance? Jihadi Group Statement Proclaims Devotion to the Islamic State," *International Business Times*, 2015, http://www.ibtimes.com/gazas-jaish-al-islam-isis-allegiance-jihadi-group-statement-proclaims-devotion-2092764
130. *JBC News*, http://www.jbcnews.net/article/101151
131. "Hamas: Rafah Clashes Terminated, 22 Confirmed Dead," *Ma'an News Agency*, 2009, http://www.maannews.com/Content.aspx?id=219107

132. *Middle East Transparent,* http://www.metransparent.com/spip.php?page=article&id_article=19987&lang=ar
133. http://alquds.co.uk/index.asp?fname=latest/data/2012-10-01-07-23-53.htm
134. *Online Jihad Exposed*, 2013, http://www.onlinejihadexposed.com/2013/02/blog-post_5091.html#more
135. *JBC News*, 2015, http://www.jbcnews.net/article/126921–مؤيدي-البغدادي-وتهدم-مسجدهم-
في-غزة-الإذاعة-حماس-تعتقل-100-سلفي-من-مؤيدي
136. *Al-Monitor*, 2013, http://www.al-monitor.com/pulse/ar/contents/articles/originals/2013/11/Ḥamās-salafist-gaza-reconciliation.html
137. *Asharq Al-Awsat*, 2014, http://aawsat.com/home/article/243411
138. *Alwatan Voice*, 2012, http://www.alwatanvoice.com/arabic/news/2012/10/20/327215.html
139. *JBC News*, 2013, http://www.jbcnews.net/article/30285
140. *Elaph*, 2014, http://www.elaph.com/Web/opinion/2014/9/940552.html
141. http://www.ammanads.com/i.html?http://sarayanews.com/
142. *Asharq Al-Awsat*, http://aawsat.com/home/article/243411
143. *Foreign Fighers: An Updated Assessment of the Flow of Foreign Fighters into Syria and Iraq*, The Soufan Group, 2015, http://soufangroup.com/wp-content/uploads/2015/12/TSG_ForeignFightersUpdate1.pdf
144. *Al-Monitor*, 2015, http://www.al-monitor.com/pulse/originals/2015/04/jordan-amman-is-nusra-militants-salafi-jihadists.html
145. http://www.saidatv.tv/news.php?go=fullnews&newsid=82336
146. *Al Arabiya*, 2013, http://goo.gl/gN1OC1
147. http://goo.gl/qOIqUG
148. *Beirut Observer*, 2015, http://goo.gl/lQGJ8R
149. *Ynet*, 2014, www.ynet.co.il/articles/0,7340,L-4585439,00.html
150. *Asharq Al-Awsat*, 2015, http://goo.gl/hdnimz
151. *JBC News,* 2014, http://goo.gl/Ry1mrJ
152. "Islamic State Conflict: 10,000 Militants Killed in Nine Months—US," *BBC*, 2015, http://www.bbc.com/news/world-middle-east-32990299
153. Laura Smith-Spark, "US Official: 10,000 ISIS Fighters Killed in 9-Month Campaign," *CNN*, 2015, http://edition.cnn.com/2015/06/03/middleeast/isis-conflict/
154. http://www.mwarid.com/i/lebanon.html?http://www.alkalimaonline.com/
155. *JBC News,* 2014, http://www.jbcnews.net/article/41260
156. *Asharq Al-Awsat*, 2015, http://aawsat.com/home/article/265181
157. *El-Dorar al-Shamia*, http://eldorar.com/node/34172
158. *Al-Monitor*, 2015, http://www.al-monitor.com/pulse/ar/contents/articles/originals/2015/02/regime-syria-daraa-southern-front-opposition.html
159. *Al-Hadath News*, http://www.alhadathnews.net/
160. *Ynet*, 2014, http://www.ynet.co.il/articles/0,7340,L-4579583,00.html

161. *Elaph*, 2015, http://www.elaph.com/Web/NewsPapers/2015/3/990194.html
162. *Elaph*, 2014, http://www.elaph.com/Web/NewsPapers/2014/3/884033.html
163. Oraib al-Rantawi, "ISIS is a Quintessential Muslim-Arab Invention," *Ad-Dustour*, http://www.addustour.com/17317
164. Hashem Saleh, "September 11 Has Not Yet Happened," *Asharq Al-Awsat*, 2014, http://aawsat.com/home/article/180956
165. Ghassan Charbel, "Small Flags," *Al-Hayat*, http://www.alhayat.com/Opinion/Ghassan-Charbel/4500691
166. Sawsan al-Abtah, "Wake Up You ISIS Supporters," *Al Ankabout*, 2014, http://www.alankabout.com/articles/61479.html
167. Aziz al-Hajj, "9/11 and the Global War on Terror," *Elaph*, 2015, http://elaph.com/Web/opinion/2015/1/972707
168. David Hudson, "President Obama: We Will Degrade and Ultimately Destroy ISIL," The White House, 2014, https://www.whitehouse.gov/blog/2014/09/10/president-obama-we-will-degrade-and-ultimately-destroy-isil
169. Zack Beauchamp, "Full Text: Obama's Oval Office Address on San Bernadino and ISIS," *Vox World*, 2015, http://www.vox.com/2015/12/6/9857270/obama-speech-address-transcript-san-bernardino-isis
170. Ghassan Charbel, *Al Hayat*, 2015, http://www.alhayat.com/Opinion/Ghassan-Charbel/6787287
171. Dr. Abd al-Hamid al-Ansari, "The Absence of Democracy as an Excuse for the ISIS Phenomenon," *Elaph*, 2014, http://www.elaph.com/Web/NewsPapers/2014/9/944912.html
172. *Alwatan Voice*, 2014, http://www.alwatanvoice.com/arabic/news/2014/06/29/560008.html
173. *Elaph*, 2014, http://www.elaph.com/Web/NewsPapers/2014/7/926140.html
174. *Asharq Al-Awsat*, 2014, http://www.aawsat.com/home/article/134821
175. *Asharq Al-Awsat*, http://aawsat.com/home/article/233566
176. *Asharq Al-Awsat*, http://aawsat.com/home/article/304236
177. http://www.all4syria.info/Archive/192368
178. http://orient-news.net/?page=news_show&id=82484
179. http://orient-news.net/?page=news_show&id=85315
180. Ibid.
181. Abdulrahman al-Rashed, "Syria and Iraq Are One State, One War," *Asharq Al-Awsat*, http://aawsat.com/home/article/383011
182. Abd al-Mun'im Sa'id, "The Upcoming War in the Gaza Strip," *al-Youm*, 2014, http://www.aawsa.com/home/article/158396
183. http://rotter.net/forum/scoops1/132646.shtml

Chapter Five: The Iranian-Arab Power Struggle: The Past Is Still Present

1. "Mapping the Global Muslim Population," Pew Research Center, 2009, http://www.pewforum.org/2009/10/07/mapping-the-global-muslim-population
2. Ibid.
3. Karim Sadjadpour, "The Supreme Leader," *The Iran Primer*, United States Institute of Peace, http://iranprimer.usip.org/resource/supreme-leader
4. *The World Fact Book*, Central Intelligence Agency, 2016, https://www.cia.gov/library/publications/the-world-factbook/geos/le.html
5. Jeffrey White, "A War Like No Other: Israel vs. Hezbollah in 2015," The Washington Institute for Near East Policy, 2015, http://www.washingtoninstitute.org/policy-analysis/view/a-war-like-no-other-israel-vs.-hezbollah-in-2015
6. http://www.orient-news.net/?page=news_show&id=87824
7. http://syria-news.com/readnews.php?sy_seq=76184
8. *Al Arabiya*, 2012, http://www.alarabiya.net/articles/2012/08/28/234698.html
9. http://www.youkal.net/2012-12-02-14-05-23/24-32/49926-
10. *Asharq Al-Awsat*, 2014, http://www.aawsat.com/home/article/146016
11. *Al Arabiya*, 2012, http://www.alarabiya.net/views/2012/11/01/246969.html
12. *Elaph*, 2012, http://www.elaph.com/Web/opinion/2012/12/778275.html?entry=opinion
13. "Special Tribunal for Lebanon," Global Policy Forum, 2008, https://www.globalpolicy.org/international-justice/international-criminal-tribunals-and-special-courts/special-tribunal-for-lebanon.html
14. http://www.mwarid.com/i/lebanon.html?http://www.alkalimaonline.com/
15. Max Fisher, "Why Wissam al-Hassan Matters for the Middle East," *The Washington Post*, 2012, http://www.washingtonpost.com/blogs/worldviews/wp/2012/10/19/why-wissam-al-hassan-security-official-killed-in-beirut-blast-matters-for-the-middle-east/
16. *Al Arabiya*, 2012, http://www.alarabiya.net/articles/2012/10/19/244697.html
17. *Al Arabiya*, 2012, http://www.alarabiya.net/views/2012/11/01/246969.html
18. "Hezbollah Leader Refuses to Hand Over Hariri Suspects," *The Guardian*, 2011, http://www.theguardian.com/world/2011/jul/03/hezbollah-leader-refuses-handover-hariri-suspects
19. Abdul Rahman Al-Rashed, "Hezbollah and the Wissam Hassan's Assasination," *Al Arabiya*, 2012, http://www.alarabiya.net/views/2012/11/03/247366.html
20. *Elaph*, 2011, http://www.elaph.com/Web/opinion/2011/8/679744.html?entry=home pagearaa
21. *Elaph*, 2011, http://www.elaph.com/Web/NewsPapers/2011/11/696559.html?entry=home pagenewspapers
22. *El-Dorar al-Shamia*, http://eldorar.com/node/60237

23. *JBC News*, 2015, http://www.jbcnews.net/article/121172
24. https://www.YouTube.com/watch?v=55qGwtDpYUI
25. *Beirut Observer*, 2016, http://beirutobserver.com/index.php?option=com_content&view=article&id=94211:2013-
26. *JBC News*, 2015, http://www.jbcnews.net/article/125714
27. Laila Bassam and Yara Bayoumy, "Lebanon Gets Hezbollah-Led Cabinet After 5-Month Lag," *Reuters*, 2011, http://www.reuters.com/article/2011/06/13/us-lebanon-government-idUSTRE75C48K20110613
28. http://www.alquds.co.uk/index.asp?fname=today\08qpt952.htm&arc=data\2012\06\06-08\08qpt952.htm
29. *Al Arabiya*, 2012, http://www.alarabiya.net/articles/2012/11/29/252505.html
30. *Asharq Al-Awsat*, 2012, http://www.aawsat.com//details.asp?section=4&article=663555&issueno=12131
31. *Asharq Al-Awsat*, 2012, http://www.aawsat.com/leader.asp?section=3&article=687400&issueno=12289
32. *Elaph*, 2012, http://www.elaph.com/Web/opinion/2012/9/764985.html?entry=asdaa
33. http://www.mwarid.com/i/lebanon.html?http://www.alkalimaonline.com/
34. *Elaph*, 2014, http://www.elaph.com/Web/opinion/2014/3/886512.html
35. *Middle East Transparent*, http://www.metransparent.com/spip.php?page=article&id_article=28835&lang=ar
36. *Asharq Al-Awsat*, 2012, http://www.aawsat.com//details.asp?section=4&article=665742&issueno=12145
37. *Asharq Al-Awsat*, 2012, http://www.aawsat.com//leader.asp?section=3&article=663911&issueno=12133
38. *Al Arabiya*, 2012, http://www.alarabiya.net/articles/2012/08/28/234698.html
39. *Asharq Al-Awsat*, 2013, http://aawsat.com/leader.asp?section=3&article=712484&issueno=12462
40. *JBC News*, 2015, http://www.jbcnews.net/article/125268
41. Ian Black, "Fear of a Shia Full Moon," *The Guardian*, 2007, http://www.theguardian.com/world/2007/jan/26/worlddispatch.ianblack
42. *Al Arabiya*, 2015, http://www.alarabiya.net/ar/iran/2015/12/11
43. "Persian in Bahrain," Joshua Project, https://joshuaproject.net/people_groups/14371/BA
44. Fred Lawson, *Bahrain: The Modernization of Autocracy*, pp.124-125.
45. http://www.todayszaman.com/tz-web/detaylar.do?load=detay&link=167742
46. http://www.saidatv.tv/news.php?go=fullnews&newsid=82381
47. *JBC News*, 2015, http://www.jbcnews.net/article/135432
48. *The World Fact Book*, Central Intelligence Agency, 2016, https://www.cia.gov/library/publications/the-world-factbook/geos/gz.html
49. https://www.paldf.net/forum/showthread.php?t=1165954

50. *JBC News*, 2015, http://www.jbcnews.net/article/111737
51. *JBC News*, 2015, http://www.jbcnews.net/article/124524
52. Ibid.
53. *JBC News*, 2015, http://www.jbcnews.net/article/124524
54. https://www.paldf.net/forum/showthread.php?t=1166597
55. *JBC News*, 2015, http://www.jbcnews.net/article/124064
56. *Al-Monitor*, 2015, http://www.al-monitor.com/pulse/ar/contents/articles/originals/2015/06/gaza-political-military-parties-emergence.html
57. Daniel Williams, "Christianity in Iraq is Finished," *The Washington Post*, 2014, https://www.washingtonpost.com/opinions/christianity-in-iraq-is-finished/2014/09/19/21feaa7c-3f2f-11e4-b0ea-8141703bbf6f_story.html
58. "Peace or a Sword?" *The Economist*, 2015, http://www.economist.com/blogs/erasmus/2015/02/christians-iraq
59. "Iran-Iraq Border," *Wikipedia*, https://en.wikipedia.org/wiki/Iran%E2%80%93Iraq_border
60. "Khorasan," *Encyclopedia Britannica*, 2015, http://www.britannica.com/place/Khorasan-historical-region-Asia
61. "Ahwazi," UNPO, 2008, http://www.unpo.org/article/7857
62. *Al Arabiya*, 2012, http://www.alarabiya.net/articles/2012/09/06/236445.html
63. "Province of Khuzestan," Iran Chamber Society, 2016, http://www.iranchamber.com/provinces/15_khuzestan/15_khuzestan.php
64. "Karbala and Najaf: Shia Holy Cities," *BBC News*, 2003, http://news.bbc.co.uk/2/hi/middle_east/2881835.stm
65. *JBC News*, http://www.jbcnews.net/article/124064
66. "Iran 'Sent Soldiers to Fight in Iraq,'" *Al Jazeera*, 2014, http://www.aljazeera.com/news/middleeast/2014/08/iran-soldiers-iraq-islamic-state-2014823161322258630.html
67. W.J. Hennigan and David S. Cloud, "Iran's Role in Iraqi Fight Against Islamic State a Quandary for US," *Los Angeles Times*, 2015, http://www.latimes.com/world/middleeast/la-fg-us-iraq-tensions-20150308-story.html
68. *JBC News*, 2015, http://www.jbcnews.net/article/108011
69. *Al Jazeera*, http://goo.gl/O5pWbl
70. http://orient-news.net/?page=news_show&id=85849
71. *JBC News*, 2015, http://www.jbcnews.net/article/112833-والنجيفي-الحشد-الشعبي-فاشل-الحشد-الشعبي-ينسحب-من-تكريت
72. http://www.aa.com.tr/ar/news/488933
73. *JBC News*, http://www.jbcnews.net/article/117865-بيانا-حول-إيران-والحشد-الشعبي-وما-يجري-في-المحافظة-4/15-شيوخ--ووجهاء-الأنبار-يصدرون
74. http://orient-news.net/?page=news_show&id=85694
75. *JBC News*, 2015, http://www.jbcnews.net/article/126034
76. *JBC News*, 2015, http://www.jbcnews.net/article/148411-

77. *Beirut Observer*, 2015, http://goo.gl/G5BI8w
78. *The World Fact Book*, Central Intelligence Agency, 2016, https://www.cia.gov/library/publications/the-world-factbook/geos/ym.html
79. http://alghadalarabi.net/ar/?Action=Details&ID=29768
80. "Security Council Demands End to Yemen Violence, Adopting Resolution 2216 (2015), with Russian Federation Abstaining," United Nations, 2015, http://www.un.org/press/en/2015/sc11859.doc.htm
81. *Asharq Al-Awsat*, 2012, http://aawsat.com/details.asp?section=4&article=672330&issueno=12189
82. *Asharq Al-Awsat*, 2012, http://www.aawsat.com/details.asp?section=4&article=693906&issueno=12335
83. "Iran's Economy, By the Numbers," *Iran Primer*, United States Institute of Peace, 2015, http://iranprimer.usip.org/blog/2015/may/11/irans-economy-numbers
84. *Asharq Al-Awsat*, 2015, http://goo.gl/xIRTgL
85. Ibid.
86. *Oil-Price.Net*, 2015, http://www.oil-price.net/
87. *Al Arabiya*, 2015, http://www.alarabiya.net/ar/saudi-today/2015/12/15
88. "Joint Statement on the Meeting Between President Barack Obama and King Salman bin Abd alAziz Al Saud," The White House, 2015, https://www.whitehouse.gov/the-press-office/2015/09/04/joint-statement-meeting-between-president-barack-obama-and-king-salman
89. "UN-Backed Action Group Agrees on Measures for Peaceful Transition in Syria," *UN News Centre*, 2012, http://www.un.org/apps/news/story.asp?NewsID=42367#.Vm_Mqb-WHIU
90. Ibid.

Chapter Six: The War in Syria

1. *The World Fact Book*, Central Intelligence Agency, 2016, https://www.cia.gov/library/publications/the-world-factbook/geos/sy.html
2. "Syria Population," *World Population Review*, 2015, http://worldpopulationreview.com/countries/syria-population/
3. *The World Fact Book*, Central Intelligence Agency, 2016, https://www.cia.gov/library/publications/the-world-factbook/geos/sy.html
4. "Alawite," *Encyclopedia Britannica*, http://www.britannica.com/topic/Alawite
5. Ibid.
6. Ibid.
7. Ibid.
8. *Asharq Al-Awsat*, 2015, http://aawsat.com/home/article/380041

9. "Syria Population," *World Population Review*, 2015, http://worldpopulationreview.com/countries/syria-population/
10. ica.com/topic/Umayyad-dynasty-Islamic-history
11. *Encyclopedia Britannica*, http://www.britannica.com/place/Damascus
12. http://www.hks.harvard.edu/news-events/news/press-releases/afghanistan-syria-and-bahrain-the-worst-elections-of-2014
13. *Asharq Al-Awsat*, 2012, http://archive.aawsat.com/details.asp?section=4&article=668125&issueno=12161#.VW_sWo2JjIU
14. https://www.YouTube.com/watch?v=x6Y7GZDb-P8
15. *Elaph*, 2011, http://www.elaph.com/Web/news/2011/10/687469.html?entry=homepage akhbar
16. *Asharq Al-Awsat*, 2011, http://www.aawsat.com//details.asp?section=4&article=647434&issueno=12024
17. https://www.YouTube.com/watch?v=ujl1WKNl9Y8
18. *Elaph*, 2011, http://elaph.com/Web/NewsPapers/2011/11/693006.html?entry=homepage newspapers
19. Joel Greenburg, "Israeli Officials Say Syria's Assad is Doomed," *The Washington Post*, 2011, https://www.washingtonpost.com/world/middle_east/israeli-officials-say-assad-is-doomed/2011/12/14/gIQAYBuEuO_story.html
20. *Asharq Al-Awsat*, 2012, http://aawsat.com/home/article/382346
21. Greg Bunro, Jayshree Bajoria, and Jonathan Masters, "Iran's Revolutionary Guards," *Council on Foreign Relations*, 2013, http://www.cfr.org/iran/irans-revolutionary-guards/p14324
22. Ibid.
23. "Quds Force," *Wikipedia*, https://en.wikipedia.org/wiki/Quds_Force
24. *El-Dorar al-Shamia*, http://eldorar.com/node/91482
25. http://www.albawaba.com/ar
26. *Asharq Al-Awsat*, 2012, http://aawsat.com/leader.asp?section=3&article=669197&issueno=12168
27. http://www.alarabonline.org/index.asp?fname=\2012\02\02-14\821.htm&dismode=x&ts=
28. *Middle East Transparent*, http://www.metransparent.com/spip.php?page=article&id_article=16781&lang=ar
29. *Asharq Al-Awsat*, 2012, http://www.aawsat.com/details.asp?section=4&article=688406&issueno=12297
30. *Beirut Observer*, http://beirutobserver.com/index.php?option=com_content&view=article&id=90820:2013-02-19-04-45-59&catid=39:features
31. *Beirut Observer*, http://beirutobserver.com/index.php?option=com_content&view=article&id=91848:2013-03-09-04-01-20&catid=41:2010-10-03-20-24-15
32. http://www.middleeasttransparent.com/spip.php?page=article&id_article=21860&lang=ar
33. http://www.beirutobserver.com/2013/06/76039/

34. Matthew Levitt, "Hezbollah: Pulled Between Resistance to Israel and Defense of Syria," *CTC Sentinel*, Compating Terrorism Center, 2015, https://www.ctc.usma.edu/posts/hezbollah-pulled-between-resistance-to-israel-and-defense-of-syria
35. http://goo.gl/14koui
36. http://www.all4syria.info/Archive/194484
37. http://www.alaraby.co.uk/politics/2015/2/13/
38. *JBC News*, http://www.jbcnews.net/article/117592
39. http://www.all4syria.info/Archive/194484
40. Ibid.
41. Philip Smyth, "The Shiite Jihad in Syria and Its Regional Effects," The Washington Institute for Near Middle East Policy, 2015, http://www.washingtoninstitute.org/policy-analysis/view/the-shiite-jihad-in-syria-and-its-regional-effects
42. *Elaph*, 2011, http://www.elaph.com/Web/news/2011/11/697072.html
43. http://www.beirutobserver.com/2013/06/77956/
44. http://www.middleeasttransparent.com/spip.php?page=article&id_article=24121&lang=ar
45. Michael Knights, "Iran's Foreign Legion: The Role of Iraqe Shiite Militias in Syria," The Washington Institute for Near Middle East Policy, 2013, http://www.washingtoninstitute.org/policy-analysis/view/irans-foreign-legion-the-role-of-iraqi-shiite-militias-in-syria
46. *Alwatan Voice*, 2012, http://www.alwatanvoice.com/arabic/news/2012/08/28/312080.html
47. http://www.middleeasttransparent.com/spip.php?page=article&id_article=21772&lang=ar
48. *JBC News*, http://www.jbcnews.net/article/23936-
49. *Elaph*, 2014, http://www.elaph.com/Web/News/2014/10/947499.htm
50. "Jaish al-Sha'bi," *Wikipedia*, https://en.wikipedia.org/wiki/Jaish_al-Sha'bi
51. *Asharq Al-Awsat*, 2013, http://www.aawsat.com/details.asp?section=4&article=716971&issueno=12495
52. Julian Border, "Iran and Hezbollah 'Have Built 50,000 Force to Help Syrian Regime," *The Guardian*, 2013, http://www.theguardian.com/world/2013/mar/14/iran-hezbollah-force-syrian-regime
53. http://www.wsj.com/articles/iran-expands-role-in-syria-in-conjunction-with-russias-air-strikes-1443811030
54. http://www.bloombergview.com/articles/2015-12-10/western-officials-iran-retreating-from-syria-fight
55. Ibid.
56. *Foreign Fighers: An Updated Assessment of the Flow of Foreign Fighters into Syria and Iraq*, The Soufan Group, 2015, http://soufangroup.com/wp-content/uploads/2014/06/TSG-Foreign-Fighters-in-Syria.pdf
57. Ashley Kirk, "Iraq and Syria: How Many Foreign Fighters are Fighting for ISIL?" *The Telegraph*, 2015, http://www.telegraph.co.uk/news/worldnews/islamic-state/11770816/Iraq-and-Syria-How-many-foreign-fighters-are-fighting-for-Isil.html

58. *Foreign Fighers: An Updated Assessment of the Flow of Foreign Fighters into Syria and Iraq*, The Soufan Group, 2015, http://soufangroup.com/wp-content/uploads/2015/12/TSG_ForeignFightersUpdate4.pdf
59. *Alwatan Voice*, 2013, http://www.alwatanvoice.com/arabic/news/2013/05/03/389159.html
60. https://www.paldf.net/forum/showthread.php?t=1106353
61. *Alwatan Voice*, 2013, http://www.alwatanvoice.com/arabic/news/2013/12/01/467201.html
62. http://www.youkal.net/2012-12-02-14-05-23/24-26/35827
63. "Internal Conflict Ruins Historical Heritage of the Middle East," *Daily Sabah*, 2015, http://www.dailysabah.com/history/2015/06/26/internal-conflicts-ruins-historical-heritage-of-the-middle-east
64. "Khalid ibn al-Walid," *Encyclopedia Britannica*, http://www.britannica.com/biography/Khalid-ibn-al-Walid
65. "Zaynab bint Ali," *Wikipedia*, https://en.wikipedia.org/wiki/Zaynab_bint_Ali
66. *Al Arabiya*, 2012, http://www.alarabiya.net/articles/2012/11/12/249204.html
67. *Alwatan Voice*, 2013, http://www.alwatanvoice.com/arabic/news/2013/04/14/382248.html
68. Syrian Network for Human Rights, http://sn4hr.org/
69. *El-Dorar al-Shamia*, http://eldorar.com/node/16956
70. Ginger Pinholster, "AAAS Satellite Image Analysis: Five of Six Syrian World Heritage Sites 'Exhibit Signifiant Damage,'" AAAS, 2014, http://www.aaas.org/news/aaas-satellite-image-analysis-five-six-syrian-world-heritage-sites-exhibit-significant-damage
71. http://www.alalam.ir/news/1470466
72. http://news.askmorgan.net/article/39983
73. http://www.all4syria.info/Archive/195016
74. "Internal Conflict Ruins Historical Heritage of the Middle East," *Daily Sabah*, 2015, http://www.dailysabah.com/history/2015/06/26/internal-conflicts-ruins-historical-heritage-of-the-middle-east
75. "Blast in Aleppo Does Major Damage to Citadel Wall," *Reuters*, 2015, http://www.reuters.com/article/2015/07/12/us-mideast-crisis-syria-aleppo-idUSKCN0PM0JW20150712
76. Syrian Economic Task Force, http://syrianeconomic.org/en/about-us/
77. http://www.all4syria.info/Archive/235531
78. "Syria Crisis 'Worsening" Amid Humanitarian Funding Shortfall, Warns Top UN Relief Official," *UN News Centre*, 2015, http://www.un.org/apps/news/story.asp?NewsID=50436#.VT_XG42JjIW
79. "More than 220,000 Dead in Syria Conflict: Monitor," *AFP*, 2015, https://en-maktoob.news.yahoo.com/more-220-000-dead-syria-conflict-monitor-084215631.html
80. "Death Toll," Syrian Network for Human Rights, http://sn4hr.org/blog/category/death-toll/
81. http://www.syriahr.com/en/2015/10/about-20-millions-and-half-killed-and-wounded-since-the-beginning-of-the-syrian-revolution/
82. *JBC News*, http://www.jbcnews.net/article/86980

83. Edwin Mora, "US Official: Chemical Weapons Use in Syria Becoming Routine," *Breitbart*, 2015, http://www.breitbart.com/national-security/2015/11/25/u-s-official-chemical-weapons-use-syria-becoming-routine/
84. "Syria Civil War: Bomb Damages Aleppo's Ancient Citadel," *BBC News*, 2015, http://www.bbc.com/news/world-middle-east-33499609
85. "Syrian Arab Republic," UNHCR, 2015, http://www.unhcr.org/pages/49e486a76.html
86. Syria Regional Refugee Response: Interagency Information Sharing Portal, UNHCR, 2015, http://data.unhcr.org/syrianrefugees/regional.php
87. Ibid.
88. "Europe: Syrian Asylum Applications," Syria Regional Refugee Response: Interagency Information Sharing Portal, UNHCR, 2015, http://data.unhcr.org/syrianrefugees/asylum.php
89. http://www.mwarid.com/i/lebanon.html?
90. *Al Arabiya*, 2013, http://goo.gl/8wSekV
91. http://www.youkal.net/2012-12-02-14-05-23/24-26/34349
92. Ibid.
93. Ibid.
94. https://www.paldf.net/forum/showthread.php?t=1126725&page=2
95. http://www.aljazeera.net/news/pages/e258b0ba-45d9-4e6e-acd0-1ef4de7654a0
96. *El-Dorar al-Shamia*, 2013, http://eldorar.com/node/34572
97. Ibid.
98. *JBC News*, http://www.jbcnews.net/article/89417
99. *Asharq Al-Awsat*, http://aawsat.com/home/article/325336
100. *Orient Net*, 2015, http://orient-news.net/?page=news_show&id=85823
101. *JBC News*, http://www.jbcnews.net/article/121316-
102. http://goo.gl/DdtIGJ
103. *El-Dorar al-Shamia*, http://eldorar.com/node/71267
104. *Asharq Al-Awsat*, 2014, http://www.aawsat.com/home/article/180931
105. http://www.middleeasttransparent.com/spip.php?page=article&id_article=31447&lang=ar
106. *JBC News*, http://www.jbcnews.net/article/118940
107. *JBC News*, http://www.jbcnews.net/article/132080
108. *AsharqAl-Awsat*,2012,http://aawsat.com/leader.asp?section=3&article=670880&issueno=12179
109. http://www.all4syria.info/Archive/192368
110. *El-Dorar al-Shamia*, http://eldorar.com/node/71267
111. http://www.all4syria.info/Archive/199156
112. *JBC News*, http://www.jbcnews.net/article/85152
113. *JBC News*, http://www.jbcnews.net/article/99369
114. "Iran Spends Billions to Prop Up Assad," 2015, *Bloomberg*

115. *Asharq Al-Awsat*, 2015, http://goo.gl/nfWqMM
116. *Elaph*, 2015, http://elaph.com/Web/opinion/2015/6/1015825.html
117. *Asharq Al-Awsat*, 2014, http://aawsat.com/home/article/381706
118. *Beirut Observer*, 2014, http://www.beirutobserver.com/2014/11
119. *Beirut Observer*, http://beirutobserver.com/index.php?option=com_content&view=article&id=89869:2013-02-01-04-44-27&catid=41:2010-10-03-20-24-15
120. Amal Saad-Ghorayeb, "Hezbollah's Iran Money Trail: It's Complicated," *Al-Akhbar English*, 2012, http://english.al-akhbar.com/node/10553
121. http://www.otv.com.lb/beta/v/episode/
122. Avi Issacharoff, "After Losing 1000 Men in Syria, Hezbolla Builds 'Security Zone,'" The Times of Israel, 2014, http://www.timesofisrael.com/after-losing-1000-men-in-syria-hezbollah-builds-security-zone/
123. http://www.soryoon.com/?p=8668
124. *El-Dorar al-Shamia*, http://eldorar.com/node/89191
125. www.youkal.net/2012-12-02-14-05-23/24-25/51828
126 http://eldorar.com/node/89191
127. *OTV*, 2014, https://www.YouTube.com/watch?v=55qGwtDpYUI
128. *JBC News*, http://www.jbcnews.net/article/125714
129. *Elaph*, 2014, http://elaph.com/Web/NewsPapers/2014/3/884014.html
130. http://www.orient-news.net/?page=news_show&id=87036
131. *JBC News*, http://www.jbcnews.net/article/125714
132. *Al Arabiya*, 2012, http://www.alarabiya.net/articles/2012/08/28/234698.html
133. http://www.jewishpolicycenter.org/57/the-iran-Ḥamās-alliance
134. http://www.beirutobserver.com/2013/08/83011/
135. http://www.youkal.net/2012-12-02-14-05-23/24-25/24312
136. *Middle East Transparent*, http://www.metransparent.com/spip.php?page=article&id_article=22708&lang=ar
137. http://www.beirutobserver.com/2013/07/80927/
138. Saidatv, 2013, http://www.saidatv.tv/news.php?go=fullnews&newsid=43145
139. *Al-Monitor*, 2015, http://www.al-monitor.com/pulse/ar/contents/articles/originals/2015/02/iran-Ḥamās-rapprochement-demands-meshaal-resignation.html
140. *El-Dorar al-Shamia*, http://eldorar.com/node/69597
141. *JBC News*, http://www.jbcnews.net/article/129718
142. *Orient-News*, 2015, http://www.orient-news.net/?page=news_show&id=87507&
143. Ibid.
144. http://all4syria.info/Archive/130995
145. http://www.youkal.net/2012-12-02-14-05-23/24-26/34349
146. https://www.paldf.net/forum/showthread.php?t=1126725&page=2
147. *El-Dorar al-Shamia*, http://eldorar.com/node/70806

148. *El-Dorar al-Shamia*, http://eldorar.com/node/80433
149. "Syrian Crisis Cost Jordan $6.6 Billion," *Middle East Monitor*, 2015, https://www.middleeastmonitor.com/news/middle-east/21754-syrian-crisis-cost-jordan-
150. *JBC News*, http://www.jbcnews.net/article/35496
151. *El-Dorar al-Shamia*, http://eldorar.com/node/71558
152. *El-Dorar al-Shamia*, http://eldorar.com/node/70250
153. http://www.ammanads.com/i.html?http://khaberni.com/
154. *Elaph*, 2014, http://www.elaph.com/Web/opinion/2014/9/940552.html
155. Jordan Offers to Arm Bedouin Tribes Against Daesh: Reports," *Albawaba News*, 2015, http://www.albawaba.com/news/jordan-offers-arm-bedouin-tribes-against-daesh-reports-709362
156. Aron Lund, "Syria's Bedouin Tribes: An Interview with Dawn Chatty," Carnegie Endowment for International Peace, 2015, http://carnegieendowment.org/syriaincrisis/?fa=60264
157. *JBC News*, http://www.jbcnews.net/article/130420
158. Lee Smith, "But Is It Good for the Druze? George Clooney and His Future In-Laws," *The Weekly Standard*, 2014, http://www.weeklystandard.com/articles/it-good-druze_791179.html
159. Faisal Irshaid, "Syria's Druze Under Threat as Conflict Spreads," *BBC News*, 2015, http://www.bbc.com/news/world-middle-east-33166043
160. "Druze in Jordan," *Wikipedia*, https://en.wikipedia.org/wiki/Druze_in_Jordan
161. http://aljumhuriya.net/en/29583
162. Firas Choufi, "Syria's Druze Reject Autonomous Statelet Despite Growing Isis Threats," *Al-Akbar English*, 2014, http://english.al-akhbar.com/node/20452
163. Leith Fadel, "Druze Continue to Ward Off Northeast Al-Sweida from ISIS; Jordanian Army Crosses Into Syria," *Al-Masdar News*, 2015, http://www.almasdarnews.com/article/druze-continue-to-ward-off-northeast-al-sweida-from-isis-jordanian-army-crosses-into-syria/
164. "Jumblat Meets Jordanian King Amid Fears for Syrian Druze," *Narharnet*, 2015, http://www.naharnet.com/stories/en/182380
165. *Allofjo*, 2015, http://www.allofjo.net/index.php?page=article&id=96725
166. 2015, http://eldorar.com/node/79510
167. http://www.all4syria.info/Archive/92203
168. *Asharq Al-Awsat*, 2014, http://aawsat.com/home/article/380041
169. *Middle East Transparent*, http://www.metransparent.com/spip.php?page=article&id_article=19841&lang=ar
170. http://orient-news.net/?page=news_show&id=4795
171. http://english.alarabiya.net/en/News/middle-east/2013/11/12/
172. "Kurds Celebrate Gains Amid Blows to Turkey's AK Party," *Al Jazeera*, 2015, http://www.aljazeera.com/news/2015/06/kurds-celebrate-gains-blow-turkey-akp-150608044425760.html

173. *JBC News*, 2015, http://www.jbcnews.net/article/158131
174. *El-Dorar al-Shamia*, http://eldorar.com/node/80977
175. The Union of Media Professional, https://www.facebook.com/www.ump
176. Ibid.
177. Barney Guiton, "'ISIS Sees Turkey as Its Ally': Former Islamic State Member Reveals Turkish Army Cooperation," *Newsweek*, 2014, http://europe.newsweek.com/isis-and-turkey-cooperate-destroy-kurds-former-isis-member-reveals-turkish-282920
178. "Report: Erdogan Trying to Hide Evidence of Supporting ISIS," *The Tower*, 2015, http://www.thetower.org/1493-erdogan-trying-to-hide-evidence-of-involvement-in-supporting-terrorism/
179. *Al-Monitor*, 2014, http://www.al-monitor.com/pulse/tr/business/2014/06/turkey-syria-isis-selling-smuggled-oil.html
180. Fazel Hawramy, Shalaw Mohammed, and Luke Harding, "Inside Islamic State's Oil Empire: How Captured Oil Fields Fuel ISIS Insurgency," *The Guardian*, 2014, http://www.theguardian.com/world/2014/nov/19/-sp-islamic-state-oil-empire-iraq-isis
181. http://english.alarabiya.net/en/News/middle-east/2014/07/03/
182. *Elaph*, 2014, http://www.elaph.com/Web/opinion/2014/11/955290.html
183. Editorial Board, "Mr. Erdogan's Dangerous Game: Turkey's Refusal to Fight Isis Hurts the Kurds," *The New York Times*, 2014, http://www.nytimes.com/2014/10/09/opinion/turkeys-refusal-to-fight-isis-hurts-the-kurds.html?_r=0
184. Paul Woodward, "Turkey Somehow Secures Release of 49 Hostages Held by ISIS," *War in Context*, 2014, http://warincontext.org/2014/09/20
185. http://www.thedailybeast.com/articles/2014/09/21
186. Editorial Board, "Mr. Erdogan's Dangerous Game: Turkey's Refusal to Fight Isis Hurts the Kurds," *The New York Times*, 2014, http://www.nytimes.com/2014/10/09/opinion/turkeys-refusal-to-fight-isis-hurts-the-kurds.html?_r=0
187. *Alwatan Voice*, 2013, http://www.alwatanvoice.com/arabic/news/2013/05/14/393581.html
188. http://www.middleeasttransparent.com/spip.php?page=article&id_article=29215&lang=ar
189. http://www.youkal.net/2012-12-02-14-05-23/24-26/43473-
190. http://www.beirutobserver.com/2014/03/93411/
191. *Elaph*, 2011, http://www.elaph.com/Web/NewsPapers/2011/11/695451.html?entry=homepagenewspapers
192. *Elaph*, 2012, http://www.elaph.com/Web/news/2012/6/740379.html?entry=Syria
193. http://www.beirutobserver.com/2013/10/86644/
194. http://www.youkal.net/2012-12-02-14-05-23/24-25/30663
195. "Key Indicators," Lebanese Republic, Central Administration of Statistics, 2015, http://www.cas.gov.lb/index.php/key-indicators-en

196. *The World Fact Book*, Central Intelligence Agency, 2016, https://www.cia.gov/library/publications/the-world-factbook/
197. Ibid.
198. "Lebanon," UNHCR, 2015, http://www.unhcr.org/pages/49e486676.html
199. *JBC News*, http://www.jbcnews.net/article/8540
200. Oliver Holmes, "New Restrictions in Lebanon Mean Syrian Refugees Live in Fear," *Reuters*, 2015, http://www.reuters.com/article/2015/04/17/us-mideast-crisis-lebanon-refugees-idUSKBN0N819Z20150417
201. "Tripoli," *Al Mashriq*, http://almashriq.hiof.no/lebanon/900/910/919/tripoli/
202. *JBC News*, http://www.jbcnews.net/article/86769
203. "Saida (Sidon) District," *Localiban*, http://www.localiban.org/rubrique551.html
204. http://www.middleeasttransparent.com/spip.php?page=article&id_article=31498&lang=ar
205. "Syria Crisis," UN Relief and Works Agency for Palestine Refugees in the Near East, http://www.unrwa.org/syria-crisis
206. Ibid.
207. "Palestine Refugees," UN Relief and Works Agency for Palestine Refugees in the Near East, http://www.unrwa.org/syria-crisis#Syria-Crisis-and-Palestine-refugees
208. Action Group for Palestinians of Syria, http://www.actionpal.org.uk/en/
209. *JBC News*, http://www.jbcnews.net/article/103260
210. *JBC News*, http://www.jbcnews.net/article/156052-102
211. "Syria Crisis," UN Relief and Works Agency for Palestine Refugees in the Near East, http://www.unrwa.org/syria-crisis
212. *El-Dorar al-Shamia*, 2014, http://eldorar.com/node/66366
213. "Lebanon," UN Relief and Works Agency for Palestine Refugees in the Near East, http://www.unrwa.org/where-we-work/lebanon
214. "Israel Providing Medical Care to al-Qaida Affiliate Fighters Wounded in Syria," *i24 News*, 2015, http://www.i24news.tv/en/news/international/middle-east/64262-150314-israel-treating
215. *Asharq Al-Awsat*, 2013, http://www.aawsat.com/leader.asp?section=3&article=716990&issueno=12495
216. Avi Issacharoff, "With Brazen Attack Inside Irael, Hezbollah Lays Down New Ground Rules," *Times of Israel*, 2014, http://www.timesofisrael.com/with-brazen-attack-hezbollah-lays-down-new-ground-rules/
217. "Iran General Died in 'Israeli Strike' in Syrian Golan," *BBC News*, 2015, http://www.bbc.com/news/world-middle-east-30882935
218. Ibid.
219. *Elaph*, 2012, http://www.elaph.com/Web/NewsPapers/2012/8/755349.html?entry=newsandreports

220. http://www.all4syria.info/Archive/195464
221. *Al Arabiya*, 2015, http://www.alarabiya.net/ar/iran/2015/12/11
222. *JBC News*, http://www.jbcnews.net/article/153293-القتال-ضد-الاحتلال-الروسي-واجب-شرعي-إخوان-سوريا
223. *JBC News*, http://www.jbcnews.net/article/153034
224. *Asharq Al-Awsat*, 2014, http://aawsat.com/home/article/448571
225. Andrew Tilghman, "US Confirms Islamic State Use of Chemical Weapons," *Military Times*, 2015, http://www.militarytimes.com/story/military/2015/08/21/isis-used-mustard-gas-makhmour-against-kurds/32116637/
226. Ibid.
227. http://www.ammanads.com/i.html?http://www.alarabiya.net/
228. http://www.middleeasttransparent.com/spip.php?page=article&id_article=31447&lang=ar
229. http://www.orient-news.net/?page=news_show&id=88221&
230. http://www.all4syria.info/Archive/192368
231. *El-Dorar al-Shamia*, http://eldorar.com/node/71267
232. "'Maybe We Live and Maybe We Die': Recruitment and Use of Children by Armed Groups in Syria," *Human Rights Watch*, 2014, https://www.hrw.org/report/2014/06/22/maybe-we-live-and-maybe-we-die/recruitment-and-use-children-armed-groups-syria
233. Ibid.
234. Ibid.
235. Ibid.
236. Ibid.
237. *Asharq Al-Awsat*, 2014, http://aawsat.com/home/article/381706
238. Idan Cohen, "Iran is Considering a Defense Agreement with Syria," *Jerusalem Online*, 2015, http://www.jerusalemonline.com/news/middle-east/iran-is-considering-a-defense-agreement-with-syria-13731
239. Abdul Wahab Badr Khan, "The Next War: Free Syria from the Iranian Occupation," *JBC News*, http://www.jbcnews.net/article/107605
240. *Asharq Al-Awsat*, 2014, http://aawsat.com/home/article/381706
241. Bandar bin Sultan, Tabq al-Asl Thanyia," *Elaph*, 2015, http://elaphjournal.com/Web/News/2015/7/1024259.html
242. Reza Kahlili, "Iran Threatens Widespread Retaliation Against US and Allies," *The Daily Caller*, 2013, http://dailycaller.com/2013/09/10/iran-threatens-widespread-retaliation-against-u-s-and-allies/
243. Fadwa al-Hatem, "Syria's Bassar al-Assad—An Expert at Buying Time," *The Guardian*, 2011, http://www.theguardian.com/commentisfree/2011/oct/31/syria-bashar-al-assad-buying-time
244. *Asharq Al-Awsat*, 2015, http://goo.gl/EAiuLT

245. http://www.ammanads.com/i.html?http://www.almasdaronline.com/
246. *Asharq Al-Awsat*, 2015, http://goo.gl/rsS8Mz
247. http://www.orient-news.net/?page=news_show&id=86406&%D8%A8%D8%A7%D9%84%D8%A3%D8%B3%D9%85%D8%A7%D8%A1
248. *The New York Times*, 2015, http://www.nytimes.com/aponline/2015/06/30/world/middleeast/ap-un-united-nations-syria.html?_r=0
249. *JBC News*, http://www.jbcnews.net/article/127626
250. *Elaph*, 2015, http://elaph.com/Web/opinion/2015/6/1015825.html
251. *JBC News*, http://www.jbcnews.net/article/125028
252. http://www.middleeasttransparent.com/spip.php?page=article&id_article=31257&lang=ar
253. http://www.all4syria.info/Archive/195458
254. 'Ali al-Amin, "In its Fifth Year, the Syrian Revolution Fights the International Community," *Middle East Transparent*, 2015, http://metranspcm.cluster011.ovh.net/spip.php?page=article&id_article=30798&var_lang=ar&lang=ar

Chapter Seven: Long Live the King: The Monarchic Regimes

1. The Gulf Cooperation Council [GCC] was established in 1981 in an agreement between Bahrain, Kuwait, Oman, Qatar, Saudi Arabia, and UAE to confront their security challenges collectively.
2. The Cooperation Council for the Arab States of the Gulf, http://www.gcc-sg.org/eng/
3. "Arab World," The World Bank, http://data.worldbank.org/country/ARB
4. The Organization of the Petroleum Exporting Countries (OPEC) was founded in Baghdad, Iraq in 1960 by five countries: Islamic Republic of Iran, Iraq, Kuwait, Saudi Arabia, and Venezuela. They were to become the founding members of the organization. These countries were later joined by Qatar (1961), Indonesia (1962), Libya (1962), the United Arab Emirates (1967), Algeria (1969), Nigeria (1971), Ecuador (1973), Gabon (1975), and Angola (2007). From December 1992 until October 2007, Ecuador suspended its membership. Gabon terminated its membership in 1995. Indonesia suspended its membership effective January 2009. Currently, the organization has a total of twelve member countries. http://www.opec.org/opec_web/en/about_us/25.htm
5. http://www.opec.org/opec_web/en/data_graphs/330.htm
6. *Petranews Jordan*, 2013, https://www.YouTube.com/watch?v=URZINR63L2E
7. "Syrian Crisis Cost Jordan $6.6 Billion," *Middle East Monitor*, 2015, https://www.middleeastmonitor.com/news/middle-east/21754-syrian-crisis-cost-jordan-66bn

8 Ibid.

9. Stephanie Ott, "Syrians at Zaatari Camp: 'We Can't Live Here Forever,'" *Al Jazeera*, 2015, http://www.aljazeera.com/news/2015/10/syrians-zaatari-camp-live-151021074641938.html

10. *JBC News*, http://www.jbcnews.net/article/139268-الزعتري-اصبح-رابع-اكبر-مدن-الاردن-صور-الديلي-تليغراف-مخيم

11. Michael Kaplan, "Syrian Refugee Crisis and Jordan Budget Deficit: Amid Economic Slowdown, Asylum Seeks Cost Country $6.6 Billion," *International Business Times*, 2015, http://www.ibtimes.com/syrian-refugee-crisis-jordan-budget-deficit-amid-economic-slow-down-asylum-seekers-2146203

12. "Syrian Crisis Cost Jordan $6.6 Billion," *Middle East Monitor*, 2015, https://www.middleeastmonitor.com/news/middle-east/21754-syrian-crisis-cost-jordan-66bn

13. http://www.orient-news.net/index.php?page=news_show&id=86538

14. Roi Kais, "US Fears Israel Would Be Dragged into War with ISIS," *Ynet*, 2014, http://www.ynetnews.com/articles/0,7340,L-4535424,00.html

15. *Alwatan Voice*, 2012, http://www.alwatanvoice.com/arabic/news/2012/10/20/327215.html

16. http://www.alquds.co.uk/index.asp?fname=today\22z498.htm&arc=data\2013\02\02-22\22z498.htm

17. http://www.ammanads.com/i.html?http://www.dampress.net/

18. Suha Ma'ayeh and Tamer El-Ghobashy, "Islamic State Lured a Son of Jordan's Elite," *The Wall Street Journal*, 2015, http://www.wsj.com/articles/islamic-state-lured-a-son-of-jordans-elite-1449015451

19. *Foreign Fighers: An Updated Assessment of the Flow of Foreign Fighters into Syria and Iraq*, The Soufan Group, 2015, http://soufangroup.com/wp-content/uploads/2015/12/TSG_ForeignFightersUpdate4.pdf

20. *Asharq Al-Awsat*, 2013, http://www.aawsat.com/leader.asp?section=3&article=718419&issueno=12507

21. *Middle East Transparent*, http://www.metransparent.com/spip.php?page=article&id_article=19965&lang=ar

22. *JBC News*, http://www.jbcnews.net/article/36384

23. *Foreign Fighers: An Updated Assessment of the Flow of Foreign Fighters into Syria and Iraq*, The Soufan Group, 2015, http://soufangroup.com/wp-content/uploads/2015/12/TSG_ForeignFightersUpdate4.pdf

24. Haweya Ismail, "Kuwait: Food and Water Security," Future Directions International, 2015, http://www.futuredirections.org.au/publications/food-and-water-crises/2384-kuwait-food-and-water-security.html

25. *Al Jazeera*, http://goo.gl/TeXXDT

Chapter Eight: Failures of the West

1. "Text: Obama's Speech in Cairo," *The New York Times*, 2009, http://www.nytimes.com/2009/06/04/us/politics/04obama.text.html?pagewanted=all&_r=0
2. Ibid.
3. *Al-Monitor*, 2015, http://www.al-monitor.com/pulse/originals/2015/03/iran-iraq-rouhani-advisor-empire.html
4. *All4Syria*, 2014, http://www.all4syria.info/Archive/197241
5. *Elaph*, 2015, http://www.elaph.com/Web/NewsPapers/2015/3/990194.html
6. *Elaph*, 2015, http://www.elaph.com/Web/NewsPapers/2015/3/989095.html
7. *Asharq Al-Awsat*, 2015, http://goo.gl/YPWwny
8. *El-Dorar al-Shamia*, 2015, http://eldorar.com/node/70980
9. *Elaph*, 2015, http://www.elaph.com/Web/NewsPapers/2015/3/990194.html
10. *Asharq Al-Awsat*, 2014, http://goo.gl/kwLMkP
11. Ibid.
12. *JBC News*, http://www.jbcnews.net/article/136304
13. Khattar Abou Diab, "The Forbidden Love Affair between Obama and Iran," Middle East Transparent, http://www.middleeasttransparent.com/spip.php?page=article&id_article=26850&lang=ar
14. Saleh al-Kalab, "These Are the Reasons Why Arabs Cannot Rely on the United States," *Asharq Al-Awsat*, 2014, http://goo.gl/llb2N9
15. Justin Fishel, "Iran Nuclear Deal Reached," *ABC News*, 2015, http://abcnews.go.com/Politics/iran-nuclear-deal-announcement-expected/story?id=29952510
16. Eyad Abu Shakra, What Is the Fate of Our [Arab] States Following the Lausanne Agreement?" *Asharq Al-Awsat*, 2015, http://goo.gl/3JsYw0
17. Mashari al-Zaidi, "Lausanne Is Yours—Not Ours," *Asharq Al-Awsat*, 2015, http://goo.gl/KuDXmJ
18. Adel Darwish, "The Nuclear Agreement with Iran Threatens Peace," *Asharq Al-Awsat*, 2015, http://goo.gl/b6uOSk
19. Jamal Khashoggi, "What Is Going to Kill Us Now: the Iranian Explosive Barrels or the Iranian Nuclear Bomb?" *JBC News*, http://www.jbcnews.net/article/135124
20. Patrick Wintour, "John Kerry Gives Syria Week to Hand Over Chemical Weapons or Face Attack," *The Guardian*, 2013, http://www.theguardian.com/world/2013/sep/09/us-syria-chemical-weapons-attack-john-kerry
21. Dr. Wahīd 'Abd al-Majīd, "Who Will Defend Obama?" http://acpss.ahramdigital.org.eg/
22. http://goo.gl/4aVsFv
23. http://www.amazon.com/The-Lost-Spring-Policy-Catastrophes/dp/1137279036

24. Andrew Green, "Why Western Democracy Can Never Work in the Middle East," *The Telegraph*, 2014, http://www.telegraph.co.uk/news/worldnews/middleeast/11037173/Why-Western-democracy-can-never-work-in-the-Middle-East.html
25. "Obama Administration Corrects Clapper's Claim that Muslin Brotherhood is 'Secular,'" *Fox News*, 2011, http://www.foxnews.com/politics/2011/02/10/administration-corrects-dni-clapper-claim-muslim-brotherhood-secular/
26. *Mapping Shari'a,* http://mappingsharia.com/?page_id=99
27. Ibid.
28. Denis MacEoin, "Tactical Hudna and Islamist Intolerance," *Middle East Quarterly*, Middle East Forum, 2008, http://www.meforum.org/1925/tactical-hudna-and-islamist-intolerance#_ftn4
29. "Hamas Offers Truce in Return for 1967 Borders," *NBC News*, 2008, http://www.nbcnews.com/id/24235665/ns/world_news-mideast_n_africa/t/Ḥamās-offers-truce-return-borders/#.VdB34f0VjIU
30. "Khaled Mashal," Awaz.tv, http://www.awaztoday.tv/profile_Khaled-Mashal_681.aspx
31. http://www.palinfo.com/site/PIC/newsdetails.aspx?itemid=118482
32. Mathew Balan, "CNN Analyst Unsure if Mass Shooter Muhammad Youssef Abdulazeez's Name is Muslim," *Newsbusters*, 2015, http://newsbusters.org/blogs/nb/matthew-balan/2015/07/16/cnn-analyst-unsure-if-mass-shooter-muhammad-youssef-abdulazeezs#.p8nybc:Xwb9
33. *Alwatan Voice*, 2014, http://www.alwatanvoice.com/arabic/news/2013/12/18/474513.html
34. *Ma'an News Agency*, 2014, http://www.maannews.net/arb/ViewDetails.aspx?ID=683242
35. "US Official: US Was Surprised by Collapse of Yemen Govt," *Daily Mail*, 2015, http://www.dailymail.co.uk/wires/ap/article-2951423/US-official-US-surprised-collapse-Yemen-govt.html?ITO=1490&ns_mchannel=rss&ns_campaign=1490
36. "Postcolonialism," *enotes*, http://www.enotes.com/topics/postcolonialism/critical-essays/postcolonialism
37. Joshua Muravchik, "Enough Said: The False Scholarship of Edward Said," *World Affairs*, 2013, http://www.worldaffairsjournal.org/article/enough-said-false-scholarship-edward-said
38. Thomas L. Friedman, "The Other Arab Spring," *The New York Times*, 2012, http://www.nytimes.com/2012/04/08/opinion/sunday/friedman-the-other-arab-spring.html?_r=0
39. Christina DiPasquale, "Advisory: Tom Friedman and Anne-Marie Slaughter on Climate Change and the Arab Spring," Center for American Progress, 2013, https://www.americanprogress.org/press/advisory/2013/02/22/54419/advisory-tom-friedman-and-anne-marie-slaughter-on-climate-change-and-the-arab-spring/
40. "Iraq 2014: Civilian Deaths Almost Doubling Year on Year," *Iraq Body Count*, 2015, https://www.iraqbodycount.org/analysis/numbers/2014/
41. Ibid.

42. Ibid.
43. http://www.worldtribune.com/2015/05/21/obama-climate-change-contributed-to-terror-groups-rise/
44. http://www.defense.gov/pubs/150724-Congressional-Report-on-National-Implications-of-Climate-Change.pdf?source=GovDelivery
45. "Pentagon Report Admits Disastrous Drought, Not Assad Caused Syrian Crisis," *Sputnik News*, 2015, http://sputniknews.com/middleeast/20150730/1025197768.html
46. Linda Qiu, "Fact-Checking Bernie Sanders's Comments on Climate Change and Terrorism," *Politifact*, 2015, http://www.politifact.com/truth-o-meter/statements/2015/nov/16/bernie-s/fact-checking-bernie-sanders-comments-climate-chan/
47. Joe Ramm, "The Link Between Climate Change and ISIS is Real," *Think Progress*, 2015, http://thinkprogress.org/climate/2015/07/23/3683536/omalley-climate-change-isis/
48. http://nypost.com/2015/11/23/prince-charles-blames-climate-change-for-isis/
49. "On Israel," Counter Extremism Project, http://www.counterextremism.com/rhetoric-category/israel
50. Bret Stevens, "Understanding the Muslim Brotherhood," *The Wall Street Journal*, 2011, http://www.wsj.com/articles/SB10001424052748703584804576143933682956332
51. David D. Kirkpatrick, "Named Egypt's Winner, Islamist Makes History," *The New York Times*, 2012, http://www.nytimes.com/2012/06/25/world/middleeast/mohamed-morsi-of-muslim-brotherhood-declared-as-egypts-president.html?_r=0
52. https://www.YouTube.com/watch?v=PHss6aaE-VA
53. Byron Tau, "Muslim Brotherhood Delegation Meets with Whitehouse Officials," *Politico*, 2012, http://www.politico.com/politico44/2012/04/muslim-brotherhood-delegation-meets-with-white-house-119647.html
54. Lauren Bohn, "The Muslim Brotherhood Comes to America," *CNN*, 2012, http://edition.cnn.com/2012/04/03/world/analysis-muslim-brotherhood/
55. Mohamed Elmenshawy, "A Successful Raid on Washington by the Muslim Brotherhood," *Shorouk News*, 2012, http://www.shorouknews.com/columns/view.aspx?cdate=11042012&id=547a1ae9-1c3f-4cd1-9e99-7f64df4b3720
56. *Islamic Encyclopedia*, http://islamicencyclopedia.org/public/index/topicDetail/id/311
57. Ibid.
58. Eric Trager, "The Administration Should Not Meet with the Muslim Brotherhood in Washington," The Washington Institute for Near Middle East Policy, 2015, http://www.washingtoninstitute.org/policy-analysis/view/the-administration-should-not-meet-with-the-muslim-brotherhood-in-washingto
59. Egyptian Revolutionary Council, http://ercegypt.org/egy/
60. Judge Waleed Sharabi, 2015, https://www.facebook.com/photo.php?fbid=767723549975871
61. "Who was Raabi'ah al-'Adawiyyah?" *Islam Question and Answer*, http://islamqa.info/en/5994

62. *Alwatan Voice*, 2013, http://www.alwatanvoice.com/arabic/news/2013/08/18/426031.html
63. "General Jim Jones, President Obama's Nation Security Advisor, Addresses J Street's First National Conference," *J Street*, 2010, https://vimeo.com/7302509
64. Daniel Pipes, "Explaining Obama's Fixation with Israel," *National Review*, 2013, http://www.nationalreview.com/article/343312/explaining-obamas-fixation-israel-daniel-pipes
65. Michael Doran, "What Now for the United States? How America Can Help the New Arab-Israel Alliance to Resist IS and Stabilize the Middle East," *Mosaic Magazine*, 2014, http://mosaicmagazine.com/response/2014/09/what-now-for-the-united-states/
66. Suleiman Taqi al-Din, "We and Palestine and the Arab Revolutions," *Elaph*, 2011, http://elaph.com/Web/NewsPapers/2011/12/701390.html?entry=homepagenewspapers
67. *JBC News*, http://www.jbcnews.net/article/34482
68. "Iran-Iraq War," *History*, http://www.history.com/topics/iran-iraq-war
69. "Iran-Iraq War (1980–1988)," GlobalSecurity.org, http://www.globalsecurity.org/military/world/war/iran-iraq.htm
70. "Although Poverty . . . Gaza Residents Flock to iPhone 5," *Al Arabiya*, 2012, http://www.alarabiya.net/articles/2012/10/16/243996.html

Chapter Nine: The Struggle for Identity: Salsa Dancing and the Niqab

1. "Umm Kulthum: The Voice of Egypt," *NPR*, 2012, http://www.npr.org/templates/story/story.php?storyId=90326836
2. "Umm Kulthum: The Lady of Cairo," *NPR*, 2010, http://www.npr.org/templates/story/story.php?storyId=124612595
3. "50 Great Voices: Explore the Nominations," *NPR*, 2010, http://www.npr.org/templates/story/story.php?storyId=114013402
4. "Umm Kulthum: The Lady of Cairo," *NPR*, 2010, http://www.npr.org/templates/story/story.php?storyId=124612595
5. Ibid.
6. Virginia Danielson, "Umm Kulthum Ibrahim," *Harvard Magazine*, 1997, http://harvard-magazine.com/1997/07/umm-Kulthūm-ibrahim
7. Farah Jassat, "Remembering Umm Kulthum: Queen of the Arabs," *The Huffington Post*, 2012, http://www.huffingtonpost.com/farah-jassat/remembering-umm-Kulthūm-q_b_1251007.html
8. *BBC*, 2015, http://www.bbc.com/arabic/middleeast/2015/05/150512_the_battle_of_the_e_muftis

9. General Iftaa' Department, The Hashemite Kingdom of Jordan, http://www.aliftaa.jo/DefaultEn.aspx
10. Fatwa-Online, http://www.fatwa-online.com/
11. Fatwa Islam, http://www.fatwaislam.com/fis/
12. http://www.jamiabinoria.net/
13. "Jamal al-Din al-Afghani," *Encyclopedia Britannica*, http://www.britannica.com/biography/Jamal-al-Din-al-Afghani
14. "Muhammad Abduh," *Wikipedia*, https://en.wikipedia.org/wiki/Muhammad_Abduh
15. "Rashid Rida," *Encyclopedia Britannica*, http://www.britannica.com/biography/Rashid-Rida
16. "Abdul Ala-Mawdudi," *Encyclopedia Britannica*, http://www.britannica.com/biography/Abul-Ala-Mawdudi
17. "Jamaat-e-Islami Pakistan," *Wikipedia*, https://en.wikipedia.org/wiki/Jamaat-e-Islami_Pakistan
18. "Shaikh Sayyid Abdul-Hasan Ali Al-Hasani Al-Nadawi," KFIP, http://kfip.org/sayyid-abul-hasan-ali-al-hasani-al-nadawi/
19. "Al Takfir wa al-Hijrah," *Encyclopedia Britannica* http://www.britannica.com/topic/al-Takfir-wa-al-Hijrah
20. Bruce Livesey, "The Salafist Movement," *Frontline*, PBS http://www.pbs.org/wgbh/pages/frontline/shows/front/special/sala.html
21. Huda al-Husseini, "ISIS Confronts al-Qaeda and Taliban in Afghanistan," *Asharq Al-Awsat*, 2015, http://goo.gl/cBoE33
22. Rana Allam, "In Egypt, the Law Itself is an Enemy of Women's Rights," *Informed Comment*, 2015, http://www.juancole.com/2015/02/itself-womens-rights.html
23. Ibid.
24. *Al-Monitor*, 2015, http://www.al-monitor.com/pulse/originals/2015/02/egypt-women-status-sisi-rule-muslim-brotherhood.html
25. Ibid.
26. "Egypt's Constitution of 2014," *Constitute*, 2014, https://www.constituteproject.org/constitution/Egypt_2014.pdf
27. http://www.unwomen.org/en/what-we-do/leadership-and-political-participation/facts-and-figure
28. *JBC News*, http://www.jbcnews.net/article/138418
29. "The Arab Social Media Report 2015," WPP.com
30. "Most Commonly Used Online Dating Websites in Saudi Arabia," *Life in Saudi Arabia*, 2015, http://life-in-saudiarabia.blogspot.com/2015/05/most-commonly-used-online-dating.html#.Vbz1iflViko
31. Topface, https://topface.com/country/saudi%20arabia/
32. LoveHabibi, http://www.lovehabibi.com/
33. SinglesAroundMe, http://saudi-arabia.singlesaroundme.com/

34. TwitterCounter, http://twittercounter.com/pages/100?version=1&utm_expid=102679131-65.MDYnsQdXQwO2AlKoJXVpSQ.1&utm_referrer=https%3A%2F%2Fwww.google.co.il%2F
35. Iraqi Civil Society Solidarity Initiative, http://www.iraqicivilsociety.org/about-us
36. *Elaph*, 2012, http://www.elaph.com/Web/news/2012/3/721608.html
37. *Middle East Transparent,* http://www.metransparent.com/spip.php?page=article&id_article=17885&lang=ar
38. Girgis Gholizade, "The 'Emo' Phenomenon and the Killing Sprees in Iraq," *Elaph*, 2012, http://www.elaph.com/Web/opinion/2012/3/723227.html?entry=opinionaraa
39. ICSSI, "Youth of Iraq: Our Personal Freedoms Are Not Guaranteed and Government Authorities Are Responsible for Nearly Half of the Violations!" *Al-Mesalla*, http://almesalla.net/Default1.aspx
40. ICSSI, "Youth of Iraq: Our Personal Freedoms Are Not Guaranteed and Government Authorities Are Responsible for Nearly Half of the Violations!" *Iraqi Civil Society Solidarity Initiative*, 2014, http://www.iraqicivilsociety.org/archives/2641
41. "Tunisian Student Stands Up to Salafists Over Flag," *Middle East & Islamic Studies Collection Blog*, Cornell University, 2012, http://blogs.cornell.edu/mideastlibrarian/2012/03/29/tunisian-student-stands-up-to-salafists-over-flag/
42. *Asharq Al-Awsat*, 2012, http://aawsat.com/details.asp?section=4&article=675678&issueno=12211
43. Ibid.
44. "Preliminary Findings by the United Nations Working Group on the Use of Mercenaries on Its Official visit to Tunisia," OHCHR, United Nations, 2015, http://www.ohchr.org/EN/NewsEvents/Pages/DisplayNews.aspx?NewsID=16219&LangID=E
45. Alice Su, "Tunisia Faces Legacy of Religion Oppression in Fight Against Radicalism," *Al Jazeera*, 2015, http://america.aljazeera.com/articles/2015/7/22/tunisia-democracy-legacy-religious-oppression.html
46. "Egyptian Activist Posts Herself Nude, Sparks Outrage," *NDTV*, 2011, http://www.ndtv.com/world-news/egypt-activist-posts-herself-nude-sparks-outrage-566321
47. Mohamed Fadel Fahmy, "Egyptian Blogger Aliaa Elmahdy: Why I Posed Naked," *CNN*, 2011, http://edition.cnn.com/2011/11/19/world/meast/nude-blogger-aliaa-magda-elmahdy
48. *Alwatan Voice*, 2012, http://www.alwatanvoice.com/arabic/news/2012/07/11/296153.html
49. Jillian Steinhauer, "Feminist Advocates Bleed and Defecate on Islamic State Flag #NSFW," *Hyperallergic*, 2014, http://hyperallergic.com/145768/feminist-activists-bleed-and-shit-on-islamic-state-flag-nsfw/
50. Aliaa Magda Elmahdy, "Ex-Muslim Women Protest Topless at Misogynistic Islamic Conference," *Arebel's Diary*, 2015, http://arebelsdiary.blogspot.com/
51. Al Azhar University, http://www.azhar.edu.eg/En/u.htm
52. *ArtsFreedom*, http://artsfreedom.org/?tag=egypt

53. *Al-Monitor*, 2014, http://www.al-monitor.com/pulse/originals/2014/04/haifa-wehbe-egypt-movie-ban-freedom-malena.html
54. *Elaph*, 2014, http://www.elaph.com/Web/Entertainment/2014/3/884078.html
55. *JBC News*, http://www.jbcnews.net/article/33372
56. Diaa Mohamed, "ECWR Calls on the Minister of Education to Refer the Teacher in Fayoum to the Public Prosecution," *The Egyptian Center for Women's Rights*, 2015, http://ecwronline.org/?p=6618
57. Shounaz Meky, "Hijab-Wearing Women Say They Are Being Turned Away at Egyptian Resorts," *Al Arabiya News*, 2015, http://english.alarabiya.net/en/perspective/2015/07/27/Hijab-wearing-women-say-are-being-turned-away-at-Egyptian-resorts.html
58. Ibid.
59. http://alquds.co.uk/index.asp?fname=today\01qpt970.htm&arc=data\2012\10\10-01\01qpt970.htm
60. *Al Arabiya*, 2012, http://www.alarabiya.net/articles/2012/11/03/247385.html
61. *JBC News*, http://www.jbcnews.net/article/123508
62. *JBC News*, http://www.jbcnews.net/article/126912
63. "Three Ways 'Open Jordan' is Trying to Change the Internet as Amman Knows It," *Albawaba*, 2015, http://www.albawaba.com/loop/three-ways-%E2%80%98open-jordan%E2%80%99-trying-change-Internet-amman-knows-it-730976
64. Ibid.
65. Elhanan Miller, "Syrian Christians Sign Treaty of Submission to Islamists," *The Times of Israel*, 2014, http://www.timesofisrael.com/syrian-christians-sign-treaty-of-submission-to-islamists/
66. "Jiyza," *Encyclopedia Britannica*, http://www.britannica.com/topic/jizya
67. *Elaph*, 2014, http://www.elaph.com/Web/News/2014/8/936418.html
68. "ISIS Fight: Mariam Al Mansouri Is First Woman Fighter Pilot for U.A.E.," *NBC News*, 2014, http://www.nbcnews.com/storyline/isis-terror/isis-fight-mariam-al-mansouri-first-woman-fighter-pilot-u-n211366
69. Mamoun Fandy, "Mariam and al-Baghdadi—the Sky and the Ground," *Elaph*, 2014, http://www.elaph.com/Web/NewsPapers/2014/9/944909.html
70. *RCSS*, 2014, http://www.rcssmideast.org/Article/2671/مريم-المنصوري#.VZrfWI0VjIU

Chapter Ten: The Internet: The Phantom Empire

1. Wikileaks, https://wikileaks.org/About.html
2. Ibid.
3. *Al Jazeera*, http://www.aljazeera.net/news/pages/53eda36c-0868-4157-8d06-91918554cf44?GoogleStatID=24

4. https://twitter.com/mujtahidd
5. Ibid.
6. "On the World Press Freedom Day: Maharat Foundation Launch 'Internet in Arab World' Report & A Campaign to Endorse Arab Prisoners of Opinion," *The Arabic Network for Human Rights Information*, 2015, http://anhri.net/?p=144042&lang=en
7. Ellen Knickmeyer and Amir Efrati, "Twitter's Fit for a Prince: Saudi Prince Alwaleed Bets $300 Million on Social Media," *The Wall Street Journal*, 2011, http://www.wsj.com/articles/SB10001424052970204791104577107733831343976
8. https://www.facebook.com/non.star.academy
9. *Moheet*, 2015, http://moheet.com/2015/04/15/2250159
10. https://www.facebook.com/tamarudegypt
11. "Tamarod Gathers 7 Million Petitions," *Egypt Independent*, 2013, http://www.egyptindependent.com//node/1793991
12. *Alwatan Voice*, 2013, http://www.alwatanvoice.com/arabic/news/2013/06/10/402974.html
13. http://www.ammanads.com/arab_newspapers.htm
14. http://www.all4syria.info/Archive/118434
15. *Elaph*, 2013, http://www.elaph.com/Web/news/2013/7/822943.html
16. "Turkey Blocks Twitter, After Erdogan Vowed 'Eradication,'" *Hurriyet Daily News*, 2014, http://www.hurriyetdailynews.com/turkey-blocks-twitter-after-erdogan-vowed-eradication.aspx?pageID=238&nID=63884&NewsCatID=338
17. *AmmanNet*, 2012, http://ar.ammannet.net/news/169645
18 *Ammon News*, 2013, http://www.ammonnews.net/article.aspx?articleno=130251
19. Ibid.
20. http://www.alquds.co.uk/index.asp?fname=online\data\2012-09-01-12-41-32.htm
21. "Turkey Blocks Twitter, After Erdogan Vowed 'Eradication,'" *Hurriyet Daily News*, 2014, http://www.hurriyetdailynews.com/turkey-blocks-twitter-after-erdogan-vowed eradication.aspx?pageID=238&nID=63884&NewsCatID=338
22. *Asharq Al-Awsat*, 2014, http://www.aawsat.com/leader.asp?section=3&issueno=12898&article=765580#.UzBBVle9bx8
23. Sawsan al-Abtah, "The Enslavement of Human Beings by Remote Control," *Asharq Al-Awsat*, 2012, http://aawsat.com/leader.asp?section=3&article=675562&issueno=12210
24. *Online Jihad Explosed*, 2013, http://www.onlinejihadexposed.com/2013/08/blog-post_21.html
25. http://www.elnashra.com/news/show/781038
26. "Hashtag Terror: How ISIS Manipulates Social Media," Anti-Defamation League, 2014, http://www.adl.org/combating-hate/international-extremism-terrorism/c/isis-islamic-state-social-media.html
27. *Reuters*, 2015, http://www.reuters.com/article/2015/03/13/us-usa-security-brennan-idUSKBN0M925R20150313
28. Deana Kjuka, "When Terrorists Take to Social Media," *The Atlantic*, 2013, http://www.theatlantic.com/international/archive/2013/02/when-terrorists-take-to-social-media/273321

29. "Terrorist Groups Recruiting Through Social Media," *CBC News*, 2012, http://www.cbc.ca/news/technology/terrorist-groups-recruiting-through-social-media-1.1131053
30. Anti-Defamation League, http://www.adl.org/
31. "Hashtag Terror: How ISIS Manipulates Social Media," Anti-Defamation League, 2014, http://www.adl.org/combating-hate/international-extremism-terrorism/c/isis-islamic-state-social-media.html?referrer=https://www.google.co.il/#.VapMIflViko
32. James Phillips, "The Message ISIS Wants to Send to America, the World," The Heritage Foundation, http://www.heritage.org/research/commentary/2014/9/the-message-isis-wants-to-send-to-america-the-world
33. Natalie Johnson, "How ISIS is Waging a 'War of Ideas' Through Social Media," *The Daily Signal*, 2015, http://dailysignal.com/2015/06/08/how-isis-is-waging-a-war-of-ideas-through-social-media/
34. J.M. Berger and Jonathan Morgan, "The ISIS Twitter Census: Defining and Describing the Population of ISIS Supporters on Twitter," The Brookings Project on US Relations with the Islamic World, 2015, http://www.brookings.edu/~/media/research/files/papers/2015/03/isis-twitter-census-berger-morgan/isis_twitter_census_berger_morgan.pdf
35. Ben Popper, "Twitter's user growth has stalled, but its business keeps improving," *The Verge*, 2015, http://www.theverge.com/2015/2/5/7987501/twitter-q4-2014-earnings.
36. J.M. Berger and Jonathan Morgan, "The ISIS Twitter Census: Defining and Describing the Population of ISIS Supporters on Twitter," The Brookings Project on US Relations with the Islamic World, 2015, http://www.brookings.edu/~/media/research/files/papers/2015/03/isis-twitter-census-berger-morgan/isis_twitter_census_berger_morgan.pdf
37. *El-Dorar al-Shamia*, 2015, http://eldorar.com/node/73939
38. https://twitter.com/activistm8/status/618827970984083457
39. Syrian Observatory for Human Rights, http://www.syriahr.com/en/
40. Humeyra Pamuk, "Turkey Has Blocked Access to Pro-Isis Websites in Its Toughest Crackdown Yet," *Business Insider*, 2015, http://www.businessinsider.com/turkey-has-blocked-access-to-pro-isis-websites-2015-7
41. Aaron Y. Zelin, "The Islamic State's Territorial Methodology," *Jihadology*, http://jihadology.net/
42. http://www.cbsnews.com/news/isis-chief-singer-and-songwriter-maher-meshaal-killed-in-syria-airstrikes-activistssa y/
43. Bryan Schatz, "Inside the World of ISIS Propaganda Music," *Mother Jones*, 2015, http://www.motherjones.com/politics/2015/02/isis-islamic-state-baghdadi-music-jihad-nasheeds
44. http://www.reuters.com/article/2015/07/17/us-mideast-crisis-beheading-idUSKCN-0PR1S320150717
45. Bryan Schatz, "Inside the World of ISIS Propaganda Music," *Mother Jones*, 2015, http://www.motherjones.com/politics/2015/02/isis-islamic-state-baghdadi-music-jihad-nasheeds

46. Diana Moukalled, "ISIS and Hollywood Illusions," *Asharq Al-Awsat*, 2014, http://archive.aawsat.com/leader.asp?section=3&issueno=12991&article=776658#.VaIzyo0VjIU
47. "Launch of the Sawab Center," US Department of State, 2015, http://www.state.gov/r/pa/prs/ps/2015/07/244709.htm
48. The Uprising of Women in the Arab World, http://uprisingofwomeninthearabworld.org/?page_id=1392&lang=en
49. The Uprising of Women in the Arab World, Facebook, https://www.facebook.com/intifadat.almar2a
50. The Uprising of Women in the Arab World, http://uprisingofwomeninthearabworld.org/?page_id=1392&lang=en
51. Ibin.
52. The Uprising of Women in the Arab World, Facebook, https://www.facebook.com/intifadat.almar2a/info?tab=page_info
53. The Uprising of Women in the Arab World, Twitter, https://twitter.com/UprisingOfWomen
54. The Uprising of Women in the Arab World, Flickr, https://www.flickr.com/photos/intifadatalmar2a/
55. Harass Map, http://harassmap.org/en/who-we-are/
56. Harrass Map, 2015, http://harassmap.org/en/
57. *JBC News*, 2014, http://goo.gl/of04UI
58. http://ar.ammannet.net/news/152336
59. Mishari al-Zaidi, "Virus of Social Media," *Asharq Al-Awsat*, 2015, http://goo.gl/BKmlDA
60. *Alwatan Voice*, 2013, http://www.alwatanvoice.com/arabic/news/2013/09/25/440189.html
61. Samir Atallah, *Asharq Al-Awsat*, 2012, http://aawsat.com/leader.asp?section=3&article=673557&issueno=12197
62. "20 Categories for Arab Social Media Award, "*Emirates 24/7*, 2014, http://www.emirates247.com/news/emirates/20-categories-for-arab-social-media-award-2014-06-17-1.553189
63. Arab Social Media Influences Summit, http://www.arabsmis.ae/#aboutpage
64. Ibid.
65. "20 Categories for Arab Social Media Award, "*Emirates 24/7*, 2014, http://www.emirates247.com/news/emirates/20-categories-for-arab-social-media-award-2014-06-17-1.553189
66. Ibid.
67. Ibid.
68. http://english.alarabiya.net/en/media/digital/2015/03/17/Arab-social-media-leaders-honored-at-Dubai-summit.ht ml
69. "Muhammad bin Rashid: Arab Social Media Influencers Summit a New Phase in Evolution of Social Media," *WAM*, 2015, https://www.wam.ae/en/news/emirates-arab/1395278071059.html
70. "Qatari Human Rights Official Defends Life Sentence for Poet Who Praised Arab Spring Uprisings," *Democracy Now!*, 2012, http://www.democracynow.org/2012/12/7/qatari_human_rights_official_defends_life

71. *Al Arabiya*, 2012, http://www.alarabiya.net/articles/2012/11/29/252462.html
72. "Omani Authorities Persecute Online Activists," *Reporters Without Borders*, 2015, http://en.rsf.org/oman-omani-authorities-persecute-online-08-04-2015,47768.html
73. http://ar.ammannet.net/?p=151770

Chapter Eleven: The Criticism of Israel: The Knight and the Dragon

1. "EU Border Assistance Mission for Rafah Crossing Point," European Union, 2005, http://eu-un.europa.eu/articles/en/article_5366_en.htm
2. "European Council Extends the Mandate of the EUBAM Rafah," European Union, 2015, http://eeas.europa.eu/csdp/missions-and-operations/eubam-rafah/news/20150702_en.htm
3. "Gaza Economy on the Verge of Collapse," The World Bank, 2015, http://www.worldbank.org/en/news/press-release/2015/05/21/gaza-economy-on-the-verge-of-collapse
4. "The Humanitarian Impact of the Blockade," OCHA, United Nations, 2015, http://gaza.ochaopt.org/2015/07/the-gaza-strip-the-humanitarian-impact-of-the-blockade/
5. "Gaza Could Become Uninhabitable in Less than Five Years in Wake of 2014 Conflict," UNCTAD, United Nations, 2015, http://unctad.org/en/Pages/PressRelease.aspx?OriginalVersionID=260
6. https://occupiedpalestine.wordpress.com/2011/05/14/Ḥamās-launches-official-website/
7. *Alwatan Voice*, 2012, http://www.alwatanvoice.com/arabic/news/2012/04/27/273522.html
8. http://www.paldf.net/forum/showthread.php?t=1032072
9. *Alwatan Voice*, 2012, http://www.alwatanvoice.com/arabic/news/2012/09/23/318915.html
10. *Alwatan Voice*, 2013, http://www.alwatanvoice.com/arabic/news/2013/06/13/404199.html
11. "Although Poverty . . . Gaza Residents Flock to iPhone 5," *Al Arabiya*, 2012, http://www.alarabiya.net/articles/2012/10/16/243996.html
12. http://www.hadhara.net/showdetail6860.html
13. http://paltimes.net/details/news/37915/المواصلات-تسمح-باستيراد-مركبات-من-مصر.html
14. William Booth, "Gaza Strip's Middle Class Enjoys Spin Classes, Fine Dining, Private Beaches," *The Washington Post*, 2015, https://www.washingtonpost.com/world/middle_east/gaza-middle-class-discovers-spin-classes-fine-dining-private-beaches/2015/08/23/7e23843c-45d5-11e5-9f53-d1e3ddfd0cda_story.html
15. "About the Crisis," OCHA, United Nations, http://www.unocha.org/syrian-arab-republic/syria-country-profile/about-crisis
16. "2015 Iraq Humanitarian Response Plan," OCHA, United Nations, 2015, https://docs.unocha.org/sites/dms/Iraq/iraq_hrp_overview.pdf
17. Ibid.

18. Ibid.
19. "Global Humanitaran Overview: Status Report," *Reliefweb*, 2015, http://reliefweb.int/sites/reliefweb.int/files/resources/GHO-status_report-FINAL.pdf
20. Ibid.
21. Elior Levy, "The Palestinian Who Opposes the Boycott Against Israel," *Ynet*, 2015, http://www.ynetnews.com/articles/0,7340,L-4667098,00.html
22. Richard Goldstone, "Reconsidering the Goldstone Report on Israel and War Crimes, *The Washington Post*, 2011, https://www.washingtonpost.com/opinions/reconsidering-the-goldstone-report-on-israel-and-war-crimes/2011/04/01/AFg111JC_story.html
23. http://unitedwithisrael.org/ki-moon-slams-Ḥamās-use-of-un-schools-for-rocket-storage-and-launching-but-still-condemns-israel/
24. David Alexander, "Israel Tried to Limit Civilian Casualties in Gaza: US Military Chief," *Reuters*, 2014, http://www.reuters.com/article/2014/11/06/us-israel-usa-gaza-id USKBN0IQ2LH20141106
25. Richard Goldstone, "Reconsidering the Goldstone Report on Israel and War Crimes," *The Washington Post*, 2011, https://www.washingtonpost.com/opinions/reconsidering-the-goldstone-report-on-israel-and-war-crimes/2011/04/01/AFg111JC_story.html
26. http://www.unwatch.org/site/c.bdKKISNqEmG/b.3820041/
27. http://blog.unwatch.org/index.php/2013/11/25/this-years-22-unga-resolutions-against-israel-4-on-rest-of-world/
28. http://www.gatestoneinstitute.org/4706/gazan-Ḥamās-war-crimes
29. Lucy Wescott, "Video Shows Gaza Residents Acting as Human Shields," *Newsweek*, 2014, http://www.newsweek.com/video-shows-gaza-residents-acting-human-shields-israeli-forces-258223
30. Holly Fletcher, "Palestinian Islamic Jihad," Council on Foreign Relations, 2008, http://www.cfr.org/israel/palestinian-islamic-jihad/p15984
31. "The Charter of Allah: The Platform of the Islamic Resistance Movement," Israel Foreign Ministry, http://fas.org/irp/world/para/docs/880818.htm
32. "Palestinian Islamic Jihad," Nation Counterterrorism Center, http://www.nctc.gov/site/groups/pij.html
33. "Hamas Covenant 1988," *The Avalon Project*, Yale Law School, http://avalon.law.yale.edu/20th_century/Ḥamās.asp
34. "Iron Dome: Defense System Against Short Range Artillery Rockers," Rafael, http://www.rafael.co.il/marketing/SIP_STORAGE/FILES/6/946.pdf
35. Ronnie Scheib, "Film Review: *In the Dark Room*," *Variety*, 2013, http://variety.com/2013/film/markets-festivals/in-the-dark-room-review-1200709477/
36. "Red Army Faction," *Wikipedia*, https://en.wikipedia.org/wiki/Red_Army_Faction
37. "Wadie Haddad," *Wikipedia*, https://en.wikipedia.org/wiki/Wadie_Haddad

38. "'Carlos the Jackal' Convicted, Sentenced to Life in Prison," *CNN World News*, 1997, http://edition.cnn.com/WORLD/9712/23/carlos/
39. https://www.mossad.gov.il/eng/Pages/default.aspx
40. "How Generational Theory Can Improve Teaching: Strategies for Working with the 'Millennials,'" *Currents in Teaching and Learning, Vol. 1, No. 1*, 2008, http://www.worcester.edu/Currents/Archives/Volume_1_Number_1/CurrentsV1N1WilsonP29.pdf
41. Darrin J. DeChane, "How to Understand the Millennial Generation? Understand the Context," *Student Pulse*, 2014, http://www.studentpulse.com/articles/878/how-to-explain-the-millennial-generation-understand-the-context
42. Erin Russell, "Millennials: The Hero Generation," *Millennial Manifesto*, 2014, http://www.millennialmanifesto.literallydarling.com/millennials-hero-generation/
43. BDS Movement, http://www.bdsmovement.net/bdsintro
44. Free Palestine Movement, http://freepalestinemovement.org/
45. https://www.facebook.com/sjpal/info?tab=page_info
46. Einelhelweh.net, 2014, http://www.einelhelweh.net/shownews.php?full=news&id_topic=9344
47. "Hamas Charter," The Jerusalem Fund, http://www.thejerusalemfund.org/www.thejerusalemfund.org/carryover/documents/charter.html?chocaid=397
48. http://www.paldf.net/forum/showthread.php?t=1079117
49. *Elaph*, 2014, http://www.elaph.com/Web/opinion/2014/1/871567.html
50. http://www.hadhara.net/showdetail6860.html.
51. http://www.alquds.co.uk/index.asp?fname=today\19qpt960.htm&arc=data\2012\04\04-19\19qpt960.htm
52. *Alwatan Voice*, 2013, http://www.alwatanvoice.com/arabic/news/2013/01/26/354287.html
53. *Elaph*, 2012, http://www.elaph.com/Web/NewsPapers/2012/6/743778.html?entry=todays article
54. David Palumbo-Liu, http://www.palumbo-liu.com/?page_id=14
55. David Palumbo-Liu, "Millenials Are Over Israel: A New Generation, Outraged Over Gaza, Rejects Washington's Reflexive Support," *Salon*, 2014, http://www.salon.com/2014/08/01/millennials_are_so_over_israel_a_new_generation_is_outraged_over_gaza_demands_change/
56. Ibid.
57. Ibid.
58. Ibid.
59. Ibid.
60. http://www.beirutobserver.com/2013/08/83011/
61. http://www.youkal.net/2012-12-02-14-05-23/24-25/24312-حزب-الله-لحماس-اخرجونا-من-سوريا
62. *El-Dorar al-Shamia*, 2014, http://eldorar.com/node/45109
63. *Asharq Al-Awat*, 2013, http://www.aawsat.com/details.asp?section=4&article=746220&issueno=12735#.UlZQblMU6So

64. http://www.saidatv.tv/news.php?go=fullnews&newsid=43145
65. *Al-Monitor*, 2015, http://www.al-monitor.com/pulse/originals/2015/04/egypt-sinai-gaza-tunnels-sanctions-sisi-terrorist.html#
66. Nicolas Pelham, "Gaza's Tunnel Phenomenon: The Unintended Dynamics of Israel's Siege," Institute for Palestine Studies, http://palestine-studies.org/jps/fulltext/42605
67. Ibid.
68. Ibid.
69. Ibid.
70. *Asharq Al-Awsat*, 2012, http://aawsat.com/details.asp?section=4&article=668496&issueno=12164
71. *Alwatan Voice*, 2012, http://www.alwatanvoice.com/arabic/news/2012/06/29/291939.html
72. *Elaph*, 2012, http://www.elaph.com/Web/NewsPapers/2012/8/756957.html?entry=todays article
73. http://www.hadhara.net/showdetail6860.html.
74. *Al-Monitor*, 2015, http://www.al-monitor.com/pulse/originals/2015/06/palestine-rafah-kerem-shalom-crossing-smuggle-goods-tunnel.html#
75. "No Revenues at the End of the Tunnel: Hamas' Deep Economic Crisis," *Albawaba Business*, 2015, http://www.albawaba.com/business/Ḥamās-economic-crisis-tunnel-523826
76. *Alwatan Voice*, 2014, http://www.alwatanvoice.com/arabic/news/2014/03/26/513627.html
77. Amir Taheri, "Gaza Strip and the Curse of Never-Ending Wars," *Asharq Al-Awsat*, 2014, http://www.aawsat.com/home/article/145481
78. Abdullah al-Obaidi, *Elaph*, 2014, http://www.elaph.com/Web/NewsPapers/2014/8/928814.html
79. http://www.all4syria.info/Archive/157514
80. *JBC News*, http://www.jbcnews.net/article/130434
81. Vasudevan Sridharan, "Egypt Building Fish Farms to Stop Smuggling in Gaza Tunnels," *International Business Times*, 2015, http://www.ibtimes.co.uk/egypt-building-fish-farms-stop-smuggling-gaza-tunnels-1517924
82. "Egypt Starts Dig On Gaza Border to Flood Tunnels," *The New Arab*, 2015, http://www.alaraby.co.uk/english/News/2015/8/31/Egypt-starts-dig-on-Gaza-border-to-flood-tunnels
83. Kaled Abu Toameh, "Gaza: Egypt Responsible for Weapons Shortage," Gatestone Insitute, 2015, http://www.gatestoneinstitute.org/5545/gaza-egypt-weapons
84. Salon Media Group, http://www.salon.com/about/
85. Truthout, http://www.truth-out.org/about-us
86. BDS Movement, http://www.bdsmovement.net/
87. "Sampling of Students for Justice in Palestine (SJP) & Other Attempts to Disrupt Freedom of Assembly and Freedom of Association of Jewish and Pro-Israel Students," AMCHA Initiative, http://www.amchainitiative.org/sjp-disruption-of-jewish-events/

88. "Muslims Torpedo UC Irvine Invited Speaker, Israel's Ambassador Oren," DemoCast, https://www.YouTube.com/watch?v=AfLs_ptJzQA
89. Benjamin Doherty, "Israel Philharmonic Orchestra Interrupted by BDS Activists," *The Electronic Intifada*, 2011, https://electronicintifada.net/blogs/benjamin-doherty/israel-philharmonic-orchestra-disrupted-bds-activists
90. "Bassam Eid: 'Pro-Palestinian Activists' are the Most Anti-Palestinian of All," *Israel Seen*, 2015, http://israelseen.com/2015/06/11/bassam-eid-pro-palestinian-activists-are-the-most-anti-palestinian-of-all/
91. "Palestinian Human Rights Activists Bassem Eid Disrupted by the BDS," South African Jewish Board of Deputies, 2015, http://www.jewishsa.co.za/general/palestinian-human-rights-activist-bassem-eid-disrupted-by-the-bds/

Chapter Twelve: What Lies Ahead: Reigns of Fear, Empire of Hope

1. *JBC News*, http://www.jbcnews.net/article/146337
2. Dr. Mamoun Fandy, "The Middle East and the End of Ideology," *Asharq Al-Awsat*, 2015, http://aawsat.com/home/article/383896/
3. Rory Jones and Tamer El-Ghobashy, "Arab League Agrees to Create Joint Military Force," *The Wall Street Journal*, 2015, http://www.wsj.com/articles/arab-league-agrees-to-create-joint-military-force-1427632123
4. "Arab Army Cheifs Conclude 2nd Joint-Arab Force Meeting," *Ahram Online*, 2015, http://english.ahram.org.eg/NewsContent/1/64/131085/Egypt/Politics-/Arab-army-chiefs-conclude-nd-jointArab-force-meeti.aspx
5. *JBC News*, http://www.jbcnews.net/article/116820-المشتركة-تهدف-لحماية-الأمن-القومي-العربي-حجازي-القوة-العربية
6. *JBC News*, http://www.jbcnews.net/article/146129
7. *El-Dorar al-Shamia*, 2015, http://eldorar.com/node/79510
8. *Al Yaum*, http://www.alyaum.com/article/4075650
9. *El-Dorar al-Shamia*, 2015, http://eldorar.com/node/80433
10. *JBC News*, http://www.jbcnews.net/article/141498
11. *JBC News*, http://www.jbcnews.net/article/143912
12. *Al Yaum*, http://www.alyaum.com/article/4075650
13. http://www.allofjo.net/index.php?page=article&id=96725
14. *JBC News*, http://www.jbcnews.net/article/138821
15. *JBC News*, http://goo.gl/GqBn3r

16. Progress Report of the United Nations Mediator on Palestine, Submitted to the Secretary-General for Transmission to the Members of the United Nations, General Assembly Official Records: Third Session, Supplement No. 11 (A/648), Paris, 1948, p. 47 and Supplement No. 11A (A/689 and A/689/Add.1, p. 5; and "Conclusions from Progress Report of the United Nations Mediator on Palestine," (September 16, 1948), U.N. doc. A/648 (part 1, p. 29; part 2, p. 23; part 3, p. 11), (September 18, 1948). http://www.jewishvirtuallibrary.org/jsource/myths3/MFrefugees.html
17. Asher Zeiger, "Abbas Says He Has No Right to Live in Safed and Has No Territorial Demands on Pre-1967 Israel," *The Times of Israel*, 2012, http://www.timesofisrael.com/abbas-says-he-has-no-right-to-live-in-safed-and-has-no-demands-on-pre-1967-israel/
18. Samir Atallah, *Asharq Al-Awsat*, 2015, http://goo.gl/FvQTmf
19. Randa Taqi a-Din, "Dark Future Awaits Middle East Youth," *JBC News*, 2015, http://www.jbcnews.net/article/145479-مستقبل-أسود-لشباب-الشرق-الأوسط
20. http://www.ammanads.com/i.html?http://www.ahram.org.eg/

ACKNOWLEDGMENTS

I WOULD LIKE TO EXPRESS A special thank-you to Rachel Monroe, a brilliant leader. I have the honor of being her friend. This book had its beginnings in a conversation I had with Rachel, who, in her determined, inspiring, and clear way, prompted me to write the book by urging me, "publish or perish!"

I would also like to thank Joyce Klein, who translated the book with professionalism and enthusiasm, and Aloma Halter, who proofread the translation. Their professional work, comments, suggestions, and feedback have undoubtedly helped to improve the book.

This book is also my way to thank my late parents, Yardena and Yosef Melamed; may their memory be a blessing. They were natives of Jerusalem, the city in which I was born and raised, and brought me up simply and with devotion. They encouraged me to widen my horizons, to give expression to my talents and my aspirations, and served as role models of diligence.

I offer my deepest gratitude to my wife, Maia Hoffman, my partner in life, in work and vision, and in the production of this book. She always challenges me to expand, to deepen, and to develop professionally and personally. Her professionalism, her insistence on and commitment to excellence, and her ceaseless striving for improvement in every area are a source of inspiration to me. This book would never have seen the light of day without her amazing commitment and the countless hours and days she spent working on it.

The principles I've discussed in this book are core values of the groundbreaking educational program I have had the honor of designing, developing, and conducting in my capacity as the fellow of intelligence and Middle East affairs at the Eisenhower Institute in Washington, DC and on the Gettysburg College campus. I extend my gratitude to Jeffrey Blavatt, the visionary executive director of the Eisenhower Institute, for offering me the platform to educate. The revolutionary program is called Inside the Middle East—Intelligence Perspectives (ITME). At the time this book is being written, I am beginning the third year of the program and it is a very exciting endeavor. To date we have graduated dozens of students. The Inside the Middle East—Intelligence Perspectives program aims to change the paradigm of the gathering, assimilation, and processing of knowledge about the Middle East in the West. ITME is training young students—tomorrow's leaders—to be interrogating, media-literate, critical thinkers who professionally gather, analyze, and process information so they can accurately understand reality in the Middle East. ITME is qualifying leaders who can interpret and understand the Middle East; have their finger on the pulse; "zoom in" and "zoom out'; accurately engage in dialogue with the Middle East and the global reality; not get sidetracked by concepts, narratives, and theories that may sound good, but detract from the ability to accurately read events and trends; and suggest effective policies. ITME is developing leaders who will be better positioned to deal with the challenges of tomorrow because they are being taught how to think, not what to think. My dream is to expand the Inside the Middle East program to other campuses and institutions to provide the leaders of today and tomorrow with the tools and skills that will enable them to accurately read and address the complex reality of the Middle East and the world.

I want also to extend my deep gratitude to Stephen F. Manfredi of the Manfredi Strategy Group, LLC. for his work as my publicist. At the time I am writing this we are just beginning our work together, I am profoundly grateful for his guidance so far. He has proven himself to be an enthusiastic and caring person and an impressive professional. I am excited to get to know him better and am confident that he will invest his heart and soul in the public relations efforts for this book. I know I will gain a tremendous amount from the experience and in advance I thank him for his immeasurable contribution to the success of this book. I would also like to thank my good friend and colleague Eli Ovits for introducing me to Stephen.

My warmest gratitude is also extended to Lucy Aharish, an amazing professional and a brave and powerful woman whom I am proud to call my colleague and friend. Lucy and i24 News offer me the stage to educate and I always tremendously enjoy our conversations in the studio. I look forward to continuing to work together to bring our message to even larger audiences. I know that together we can help more people truly understand the Middle East and navigate this complicated region which is close to both of our hearts. Lucy's attitude, path, and career can serve as a role model for many young women and I am profoundly moved and honored to know that she thinks highly of me.

This book would not have been possible without the relentless commitment and dedication of Julia Abramoff, senior editor, Skyhorse Publishing, Inc. She is a consummate professional and I am deeply lucky to have had her on my side. I'll bet she never thought from our first conversation in August 2014 that we would embark on such a journey! We cannot thank her enough for her round-the-clock commitment and dedication. Julia said that she learned a lot throughout the editing process. I am honored to know that, and I can say that she taught me a lot about striving for excellence. Her uncompromising professionalism is matched by her sweet and caring demeanor. I am truly thankful that I had the opportunity to work with her and learn from her and I hope our paths will continue to intersect.

INDEX

B

C

O

P